INSPIRE / PLAN / DISCOVER / EXPERIENCE

MOROCCO

MOROCCO

CONTENTS

DISCOVER MOROCCO 6

EXPERIENCE MOROCCO 70

NEED TO KNOW 312

Left: colourful baskets for sale in a souk
Previous page: sand dunes in the Erg Chebbi desert

DISCOVER

Night market, Jemaa el-Fna, Marrakech

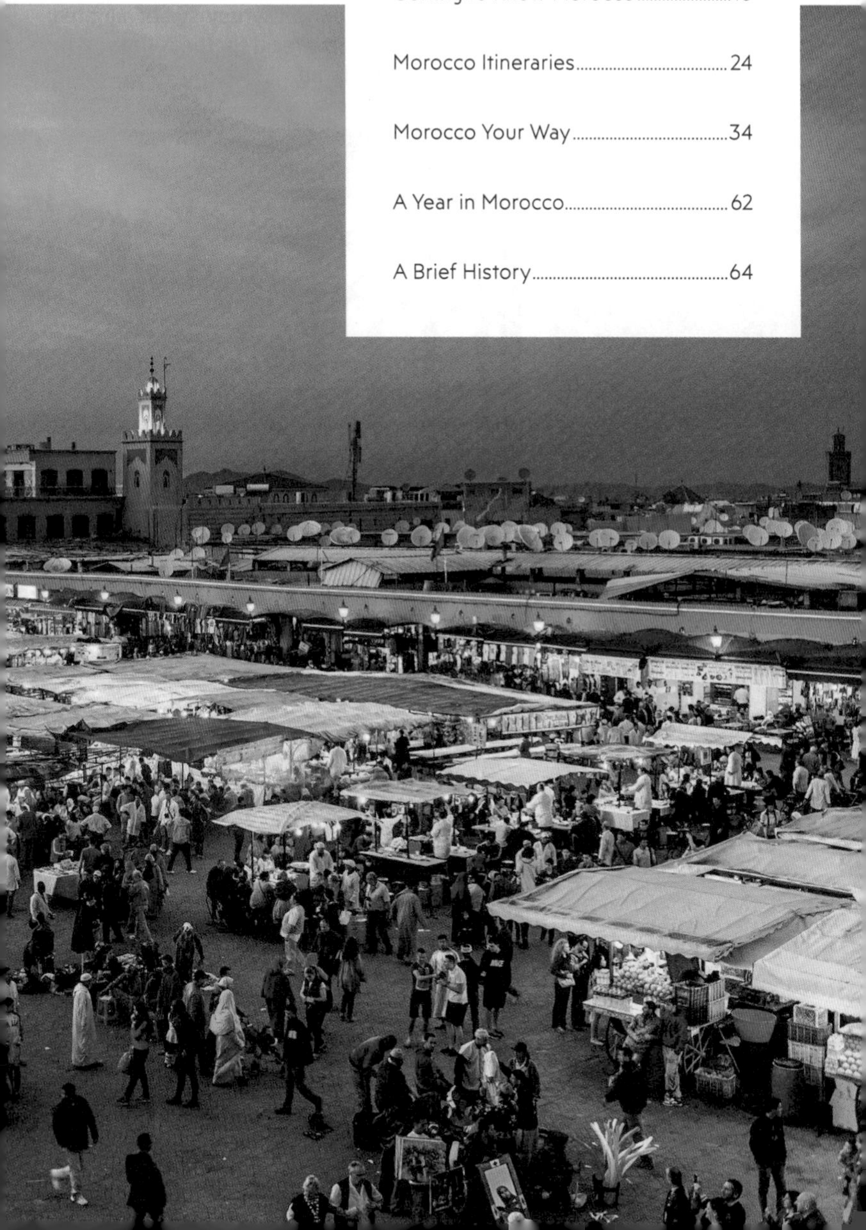

WELCOME TO
MOROCCO

Bustling souks full of glittering goods, heady with the smell of spices. Shady palm oases and rolling seas of scorching sand dunes. Snow-capped mountain passes, ancient walled cities and an endless supply of syrupy-sweet mint tea; Morocco is a veritable feast for the senses just waiting to be explored.

1 The magnificent red mud-brick *ksar* of Aït Benhaddou, a striking example of southern Moroccan architecture.

2 Dried roses from the Dadès Valley, sold throughout Morocco.

3 The busy square at Jemaa el-Fna, Marrakech.

Rooted in tradition yet strongly drawn to the modern world, Morocco is a country of stark contradiction and dazzling diversity. Over the centuries, its African, European and Middle Eastern roots have become deeply intertwined, resulting in a unique cultural richness particular to this vibrant corner of the world.

The most breathtaking natural scenery, including the rugged landscapes of the High Atlas and Middle Atlas mountain ranges, the enclosed green valleys of the Rif, and the palm groves and Kasbah-guarded gorges of the southern oases, is concentrated in the upper half of the country. With a car, or by making use of the country's bus and rail network, it is possible to see the very best of Morocco in a couple of adventure-packed weeks.

The north, too, is where you will find Morocco's most fabulous cities, including the imperial quartet of Fes, Marrakech, Meknès and Rabat. All four have historic walled medinas and magnificent mosques and palaces. Equally atmospheric are Morocco's coastal cities, including the bohemian crossroads of Tangier, laidback Essaouira and art deco Casablanca.

This guide breaks Morocco down into easily navigable chapters, with detailed itineraries, expert local knowledge and comprehensive maps to help you plan your perfect trip. Whether you are here for a relaxing weekend getaway or an ambitious country-wide tour, this Eyewitness guide will ensure that you see the very best the country has to offer. Enjoy the book, and welcome to Morocco.

REASONS TO LOVE
MOROCCO

Winding streets in ancient cities, colourful souks, precipitous mountain peaks and vast desert dunescapes. There are so many reasons to visit this vibrant and intoxicating country. Here are some of our favourites.

1 MEDIEVAL MEDINAS

A medina is an historic old city, of which Morocco has many. Laced with twisting alleys and full of hidden treasures, they are fabulous places to explore and lose yourself in time.

ESSAOUIRA 2

This small blue-and-white city on the Atlantic coast has long been associated with music and the arts, and is famed for its laidback, sea-salted, bohemian charm *(p126)*.

3 MOROCCAN CUISINE

From slowcooked meat tagines to freshly picked figs with homemade yogurt, Moroccan food is often simple but packed with flavour from local herbs, spices and regional ingredients.

MOROCCAN CHIC 4
Fashion designers the world over have found inspiration in the vibrant colours and sumptuous textures of Morocco, from Yves Saint Laurent to Tom Ford.

THE MAGIC OF JEMAA EL-FNA 5
Every night storytellers entrance audiences, charmers cast spells and Gnaoua musicians play on Marrakech's main square. It is the most otherworldly of places *(p236)*.

HIKING IN THE HIGH ATLAS 6
The High Atlas mountains offer numerous trails suitable for both beginners and experts, taking in isolated mountain villages and spectacular scenery *(p224)*.

RIADS 7
A riad is a traditional townhouse with a courtyard garden. In recent years, many have been turned into intimate boutique hotels brimming with Moroccan charm.

CINEMATIC LANDSCAPES 8
You may experience *déjà vu* in Morocco - the country's stunning scenery has starred in countless TV shows and blockbusters, from *Gladiator* to *Game of Thrones* (p52).

9 MINT TEA
Made with fresh mint, Moroccan tea is refreshing even in the hottest weather. Moroccan hospitality is such that visitors may be offered it dozen times a day or more.

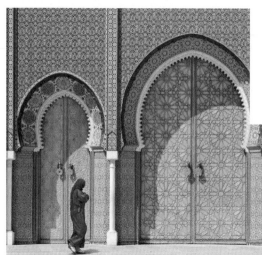

10 AMAZING ARCHITECTURE

Most mosques may be out of bounds, but there are plenty of other historic buildings, from tombs to royal palaces, lavishly adorned with colourful tiling and intricate plasterwork.

SURFING THE ATLANTIC COAST 11

The Atlantic swell on Morocco's windswept southern shores is legendary. For something really special head down to the picturesque surfers' enclave of Sidi Ifni *(p304)*.

THE SOUKS OF MARRAKECH 12

Every town and city has souks selling all manner of goods; the best are in the dusky-pink city of Marrakech *(p238)*. Here you will find the most appealing mix of trinkets and treasures.

EXPLORE
MOROCCO

This guide divides Morocco into 13
colour-coded sightseeing areas, as
shown on the map below. Find out
more about each area on the
following pages.

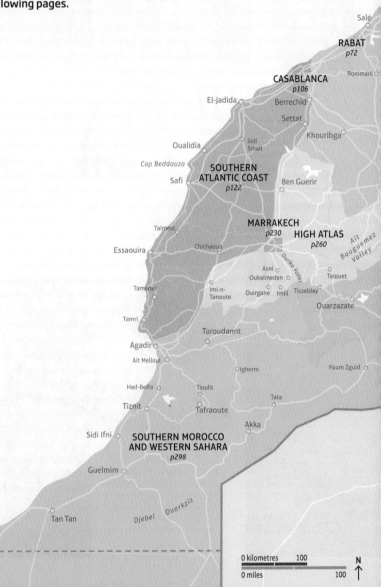

Atlantic Ocean

Salé

RABAT
p72

Rommani

CASABLANCA
p106

El-Jadida
Berrechid
Settat
Khouribga

Oualidia
Sidi Smail

Cap Beddouza

Safi

SOUTHERN ATLANTIC COAST
p122

Ben Guerir

Talmest

MARRAKECH
p230

HIGH ATLAS
p260

Aït Bouguemez Valley

Essaouira
Chichaoua
Ourika Valley

Asni
Oukaïmeden
Telouet

Tamanar
Imi-n-Tanoute
Ouirgane
Imlil
Tisselday

Tamri
Ouarzazate

Taroudannt

Agadir
Aït Melloul

Igherm
Foum Zguid

Had-Belfa
Tioulit
Tata

Tiznit
Tafraoute

Akka

Sidi Ifni
SOUTHERN MOROCCO AND WESTERN SAHARA
p298

Guelmim

Tan Tan
Djebel Ouarkziz

0 kilometres   100

0 miles   100

N

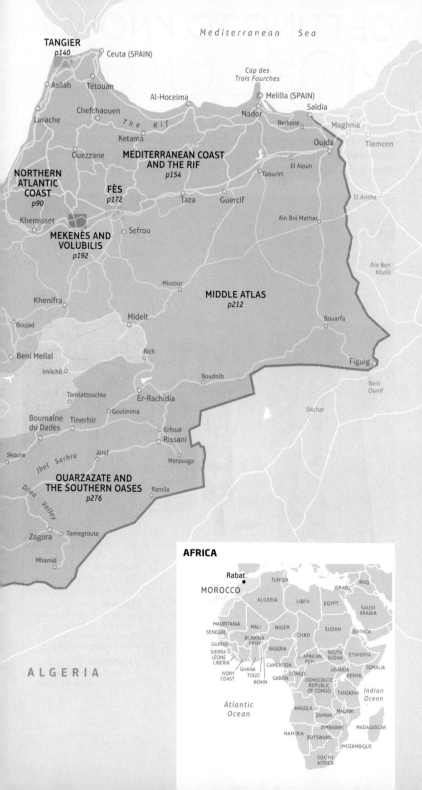

SPAIN

Mediterranean Sea

TANGIER
p140

Ceuta (SPAIN)

Asilah

Tétouan

Cap des
Trois Fourches

Al-Hoceima

Melilla (SPAIN)

Chefchaouen

Nador

Saïdia

Larache

The Rif

Berkane

Maghnia

Ketama

Oujda

Tlemcen

Ouezzane

MEDITERRANEAN COAST
AND THE RIF
p154

El Aioun

Taourirt

El Aricha

NORTHERN
ATLANTIC
COAST
p90

FÈS
p172

Taza

Guercif

Khemisset

Ain Bni Mathar

MEKENÈS AND
VOLUBILIS
p192

Sefrou

Missour

Aïn Ben
Khelil

Khenifra

MIDDLE ATLAS
p212

Boujad

Midelt

Bouarfa

Beni Mellal

Rich

Figuig

Imilchil

Boudnib

Beni
Ounif

Tamtattouchte

Béchar

Er-Rachidia

Boumalne
du Dadès

Tinerhir

Goulmima

Skoura

Jbel Sarhro

Alnif

Erfoud

Rissani

Merzouga

OUARZAZATE AND
THE SOUTHERN OASES
p276

Ramlia

Draa Valley

Zagora

Tamegroute

Mhamid

ALGERIA

AFRICA

Rabat

MOROCCO

TUNISIA

ALGERIA

LIBYA

EGYPT

ISRAEL

IRAQ

SAUDI
ARABIA

MAURITANIA

MALI

NIGER

CHAD

SUDAN

ERITREA

SENEGAL

GUINEA

BURKINA
FASO

NIGERIA

SIERRA
LEONE
LIBERIA

IVORY
COAST

GHANA
TOGO
BENIN

CAMEROON

C. AFRICAN
REP.

SOUTH
SUDAN

ETHIOPIA

SOMALIA

CONGO

GABON

UGANDA

KENYA

DEMOCRATIC
REPUBLIC
OF CONGO

TANZANIA

*Indian
Ocean*

ANGOLA

ZAMBIA

MALAWI

*Atlantic
Ocean*

NAMIBIA

ZIMBABWE

BOTSWANA

MADAGASCAR

MOZAMBIQUE

SOUTH
AFRICA

GETTING TO KNOW
MOROCCO

Where you go in Morocco depends on what kind of trip you are planning. Rest and relaxation are best found in Marrakech, Essaouira and Agadir; Fès and Meknès are great for history and culture enthusiasts, while the High Atlas and Southern Oases are hubs for activities and adventures of all sorts.

RABAT

PAGE 72

The ever-evolving Atlantic port of Rabat is both an ancient imperial city and Morocco's modern capital and administrative centre. It combines an ancient walled medina by the sea with an inland city of domes and minarets, sweeping terraces, modern structures and grand public buildings. In the Musée de l'Histoire et des Civilisations and Mohammed VI Museum of Modern and Contemporary Art, Rabat has two of the country's best museums, while ancient history is represented by a sedate medina and the atmospheric Chellah Necropolis filled with hidden treasures.

Best for
Historical treasures and imperial architecture

Home to
The Mausoleum of Mohammed V, Chellah Necropolis and Mohammed VI Museum of Modern and Contemporary Art

Experience
Bartering for bargain carpets in the bustling souks of the medina

PAGE 90

NORTHERN ATLANTIC COAST

Stretching north of Rabat to the outskirts of Tangier's sprawling metropolis, this little visited region is the best place to discover Morocco's rich Phoenician, Roman, Portuguese and Spanish heritage. It combines soft-sand beaches, coastal lagoons, epic forests and peaceful fishing towns with some of the oldest archaeological sites in the country. Highlights include the old pirate stronghold of Salé and the small, artsy Andalusian-style town of Asilah.

Best for
Archaeological sites and low-lying coastal wetlands

Home to
The characterful coastal cities of Asilah and Salé

Experience
The bountiful produce of the local countryside at Ksar el-Kebir's Sunday market

PAGE 106

CASABLANCA

The commercial and financial capital of Morocco, this modern and somewhat brash city is brimming with energy and verve. Largely developed by the French in the early 20th century, it retains a wonderful legacy of Art-Deco architecture; crumbling Mauresque masterpieces line wide, tree-lined avenues. Casablanca is home to more skyscrapers than minarets, although its famed Hassan II Mosque is the country's largest and most impressive – not to mention the only mosque in Morocco that can be visited by non-Muslims.

Best for
Boutique shopping, fine dining and a vibrant nightlife

Home to
Hassan II Mosque and Art-Deco architecture

Experience
Sipping cocktails and listening to live music at one of the many stylish bars in Ain Diab

→

PAGE 122

SOUTHERN ATLANTIC COAST

The coastline south of Casablanca is dotted with many small towns, some of which were built by the Portuguese. Many of these places, such as El-Jadida and Oualidia, are popular local resorts. Most visitors content themselves with a short trip to Essaouira, a compact walled city on the sea. With its lovely old medina and a slightly bohemian air, it's a great place to enjoy fresh seafood and cold beer while watching the sun sink beyond the ramparts.

Best for
Fresh seafood and coastal retreats

Home to
Serene seaside towns Essaouira and El-Jadida

Experience
An extravaganza of North African arts, music and culture at the annual Gnaoua Festival in Essaouira

PAGE 140

TANGIER

The meeting place between North Africa and Europe, Tangier is unlike anywhere else in Morocco. It is boisterous, brash and even slightly seedy, but nonetheless absolutely fascinating. It has a rich tradition of providing refuge to maverick Western writers, artists and musicians, from the likes of Henri Matisse to Mick Jagger, and even today the alleys of the old medina seem to hold their secrets tight. Recent investment has furnished the city with a new port, marina and swish hotels in a bid to bolster tourism, but the city's raffish charm remains very much intact.

Best for
Ocean views, literary hotspots and cultural crossroads

Home to
The American Legation Museum and the legendary Café Hafa

Experience
Sipping mint tea and watching the world go by from the Petit Socco, where the Beat writers hung out

MEDITERRANEAN COAST & THE RIF

East of Tangier and beyond the Spanish enclave of Ceuta, the coast is punctuated by sweeping beaches of golden sand and, from Wadi Laou to Al-Hoceima and Saïdia, by secluded bays beneath rocky cliffs. Inland, the Rif presents a great variety of landscapes, including high, steep valleys where almond trees blossom and oleanders flower, mountain roads that command wild and magnificent vistas, forests of cedar, fir and oak, and isolated villages with pitched tin roofs.

Best for
Idyllic beaches, atmospheric medinas and lush mountains

Home to
The picturesque medinas of Tetouan and Chefchaouen

Experience
Scenic hiking routes through the Zegzel Gorge and the mountains of the Rif

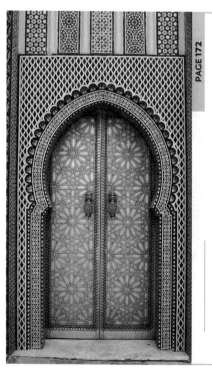

FÈS

Fès is home to the most stunning, not to mention expansive, of all Morocco's historic medinas. In fact, it is the world's largest living medieval city. Enclosed within defensive walls, old Fès, or Fès el-Bali, is an impossible compress of buildings intersected by a vein-like network of the tightest of alleys. In this labyrinth it feels like the city is sheltered from time, as visitors lose themselves in fascinated exploration. To the south, the open spaces and vast squares of Fès el-Jedid, the city's new town, include the royal palace and Jewish Quarter.

Best for
Imperial architecture and a medieval medina

Home to
The Bou Inania Medersa, Musée Dar el-Blatha and Fès el-Jedid

Experience
Trying to navigate the winding alleys and narrow passageways of Fès el-Bali

→

PAGE 192

MEKNÈS & VOLUBILIS

The smallest of Morocco's four imperial cities, Meknès is less impressive than Fès but still boasts an attractive medina, as well as the enormous Bab Mansour gate that leads into the heart of the old city and, in the Mausoleum of Moulay Ismaïl, one of the few holy shrines that is open to non-Muslims. Meknès is also the jumping off point for the hilltop pilgrimage town of Moulay Idriss and for Morocco's most impressive Roman ruins, at Volubilis.

Best for
Holy sites and Roman ruins

Home to
The Mausoleum of Moulay Ismaïl, Moulay Idriss and Volubilis

Experience
Journey back in time to ancient Rome as you explore the magnificent ruins at Volubilis

PAGE 212

MIDDLE ATLAS

A wild region of rare beauty, the Middle Atlas is surprisingly little visited. The great cedar forests that cover the mountainsides between deep valleys stretch as far as the eye can see. Bordered by the fertile plain of the Saïs and the cities of Fès and Meknès, the mountainous heights of the Middle Atlas are the territory of Berber tribes, whose population is thinly scattered over the area. While there are few must-see sites, it is a wonderful region for some leisurely driving tours and scenic trekking routes.

Best for
National parks and long, meandering scenic drives

Home to
Cascades d'Ouzoud and Jbel Tazzeka National Park

Experience
Monkeying around with Barbary macaques

MARRAKECH

Morocco's most colourful and magical city, pink-walled Marrakech is the archetypal melting pot. It mixes North African tribal culture with high fashion, medieval souks with stylish boutique riads, and age-old traditions of saints and spiritualism with a pulsating nightlife. Enjoy languid, sun-drenched days beside the pool and pampering sessions at a traditional hammam or destination spa. Adventure into the bustling souks and exprience the magic of Jemaa el-Fna by night. From here, waterfall treks, desert adventures and breathtaking mountain passes are just a day trip away.

Best for
Bargain hunting, boutique shopping and opulent riad living

Home to
The bustling square of Jemaa el-Fna, souks of all shapes and sizes, and tranquil escapes such as the Majorelle Gardens

Experience
Al fresco dining at Jemaa el-Fna night market

→

PAGE 260

HIGH ATLAS

Extending from the plains of the Atlantic seaboard to the Algerian border, the High Atlas forms an almost impregnable barrier some 800 km (500 miles) long and 100 km (60 miles) wide. The largest massif in the Atlas chain, this is the highest mountain range in North Africa. It is also surprisingly accessible, with two roads out of Marrakech snaking over breathtaking mountain passes and winding their way between the peaks in a series of sharp switchbacks. Veer away from the main drag and you will find quiet villages and towering kasbahs, still inhabited by Berber tribes.

Best for
Stunning mountain views and high-altitude trekking

Home to
Morocco's highest peak, Jbel Toubkal, and the Aït Bouguemez Valley

Experience
Descending from dizzying heights at Oukaïmeden, Africa's highest skii resort

PAGE 276

OUARZAZATE AND THE SOUTHERN OASES

Arguably the most rewarding region of Morocco to explore, this is where the southern edge of the High Atlas mountains meets the desert. A landscape cut by steep canyons and studded with arid hills, it is criss-crossed by wadis where shade-giving date palms grow in profusion. Eventually everything gives way to the sand. A succession of isolated fortified kasbahs tells the story of ancient trading routes. Here, the light is intensely bright and the colours sumptuously rich.

Best for
Desert trekking, lush oases and ancient kasbahs

Home to
The majestic hill-top Ksar of Aït Benhaddou

Experience
Sleeping out under the stars in the dunes of Erg Chebbi desert

PAGE 298

SOUTHERN MOROCCO AND WESTERN SAHARA

The vast southwestern region of Morocco is rarely explored by visitors, with the exception of the popular coastal resort city, Agadir. Those who venture further will find a variety of spectacular landscapes. The fertile Souss plain, dominated by stony desert and dotted with shady palm oases, is bordered by the rugged Anti-Atlas. At the coast, sheer cliffs give way to large areas of dunes linking Morocco to the Sahara and the Republic of Mauritania.

Best for
Desert landscapes and the wild, windswept beaches of the far south

Home to
Agadir, Souss-Massa National Park and Sidi Ifni

Experience
Lazy days at Agadir city beach, or surfing Atlantic rollers on vast stretches of wild coastline

←

1 Mausoleum of Moulay Ismaïl, Meknès.

2 Hassan II Mosque by night.

3 Herbs and ingredients for sale on Rahba Kedima, Marrakech.

4 Tranquil Majorelle Garden, Marrakech.

From grand imperial cities to mountain escapes, Morocco has more than enough to keep visitors occupied. Whether you're planning a short city break or several weeks spent in serious exploration, you will be rewarded handsomely for your efforts.

2 WEEKS

A Grand Tour of Morocco

Day 1

For your first unforgettable hit of Morocco, head straight to Marrakech's main square, Jemaa el-Fna *(p236)*. From here endless souks weave away from the main thoroughfare. Once you've had your fill of bargaining, escape to the Jardin Secret *(p246)* for lunch with a view on the terrace café, before heading back to the action. At night, the square is transformed into a vibrant food market with an infectious party atmosphere.

Day 2

Revisit Jemaa el-Fna in the morning, when food stalls have been replaced by sellers of orange juice squeezed to order. Pass by the Koutoubia Mosque *(p234)*, and weave your way to the Ben Youssef Medersa *(p240)*, the largest Islamic college in Morocco. Refuel at one of the many cafés in the fashionable Mouassine quarter *(p248)* and dine in the medina.

Day 3

Visit the breathtaking ensemble of buildings and gardens at the ruined Palais el-Badi *(p252)*. Eerier still, are the nearby Saadian Tombs *(p256)*. Stop for lunch at one of the friendly cafés around the Rahba Kedima *(p238)* before heading to the charming Majorelle Garden *(p242)*. Afterwards, make the short walk into central Guéliz *(p257)* and explore the quirky shops, cafés and galleries on the side streets off Avenue Mohammed V.

This lively area is full of hip eateries, such as the chic Kechmara *(3 Rue de la Liberté)*. After sundown, take in the view from the rooftop Skybar at Hotel La Renaissance.

Day 4

Depart Marrakech in the morning. You could hire a car, but it is also easy to get around Morocco by train or bus. Arrive in Casablanca by early afternoon to join a tour of the super-sized Hassan II Mosque *(p110)*. Take a walk around downtown to admire Casablanca's rich legacy of Art-Deco architecture, and dine on fine Moroccan cuisine at La Squala *(p116)*. Afterwards, drop by Rick's Café, the club inspired by the 1942 classic, *Casablanca*.

Day 5

Push on up the coast to the modern capital of Rabat. Aim to arrive mid morning and grab a bite to eat in the medina while exploring the whitewashed alleyways of the Ouidaïa Kasbah *(p88)*. Entered through the imposing Almohad gate, Bab Ouidaïa, this historic citadel is the oldest part of the city. From the old to the new, head to the Mohammed VI Museum of Modern and Contemporary Art to take in the works of Morocco's modern artists *(p80)*. Later, enjoy some excellent Moroccan cuisine at the reliable and welcoming La Koutoubia *(p83)*.

→

Day 6

After breakfast, head inland to Meknès. Swing by the Mausoleum of Moulay Ismaïl (p196), the most important place of worship in the city, and admire the view of Meknès from the top of the spectacular Bou Inania Medersa (p205), a fine example of Merinid architecture. After lunch, while away the hours at the Musée Dar Jamai. For spectacular panoramic views, dine at Le Collier de la Colombe.

Day 7

A short trip from Meknès is Volubilis (p198), Morocco's most impressive Roman-era site. Stop by Moulay Idriss (p203) for a late lunch and spend the afternoon exploring this holy hilltop town. Next stop Fès. On arrival, settle into your hotel and treat yourself to dinner at one of the finest riads in the ancient medina – Dar Tajine.

Day 8

Fès is not a city to be rushed. After a heady pace of almost a city a day, take the foot off the gas and revel in your surroundings. Meander through the ravine-like alleys of the medina and take in the sights, sounds and smells of this ancient city. Start with Fès el-Jedid (p180) before tackling the map-defeating maze of Fès el-Bali. Stop for mint tea and graze on street food along the way. For an unforgettable evening, enjoy cocktails and dinner at l'Amadier Palais Faraj overloooking the medina.

Day 9

After breakfast, explore the intricate El-Attarine and El-Cherratine medersas (p189), then on to the famous Café Clock (7 Derb el-Magana) for a pick-me-up – it often hosts live music, Moroccan culture classes, calligraphy workshops, and even cooking courses. Once sufficiently refuelled, explore the Musée Dar el Blatha (p176) before heading to la Maison Bleue (2 Place Batha) for dinner.

Day 10

Time to reverse your route and head back towards Marrakech. This is about an eight-hour journey through the rolling

① Leather Tanneries in Fès.
② Bou Inania Medersa, Meknès.
③ Roman Ruins at Volubilis.
④ Jemaa el-Fna, Marrakech.
⑤ Moroccan sweet mint tea.
⑥ Rafting at Cascades d'Ouzoud.

hills of the Middle Atlas. Break the journey in the quaint mountain town of Beni Mellal (p226) at the foot of Jbel Tassemi. On arrival back in Marrakech, enjoy a leisurely evening stroll through the city centre.

Day 11

Just a short day trip from Marrakech are the Cascades d'Ouzoud (p216). Many tour operators offer full day and half-day trips to suit your needs, usually with a lunch stop at a local riad or restaurant included. After a day's exploration, indulge in a trademark Moroccan hammam experience on your return to the city.

Day 12

Rise early and travel to the seaside town of Essaouira (p126). Wander through the winding streets and bastions of the medina, and be sure to stop by shop-lined Rue Attarine to search for some bargains. When hunger strikes, treat yourself to a straight-from-the-sea lunch of freshly caught sardines grilled at the port. Spend the afternoon walking along

the sea wall and admiring the view from the ramparts. Watch the sunset from the rooftop bar at the Taros café, then dine at one of the many restaurants on Rue Skala.

Day 13

After a hearty breakfast, head to the surf beach at Sidi Kaouki (p132), one of Morocco's top surfing locations. Take lessons from a qualified instructor (often a generous picnic lunch is provided), or if you're already a seasoned surfer, hit the waves for the rest of the day. You'll soon work up an appetite, so dine at Le Chalet de la Plage, a beachside seafood restaurant in town with fine views.

Day 14

Return to Marrakech in time for a lunch. Before departing the city, take a petit taxi to the Agdal Gardens (p258), an expansive 12th-century botanical garden south of the medina. The Saadian pavilion commands breathtaking views across the city to the north, and the snow-capped peaks of the High Atlas to the south – a perfect scene on which to end your trip.

→

1 Sunset over Aït Benhaddou.

2 Winding streets within the fortified walls of Aït Benhaddou.

3 The set of *Cleopatra* (1999) at the Atlas Studios, Ouarzazate.

4 Colorful tiles on a fountain in Taourirt Kasbah, Ouarzazate.

Few things say "North Africa" quite like the Sahara. This itinerary combines the colour and intensity of Morocco's vibrant cities with mountain passes and sand. Lots of sand. The route is possible by public transport or car.

10 DAYS

in the Valleys and Kasbahs of Southern Morocco

Day 1

After spending a few days taking in the sights of Marrakech *(p231)*, set off early for Agadir *(p302)*. The mild climate and coastal air here are a pleasant treat after the sweltering heat of Marrakech. After lunch at one of the many restaurants overlooking the marina, head for the Polizzi Medina, which teems with restaurants and craft workshops. Admire the Berber exhibits in the Musée Municipal du Patrimoine Amazigh, and stroll through the Vallée des Oiseaux on your way to the beach for the rest of the afternoon. For dinner, book a table at El Toro (no. 7 Front de Mer), which serves Spanish-Moroccan fushion dishes right on the beach promenade.

Day 2

To make the most of the day, rise early for the hour drive down the coast to the Souss Massa National Park *(p308)*. In contrast to the busy beachfront bars and restaurants of Agadir, this tranquil nature reserve offers a taste of unspoiled Morocco, playing host to hundreds of migratory birds from southern Spain and France. Pack a picnic and spend the day exploring some of the scenic trails. With the exception of the tiny fishing villages that line the coast, you are likely to have a free run of the place. Most of the nearby hotels offer hammam and spa facilities, a perfect antidote to a hard day of hiking.

Day 3

After breakfast at your hotel, head east on the N10 to the town of Taroudannt *(p306)* where, behind the mighty red-ochre ramparts are scenes of traditional Berber life. In the souks, situated between the two main squares, you can pick up all manner of exquisitely crafted souvenirs. About 37 km (23 miles) southeast of the town is the spectacular Tioute Kasbah which dominates the palm groves – a perfect location for picnic with a view. Head back to Taroudannt and dine in the the spectacular gardens of the Dar el-Hossoun.

Day 4

After breakfast push on to Ouarzazate *(p282)*, where the mountains meet the desert. The town also happens to be the unlikely hub of Morocco's film industry. Visit the CLA and Atlas film studios, where hundreds of Hollywood movies have been shot, and enjoy exploring this delightful sleepy town, home to the Taourirt Kasbah. In the late afternoon, drive 30 km (19 miles) north on the N9 to the fortified village of Aït Benhaddou *(p280)*. The added bonus of an overnight stay here means you get to see the amazing mud-walled fortress at sunset when it glows bright red and – if you are an early riser – at sunrise, when it is at its most glorious. →

Day 5

Depart Aït Benhaddou and head east into the Dadès Valley, also known as the Valley of the Kasbahs, because so many of the mud-walled fortresses line the way. This is a wonderful road to navigate, full of switchbacks and bizarre rock formations. There are plenty of stunning spots to pause at en route, and it is worth exploring the side roads for more fabulous scenery. Stay the night in Boulmalne du Dadès at the idyllic Xaluca Dadès Hotel *(p289)*, where a warm welcome and mountains of delicious continental and Moroccan cuisine make for a memorable – and filling – dining experience.

Day 6

Another early start, this time following the road north out of town, to Todra Gorge *(p290)*. Park up and take the opportunity to wander through some spectacular, canyon-like scenery. Return the way you came and carry on east and then south at Er-Rachida, through Erfoud to Rissani (p297). This is a small village with a few kasbahs and a lively souk,

worth a brief stop for lunch. Aim to halt for the night at Merzouga (p296), a small village that is the access point for the majestic Erg Chebbi dune fields. Take your pick of the hotels and guesthouses that line the western fringe of the dunes.

Day 7

Desert trips, from excursions of a few hours to expeditions lasting several days, can be arranged in Merzouga. These can involve anything from trekking on foot to travelling on camelback, dune buggy or four-wheel drive, among other adventurous modes of transport. To experience the undulating dunescapes and infinite stillness of the Erg Chebbi at its best, opt for an overnight stay. Accommodation options range from basic camps, to plush, fully furnished luxury tents with ensuite facilities. Whichever you choose, you will no doubt be humbled by the vast, shifting expanse of apricot-coloured sand, illuminated in the glow of the setting sun. By night, millions of twinkling stars and planets are visible as they dance across the dark desert sky.

1 Steep canyons in Todra Gorge.
2 The verdant Dadès Valley.
3 City Walls of Taroudannt.
4 Colourful spices for sale in a souk.
5 Walking on the Erg Chebbi dunes.
6 Jemaa el-Fna, Marrakech.

Day 8

On departing the desert, leave Merzouga and retrace your route to Er-Rachida. Continue north through the striking scenery of the Ziz Gorge *(p294)* and on up to Azrou *(p222)* for a lunch stop and short stroll around the town and its beautifully painted streets and doorways. This is about a five-hour drive in total, over the course of which, the landscape transitions from parched desert to rocky mountain terrain, until finally you emerge in the lush green valleys of the Middle Atlas. At Azrou, strike northeast on the N8 highway for the nearby town of Ifrane *(p222)*. Surrounded by dense forest, it is far cry from the scenery you woke up to this same morning.

Day 9

From your base in Ifrane, spend a few hours touring the three attractive lakes of Dayet Aouam, Dayet Ifrah and Dayet Hachlaf *(p228)*. Depart Ifrane in the early afternoon and head southwest on the N8, via Beni Mellal *(p226)* and then turn off the highway to climb through wooded hills to reach Bin el-Ouidine, a village that sits on the banks of the largest lake in Morocco. You will find comfortable rooms and a warm welcome at the lakefront hotel and restaurant, Tigmi Dar Samy. Dine on the terrace and enjoy an evening dip in the pool.

Day 10

After breakfast, drive to the nearby Cascades d'Ouzoud *(p216)*, a thundering waterfall in the heart of the Middle Atlas. Spend a few hours exploring the scenery around these famous waterfalls. A quick dip in the plunge pool is a great way to cool off in the afternoon heat; be warned, the water is surprisingly cold. Riverside cafés and fruit stands serve basic snacks, but keep an eye out for the roaming local apes – they will snatch at anything edible. From here it is a drive of a couple of hours back to Marrakech. Have one last dash around the souks to dispose of those remaining dirhams, and indulge in a farewell meal of couscous and tagine overlooking the nightly dramatics at Jemaa el-Fna.

7 DAYS

In Tangier and the Mediterranean Coast

Day 1

Start your first day in Tangier *(p140)* by wandering the winding streets of the city's ancient medina. Pause for coffee on the legendary Petit Socco *(p146)* before visiting the American Legation *(p147)* for a crash course in the city's louche history. When you've had your fill of antiquity, head up the hill to the peaceful kasbah *(p144)*, where you'll find a handful of home-grown boutiques – perfect for souvenir shopping. Experience the modern side of Tangier with a walk along Rue de la Liberté *(p150)* as the sun sets. Try to reserve a table at Populaire Saveur du Poisson *(p151)*, known locally as Popeye's, and relish a terrific six-course set menu.

Day 2

Head out of Tangier and along the coast. You can do this by public transport but this part of Morocco is best enjoyed with your own transport, so renting a car is a good idea. After looping around the Spanish enclave of Ceuta *(p166)* the coastal road passes through a string of glitzy new resorts before reaching M'diq. Once a fishing village, this is now fast becoming the place to go on Morocco's Mediterranean coast and has a host of beachfront cafés that are perfect for a spot of lunch. Afterwards, swing inland and climb up to Tetouan, where you can stop for the night.

Day 3

Take most of the day to explore the whitewashed charms of Tetouan *(p158)*, which feels more Andalucían than Arabic. Meander in the *mellah*, the old Jewish quarter, and take a look at the former grand railway station, which is now a museum of art. Break for a seafood lunch at the Esquina de Pescado *(43 Avenue Chakib Arsalan)* before continuing your exploration. In late afternoon say your goodbyes and head south on route N2 for Chefchaouen.

1 Blue painted walls of the old Medina in Chefchaouen.

2 Musicians playing at Tangier's stunning Kasbah.

3 Modern Art Center of Tetouan.

4 Tangier's winding medina.

5 Refreshing mint tea, a Moroccan staple.

Day 4

Beautiful hill town Chefchaouen *(p160)* is perfect Instagram material, with its tangle of blue-painted streets tumbling between two peaks. It is a glorious place to spend the day – wander the medina and the Quartier al-Andalus, sit on central Place Uta el-Hammam, sip mint tea and watch the world go by. There are plenty of decent places to eat and lots of characterful accommodation.

Day 5

After an early, hearty breakfast leave Chefchaouen and drive east on route N2. Head for Al-Hoceima *(p167)*, some 210 km (126 miles) away, which should take you just under five hours. This is one of Morocco's most spectacular roads, passing through the heart of the Rif Mountains, with stunning views of the deep slopes below and distant high peaks. You'll have plenty of opportunities to stop and take photos.

Day 6

Enjoy a leisurely morning after a day on the road. Al-Hoceima is a quiet sea-side town with a strong Berber character, home to a small but lively fishing harbour and lovely sandy beaches. Better still, it's a good base for exploring neighbouring Al-Hoceima National Park. Full of rocky canyons covered by forests, the national park is a haven for bird- and wildlife and makes for great exploration in the afternoon.

Day 7

Set off for Tangier by following Route N16. This hugs the southern fringes of Al-Hoceima National Park before closely following the coast all the way back to Tetouan and providing yet more fabulous scenery. You can pick up the main highway back to Tangier before enjoying a reviving mint tea at Café Hafa *(p145)*.

Roaming the Rif

The Rif is the most northerly of Morocco's mountain chains. Its peaks aren't as high as the Atlas but the landscape is a patchwork of verdant greens, with views of the azure Mediterranean. Hillside towns, such as the pastel-blue Chefchaouen *(p160)*, make a good base from which to explore neighbouring valleys.

←

Lush vegetation on the rolling hills of The Rif

MOROCCO FOR
CHALLENGING LANDSCAPES

With mountain ranges towering to heights of over 4,000 m (13,130 ft), extensive Atlantic and Mediterranean coastlines and vast areas of desert, the landscape of Morocco is nothing if not varied. It is possible to pass between snow-capped peaks and steep-sided sand dunes in the same day.

Palm Oases

The roads south of the High Atlas link numerous and often extensive palm oases. These are fed either by rivers flowing down from the mountains or by the underground water table. Set in hostile surroundings, the oases are a fragile ecological environment that only survives thanks to careful human maintenance. They mostly support date palms, whose fruit is harvested each autumn. Some of the largest palm oases can be found near the city of Tinerhir *(p291)* and around Tafilalt *(p296)*.

→

A palm tree forest growing around a village in Morocco

↑ Snow-capped peaks and wild terrain in the Atlas Mountains

Experience the Mountain Air

The Atlas Mountains range in a diagonal right across Morocco. To the north are the low-rise Middle Atlas, blanketed with Aleppo pine and Atlas cedar. Towns like Ifrane *(p222)* offer easy trekking between remote Berber mountain villages. Further south are the soaring peaks of the High Atlas. Several dizzying roads pass through the peaks, notably the Tizi-n-Tichka *(p272)*. Serious hikers should head to Imlil *(p271)* for the highest peak, Mount Toubkal.

> **INSIDER TIP**
> **Desert Dust**
>
> Be mindful of your impact on the desert environment and wildlife when choosing your tour operator. Opting for a traditional camel-ride over a 4WD lessens disruption to the fragile ecosystem.

Enter the Sahara

Almost half of the territory of Morocco is desert. Only the truly intrepid venture into the remote southern Sahara provinces. South of the High Atlas, however, well-worn trails wind down to spectacular dune fields at Mhamid *(p288)* and Merzouga *(p296)*. Here, vast shifting seas of sands roll away to the Algerian border and beyond. There is even the opportunity to join a desert camp and sleep under the clear skies and the stars.

↑ Camping in the desert *(inset)*, and sunset over the Erg Chebbi dunes

Sandboarding

For those who make it all the way down to where the grand Sahara begins at Merzouga *(p296)* in the Southern Oases, several companies offer the opportunity to go sandboarding. If you have never done it before, it involves hiking through the warm sand to reach the top of the steep dunes, then mounting a board and whizzing down at high speed. These excursions can often be paired with camel trekking, star gazing and camping in the desert dunes.

Sandboarding down the steep slopes of the Sahara Desert ↓

MOROCCO FOR
OUTDOOR ADVENTURES

Morocco's dramatic natural environments and great topographical diversity make it a great destination for all manner of adventure sports and activities from sandboarding to skiing. Day trips to these outdoor playgrounds can be easily arranged from the major tourist hubs of Marrakech and Fès.

Skiing and Snowboarding

Few would associate Morocco with winter sports, but the country has several high-altitude resorts, including Ifrane *(p222)*, near Fès, and Oukaïmeden *(p268)*, near Marrakech. Close enough for a day trip to the city, Oukaïmeden also has accommodation for anyone who wants to make an early start on the pistes.

→

Descending the rocky slopes of the High Atlas

Hiking and Trekking

Morocco offers all grades of trekking, from gentle trails through forests and valleys in the undulating terrain of the Rif and Middle Atlas, through to high-altitude expeditions in the High Atlas that require porters and camel, mule or vehicle support. Some of the most popular routes are around Jbel Toubkal *(p274)*, Morocco's highest mountain, and the Aït Bouguemez Valley.

CAMEL WELFARE

As tourism continues to increase in Morocco, camels are more at risk of suffering from neglect and abuse. If you see an animal being treated badly by their handler, refuse the ride. You can also file a report to the Ministry of Tourism.

↑ Hikers trekking through the arid High Atlas terrain

Up, Up and Away!

Enjoy a bird's-eye view of the sprawling city of Marrakech and surrounding desert and the foothills of the Atlas Mountains from the lofty heights of your very own hot air balloon. Several companies based in Marrakech offer dawn departures that allow you to take in the sunrise as you float above the city. A traditional Moroccan breakfast is usually included in the deal.

↑ Balloons above Marrakech *(inset)* and the Sahara

Marine Mammals

Bordering both the Atlantic Ocean and the Mediterranean Sea, Morocco's coastline is home to an abundance of marine wildlife. Dolphins and porpoises can be spotted all along the coast, while the Strait of Gibraltar is a great place to see sperm whales and orcas. Hop on a boat tour from Tangier between April and July for the best chance of seeing them in the wild.

←

Wild orcas swimming in the Strait of Gibraltar, home to a wide variety of marine life

MOROCCO FOR
WILDLIFE
ENCOUNTERS

From vast expanses of forests and arid desert to towering mountain plateaus and miles of coastline, Morocco's tremendous diversity of habitats supports a wide range of fascinating species of mammals and birdlife. Skip the zoos and venture into the wild to see these magnificent creatures.

Monkeying Around

The macaque, or Barbary ape, is North Africa's only monkey. Three-quarters of the population lives in the cedar forests of the Middle Atlas. Macaques are also found in the Rif and the High Atlas (and on the Rock of Gibraltar). The animals live in colonies of 10 to 30 individuals, consisting of adults and young monkeys of both sexes; troops are matriarchal, with the male monkeys helping rear the young. The easiest way to see them is on a day trip from Marrakech to the Cascades d'Ouzoud *(p216)*.

→

A lone macaque relaxes in the treetops, Morocco's only species of monkey

Dinky Desert Foxes

The fennec fox, the smallest of its species in the world, abides in some of Morocco's harshest desert environments. Measuring around 20 cm (8 inches) long when fully grown, and with super-size ears, the nocturnal fennec fox is as elusive as it is adorable. Only a lucky few will stumble across them in the wilds of the Western Sahara. However, they can be more easily glimpsed on an over-night desert stay, when they venture out of their dens dug in the sand and come surprisingly close to the camps. Beware of roadside petting zoos that allow tourists to pet captive fennecs; species numbers have declined dramatically because of this behaviour.

$\rightarrow$

A tiny fennec fox, famous for its minature size and large ears

Birds of a Feather

With over 460 recorded species, Morocco is a bird-watcher's paradise. Souss Massa National Park *(p308)*, Oualidia *(p136)*, and Moulay Bousselham *(p101)*, host migrant species such as flamingoes, egrets, and the near extinct bald ibis in October and March–April.

$\leftarrow$

Inquisitive male Seebohm's Wheatear perches on a rock

NATIONAL PARKS AND NATURE RESERVES

There are 11 national parks in Morocco, all of which support indigenous wildlife. Souss Massa *(p308)* holds captive-breeding programmes for four threatened North African species including the scimitar oryx and the dorcas gazelle, and is in the process of reintroducing the North African ostrich. Ifrane National Park *(p228)* is home to a population of Barbary apes, while Merja Zerga is a Permanent Biological Reserve that welcomes masses of migrating birds.

INGENIOUS DESIGN

Before the days of air-conditioning, Moroccan buildings were constructed to withstand intense heat. Townhouses, known as riads, still consist of an open central courtyard to aid ventilation, while thick, windowless exterior walls keep the heat out. Mosques and public buildings often contain a system of fountains and open channels that, in combination with natural ventilation, creates a cooling effect.

The splendid courtyard and ablution pool in Ben Youssef Medersa ↑

MOROCCO FOR
AMAZING ARCHITECTURE

Traditional Moroccan architecture is like a jewellery box, where an often plain exterior hides fabulous riches within. Mosques and *medersas* typically present blank faces to the street but once inside a riot of ornamentation awaits. In Morocco, it pays to be nosey and stick your head through the door.

Fabulous Fondouks

The *fondouk* is the ancestor of the hotel, a medieval merchants' hostel with a courtyard surrounded by stables on the ground floor and rooms above. Travellers to Chefchaouen (p160) can still stay in an original *fondouk*. Many have now been coverted into shops, yet the Fondouk el-Nejjarine (p185) in Fès has become a museum of wooden arts.

←

The splendid galleried interior of the Fondouk el-Nejjarine, now a museum

Magnificent Mosques and Medersas

Non-Muslims are not allowed inside mosques in Morocco and have to be content with admiring their distinctive, square-shaped minarets from the sidelines. The exception is the modern Hassan II Mosque *(p110)* in Casablanca, which non-Muslims can visit as part of a guided tour. Non-Muslims can also visit any of the many *medersas* (Koranic schools) found in most cities. These are often filled with exquisite architectural ornamentation. Don't miss the Bou Inania Medersa *(p205)* in Fès, which also has a minaret, and the Ben Youssef Medersa *(p240)* in Marrakech – the largest *medersa* in Morocco.

Rock the Kasbah

The kasbah (also sometimes called a *ksar*; plural *ksour*) is a fortified dwelling typically found in the tribal south. They are made of mud-brick, and the upper parts of the walls are often decorated with geometric patterns and incised motifs. They can be quite small, meant for a single family, or, as in the case of the Aït Benhaddou *(p280),* they can sprawl up hillsides and accommodate whole villages.

→

One of the tower structures that form part of the magnificent Aït Benhaddou

Art Deco à la Mode

French rule in the early 20th century left Morocco's cities with a legacy of elegant modernist architecture. Casablanca is packed full of stunning Art-Deco buildings such as the beautiful tiled façade of Hôtel Guynemer on Rue Mohamed Belloul or the iconic Cinema Rialto on the corner of Rue Mohammed el Qorri *(p114)*.

←

Art Deco façade of the imposing Casablanca Cathedral

The Souks of Marrakech

Every medina has areas dedicated to buying and selling known as souks (bazaars). Some of the most extensive souks are in Marrakech where, as is typical, they are organised by trade. The colour, smells and sounds are mesmerizing, and a day spent in the souks is one of the most rewarding things you can do in Morocco, whether you are buying or not.

$\rightarrow$

Exploring one the many bustling souks in Marrakech

MOROCCO FOR
MEDIEVAL MEDINAS

Medina in Arabic simply means city, although in Morocco today it is usually taken to mean the "old city". These atmospheric tangles of narrow winding streets and alleys, enclosed within high defensive walls, are a perfect place to take in the sights, sounds and smells of Morocco.

Get Lost in Fès el-Bali

The best-preserved and most sprawling Medina in Morocco belongs to Fès el-Bali, or old Fès. It may seem choatic on arrival, but there is still a sense of order. The grand mosque is at the centre, different religious and ethnic groups have their own areas, and activities are located according to a social and commercial hierarchy. Despite this, any first-time visitor will inevitably get lost, which is all part of the experience.

Locals at work in the historic tanneries of Fès el-Bali ↑

Chefchaouen Blues

With its blue- and white-washed buildings and mediterranean-style terracotta roofs, the Rif city of Chefchaouen (p160) looks more like a Greek island village than a Moroccan city. Fortunately the medina is much smaller than the maze-like Fès el-Bali, and the pace of life notably calmer. The cobbled lanes are lined with quirky cafés, and shops are filled with local handicrafts. Relax in the blue hues or venture into the tranquil greenery of the hills that surround this beautiful city.

← The famously blue walls and steps of the city of Chefchaouen, peppered with plants

PRETTY IN PINK

The more perceptive visitor may have noticed that every building in Marrakech medina is painted pink. Why? It's the law, introduced during the era of French rule. The colour is actually ochre, the colour of the earth from which bricks were made in the past. Modern buildings still uphold this pink paint tradition, making the city a photographer's dream, particularly in the morning and evening light. Once you've captured the so-called Rose City, head to the Blue Pearl of Morocco, Chefchaouen.

💬 INSIDER TIP
Guide or No Guide?

You may be approached in the medina by a local offering their services as a guide. This usually means they want to take you shopping and earn a commission on any sale. Unless you really are looking for something in particular, just say no.

The Ancient Walls of Taroudannt

Taroudannt's well-preserved walls are a reminder of the time when the mountain city was a stop-off on the trans-Saharan trading route. Unlike in other Moroccan cities, it is possible to walk along the top of a stretch of these walls. The view from up there is particularly lovely at sunset.

→ Passing through a gateway in the city walls of Taroudannt

NAVIGATING THE MEDINA

Almost all of Morocco's Medina's have the same layout. The typical medina (meaning "town" in Arabic) consists of a densely packed urban conglomeration enclosed within defensive walls set with lookout towers. The tangle of narrow winding streets and countless alleyways turns the layout of a medina into a labyrinth. The centre of the medina is cut through by wide avenues running between the main gateways and other main streets, which, as a defensive measure, are either angled or closed off by houses or projecting walls.

THE LAYOUT OF A MEDINA

Despite their apparent chaos, medinas are laid out according to a certain set of considerations. The mosque is always located at its heart. Other features include the separation of different religious and ethnic groups, the distinction between home and the workplace, and the location of activities according to a social and commercial hierarchy. Every medina is laid out according to these factors.

THE QUARTERS

The quarters of a medina are no more than loosely defined areas. A quarter, or *hawma*, is really just a communal space consisting of several small streets and alleyways, and it is the focus of the inhabitants' material and spiritual life. Each quarter has a communal oven, a hammam (steam bath), a Koranic school, and a grocer's shop selling basic goods, which is always located in one of the smaller streets.

Did You Know?

The medina of Fès el-Bali is said to be the best-preserved medieval town in the Arab world.

Townhouses, or riads, are arrange around a central courtyard

Roof terrace

Street partly blocked by a house

← Jemaa el-Fna, at the heart of Marrakech Medina, and the souks branching off it *(inset)*

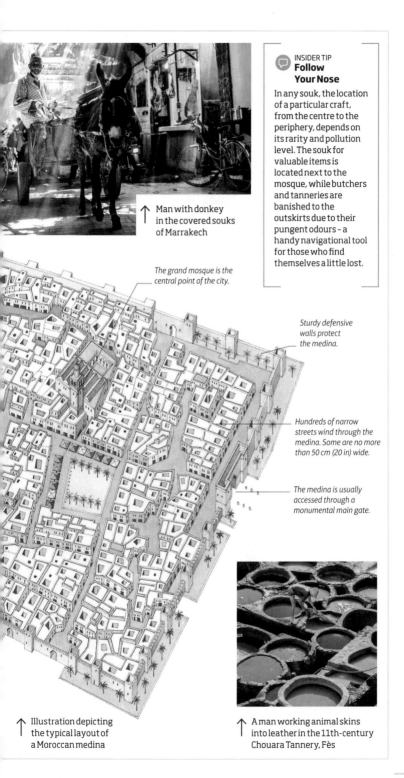

Man with donkey in the covered souks of Marrakech

INSIDER TIP
Follow Your Nose

In any souk, the location of a particular craft, from the centre to the periphery, depends on its rarity and pollution level. The souk for valuable items is located next to the mosque, while butchers and tanneries are banished to the outskirts due to their pungent odours – a handy navigational tool for those who find themselves a little lost.

The grand mosque is the central point of the city.

Sturdy defensive walls protect the medina.

Hundreds of narrow streets wind through the medina. Some are no more than 50 cm (20 in) wide.

The medina is usually accessed through a monumental main gate.

Illustration depicting the typical layout of a Moroccan medina

A man working animal skins into leather in the 11th-century Chouara Tannery, Fès

Seafood Galore

Morocco's coastal position means sardines, anchovies, prawns and mackerel are just some of the fresh offerings you will find on menus. Fish such as bream and bass are typically marinated in a spicy mixture called chermoula and are usually cooked and served whole. In Essaouira, the freshest fish is served straight off the boats in the port *(p126)*.

←

A delicious plate of oysters and lime, straight from the sea

MOROCCO FOR
FOODIES

Eating in Morocco is an absolute joy, so make sure you pack an appetite. Restaurant meals can be elaborate affairs of multiple courses, but there is even more fun to be had grazing on street food from small medina stalls, harbourfront grills and market squares.

TOP 4 MUST TRY DISHES

Merguez
Spicy mutton or beef sausage, often used in a tagine or couscous dish.

Pastilla
Pastry pie filled with chicken or pigeon, almonds and eggs, and dusted with icing sugar.

Harira
A spicy lamb broth made with tomatoes, red lentils, chickpeas and other pulses.

Mechoui
A whole sheep or lamb slowly spit-roasted on a barbecue until the meat becomes incredibly tender.

Tajines and Couscous

The twin staples of Moroccan cuisine are tajines and couscous. A tajine is a slow-cooked stew, typically involving a meat and fruit combination, such as lamb with prunes or apricots, or chicken with lemon or olives. Couscous, the Moroccan national dish, is a semolina-based grain, which is typically served with stew.

→

A sumptuous array of tagines and couscous traditional dishes

Dining on the Square

The variety of foods sold from small stalls or handcarts around Morocco is endless. The best place to sample the greatest range is at Marrakech's Night Market, which takes over half of the city's main square each evening. Over 40 stalls fire up their gas burners to prepare grilled meats, fried fish, griddled veg and many more wild and wonderful dishes unique to Morocco. It's easy to be overwhelmed with choice, so to sample local favourites, look for the stalls that attract the greatest numbers.

→

Street food at the Night Market in Marrakech

Fine Dining

Morocco's imperial cities are now home to a number of restaurants serving up innovative, contemporary dishes with locally sourced ingredients, whilst honouring the country's vibrant culinary traditions. Headed up by Yannick Alléno and his team of talented chefs, La Grande Table Marocaine at the Royal Mansour in Marrakech is often hailed as the best in the country.

←

Traditional sweet Moroccan pastries

Mint Tea

To help with digestion, herb-infused teas are sipped at the end of the meal. Those herbs might be lemon-scented verbena or wormwood, but most usually it's mint. Authentic Maghrebi mint tea is made with spearmint leaves and sugar. The tea is served hot and very sweet, and you glass is never allowed to be empty. Tea is consumed socially throughout the day in Morocco.

→

Two glasses of refreshingly sweet Moroccan mint tea

Moroccan Must-buys

Shoppers should consider Moroccan leather, and bags make great souvenirs. Soft leather is also used for babouches; striking slippers with pointed toes. Local ceramics vary from city to city; Marrakech favours single colours, Fès prefers blue patterns. Moroccan argan oil is a popular beauty product – pick it up cheap in Essaouira (p126) and Taroudannt (p306).

→

Gorgeous coin-studded leather bags for sale in Marrakech

MOROCCO FOR
SHOPPERS

Morocco's souks represent commerce at its most intoxicating, with thousands of small shops crammed together and bursting with evocative colour and pattern. In Morocco's cities, smart and sophisticated boutiques selling unique designer items are equally tempting. Where will you begin?

HONE THOSE HAGGLING SKILLS

Haggling is expected – and encouraged – across all items in the souk, except for food. Sellers enjoy the friendly bartering, often performing a series of dramatics before settling on a price. Be polite and playful, yet firm; offer as little as a third of the stated price (don't be put off by the laughter that will inevitably ensue) and expect to eventually pay around half. Anything higher and you are likely being ripped off. Avoid entering negotiations if you're unsure that you will make a purchase.

Shopping the Souks

Chunky jewellery, silk kaftans, brass lightshades – it is impossible to explore a souk and not buy something you never knew you wanted. The most extensive and enticing souks are in Fès, Marrakech and Rabat. Safi (p136) is great for pottery, while Azrou (p222) is the place for rugs.

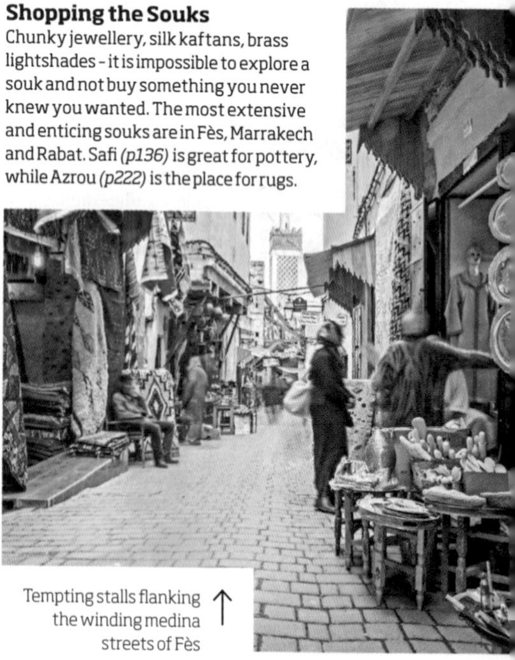

Tempting stalls flanking the winding medina streets of Fès ↑

Modern Moroccan Styles

It's not just about labyrinthine souks packed with trinkets and treasures. Away from the souks, the modern city centres in Marrakech (p230), Rabat (p72), Casablanca (p106) and Tangier (p140) are full of bijou boutiques and curated concept shops selling contemporary Moroccan fashion, accessories and homeware. Look for clothing, candles, soaps, scents and gorgeous jewellery by young local talent. If you're in Marrakech, head to the boutique at the fabulous El Fenn hotel (www.el-fenn.com).

← Perusing the wares in a modern ceramics shop in Marrakech

TOP 5 SHOPPING EXPERIENCES

33 Rue Majorelle
⌂ 33 Rue Yves Saint Laurent, Marrakech
Chic goods made by local artists and up-and-coming designers.

Elizir Gallery
⌂ 22 Avenue d'Istiqlal, Medina, Essaouira
Retro store piled high with vintage furniture and knick-knacks.

Las Chicas
⌂ 52 Kacem Guenoun, Bab Kasbah, Tangier
An eclectic emporium stocked with everything imaginable.

Les Mystères de Fès
⌂ 53 Derb Bin Lemsarri, Medina, Fès
A 13th-century riad stuffed with antiques and vintage pieces.

Souq Cherifia
⌂ Rue Mouassine, Marrakech
Pieces by young, edgy Moroccan designers.

↑ Vibrantly patterned carpets displayed in Marrakech's souks

Carpets Galore

Berber carpets are unique, coming in all shapes, sizes and patterns, depending on their region. Good places to find them are Marrakech and the souks of the Middle and High Atlas. City carpets are typically woven in Rabat, Salé and Casablanca and feature perfectly symmetrical patterns. Pick one up at the Tuesday carpet market in Khemisset (p210).

Masterpieces in Marrakech

Marrakech is the art hub of Morocco and, more broadly, North Africa. The scene here centres around the new city neighbourhood of Guéliz (p257), which has a dynamic and diverse feel that befits an artistic heart. The side streets surrounding Place Abdel Moumen in particular are jam-packed with cutting-edge independent galleries. Any art tour should include the refined, New York-loft-like David Bloch Gallery (Rue des Vieux Marrakchis), Galerie 127 (127 Avenue Mohammed V), a centre for African photography, and Matisse Gallery (Passage Ghandouri, off Rue Yougoslavie), which exhibits the big-hitters of Moroccan art.

↑ Exhibition by Carlos Mare and Vincent Abadie Hafez at the David Bloch Gallery

MOROCCO FOR
ART LOVERS

Countless artists from Europe and America have found inspiration in Morocco, creating great masterpieces based on their travels. Today, the country inspires local artists and their works are rightly showcased in an increasing number of chic private galleries across the country.

Art by the Sea

The stunning light in the coastal city of Essaouira (p126) has long attracted artists, whose works have gained international plaudits. The artists share a vibrant "tribal", almost Aboriginal, style that draws on Arab-Berber history. It's hard to resist their cheerful, bright colours, swirling shapes and evident affection for the city. The best place to see their work is at Essaouira's Galerie Damgaard (p129), which has been at the forefront of promoting the group's work since the 1980s.

←

This bright painting, by Mohammed Tabal, is typical of Essaouira's style

↑ Inside the beautiful Villa des Arts in the modern capital of Rabat

Contemporary Capital

As well as being home to the impressive Villa des Arts (p116), Morocco's inaugural Museum of Modern and Contemporary Art (p80) opened in Rabat in 2014. While hosting a blockbuster programme of temporary exhibitions, it's permanent collection offers a useful crash-course in Morocco's history of fine art.

Land of Inspiration

From Eugène Delacroix to Henri Matisse, artists have been drawn to Morocco by its stunning light and dramatic scenery. Perhaps you'll be inspired to paint your own master-piece - observe life in the city of Tangier (p140), or head to the utterly enchanting Majorelle Garden (p242) established by French artist Jacques Majorelle.

→

Fanatics of Tangier (1832) by Eugène Delacroix

TOP 5 UNIQUE ART SPACES

Atelier 21
⌂ 21 Rue Abou Al Mahassine Royani, Casablanca
One of Casablanca's leading contemporary galleries, exhibiting Moroccan artworks.

Green Olive Arts
⌂ 18 Avenue Mohammed ben Abderrahman, Tetouan
Artist residency and collaborative space celebrating local art.

Al Maqam
⌂ Douar Lamgassem, Tahannaout
The studio of famed artists Mohammed Mourabiti and Mahi Binebine.

Riad Yima
⌂ 52 Derb Aarjane, off Rahba Lakdima, Medina, Marrakech
Anglo-Moroccan artist Hassan Hajjaj displays his Warhol-esque pop art in this quirky riad.

Voice Gallery
⌂ 366 Sidi Ghanem, Marrakech
Cool gallery focusing on African art.

Marrakech in the Movies

Alfred Hitchcock's famed thriller *The Man Who Knew Too Much* (1955), starring James Stewart and Doris Day, features scenes in Jemma el- Fna *(p236)* and at the opulent Mamounia Hotel *(p251)*. City sights including the Ben Youssef Medersa *(p240)* also appear in *Hideous Kinky* (1998), starring actress Kate Winslet.

←

Brenda De Banzie and James Stewart in *The Man Who Knew Too Much*

MOROCCO ON
SCREEN

Fan of the silver screen? Morocco won't disappoint. The drama and diversity of its natural landscapes has landed the country several starring roles in blockbuster films and series. It's stood in for all manner of locations, including Egypt, Mombasa, Tibet, Troy and even Mars.

MARRAKECH INTERNATIONAL FILM FESTIVAL

Movie buffs and the rich and famous descend upon the imperial city *(p230)* for the Marrakech International Film Festival in December. Film fans can enjoy open-air screenings of classic Hollywood films, gritty arthouse productions, star-studded world premiers and special events throughout the city. It's also great for celeb-spotting.

→

John Hannah, Rachel Weisz and Brendan Fraser in *The Mummy*

Hollywood in the Desert

The desert city of Ouarzazate *(p282)* is known as "Morocco's Hollywood" and its film studios have hosted film crews for *The Mummy* (1999), *Star Wars* (1977) and *Gladiator* (2000) to name a few. When they're not in use, you can explore the sets, including a replica Roman Colosseum and an ancient Egyptian temple.

↑ Inside Rick's Café, inspired by Hollywood classic *Casablanca*

A Common Misconception

Ironically, the one famous film with a Moroccan connection, *Casablanca* (1942), was not shot here. Like countless others, the movie was shot almost entirely at Warner Bros. Studios in Burbank, California. In spite of this, you can still get a flavour of the romantic drama in the Moroccan city. Step back in time at Rick's Café *(p118)*, designed to recreate the bar made famous by Humphrey Bogart and Ingrid Bergman. Here's looking at you, Casablanca.

Did You Know?

Orson Welles stayed at Essaouira's Hôtel des Îles when filming *Othello* (1951). He met Winston Churchill here.

Game of Thrones

Blockbuster swords and dragons series *Game of Thrones* (2011–19) had a number of scenes filmed here in Morocco. Coastal Essaouira *(p126)* stood in for the fictional city of Astapor, also known as the Red City, with several scenes shot on the old fortified sea walls. The mud-walled kasbah of Aït Benhaddou *(p280)* was used to represent the slavers' city of Yunkai. Further scenes were shot in the arid deserts surrounding Ouarzazate *(p282)*.

↑ Fortress-turned-film set Aït Benhaddou, used in *Game of Thrones (inset)*

Hendrix and Essaouira

Jimi Hendrix spent a week in Essaouira in July 1969. His visit has inspired a thriving local "Hendrix-stayed-here" cottage industry. In fact, the only place he stayed was the Hôtel des Îles, near the port. This has not stopped the village of Diabat making the most of his visit. Here you will find the Café Hendrix, which is adorned with a large mural of the famous musician.

$\rightarrow$
Brightly coloured mural of Jimi Hendrix, located in Diabat

MOROCCO ON THE
HIPPY TRAIL

From the mid 1960s to the early 1970s, Morocco became part of the hippy movement. The free-spirited hung around the medinas in search of enlightenment and inspiration, as well as a good time. Today, Morocco still appeals to travellers looking to lose (or find) themselves in local culture.

MUSIC FESTIVALS

Morocco's homegrown musicians are joined by international artists for a whole host of annual music festivals. Chief among them is the Gnaoua World Music Festival (p129), which has been taking place in Essaouira since 1998. Also regularly attracting big international names are the Fès Festival of World Sacred Music, which has expanded its remit beyond the spiritual to embrace rock and pop, and Rabat's contemporary Mawazine Festival, which is one of the largest music festivals in the world.

Hanging out at the Café Baba

As the closest point to Europe, everyone passed through the once lawless city of Tangier. The cafés on the Petit Socco (p146) were, and still are, the places to meet. The same goes for Café Baba, also in Tangier, which was once a popular haunt of writers and musicians.

The pastel blue walls of Café Baba, adorned with ↑ photographs of musicians

Coastal Vibes

About 19 km (12 miles) north of Agadir is the small fishing village of Taghazout, where surf culture dominates. A popular spot for visitors seeking to escape the cities, it was colonized by the hippy movement in the 1970s, and still retains much of its bohemian charm. Nearby Banana Village and Paradise Valley (a worthwhile day trip for rock pools and waterfalls) attract many backpackers seeking adventures on the road less travelled – not so easy these days with tourism on the rise.

← Relaxing by the sea near near tranquil Taghazout, a surfing paradise

TOP 4 MOROCCAN INSPIRED TRACKS

"Marrakesh Express" by Crosby, Stills and Nash
Inspired by a trip songwriter Graham Nash made by train from Casablanca to Marrakech in 1966.

"Jealous Guy" by John Lennon
The Beatles spent time in Morocco and an early version of this Lennon song was called "On the Road to Marrakesh".

"Continental Drift" by The Rolling Stones
The Stones recorded with Morocco's Master Musicians of Jajouka on their 1989 Steel Wheels album.

"No Quarter" by Robert Plant and Jimmy Page
The video to accompany this 1994 recording was filmed on Jemaa el-Fna.

The Rolling Stones at Jemaa el-Fna

In March 1967 the Rolling Stones took up temporary residence at the Es Saadi hotel in Marrakech. They made field recordings of local Gnaoua musicians in Jemaa el-Fna, the descendents of whom still play on the square most evenings (p236). There are also concerts of local musicians four nights a week at Café Clock in the Kasbah, a funky venue that keeps the creative spirit of Marrakech burning.

↑ A performance by Gnaoua musicians in Jemaa el-Fna

Did You Know?

On Legriza Beach there stands a monumental sandstone arch, formed from years of erosion.

MOROCCO FOR
BEACHGOERS

With over 1,930 km (1,200 miles) of combined Mediterranean and Atlantic coastline, Morocco has no shortage of beaches. Other than a few resorts, much of this coastline is relatively undeveloped, particularly in the south. For those seeking watersports, Morocco is also a major centre for surfing.

Bustling Beach Resorts

The premier Moroccan beach resort is Agadir *(p302)* thanks to its long, wide, white-sand beach and year-round sunshine. It has plenty of good hotels and lots going on when it comes to eating, drinking and nightlife. Further north on the Atlantic coast, locals flock to the pretty town of Asilah *(p94)* in the summer months, turning the quiet town into a thriving resort. On the Mediterranean, Tamuda Bay has a lovely beach that slopes gently into the sea.

$\longrightarrow$

Palms trees, modern hotels and a glorious sandy bay at Agadir

Watersports on the Atlantic Coast

A number of spots along Morocco's Atlantic coast rate highly among the global surf community. These include Mehdya (p98) near Rabat, Sidi Kaouki (p132) near Essaouira, and further to south, the small, sleepy town of Sidi Ifni (p304). Further south still, Dakhla has a lagoon renowned for watersports, including kite surfing. Strong winds and currents mean that these places are best suited to experienced surfers. Less demanding watersports and other activities are offered at resorts such as Agadir (p302).

←

Gliding along the waters of Dakhla's lagoon, an area famous for its powerful winds

> **INSIDER TIP**
> **Beach Dress Code**
>
> Bikinis are fine at resorts but on more remote beaches it's customary for women to wear a sarong when not in the water. Pack a wetsuit for watersports: the Atlantic's chill may suprise you.

↑ A surfer exits the water after a hard day's surfing

Off the Beaten Track

If you really want to lose the crowds, head south. There are countless excellent beaches beyond Agadir, including the secluded Plage Sauvage and Legriza, both near Sidi Ifni (p304). The area is not the most accessible, which is why it has remained a haven for those desiring peace. One of the country's longest and loveliest stretches of sand is at Saïdia (p170), on the north coast not far from the Algerian border.

↑ Crystal-clear water in a secluded cove near the town of Saïdia

Go Public with the Locals

Bathing is a huge part of Moroccan culture, so it's not surprising that every town and city has its bathhouse. The advent of domestic plumbing means public bathhouses are more about socialising than getting clean. Join the locals at the famous Hammam El Bacha *(20 Rue Fatima Zohra, Medina)* in Marrakech *(p230)*; it was built for the servants of the ruler of Marrakech, who resided in the nearby Dar El Bacha. In Fès *(p172)*, the Hammam Aïn Azleten *(Talâa Kebira)* and Hammam Sidi Azouz *(Talâa Seghira, opposite Hôtel Lamrani)* both offer an authentic experience in the Medina.

→
Intricate tilework at a public bathhouse

MOROCCO FOR
HAMMAMS AND SPAS

The Moroccan hammam experience is certainly one that ought not to be missed. Ranging from simple one-room saunas to elaborate hammam complexes, and offering massages, facials and – if you're feeling brave – an invigorating full body scrub down, this is the perfect way to unwind.

Plush Private Hammams

A wave of boutique hammams catering for travel-worn tourists has swept across the country. Those seeking a high-end hammam experience should consider staying in a larger riad or hotel with a hammam on site, such as La Sultana Marakkech *(www.lasultanahotels.com)*. These private hammams are dedicated to pampering, with steam rooms, plunge pools and treatment rooms galore. Alternatively ask staff for local recommendations.

↑ Relaxing at the luxury La Sultana Marrakech hotel

← A massage table sprinkled with rose petals and lit by candlelight at a luxury riad spa in Fès, northern Morocco

Indulge at a Destination Spa

Morocco offers an exceptional selection of spa treatments, often incorporating locally sourced natural oils, such as Rose Absolute from around the Dadès Gorge *(p290)* and native argan *(p138)*. Head to Agadir *(p302)* for seawater spas, while yogis will enjoy the specialist Om Yoga camp in Casablanca *(2 Rue Golfe des Comores)*. There's also the thermal centre at Moulay Yacoub *(Vichy Thermalia Moulay Yacoub, Fès Principale)*. In and around Marrakech has the greatest number of retreats, typically attached to luxury hotels.

← A tranquil, illuminated hammam pool beneath the Hassan II Mosque, Casablanca

MOROCCAN MASSAGE

An essential part of the hammam experience is a massage. Not for the faint-hearted, this involves being rubbed down with fragrant essential oils, followed by a vigorous all-over kneading. The full treatment takes about an hour and leaves you with limbs like jelly. There is usually a strict separation of the sexes when it comes to massage: masseurs for men, masseuses for women. Men typically wear shorts (or wrap a towel around themselves) while women tend to go naked. Swimwear or underwear is permitted if you don't want to bare all.

Did You Know?

Storks are thought to be reincarnations of *marabouts* (holy men) and so are viewed as sacred.

MOROCCO FOR
SPIRITUALITY

Although Morocco is a Muslim country, many people retain beliefs that are outside the mainstream religion. The cult of saints and holy men is strong, and the practising of spiritualist rites (zikrs) is a spectacle for any visitor looking to experience Morocco's colourful spiritual life.

Tombs of Holy Men

Followers of holy men *(marabouts)* gather eagerly to make pilgrimages to their tombs and receive blessings *(baraka)*. These small mausoleums, which are often covered with a white dome, can be seen throughout Morocco. A charming example in Marrakech are the Saadian Tombs *(p256)*, tucked away in a peaceful garden. Some important shrines - or *zaouias* - are the subject of mass pilgrimages known as *moussems*. These gatherings are both spiritual and commercial occasions and are well worth attending. If you're in Fès in late summer, make time to join the *moussem* at the Zaouia of Moulay Idriss II *(p188)*.

↑ Worshipping at the tomb of Moulay Idriss I in Meknès

Moroccan Blues

Gnaoua is both a type of music and the name of those who play it. The Gnaoua people trace their ancestry back to sub-Saharan Africa, though they were taken north by slave traders. The favoured instrument of the Gnaoua musicians is the gimbri, a long-necked lute that produces hypnotic sounds. They are best experienced at Essaouira's Gnaoua World Music Festival (p129). You can also hear them year-round at Jemaa el-Fna in Marrakech (p236).

←

Gnaoua musicians performing in the streets of Essaouira

THE MOUSSEM

Moussems are festivals held in honour of saints and holy men and are typically rural affairs, although some have acquired national significance. The largest include the Moussem of Moulay Idriss held in Moulay Idriss (p202) and the Moussem of Moulay Idriss II in Fès (p188). Some are attached to the lunar calendar so they change date.

↑ Playing a gimbri, an instrument favoured by the Gnaoua people

Medicine and Magic

Moroccans have a strong belief in the power of ritual and charms. Exorcists in the south do a good business battling *jinns* – the spirits that bring bad luck. Look out for traditional herbalist stalls in the souks of Fès el-Bali (p185) and Marrakech (p238), where vendors demonstrate the powers of their wares.

700dh/K

↑ Assorted spices and herbs for sale in Marrakech's medina

A YEAR IN
MOROCCO

JANUARY

Yennayer, the Amazigh New Year *(12–13 Jan)*. Traditional Berber celebration of the new crop year in Agadir, Tiznit and the Middle Atlas.

△ **Marrakech Marathon** *(late Jan)*. See Marrakech at a blur as you race around the city.

FEBRUARY

△ **Almond Blossom Festival** *(2nd week in Feb)*. Held in hilltop Tafraoute, Morocco's largest producer of almonds.

Moussem of Sidi ben Aïssa *(late Feb–early Mar)*. One of Morocco's most spectacular saint's festivals, held in Meknès.

MAY

△ **Rose Festival** *(varies)*. Celebrating the rose harvest at El-Kelaa M'Gouna.

Trans-Atlas Marathon *(late May)*. 273 km (170-mile) race through the High Atlas.

Mawazine Festival *(May/June)*. Rabat pop and rock festival, with past headliners such as Rihanna.

JUNE

Fès Festival of World Sacred Music *(late Jun)*. An excellent world-music festival. Previous participants have included Björk and Patti Smith.

△ **Gnaoua World Music Festival** *(late Jun)*. Four-day festival of pop, jazz and world music held in Essaouira.

SEPTEMBER

Oasis Festival *(mid-Sep)*. A techno dance-fest held just outside Marrakech.

△ **Imilchil Marriage Festival** *(mid-Sep)*. Celebrated by Middle Atlas Berber tribes.

Jazz au Chellah *(late Sep)*. Five-day East-meets-West jazz festival held in Rabat.

OCTOBER

△ **Salon du Cheval** *(mid-Oct)*. A top international horse show held at El-Jadida on the Atlantic Coast.

Erfoud Date Festival *(varies)*. This three-day carnival is held in the Southern Oases, and takes place just after the date harvest.

MARCH

Beyond Sahara (*early Mar*). This music, culture, travel and wellbeing festival is held in locations across Morocco.

△ **Maroc Classic** (*mid-Mar*). An epic cross-country classic car rally.

APRIL

△ **Marathon des Sables** (*early Apr*). Extreme endurance seven-day foot race over 241 km (150 miles) of desert.

Festival International De Merzouga (*early Apr*). A festival of music and culture.

Jazzablanca (*mid-Apr*). Long-running jazz festival that takes place in Casablanca.

JULY

Timitar Music Festival (*early Jul*). A vibrant African music festival hosted in Agadir.

△ **Asilah Festival** (*varies*). Coastal arts festival involving mural painting in Asilah medina.

Festival of Popular Arts (*varies*). Berber musicians and dance troupes from across Morocco perform in Marrakech.

AUGUST

Alegria Festival (*mid-Aug*). An arts and music festival held in Chefchaouen in the Rif.

△ **Moussem of Moulay Idriss** (*late Aug*). This annual Moussem is held in Morocco's most important pilgrimage site, the town of Moulay Idriss.

NOVEMBER

Independence Day (*18 Nov*). Colourful parades and street parties mark Morocco's 1944 declaration of independence from French and Spanish colonial powers.

△ **Marrakech International Film Festival** (*last week Nov, first week Dec*). A glam affair heaving with celebs, parties and film events.

DECEMBER

△ **Tan Tan Moussem** (*early Dec*). An amazing gathering of thousands of Berber tribes in Southern Morocco to celebrate nomadic tradition and culture.

Olive Tree Festival (*mid-Dec*). This agricultural festival celebrating the noble olive is held in the Rif town of Rafsaï, north of Fès.

A BRIEF
HISTORY

Morocco is an ancient and diverse kingdom. Its origins are distinctly Berber, Arab and African, and since the 7th-century arrival of Islam, the country has been an important power on the global stage. Many cultures have combined to form Morocco today, and the influence of each is still tangible today.

Pre-Islamic Morocco

For over 40,000 years Morocco has been a bridge between the African and European continents. Archaeological finds prove that it was settled by the Berbers in the remote past but little is known of the first pre-Arab inhabitants of North Africa, who may have come from Eurasia and the Middle East.

The Phoenicians established trading posts along the Moroccan coast, which were later taken over by forces from Carthage (in modern Tunisia). In 146 BC, the Romans extended their control westwards over the northern half of Morocco. It became part of a region they called Mauretania and its

1 The port city of Safi in 7th-century Morocco. ↑

2 The arrival of fearless Phoenician navigators.

3 A mosaic depicting the labours of Hercules, found in of Volubilis.

4 A Berber general during Morocco's conquest of Spain.

Timeline of events

8000–7000 BC
Youssef ben Tachfin founds Marrakech and starts to expand his Almoravid empire

c 1000 BC
Arrival of the Phoenicians, who established trading posts along the coast

c 400 BC
Berber tribes unite to establish a kingdom, which would ultimately become known as Mauretania

46 BC
Roman Emperor Claudius annexes the Berber kingdom

southern frontier lay at the level of Rabat. In the 3rd century, however, Christianity began to spread and Roman domination was severely diminished. Religious unrest and local uprisings gradually extinguished the hold of all the ancient civilizations.

The Arrival of Islam

From the end of the 7th century, a new set of invaders, and a new religion, began to make its mark on Morocco. In 705, Moussa ibn Nosaïr brought the territory from Tangier to the Draa valley under the control of the Arab Islamic Umayyad caliph in Damascus. He then turned his attention to Europe, initiating the conquest of Spain in 711.

Back in Arabia, opposing sides battled for the right to rule the Islamic empire. One of those on the losing side, Idriss ibn Abdallah, fled as far west as he could, ending up in Morocco. In 789, the Aouraba (a Berber tribe) made him their leader. Idriss carved out a small kingdom, and set about building a new city, Fès. He died soon afterwards, and was succeeded by his son, Idriss II (793–828), who made Fès the Idrissid capital. The Idrissids are considered to be the first of Morocco's ruling dynasties.

WHERE TO SEE PRE-ISLAMIC MOROCCO

Lixus (p100), on the North Atlantic coast, was a Phoenician settlement, although the ruins that can be visited there date from the Roman era. There are more Roman remains at nearby Banasa (p104), but the finest site by far is Volubilis (p198), which includes the extensive remains of a major town.

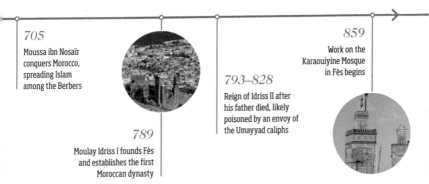

705
Moussa ibn Nosaïr conquers Morocco, spreading Islam among the Berbers

789
Moulay Idriss I founds Fès and establishes the first Moroccan dynasty

793–828
Reign of Idriss II after his father died, likely poisoned by an envoy of the Umayyad caliphs

859
Work on the Karaouiyine Mosque in Fès begins

نسوا حظا مما
ذكروا به ولا تزال
خطاب

Morocco and Andalusia

At the death of Idriss II, the kingdom was divided between his two sons, and then between their descendants. There were challenges from dynasties in Tunisia and Egypt, and from Andalusia in Spain. Unexpectedly, the next empire rose from the south. A tribe of nomadic Berbers came out of the Sahara to launch a crusade for a pure Islamic state. Their leader was Youssef ben Tachfin and he founded Marrakech, which became Morocco's second capital and the powerbase for a new dynasty, the Almoravids (1062–1147). The Almoravids extended their empire across the Mediterranean, and it was during their reign that the arts and crafts of Andalusia were imported into Morocco.

One Dynasty After Another

In opposition to the increasingly decadent Almoravids, the Almohads (1121–1269) emerged from Tin Mal, a narrow valley in the High Atlas, and took control of the main cities of Morocco and Andalusia. Far from being zealots, they proved enlightened rulers, reorganizing the empire's administration and economy, founding universities and encouraging a flourishing intellectual

① Ancient script, thought to date from 10th–11th century.

② Painting of the Chellah Necropolis, Rabat.

③ Tapestry depicting Portuguese King Alfonso's taking of Asilah.

Did You Know?
The imperial cities of Fès, Marrakesh, Meknes and Rabat have all served time as the capital of Morocco.

Timeline of events

1062
Youssef ben Tachfin founds Marrakech and starts to expand his Almoravid empire

1107–42
Andalusian culture takes root in Morocco during the reign of Ali ben Youssef

1130–63
Abd el-Moumen, the first Almohad caliph, conquers as far as Tripoli

1212–69
Decline of the Almohad dynasty and loss of territories in Andalusia

life. Theirs was an age of unequalled splendour. Ultimately, they were driven out of Andalusia by the Spanish Christian princes, and so began a cycle of Moroccan history in which revolutionary nomads wrenched power from corrupt city-dwellers, only to become bloated and complacent themselves, and ripe for the next army to march down from the mountain passes.

A Shrinking Empire

Next in line were the Merinids (1248–1465), who gained control of the major cities and fertile plains from 1248, although it was not until 1269 that they conquered Marrakech. They were unsuccessful in their attempts to regain territory on the Iberian peninsula and even lost the Moroccan region of Ceuta to the Portuguese. They were, however, competent domestic rulers and great builders. Many of the finest of Morocco's exquisite *medersas*, such as the Bou Inania in Fès, were built in the Merinid era. Inevitably, crises of succession and another emerging Berber dynasty gradually undermined their authority. On this occasion, with the waning of dynastic power within Morocco, Europe took its chance to intervene.

↑ An inscribed gold coin from the era of the Almohad dynasty

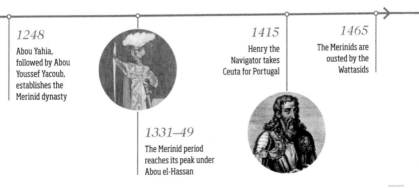

1248
Abou Yahia, followed by Abou Youssef Yacoub, establishes the Merinid dynasty

1331–49
The Merinid period reaches its peak under Abou el-Hassan

1415
Henry the Navigator takes Ceuta for Portugal

1465
The Merinids are ousted by the Wattasids

European Domination

With the expulsion of the last Muslim forces from Andalusia in 1492, the Spanish moved into northern Morocco and the Portuguese seized towns on the Atlantic coast. The response was led by the Beni Saad tribe from the Draa valley, which established the Saadian dynasty (1525–1659).

Like those before them, the Saadians ultimately declined and were replaced by the Alaouites, the seventh and present ruling group. It took ten years for the dynasty's founder, Moulay Rachid (1664–72), to bring the country under his control.

When Moulay Abdel Aziz ascended the throne in 1894, France already had an imperial presence in Algeria and Tunisia, and aimed to secure a free hand in Morocco. In 1907 French forces occupied Casablanca. Subsequent uprisings led the French to impose a protectorate through the Treaty of Fès in 1912.

The Fight for Independence

Morocco was divided into two zones: a French zone, covering the largest part of the country, and a Spanish zone, in the north and south. Tangier was an international free city. A new ruler,

↑ A depiction of French colonial rule, established in Morocco in 1912

Timeline of events

1525
The Saadians take Marrakech and make it their capital

1757–90
Rule of Sidi Mohammed Ben Abdallah who establishes his capital in Rabat

1912
The signing of the Treaty of Fès, through which the French impose a protectorate

1927
Reign of the sultan Mohammed ben Youssef, (later Mohammed V) begins

Mohammed V, drew a following of young nationalists, who set up the Istiqlal (Independence) Party. The French responded by forcing Mohammed V into exile. But international opinion no longer supported the colonial powers, and the United Nations stepped in. After negotiations with France, the deposed sultan made his triumphant return from exile as King Mohammed V.

Morocco Today

Today, Morocco is a constitutional monarchy. The head of state since 1999, King Mohammed VI (grandson of Mohammed V), rules through an elected parliament. It is a Muslim state based on Islamic law, although – certainly in the cities – few people appear to be overtly religious. The country has strong economic and political ties to the West, and old adversaries France and Spain are Morocco's primary trade partners, as well as their primary foreign investors. Blessedly free of the political turmoil that has raged elsewhere in North Africa, present-day Morocco marries modern Mediterranean culture with a rich Islamic heritage, underlaid with ancient tribal Berber customs and practices. It makes for a complex and intoxicating mix.

1 Painting depicting negotiations in the 1600s.

2 Moroccan and French leaders at the end of WW2.

3 Kofi Annan of the UN meets King Hassan II.

4 King Mohammed VI and Emmanuel Macron.

Did You Know?

In 1777, Morocco became the first country to recognize the USA as an independent nation.

1956

The French Protectorate officially ends, and Morocco celebrates its independence

1999

Death of King Hassan II. His son, the current reigning monarch, is crowned Mohammed VI

2004

The Al-Hoceima earthquake kills more than 500 people in Northern Morocco

2011

Moroccans protest in Rabat for months to demand constitutional reform

EXPERIENCE

Striking blue medina of Chefchaouen

RABAT

Following the defeat of Alfonso VIII of Castel at the Battle of Alarcos in 1195, the caliph Yacoub el-Mansour embarked on the construction of a great and splendid city that was to be known as Ribat el-Fath (Camp of Victory). The Almohads' defeat at the Battle of Las Navas de Tolosa in 1212 weakened their power and led to the city's decline.

In 1610, Philip III of Spain expelled from his kingdom the remaining Moors, who fled to the cities of the Maghreb, with many settling in Rabat. The city then became the capital of a minor and relatively autonomous coastal republic. Funds brought by the Andalucian refugees were put towards a flotilla of privateers that preyed on European shipping. The "Republic of Bou Regreg", as it was known, was then annexed to the sherif's kingdom in 1666, although piracy was not brought to an end until the mid-19th century. In 1912 Marshal Lyautey made Rabat the political, administrative capital of Morocco.

RABAT

Must Sees

1. Mausoleum of Mohammed V
2. Chellah Necropolis
3. Mohammed VI Museum of Modern and Contemporary Art

Experience More

4. City Walls
5. Bab Oudaïa
6. Place du Souk el-Ghezel and Rue Hadj Daoui
7. Musée des Oudaïa
8. Rue des Consuls
9. Rue Souk es-Sebat
10. Rue Souïka
11. Andalusian Wall
12. Hassan Tower
13. Ville Nouvelle
14. Musée de l'Histoire et des Civilisations
15. Bab el-Rouah
16. Dar el-Makhzen

Eat

1. Dar Zaki
2. La Koutoubia
3. Cosmopolitan

Stay

4. L'Alcazar
5. Le Pietri Urban Hotel

Plage de Salé Ville

D **E** **F**

BAB AL-BAHR

AVENUE SIDI BEN ACHIR

AVE DES FORCES ARMÉES ROYALES

RUE AL YACHI

RUE MADARIS

AVENUE FES

AVENUE FES

AVENUE SIDI BEN ACHIR

RABAT

1

Wadi Bou Regreg

Wadi Bou Regreg

Bab el Bahr

TARIK EL MARSA

MELLAH

Andalusian Wall ⑪

RUE OUQQASA

BOULEVARD HASSAN II

PLACE SIDI MAKLOUF

Pont Moulay Hassan

Pont Hassan II

2

PLACE DU MELLAH

Place du 16 Novembre

RUE MELILYA

RUE ABDELMOUMEN

RUE ES SAÂDINE

BOULEVARD

EL ALAOUIYNE

Jardin Tour Hassan

Hassan Tower

⑫

ABI REGREG

RUE MOULAY RACHID

R. EL MOUAHHIDINE

Hassan Mosque

Mausoleum of Mohammed V ①

PLACE MELILYA

QUARTIER HASSAN

RUE EL MARINIYNE

RUE DE LA TOUR HASSAN

AL-SAHAT AL-KABIRA

R.P.LUMUMBA

RUE MOULAY

RUE MAKKA

RUE DE TUNIS

RUE IDRISS EL AKBAR

3

RUE DU

AVENUE MOULAY

Tour Hassan 🕌

RUE DE

RUE

Place Al-Joulane

PLACE EL JOULANE

PLACE EL OUAHDAH EL IFRIQYAH

RUE D'OUJHRANE

RUE ISMAÏL

PLACE A. LINCOLN

ROUTE AÏN HOUALLA

ABOU EL MARINI

PLACE MOULAY HASSAN

RUE ELAZAÏR

ℹ

PLACE MOULAY ALI CHÉRIF

RUE D'ANNABA

RUE CHELLAH

BLVD TARIQ IBN ZIAD

HASSAN

RUE

② ABD EL AZIZ

MOULAY

⑭ **Musée de l'Histoire et des Civilisations**

PLACE MOULAY ALI CHÉRIF

RUE BEN TACHINE

RUE PATRICE

AVENUE DE MEKNÈS

RUE DE FÈS

AVE DE

AVENUE DU PRÉSIDENT ROOSEVELT

AVENUE DE MARRAKECH

4

AVENUE

AVENUE

LUMUMBA

MOHAMMED

MOULAY ALICHÉRIF

RUE D'OUARZAZATE

AVE ES SAQUIRA

V

QUARTIER ADMINISTRATIF

CITÉ KHALIFA

Mechouar

YACOUB EL MANSOUR

BLVD MOUSSA IBN NOSSAIR

Chellah Necropolis ②

5

AVENUE OUARZAZATE

Bab Zaer

0 metres 500

0 yards 500

N

D **E** **F**

❶ 🖐 🗺

MAUSOLEUM OF MOHAMMED V

📍E3 **🏠Boulevard El-Alaouiyine** **🕐9am–6pm daily**

This complex on the edge of the Nouvelle Ville stands as a monument to the reign of Morocco's Alouite dynasty, which has held power since 1664. It comprises a mosque, museum and the mausoleum of the father (the late Hassan II) and grandfather of the current king.

Raised in memory of Mohammed V, the father of Moroccan independence, this majestic building was commissioned by his son, Hassan II. It was designed by the Vietnamese architect Vo Toan and built with the help of 400 Moroccan craftsmen. The group of buildings that make up the mausoleum include a mosque and a museum devoted to the history of the Alaouite dynasty. Visitors enter onto a mezzanine gallery from which they can view the sarcophagus and admire the exquisite decoration of the chamber.

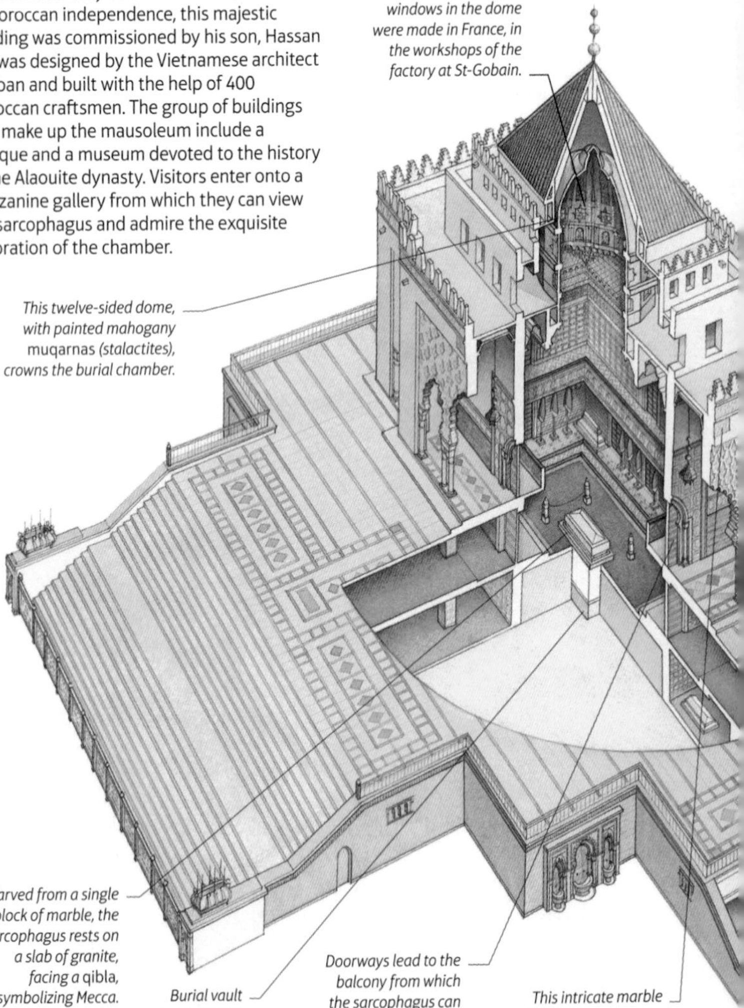

The stained-glass windows in the dome were made in France, in the workshops of the factory at St-Gobain.

This twelve-sided dome, with painted mahogany muqarnas (stalactites), crowns the burial chamber.

Carved from a single block of marble, the sarcophagus rests on a slab of granite, facing a qibla, symbolizing Mecca.

Burial vault containing the body of Mohammed V

Doorways lead to the balcony from which the sarcophagus can be viewed below.

This intricate marble frieze features a song of holy praise carved in Maghrebi script.

↑ The Mausoleum's intricately decorated chamber and Moorish-style fountain *(inset)*

The doorways on the four sides of the mausoleum are fronted by slender columns of Carrara marble.

This fountain is embellished with polychrome zellij tilework and framed by a horseshoe arch.

These large candelabra, with slender vertical shafts, are made of pierced and engraved copper.

Main entrance

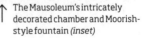

↑ A guard on horseback watches over the entrance to this sacred building.

MOHAMMED V

In the rest of the Arab world monarchies were replaced by authoritarian republican regimes (as in Iraq, Egypt, Yemen and Tunisia). In Morocco, however, Mohammed V's patriotic sentiment united the country behind a monarchy. A pious and outward-looking Muslim, the king encouraged the emancipation of women, the education of his people, and agrarian reform.

Did You Know?

Women feed eggs to the sacred eels in the Chellah basin in the hope of becoming pregnant.

Ancient Roman ruins of ↑
Sala Colonia sit within the
Islamic Chellah complex

2 ⊘

CHELLAH NECROPOLIS

⊙ E5 ⚑ Southeast of the city. Access via Bab Zaer, best reached by taxi ⏱ 9am–6pm daily

One of Morocco's most intriguing historical ruins, the Chellah is a sacred walled burial ground, dotted with ruined tombs, crumbling temples and imposing minarets topped with storks nests.

Just a short walk from Rabat's bustling medina, the once magnificent – now distinctly eerie – Chellah Necropolis houses Roman ruins and a medieval Muslim burial ground. It was Abou Yacoub Youssef, the first Merinid caliph, who first chose this as the site of a mosque in 1284. Abandoned in 1154 and damaged further by the Lisbon earthquake in 1755, it was listed as a World heritage Site in 2012. Today this overgrown labyrinth of rock and rubble is a fascinating place to explore.

Sala Colonia

Archaeological excavations revealed the remains of a once prosperous Roman city, known as Sala Colonia. Still visible today is the *decumanus maximus*, the main thoroughfare that crossed from east to west, leading to the port. From the forum, a road to the right leads towards the Merinid necropolis.

↑ Ancient archway at the abandoned Chellah Necropolis

↑ The imposing 13th-century Almohad gate flanked by two towers marks the entrance to the necropolis

JAZZ AU CHELLAH

For five days in September crowds descend on this ancient site for a series of ten concerts held here during the annual Chellah jazz festival. Founded in 1996 and moving to this site in 2005, it brings artists from the European Union to meet and play with local Moroccan musicians. Find out more at *www. jazzauchellah.eu*.

3

MOHAMMED VI MUSEUM OF MODERN AND CONTEMPORARY ART

C4 ⌂ Corner of Avenue Moulay Hassan & Avenue Allal Ben Abdellah
🕐 10am–6pm Wed–Mon 🌐 museemohammed6.ma

Opened in October 2014, this is the first museum in Morocco devoted to modern art. Known as the MMVI, its many exhibits are testament to the country's ongoing contribution to the contemporary art world.

Inaugurated by King Mohammed VI, this museum that bears his name is housed in an elegant modern building that offers a fresh take on traditional Moroccan architecture. It was designed by local architect Karim Chakor and took a decade to build at a cost of approximately $23 million. The ground floor is used for temporary exhibitions, which to date have included major shows of Goya, Giacometti, Picasso and contemporary African art. In 2020 the museum will have an exhibition devoted to the French romantic painter Eugène Delacroix, who famously painted in Morocco in the 19th century. The permanent collection, which is displayed in a series of galleries on the second floor, consists of works by some of the most important Moroccan artists of the last hundred years.

Must See

↑ Sculptures by Moroccan artist Abdeljalil Saouli and exterior murals by Chaïbia Talal

Contemporary Moroccan Artists

Lalla Essaydi

▽ Born in Marrakech in 1956, Essaydi champions women, most famously in her series of large-scale photographic works of female subjects in which their clothing and bodies, along with the walls and other surfaces around them are covered in densely written calligraphic henna.

Farid Belkahia

Considered one of the most important of modern Moroccoan artists, Belkhahia, was born in Marrakech in 1934 and died in 2014. His early works were completed mostly in oils, but he later became known for painting on leather and incorporating symbols and imagery from Berber traditions.

Mohammed Ben Ali Rbati

▷ Regarded as the father of Moroccan painting, Rbati had no formal arts training. His talent emerged while working as a cook for the Irish painter Sir John Lavery. Rbati used watercolours to depict stylised street scenes set in his native city of Tangier.

Mohammed Melehi

Born 1936 in Asilah, Melehi trained as a painter in Tétouan before continuing his studies overseas. He became an influential teacher back in Morocco and a pioneering modernist working in bright colours with a recurring motif of a hard-edged wave.

Hassan Hajjaj

Born in Larache, Hajjaj lived in the UK as a child and his life since has been split between the two countries. Labelled a Moroccan Andy Warhol, his work includes photographic portraits, video and hand-crafted objects fashioned out of recycled materials.

Did You Know?

Islam discourages the depiction of people in art, favouring instead calligraphy and abstract pattern.

← Works by Abdelkbir Rabl (left) and Mohamed Romain Atallah on display before the museum's official opening

EXPERIENCE MORE

④

City Walls

⑨ B3 🏛 In the north of the city, accessible via Place du Souk el-Ghezel and Place de l'Ancien Sémaphore

Separated from the medina by Place du Souk el-Ghezel, the Oudaïa Kasbah is defended by thick ramparts. These were built mostly by the Almohads in the 12th century, and were restored and remodelled in the 17th and 18th centuries by the Moriscos (Muslim refugees from Andalusia) and the Alaouite kings.

Most of the Almohad walls that face on to the sea and run inland survive. The walls surrounding the Andalusian Garden date from the reign of Moulay Rachid (founder of the Alaouite dynasty). The Hornacheros (Andalusian emigrants) who occupied the kasbah and rebuffed attacks from both sea and land rebuilt the curtain wall in several places and constructed the Pirates' Tower, whose inner stairway leads down to the river. They also pierced the walls of the old Almohad towers with embrasures to hold cannons and dug a system of underground passages leading from within the kasbah to the exterior.

The city walls are built of rough-hewn stone covered with a thick coating of ochre plaster. They are set with imposing towers and bastions, which are more numerous along the stretch of the walls facing the sea and the river. The walls are surmounted by a rampart walk bordered by a low parapet; part of the rampart walk survives.

This sturdy building and sophisticated military construction defended the pirates' nest and withstood almost all attacks from European forces.

---

⑤

Bab Oudaïa

⑨ C1 🏛 Oudaïa Kasbah, leads to the kasbah from Place du Souk el-Ghezel

The main entrance into the kasbah, Bab Oudaïa towers over the cliffs that line the Bou Regreg, dominating Rabat's ancient medina. This monumental city gate, built in dressed stone of red ochre, is considered one of the finest

examples of typical Almohad architecture. But the particular design and conception of this 12th-century gateway make it more of a decorative feature than a piece of military defence work. Flanked by two towers, it is crowned by a horseshoe arch. The inner and outer façades are decorated with rich ornamentation carved in relief into the stone as the base of the parapet. Above the arch, two bands with interlacing lozenges are outlined with floral decoration. Both sides of the gate are crowned with calligraphy.

The gatehouse of the former Oudaïa Palace was also a defensive feature, as well as a tribunal. Today, the gatehouse serves as an exhibition hall.

←

The sun beating down on the ancient walls of the Oudaïa Kasbah

> **Bab Oudaïa towers over the cliffs that line the Bou Regreg, dominating Rabat's ancient medina.**

6

Place du Souk el-Ghezel and Rue Hadj Daoui

📍 C1

A convenient place to start exploring Rabat's medina is Place du Souk el-Ghezel (Wool Market Square), so named because of the market once held here. This was also the place where Christian prisoners were once sold as slaves. Today, fine carpets made in the city are auctioned here every Thursday morning.

Rue Hadj Daoui, southwest of Place du Souk el-Ghezel, leads into the residential area of the medina, where the streets are quieter and the houses built by the Moriscos are still visible.

The unmistakable mark the Moriscos made on Rabat can be seen in the architecture: for example, semicircular arches and ornamental motifs such as pilasters consisting of vertically arranged mouldings that decorate the upper parts

←

Bab Oudaïa, the kasbah's monumental city gate, built in the 12th century

of doors. The smaller houses are of simple design, most of them built of stone rendered with limewashed plaster. Most of the richer houses tucked away in the different quarters of Rabat are built around a central courtyard, like those in other Moroccan medinas, and have a refined elegance.

Walking west along Rue Hadj Daoui leads to Dar el-Mrini, a fine private house built in 1920 and transformed into an exhibition and conference centre.

7

Musée des Oudaïa

📍 C1 🏛 Oudaïa Kasbah, accessible via a gateway in the southwestern walls 🔒 For renovation

In the 17th century, Moulay Ismaïl built a small palace within the kasbah. This would become the residence of the first Alaouite sultans while they were based in Rabat, as an inscription on the wooden lintels of the central patio indicates: "Unfailing fortune and brilliant victory to our lord Smaïl, leader of the faithful."

The palace was completely restored and slightly altered during the Protectorate, and has since undergone further phases of restoration and renovation. Since 1915, the palace has housed the Musée des Oudaïa. Though the museum is currently closed, the grounds may still be explored.

EAT

Dar Zaki
Fine Moroccan cuisine with a local twist.

📍 C2 🏛 23 Rue Moulay Brahim 📞 (0537) 70 27 33 🕐 Sun

💲💲💲

La Koutoubia
A Rabat classic since 1955, offering excellent Moroccan dishes.

📍 D4 🏛 10 Rue Pierre Parent 📞 (0537) 70 10 75 🕐 3-7pm daily

💲💲💲

Cosmopolitan
Serving seasonal French cuisine cooked to perfection, this elegant restaurant is one of the top places to eat in Rabat. The menu changes daily

📍 B4 🏛 Ave Ibn Toumert & Rue Abou Abbas El Guerraoui 📞 0537 20 00 28

💲💲💲

The palace as it is today consists of a main building arranged around an arcaded courtyard. The four sides of the courtyard lead off into large rectangular rooms with marble floors and geometrically coffered ceilings. The surrounding buildings include a prayer room for private worship, a hammam (steam bath) and a tower. A beautiful garden laid out in the Andalusian style gives the palace the status of a princely residence.

8

Rue des Consuls

📍 C2 🏛 Eastern part of the medina

Running through the medina, Rue des Consuls begins at the Wool Market in the north and leads towards the Andalusian Wall in the south. Up to the time of the Protectorate, this street was where all foreign consuls in Rabat lived. Covered with rushes and a glass roof, the street is lined with the shops of craftsmen and traders, making it the liveliest quarter in the medina.

South of Rue Souk es-Sebat the street changes name to Rue Ouqqasa, which borders the mellah (Jewish quarter). In Rue Tariq el-Marsa is the Ensemble Artisanal, selling Moroccan crafts, and, a little further on, is a restored 18th-century naval depot.

9

Rue Souk es-Sebat

📍 C2 🏛 In the medina

This thoroughfare begins at the Great Mosque and ends at Bab el-Bhar (Gate of the Sea), crossing Rue des Consuls. Covered by a rush trellis, this lively street is packed with leatherworkers, jewellers, fabric merchants and traders in all sorts of other goods.

10

Rue Souïka

📍 C2 🏛 In the medina
🕌 Great Mosque: closed to non-Muslims

Running southwest from Rue Souk es-Sebat, Rue Souïka (Little Souk Street) is the main artery through the medina. Lined with busy restaurants and small shops selling all manner of goods, the street throngs with people most of the day, the air fragranced with the heady perfume of the spice merchants' wares.

At the intersection with Rue de Bab Chellah stands the Great Mosque, built between the 13th and 16th centuries and restored during the Alaouite period. The mosque's most prominent feature is the minaret, completed in 1939. It is built of ashlars (blocks of hewn stone), decorated with dressed stone, and pierced with openings in the shape of lobed arches.

Opposite the mosque is a 14th-century fountain with a pediment of intersecting arches. On the corner of Rue Sidi Fatah, is the Moulay Sliman Mosque, or Jamaa el-Souika, built on the site of an earlier place of worship.

11

Andalusian Wall

📍 D2 🏛 Between Bab el-Had and Place Sidi Makhlouf

In the 17th century, the Moriscos – Muslim refugees from Andalusia – found the

→

The prestigious Hassan Tower overlooking the remains of Hassan Mosque

←

The glass roof over
the bustling Wool Market
on Rue des Consuls

medina undefended and so
encircled it with a defensive
wall. Named for its builders,
the Andalusian Wall stands
about 5 m (16 ft) high and
runs in a straight line for
more than 1,400 m (4,595 ft)
from Bab el-Had (Sunday
Gate) in the west to the *borj*
(small fort) of Sidi Makhlouf
in the east. The wall is set
with towers placed at regular
intervals and is topped by a
rampart walk. This is protected
by a defensive parapet that
the Andalusians pierced with
numerous narrow slits known
as loopholes.

To the east of the wall, they
built the Bastion Sidi Makhlouf,
a small, irregular fort that
consists of a platform resting
on solid foundations, with a
tower close by. They also built
embrasures over two of the
Almohad gates, Bab el-Alou
and Bab el-Had.

Bab el-Had was once the
main gateway into the medina.
Dating from the Almohad
period (1147–1248), it was
rebuilt by Moulay Sliman in
1814. On the side facing
Boulevard Misr, one of the
gate's two pentagonal towers
stands close to the Almohad
walls, which
probably date from
1197. Bab el-Had
contains several

small chambers intended to
accommodate the soldiers who
were in charge of the guard,
the armouries and the billeting
of the troops.

___

12

Hassan Tower

📍 E2 🏛 Rue de la Tour
Hassan 🔒 To the public

For more than eight centuries,
the Hassan Tower, built by
Yacoub el-Mansour in about
1196, has stood on the hill
overlooking Wadi Bou Regreg.
Best seen as you approach
Rabat by the bridge from
Salé, it is one of the city's
most prestigious monuments
and a great emblem of Rabat.

The construction of this
gigantic mosque, of dimensions quite out of proportion
with the population of Rabat
at the time, suggests that the
Almohad ruler had grand
intentions to make the city
his new imperial capital.

An alternative interpretation
is that the Almohads were
attempting to rival the magnificent Great Mosque of Córdoba,
the former capital of the
Islamic kingdom in the West.
Either way, after the death of
Yacoub el-Mansour in 1199,
the unfinished mosque fell into
disrepair. All but the mosque's
minaret was destroyed by an
earthquake in 1755.

The Hassan Mosque was
built to a huge rectangular
plan, larger than that of the

Great Mosque of Córdoba by
several metres. It was the
largest religious building in
the Muslim West, inferior only
to the Great Mosque of
Samarra in Iraq.

A great courtyard lay at the
foot of the tower, while the
huge prayer hall was divided
into 21 avenues separated by
lines of gigantic columns
crowned with capitals. Remains
of these imposing stone
columns survive and still
convey an impression of
infinite grandeur.

The minaret, a square-sided
tower, was to have surpassed
the height of the Koutoubia
Mosque *(p234)* and the Giralda
in Seville, but it was never
completed. Even unfinished,
its size is still impressive. Each
of its four sides is decorated
with blind lobed arches.
On the topmost level of the
minaret, extended interlacing
arches form a *sebkha* motif
(lozenge-shaped blind fret-
work). The interior is divided
into six levels, each of which
consists of a domed room,
and is linked and accessed
by a continuous ramp.

It was from the Hassan
Tower that Mohammed V
conducted the first Friday
prayers after independence.

⓭
Ville Nouvelle

⚲ C3

During the 44 years of the Protectorate, Marshal Lyautey and the architects Prost and Ecochard built a new town in the empty part of the extensive area enclosed by the Almohad walls. Laying out wide boulevards and green spaces, they created a relatively pleasant town with a spacious feel. Avenue

A NEW CULTURAL CAPITAL

Rabat is currently in the process of transforming itself. The banks of the Bouregreg River are the site for a large development that will include a revamped archaeological museum, an arts centre and a national archive building, along with malls, a hotel and a residential district. The crowning glory will be a new Grand Theatre. Its fluid lines, inspired by the river, are already taking shape.

Mohammed V, the main avenue, runs from the medina to the El-Souna Mosque, or Great Mosque, which was built by Sidi Mohammed in the 18th century. The avenue is lined with residential blocks in the Hispano-Maghrebi style. They were built by the administration of the Protectorate, as were the Bank of Morocco, the post office, the parliament building and the railway station. The Bank of Morocco also houses the **Musée Bank Al Maghrib**, which displays a coin collection, plus Moroccan and Orientalist paintings.

Rue Abou Inan leads to the **Cathédrale Saint-Pierre**, a pure white building dating from the 1930s.

Musée Bank Al Maghrib
⚲ Bank of Morocco, Rue du Caire **⏰** Times vary, check website **🌐** bkam.ma/musee

Cathédrale Saint-Pierre
⚲ Place du Golan **☎** (0537) 72 23 01 **⏰** 9am–noon & 3–6pm daily

Palms lining Avenue Mohammed V and the towers of Cathédrale Saint-Pierre *(inset)* ↓

⓮ ♿
Musée de l'Histoire et des Civilisations

⚲ D4 ⌂ 23 Rue el-Brihi (behind the Grand Mosque, opposite the Chellah Hotel) **☎** (0537) 70 19 19 **⏰** 10am–6pm Wed–Mon (last admission 45 mins before closing) **🔒** Public hols

Formerly known as the Musée Archéologique, this institution reopened in 2017 with a new name following a period of modernization. It holds the most extensive collection of archaeological artifacts in the country, displayed in a building constructed in the 1920s under French rule.

The museum presents a chronological tour through the history of Morocco, from prehistory to the Islamic era. An alternative thematic route allows visitors to explore the collection through a specific focus on marble and bronze

> The intricate façade of Dar el-Makhzen intrigues visitors with its arched brass gate detailed with mosaic tilework and carved cedar wood.

↑ Guards flanking the entrance to the Dar el-Makhzen (royal palace)

statuary, which comes mainly from Volubilis (p198) and which demonstrates the wealth enjoyed by Morocco's Roman towns (p105). Notable objects include an *ephebe* (young soldier) wearing a crown of delicately carved ivy, the so-called *Dog of Volubilis*, which dates from the reign of Hadrian (early 2nd century) and was designed to be accompanied by a human figure, and a bust of Juba II, which dates from 25 BC and is probably from Egypt.

15
Bab el-Rouah

📍 C4 🏛 Place an-Nasr
🕐 Gallery: daily during exhibitions

A sturdy and imposing Almohad gateway, Bab el-Rouah, the Gate of the Winds, dates from the same period as Bab Oudaïa (p82).

The entrance is decorated with the outline of two horse-shoe arches carved into the stone and surrounded by a band of Kufic calligraphy. The interior contains four rooms with elegant domes, now used for exhibitions.

16
Dar el-Makhzen

📍 B5 🏛 In the northwest of the city 🕐 To the public

An extensive complex enclosed within its own walls, the Dar el-Makhzen (royal palace) is inhabited by about 2,000 people. Although members of the public are forbidden from

entering the palace itself, the exterior is of interest in its own right. Built on the site of an 18th-century royal residence, the palace was completed in 1864 but was constantly enlarged thereafter; today, it even includes a race-course. The intricate façade of Dar el-Makhzen intrigues visitors with its arched brass gate detailed with mosaic tile-work and carved cedar wood.

The palace now houses the offices of the Moroccan government, the Supreme Court, the prime minister's offices, the Ministry of Habous and Islamic Affairs (the branch of government responsible for religious organizations), and the El-Fas Mosque. The *méchouar*, a place of public assembly, is the venue for major gatherings, including the *bayaa*, a prestigious ceremony at which senior government ministers swear their allegiance to the king. Traditionally, the king would reside in the former harem, though the current king, Mohammed VI, stays in his own private residence.

Besides private buildings, the palace also includes an extensive and immaculately kept garden, planted with various species of trees and with flowers in formal beds.

A SHORT WALK
THE OUDAÏA KASBAH

Distance 0.7 km (0.4 miles) **Time** 7 minutes

The kasbah takes its name from the Oudaïas, an Arab tribe with a warrior past that was settled here by Moulay Ismaïl (1672–1727) to protect the city from the threat of rebels. As you wander, look up to see part of the city walls that surround this hilltop "fortress", and Bab Oudaïa, the gate that pierces it, which dates from the Almohad period (1147–1248). On Rue Jamaa, the main thoroughfare of this picturesque district, stands the El-Atika Mosque. This imposing sanctuary was built in the 12th century, and is the oldest mosque in Rabat.

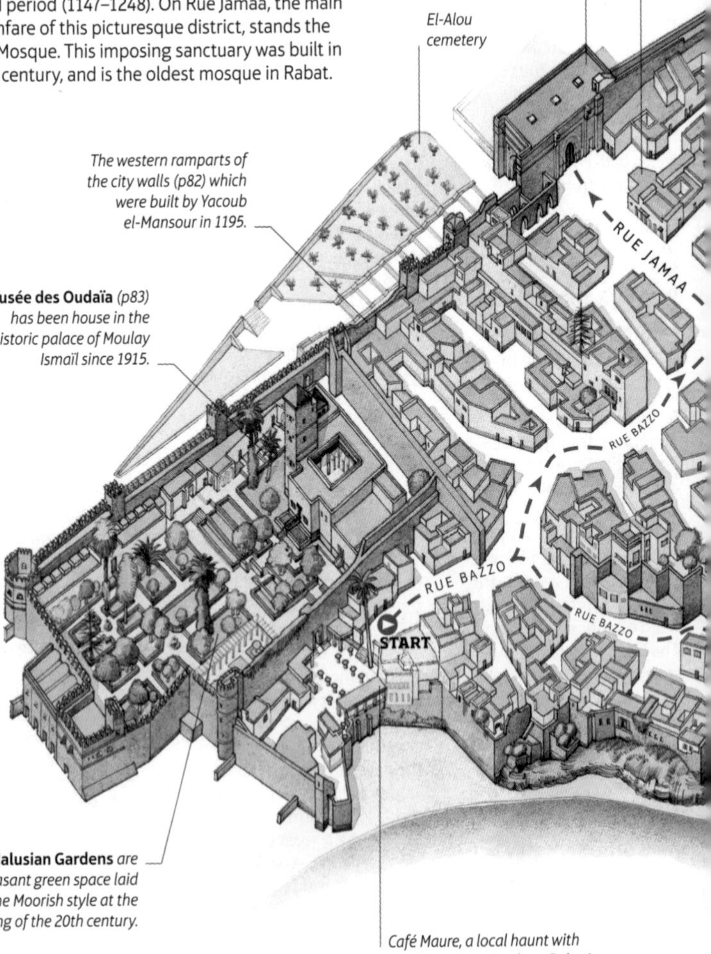

Fountain

*The 12th-century **Bab Oudaïa** (p82), an archetypal example of Almohad military architecture.*

El-Alou cemetery

The western ramparts of the city walls (p82) which were built by Yacoub el-Mansour in 1195.

Musée des Oudaïa *(p83) has been house in the historic palace of Moulay Ismaïl since 1915.*

RUE JAMAA

RUE BAZZO

RUE BAZZO

START

RUE BAZZO

RUE BAZZO

The **Andalusian Gardens** *are a pleasant green space laid out in the Moorish style at the beginning of the 20th century.*

↑ Illustration of the route around the Oudaïa kasbah

Café Maure, a local haunt with excellent views , is where Rabatis come to relax and pass the time.

The walled Rabat medina, which is filled with dozens of traditional shops

Locator Map
For more detail see p72

Blue or white lime-washed houses, that were built in the late 17th to early 18th centuries, line the narrow kasbah streets.

Almohad walls

The prayer hall of the **El-Atika Mosque**, which was founded in about 1150 by Abd el-Moumen and is Rabat's oldest monument.

Did You Know?

Most of the 2001 film *Black Hawk Down*, starring Josh Hartnett, was filmed in and around Rabat.

RUE JAMAA

FINISH

Pirates' Tower

Carpet workshop

The platform of the former Oudaïa signal station, which was built in the 18th century by Sultan Sidi Mohammed ben Abdallah.

0 metres   50
0 yards   50   →N

RABAT

The Oudaïa Kasbah

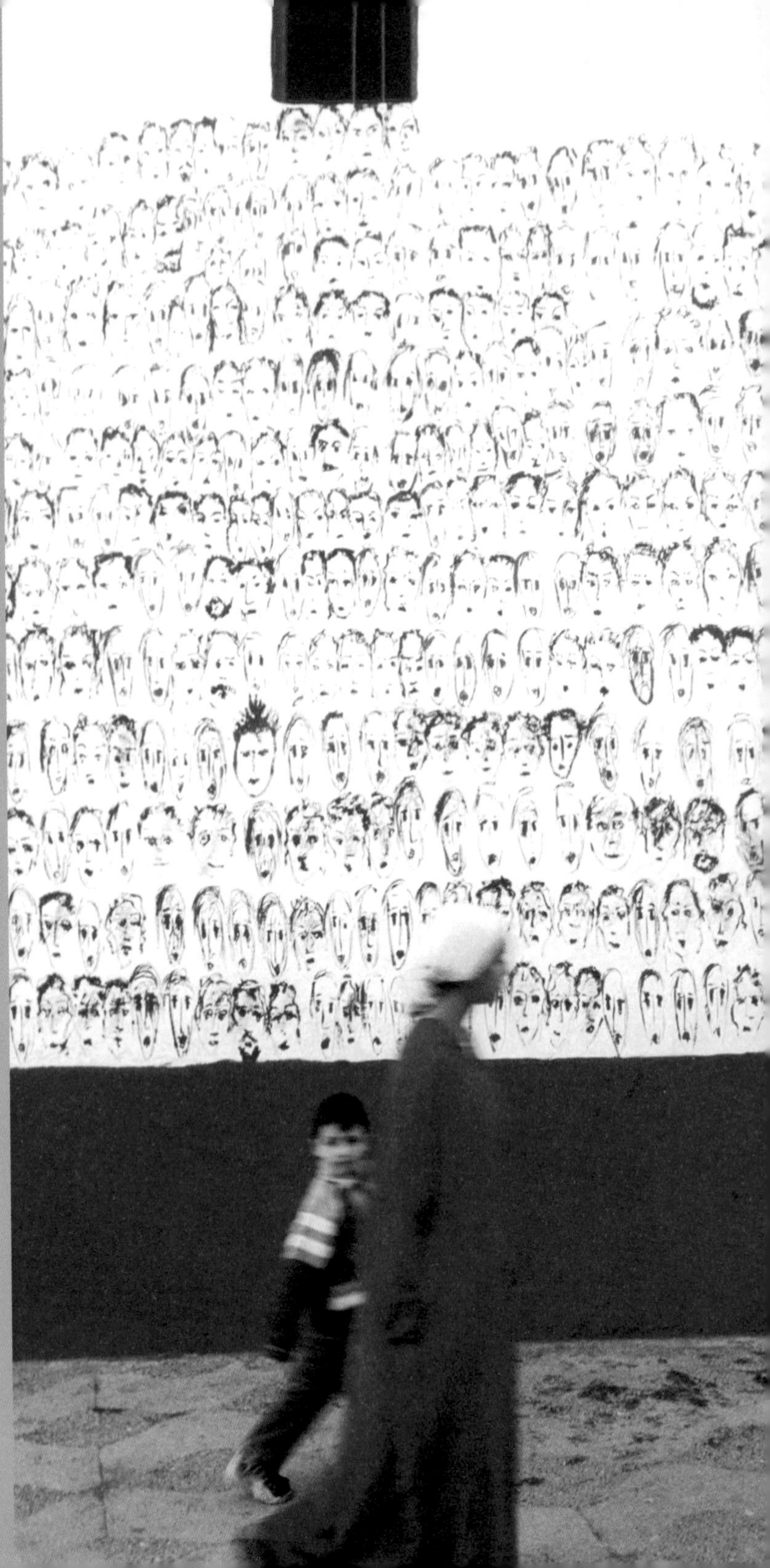

Murals adorn the walls in the town of Asilah

NORTHERN ATLANTIC COAST

To explore Morocco's North Atlantic Coast is to travel back in time, since the heritage of the Phoenicians and the Romans, the corsairs, the Portuguese and the Spanish, as well as that of the French colonial period is ever-present alongside the modern prosperity brought by agriculture, port activity, trade and tourism.

For 250 km (155 miles), scenic roads skirt the coastline and sandy bays, following the course of the old Roman road linking the ancient city of Sala Colonia, known today as Chellah *(p78)*, to the settlments of Banasa, Lixus and Tangier.

Over the centuries, the Atlantic Ocean has shaped the history of these coastal towns: occupied from Phoenician times and into the Roman period, they have attracted pirates, invaders and Andalusian, Spanish and French occupiers, each of whom left their mark. It is also the ocean that gives the region its gentle, moist climate (strawberries, bananas and tomatoes are grown here in abundance) and drives industry from Kenitra to Tangier, where the busy port handles cargo bound for Europe and beyond.

NORTHERN ATLANTIC COAST

Must Sees

1. Asilah
2. Salé

Experience More

3. Sidi Bouknadel
4. Mehdya
5. Forest of Maâmora
6. Kenitra
7. Thamusida
8. Lixus
9. M'Soura Stone Circle
10. Moulay Bousselham
11. Larache
12. Ksar el-Kebir
13. Souk el-Arba du Rharb
14. Banasa

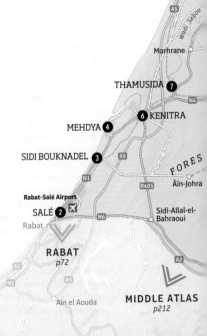

Atlantic Ocean
Sidi-el-Hachemi
A5
Wadi Sebou
Morhrane
THAMUSIDA 7
N4
6 KENITRA
MEHDYA 4
SIDI BOUKNADEL 3
A5
FORES
N1
Aïn-Johra
R405
Rabat-Salé Airport
SALÉ 2
N6
Sidi-Allal-el-Bahraoui
Rabat
RABAT
p72
A2
A1
A5
N1
Aïn el Aouda
MIDDLE ATLAS
p212
0 kilometres 20
0 miles 20
N

→

Gentle waves lapping
against the city ramparts
that surround Asilah

❶

ASILAH

🅰 D1 🚆🚌 From Tangier or Rabat

Established by the Phoenicians, Asilah was a prominant
town in the pre-Roman and Roman periods. In 1471
it was captured by the Portuguese and became an
important centre of trade. Asilah came under Moroccan
control in 1691, during the reign of Moulay Ismaïl.
Today, this small Andalusian-style town has a relaxed
atmosphere and a well-maintained medina. The narrow
streets are paved or limed, and lined with houses
fronted by balconies. The town is frequented by
painters, who mark the walls with signs of their
passing, particularly during the Asilah Festival.

①
Medina

Asilah's medina may be on the
small side, but it has rightfully
gained a reputation for its
tranquility and cleanliness, a
suitable balm to the bustle of
nearby Tangier. Enclosed within
walls built by the Portuguese
in the 15th century, the medina
is entered by two main gates,
the Bab el-Kasaba and the
bastion-like Bab el-Homar
(Land Gate), the latter decorated with a Portuguese royal
coat of arms. The streets within
are narrow and winding, and
the houses are painted white
with blue decorative touches.
At the southern end of the
ramparts is the *koubba* (shrine)
of Sidi Mamsour, which is off
limits to non-Muslims, but it is
also a good spot for views out
to sea, particularly at sunset.

---

②
Palais de Raissouli

🅰 Medina

Moulay Ahmad Er-Raissouli
was the last of the Barbary
pirates. He made a career out
of kidnapping prominent
officials and holding them to
ransom for vast sums of
money. One of his most
famous captives was Walter
Harris, a *London Times* writer,
who he held for three weeks
before releasing him. It was
said that Er-Raisouli was well-
educated and could be quite
charming, but he was also
capable of great cruelty. On
one occasion, he returned the
head of an envoy in a basket
of melons. His grand palace
has been beautifully restored,
complete with a glass-fronted
terrace overlooking the ocean.
The palace is open to visitors
during the Asilah Festival,
when this otherwise sleepy
seaside town bursts into life.

↑ Colourful Moroccan
ceramics on display
in Asilah's medina

ASILAH FESTIVAL

Asilah has long been synonymous with art, and many artists choose to live here. Their numbers are swollen every July during the Asilah Festival of art. Every year the locals freshly whitewash the medina and visiting artists are invited to create street art using the walls as a canvas.

③

Centre de Hassan II Rencontres Internationales

🏠 Medina ⏰ 8:30am-5pm daily (to 8pm summer)

The "Centre for International Encounters" functions as a community hub, exhibition space and meeting place for local and international artists

visiting the town of Asilah. Located in an attractive, modern low-rise building just inside the unassuming Bab el-Kasaba at the entrance to Asilah's medina, the Centre de Hassan II Rencontres Internationales regularly hosts temporary and returning art and sculpture exhibitions in its many gallery spaces. The venue comes into its own each summer when it becomes the hub for the annual Asilah Festival.

④

Church of San Bartolome

🏠 Ave. du Prince Héretier

This twin-towered church, built in the Hipano-Moorish style, would not look out of place on an Andalusian plaza. It is a functioning Catholic church, and is looked after by resident nuns who are happy for visitors to look around the enchanting interior.

SHOP

Central Market

Tucked beside the medina walls, Asilah's small central market mixes fruit and vegetables with souvenirs. Visit on a Thursday for weekly market day, when the number of stalls swells in size. A row of restaurants at the market serve fish and seafood dishes.

🏠 Avenue Mohamed VI, Medina ⏰ 8am-8pm

Ⓓⓗ Ⓓⓗ Ⓓⓗ

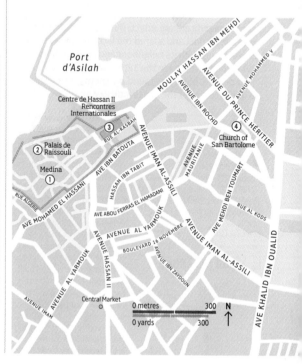

↑ Boats moored in Salé's peaceful Bou Regreg Marina

❷

SALÉ

🅰C2 🏠West of Rabat, on the right bank of Wadi Bou Regreg ✈Rabat-Salé, 10 km (6 miles) on the Meknès road 🚌🚊Route de Casablanca ℹRabat (0537) 66 06 63

Founded in the 11th century, Salé was fortified and embellished by the Merinids with a *medersa*, a mosque and a magnificent aqueduct. During the Middle Ages it was a busy port and shared the lucrative business of privateering with its neighbour and rival Rabat (*p72*). When piracy ended in the 18th century, the town went into decline, but it has found prosperity once again, as a major centre of the crafts industry.

① City Walls

Unlike largely modern, secular Rabat across the river, Salé retains its medieval, spiritual character. It has a well-defined medina, wrapped all the way around by its fortified walls,

Did You Know?

Salé was the more important city until the French made Rabat their capital in the 20th century.

which are remarkably well preserved for their age. The walls are pierced by nine gates, the largest of which is Bab Bou Haja, the main entrance to the medina, near the Bab Lamrissa tram stop. Close by, on the southeastern side, is the rather impressive 13th-century Bab el-Mrisa (Gate of the Sea), which takes the form of a horseshoe arch flanked by two square towers. This was the entrance to the maritime arsenal built by Yacoub el-Mansour, and a canal linking Wadi Bou Regreg to the harbour passed through it, allowing ships to sail right into the city, probably fresh from plundering the high seas. It has long since silted up.

② The Souks

Salé's *kissaria* and souks are brimming with artisans and traders. Entering the medina via Bab Bou Haja, to the right is the *mellah*, while the souks are at the end of Rue Bab el-Khebbaz, which emerges onto a square beside a *kissaria* for textiles. To the north is the Souk el-Kebir (Grand Souk), for leather, carpets and household items, and the Souk Haddadin, for metalwork. To the west, Rue Kechachin is home to carpenters and stonemasons.

STAY

The Repose
This four-room retreat in the heart of the medina offers a stunning roof-top sun terrace, cooking classes and vegetarian and vegan cuisine.

🏠17 Zankat Talaa, Ras Cherja, Medina
🌐therepose.com

③ ⑤

Medersa Abou El Hassan

🏛 Rue de la Grande Mosquée
🕐 8:30am-5pm daily

At the heart of the medina is the Grand Mosque, which dates from the early 11th century, making it one of the oldest in Morocco. It is also one of the largest in the country. This is closed to non-Muslims. Next to the mosque is a *medersa*, founded in 1341 by the Merenid ruler Abou el-Hassan and open to both Muslims and non-Muslims. Much like the Bou Inania Medersa in Fès *(p178)* and Ben Youssef Medersa in Marrakech *(p240)*, it features sumptuous Merenid architecture and decoration. Unlike the other two, visitors can usually ascend to the upper level to visit the old student cells. From the roof there are splendid views across the river to Rabat.

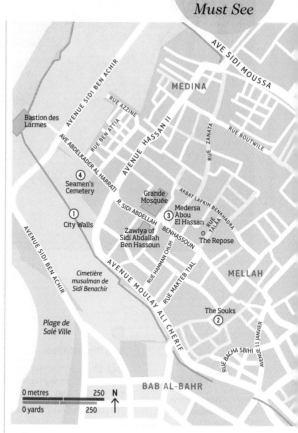

④

Seamen's Cemetery

🏛 Avenue Hassan II
🚫 Non-Muslims

Immediately west of the Grand Mosque (which only muslims are permitted to enter) is the Zaouia of Sidi Abdallah ben Hassoun, patron saint of Salé, boatmen and travellers. He is the focus of a *moussem* (festival) held each year on the eve of his birthday,

which is marked by a candlelit procession through the town. Just beyond the shrine is the Seamen's Cemetery, which is dotted with more shrines of such holy men as Sidi ben Achir. In the 16th century, he was credited with the power to calm the waves, allowing vessels to dock safely.

SALÉ ROVERS

Feared throughout 17th-century Europe, Salé was founded as an independent pirate republic by a Dutchman named Jan Janszoon van Haarlem, more commonly known as Murat Reis the Younger. He presided 18 ships, which plundered the Atlantic trading routes, captured the island of Lundy off the English coast, and raided places as far away as Ireland, Corsica, and Sardinia.

← The setting sun casts shadows over the Seamen's Cemetery

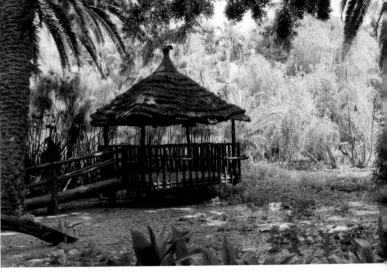

EXPERIENCE MORE

EAT

Restaurant Merzouga

This restaurant is favoured by locals. Among the varied menu, highights include excellent fried-fish dishes, always prepared with the day's catch fresh off the boat.

C2 1 ère Rue Front de Mer, No 84 Mehdya Plage (0537) 38 98 71

Dh Dh Dh

Relais Maâmora

A family-friendly retreat offering activities such as archery and paintball, plus a working farm. The on-site restaurant serves Moroccan and international cuisine.

C2 Sidi Allal El Bahraoui relaismaamora.com

Dh Dh Dh

3

Sidi Bouknadel

C2 10 km (6 miles) north of Salé on the N1 to Kenitra Rabat

The serene **Jardins Exotiques** (tropical gardens) just outside Sidi Bouknadel were laid out in 1951 by the horticulturist Marcel François and are today owned by the state. Some 1,500 species native to the Antilles, South America and Asia grow in the garden.

Two kilometres (1.25 miles) to the north is the **Musée Dar Belghazi**, with a collection of fine objects including jewellery, kaftans, marriage belts, carved wooden doors, pottery and musical instruments. The museum was established by a master woodcarver, with bequests from artists and collectors.

Jardins Exotiques

Autumn & winter: 9am-5:30pm; spring & summer: 9am-7:30pm

Musée Dar Belghazi

Km 47, Route de Kenitra (0537) 82 21 78
9am-5pm daily

4

Mehdya

C2 39 km (24 miles) from Salé on the N1 to Kenitra, at km 29 turning onto the Mehdya-Plage road Kenitra, then by taxi

This small coastal resort is much frequented by the inhabitants of Rabat and Kenitra. On the estuary of Wadi Sebou, it stands on the site of what may have been a Carthagenian trading post in the 5th century BC, and then an Almohad naval base. Later, the town was occupied by the Portuguese, the Spanish and the Dutch, and finally captured by Moulay Ismaïl *(p196)* at the end of the 17th century.

The kasbah, which stands on the plateau, still has its original walls and its moated bastions. The monumental gate, built by Moulay Ismaïl, leads to the governor's palace.

The **Sidi Boughaba Lake**, along the Mehdya Plage road, is a large bird sanctuary: thousands of birds rest here during their migration between Europe and sub-Saharan Africa.

← A wooden hut overlooking one of the many quiet spaces in the Jardins Exotiques

Although the forest is now planted mostly with eucalyptus, which grows much faster than other species, large tracts of it are still covered with cork oak, which is grown for its bark. At a factory in nearby Sidi Yahia, eucalyptus wood is turned into a pulp that is used in the production of paper and the manufacture of artificial silk.

Being intensively exploited and degraded by the grazing of cattle, sheep and goats, the forest is becoming increasingly bare. However, enough cover remains to allow a refreshingly cool walk in summer, when wood pigeons, kites, rollers and spotted flycatchers can be seen among the trees.

Sidi Boughaba Lake

🛈 National Education Centre for Environmental Education of Sidi Boughaba; (0537) 74 72 09; open 9am–3:30pm Mon–Fri

⑤
Forest of Maâmora

🅰 D2 🅰 East of Rabat on the N1 to Kenitra or the N6 to Meknès

The Forest of Mamora, between Wadi Sebou and Wadi Bou Regreg, covers an area 60 km (37 miles) long and 30 km (19 miles) wide.

⑥
Kenitra

🅰 C2 🅰🅰 Rabat

Established in 1913 in the early days of the French Protectorate, from 1933 to 1955 this town was known as Port Lyautey. Nowadays, Kenitra consists of distinct districts: residential areas

with villas, a European-style town centre and less affluent suburban areas.

In the harbour, on the right bank of Wadi Sebou, regional produce from the Rharb (such as rice, sugar beet, citrus fruit, cork, cotton, cereals and pulp for papermaking) is unloaded for use in local industries.

Once a marshy area that was rife with malaria (but still used for extensive stock-farming), the alluvial plain of the Rharb has been completely transformed by irrigation. It is now one of Morocco's most important agricultural areas.

⑦
Thamusida

🅰 C2 🅰 55 km (34 miles) northeast of Rabat, 17 km (10.5 miles) northeast of Kenitra on the N1 (Kenitra North exit)

On the N1, at the milestone reading "Kenitra 14 km, Sidi Allal Tazi 28 km", a track heading westwards leads to this ancient site on Wadi Sebou, inhabited by the Romans from the 2nd century BC to the 3rd century AD.

Part of the ancient city walls can still be seen, along with the outline of the Roman army camp (with streets intersecting at right angles) and the site's major feature, the *praetorium* (headquarters), with columns and pilasters. To the northeast, the remains of Roman baths and a temple with three chambers, or *cellae*, can be made out. North of Wadi Sebou are the vestiges of the old harbour docks.

SEA FISHING

The Moroccan coastline faces both the Atlantic and the Mediterranean, with access to some of the world's richest fishing grounds. Bringing in the largest catches in the whole of Africa, Morocco's fishing industry employs some 200,000 people, with exports worth over $600 million per year. But modern methods have not replaced traditional ways completely, as small-scale fishing is still a way of life for many.

STAY

Hay Essalam

A variety of rooms are available at this well-located budget hotel, some with en suite bathrooms, balconies, and air-con. Guests can choose from the many surrounding cafés or perch on the roof terrace.

⬛D1 🏠9 Avenue Hassan II, Larache
📞(0539) 91 68 22

(Dh) (Dh) (Dh)

La Maison Haute

More a guesthouse than a hotel, this quaint little lodging on the hilltop affords a glimpse into the real Morocco, as well as panoramic views of Larache. As the name implies, there are plenty of stairs.

⬛D1 🏠Derb Ibn Thami, Larache 🌐lamaisonhaute.free.fr

(Dh) (Dh) (Dh)

---

⑧ Lixus

⬛D1 🏠5 km (3 miles) northeast of Larache on the N1 🚌From Larache

This ancient site, which commands a view of the ocean, of Wadi Loukkos and of Larache, is a UNESCO World Heritage Site. According to legend, Lixus was the site of the Garden of the Hesperides, from which Hercules was tasked with stealing golden apples as one of his Twelve Labours. In the 1st century AD, the Roman writer Pliny described Lixus as the most ancient Phoenician colony in the western Mediterranean.

In the 7th century BC the Phoenicians established a trading post here, serving as a stage on the Gold Route. After it had been taken by the Romans between AD 40 and 45, Lixus became a centre of the manufacture of *garum* – sauce made with scraps of fish marinaded in brine from salting vats and Morocco's major industry in Roman times. The Romans abandoned Lixus at the end of the 3rd century AD. The wall built around the city at that time reduced its inhabited area by half.

The vats in which meat and fish were salted and *garum* was made can be seen dotted around the edges of the site. In the amphitheatre, with its circular arena, public games took place.

The Acropolis above the town has its own walls; only on the western side, where there is a sheer drop, do they coincide with the town walls. An apsidal building, preceded by an atrium with a cistern, has been excavated. The Great Temple (1st century BC–1st century AD), to the south, features an arcaded *area* (courtyard). The *cella*, where the god dwelt, on the axis of the peristyle, backs onto an apsidal wall; opposite is a large semicircular apse with a mosaic floor.

---

⑨ M'Soura Stone Circle

⬛D1 🏠El-Utad to Chouahed 27 km (17 miles) southeast of Asilah on the N1, then R417 towards Tetouan

This Neolithic site is reached via a 7-km (4-mile) track running from Sidi el-Yamani towards Souk et-Tnine. Perhaps the burial place of an important local ruler, it consists of around 200 monolithic standing stones ranging in height from 50 cm (20 inches) to 5 m (16 ft) and surrounding a large

tumulus (a mound of earth raised over a burial area). Unique in the Maghreb and the Sahara, particularly in terms of its sheer size, this monument is reminiscent of those seen in Spain. The types of pottery – decorated with impressions of *cardium* shells – and bronze weapons brought to light by excavations on the site are also identical to Spanish examples.

---

⑩ Moulay Bousselham

🗺 D1 🚗 48 km (30 miles) south of Larache 🚌🚕 From Café Milano

The small, single-street town of Moulay Bousselham is a very popular coastal resort with Moroccans. It has an attractive crescent of beach sheltered by cliffs, although the currents there can be dangerous. The mosque and the tomb of the 10th-century holy man who gives the town its name tower above the ocean and the adjacent Merja Zerga (Blue Lagoon). They are the focus of one of the largest of the region's religious festivals, which takes place each July, making Moulay Bousselham a major place of pilgrimage and attracting many followers.

Adjoining the lagoon is the Merja Zerga National Park, a large wetland area that draws birdwatchers from all over the world. Boat trips can be organized to see the thousands of birds – rare species of gulls and terns, marsh owls, herons, pink flamingoes, gannets, sheldrake, marsh harriers and peregrine falcons – that come to the lagoon on their migrations in December and January. The trips depart from the small fishing harbour.

←

Ruins of the ancient colony of Lixus, abandoned by the Romans in the 3rd century AD

↑ Waves crashing against the walls of Laqbibat Castle in Larache

⑪ Larache

🗺 D1 🚌 From Tangier, Rabat

Set a little way back from major roads, Larache is both an Andalusian and an Arab town. The modern part of the town bears obvious signs of the Spanish Protectorate (1911–56), during which time Larache was held by Spain.

Established in the 7th century by Arab conquerors, by the 11th century Larache was an important centre of trade on the left bank of Wadi Loukkos. In the 16th century it was used as a base by corsairs from Algiers and Turkey, and was subject to reprisals by Portuguese forces from Asilah. The town passed to Spain in 1610 and was then taken by Moulay Ismaïl at the end of the 17th century.

The medina is reached from Place de la Libération, a very Spanish plaza, and through Bab el-Khemis, a brick-built gate roofed with glazed tiles. In the fabrics souk – the *kissaria* (Socco de la Alcaicería) – a market offers a wide range of goods. Narrow streets lined with houses with floral decoration lead down towards the harbour. Bab el-Kasba separates the southern edge of the fabrics souk from Rue Moulay el-Mehdi, a street covered with overhead arches and leading to an octagonal minaret and a terrace overlooking the meandering Wadi Loukkos, the salt-marshes and the Lixus promontory.

On the route to Lixus is the Château de la Cigogne (Stork's Castle), a fortress that was built in 1578 by the Saadian rulers and then remodelled by the Spanish in the 17th century. It is closed to the public.

It is a pleasant stroll along the seafront, which has come to be known as the "balcony of the Atlantic". Nearby is the Moorish market. The Catholic Cemetery is where you will find the final resting place of celebrated French writer Jean Genet (1910–86), his grave placed to face the ocean.

> According to legend, Lixus was the site of the Garden of the Hesperides, from which Hercules was tasked with stealing golden apples as one of his Twelve Labours.

Sun setting over the hilltop town of Larache

↑ Intricate ceramic handicrafts on display at the Sunday souk in Ksar el-Kebir

South of the forum rises the capitol, where several altars stand before the temple's five *cellae* (chambers). In the public baths, the various rooms for the Roman ritual of bathing – robing rooms, a *caldarium* and a *tepidarium* (hot and warm rooms) with underfloor heating, and a *frigidarium* (cold room) – can easily be distinguished, along with wall paintings and a herringbone brick floor.

A famous document engraved on bronze was discovered at Banasa. Known as the Banasa Table, it was an edict by which Caracalla granted the province relief from taxes in return for lions, elephants and other animals that the emperor desired for public spectacles in Rome.

From the N1 or freeway, Banasa is reached by taking the R413, then, 3 km (2 miles) before Souk Tleta du Rharb, by turning off onto the P4234. As it approaches the site, the road is reduced to a track.

12 Ksar el-Kebir

D1 Moulay el-Mehdi, 3 km (2 miles) From Tangier

This sizable country town, surrounded by extensive olive plantations and citrus groves, takes its name from a great fortress, which, during the Almoravid and Almohad periods, controlled the road leading to the ports along the Straits of Gibraltar.

It was at Wadi el-Makhazin nearby that the Battle of the Three Kings took place in 1578. The conflict has been described as the "last crusade undertaken by the Christians of the Mediterranean". It was instigated by the Saadian sultan El-Mutawakkil, who, having been driven from Morocco, was zealous for a crusade. In alliance with Sebastião I, the king of Portugal at the time, he made a bid to win back his kingdom. Sebastião, Al-Mutawakkil and their opponent, the Saadian sultan Abd el-Malik (who was victorious over the invaders), all died in the battle. Moulay Ahmed, brother of Abd el-Malik, succeeded him, becoming known not only as Ahmed el-Mansour (the Victorious) but also as Ahmed el-Dhebi (the Golden), because of the ransom that he exacted.

13 Souk el-Arba du Rharb

D2 Rabat or Tangier

A major agricultural centre on the northwest border of the Rharb region, Souk el-Arba du Rharb is especially busy on Wednesdays, when the weekly market is held. The town's position on the intersection of roads leading to Tangier, Rabat, Meknès and the coastal town of Moulay Bousselham has made it a key staging post throughout history.

14 Banasa

D2 103 km (64 miles) northeast of Rabat on the N1 or Rabat-Tangier freeway (Kenitra North exit)

This ancient town, an inland port on Wadi Sebou and the most developed in Mauretania Tingitana, was a centre of ceramic production from the 3rd century to the 1st century BC. A Roman colony from 33 to 25 BC, Banasa was a prosperous and bustling commercial town until the end of the 3rd century AD.

The entrance to the town, through a vaulted gateway, leads to the basilica and the paved and arcaded forum.

ROMAN MOROCCO

The Roman Empire stretched across North Africa to the Atlantic coast. The region that encompassed present-day Algeria and northern Morocco was known as the province of Mauretania Tingitana. By the 4th century, imperial rule disintegrated due to attacks by East Germanic tribes known as the Vandals. The legacy of Roman rule in Morocco lives on in sites dotted around northern Morocco.

VOLUBILIS

Originally founded by Berbers, Volubilis (p198) later became the Roman capital of Mauretania. It grew rapidly from the 1st century with a number of major public buildings, including a forum, a basilica and a capitol, which served as the city's religious centre. It is Morocco's most extensive archaeological site.

LIXUS

Its location at the far reaches of the Roman Empire led Mauritania to be associated with legendary journeys. The colony of Lixus (p100) was connected to the mythical labours of Hercules. Here was said to be the Garden of the Hesperides, to which Hercules was dispatched, as his penultimate labour, to pick golden apples.

THAMUSIDA

North of modern-day Rabat, Thamusida (p99) was originally a Berber settlement, later occupied by the Romans during the reign of Augustus (63 BC-14 AD). Excavations in the 20th century unearthed the walls of the docks, as well as baths and a temple.

SALA COLONIA

Visitors to the Islamic-era Chellah Necropolis (p78) can also visit the same site's Roman-era ruins. Excavations here reveal distinctive Roman architectural elements, including a triumphal arch, public square and a *decumanus maximus* (main thoroughfare).

ROMAN CITIES

Mauritania's cities were bustling centres of trade and administration, as well as garrison towns. As was the case in Rome, the focal point of the city was the forum (a market place and public area) and the basilica, simultaneously a monetary exchange, law court and meeting place. The capitol was the city's religious centre.

↑ Ancient ruins of Volubilis, the Roman capital of Mauretania Tingitana

Mosaics adorn the floor ↑ of a ruined building at the site of Volubilis

CASABLANCA

In the 7th century, Casablanca was no more than a small Berber settlement clinging to the slopes of the Anfa hills. However, for strategic and commercial reasons, it was already attracting the attention of foreign powers. In 1468, the town was sacked by the Portuguese, who wrought wholesale destruction on the city's privateer ships. Then, in the 18th century, with the sultanate of Sidi Mohammed ben Abdallah, Dar el-Beïda (meaning "White House" – "Casa Blanca" in Spanish) it acquired a new significance. This was thanks to its harbour, which played a pivotal role in the sugar, tea, wool and corn markets of the Western world.

It was in the 20th century, under the French Protectorate *(p68)*, that Casablanca underwent the most profound change. Against expert advice, Marshal Lyautey, the first resident-governor, proceeded with plans to make Casablanca the country's economic hub. To realize this vision, he hired the services of town planners and modernized the port. For almost 40 years, the most innovative architects worked on this huge building project. Casablanca continued to expand even after independence (1956). Futuristic high-rise buildings and a colossal mosque sending its laser beams towards Mecca once again expressed the city's forward-looking spirit.

CASABLANCA

Must See

❶ Hassan II Mosque

Experience More

❷ Avenue des Forces Armées Royales
❸ Place des Nations Unies
❹ Boulevard Mohammed V
❺ Place Mohammed V
❻ Parc de la Ligue Arabe
❼ Villa des Arts
❽ Abderrahman Slaoui Foundation Museum
❾ Old Medina
❿ Quartier Habous (New Medina)
⓫ Port
⓬ Corniche d'Aïn Diab
⓭ Anfa
⓮ Casablanca Twin Center
⓯ Mohammedia
⓰ Musée du Judaïsme Marocain

Eat

① La Sqala
② Taverne du Dauphin
③ Le Cabestan

Drink

④ Petit Pouchet
⑤ Sky 28

Stay

⑥ Riad Jnane Sherazade
⑦ Hyatt Regency
⑧ Le Doge Hotel & Spa

Greater Casablanca

Atlantic Ocean

Mohammedia ⑮

CASABLANCA

PLAGE DE AIN SEBAA

AIN HARROUDA

③ Area of main map

ROCHES NOIRES

SIDI MOUMEN

Casablanca Mohammed V International Airport

⑫ Corniche d'Ain Diab

LITTORAL

Tit Mellil

⑯ Musée du Judaïsme Marocain

SIFI MAÂROUF

0 km   5
0 miles   5

N

ABDALLAH

BOULEVARD DES

RUE JEMA ECH CHLEUH

EL ALAOUI

① Port ⑪

Old Medina ⑨

Chleuh Mosque

Bab el-Marsa

Bab Marrakech

OLD MEDINA

ALMOHADES

Casa Port Railway Station

BLVD HOUPHOUET-BOIGNY ②

BOULEVARD MOULAY ABDERRAHMANE

Avenue des Forces Armées Royales ②

AVENUE DES FORCES ARMÉES ROYALES

PLACE ZELLAGA

AVENUE DES FORCES

RUE DE TOULON

ARMÉES ROYALES

⑦ Pl Nation Unies

Colis Postaux 🖂

RUE A. BEN ABDALLAH

AVENUE DES FORCES

Place des Nations Unies ③

BLVD MOHAMMED V

AVE HOUMANE

AVE MOHAMMED V ④ ℹ

Marché Central 🖼

BLVD HASSAN SEGHIR

RUE AHMED FARIS

BOULEVARD DE LA RÉSISTANCE

RUE DE KARACHI

Mohamed Diouri 🖼

RUE TAIEB ABDELKARMI

La Résistance 🖼 ③

HASSAN I

RUE

Abderrahman Slaoui Foundation Museum ℹ ⑧

⑧

DE PARIS

ABDALLAH

EL FETOUAKI

Boulevard Mohammed V ④

MOHAMED

RUE DE KARACHI

RUE MAGELLAN

BOULEVARD EMILE ZOLA

RUE DU PARC

RACHIDI

Place Mohammed V ⑤

HASSAN II

RUE DU PR MOUL.

AVENUE

PL. DU 20 AOÛT

FONCIÈRE

SMIHA

Place Mohammed V 🖼

BLVD DU

LALLA YACOUT

PL. DE LA VICTOIRE

BLVD DE KHOURIBGA

BLVD YOUSSEF IBN TACHFINE

AVE SLAOUI

RUE

BLVD A. REITZER

RD-PT MERS SULTAN ℹ

MOSTAFA EL MAANI

ELMESKINI

RUE

BLVD DE LA RÉSISTANCE

RUE BARATHON

AVE OULED ZIANE

AVE MERS SULTAN

AVE OMAR

RAHAL

BD

RUE BAALABAK

BLVD LAKEN

DE STRASBOURG

RUE BARATHON

Parc de la Ligue Arabe ⑥

YOUSSEF

RUE D'AGADIR

RUE MOSTAFA EL MAANI

RUE DE REIMS

RUE HADJ AMAR

BOULEVARD

RIFFI

D'ALSACE

OU IDER

RUE DE LIBOURNE

RUE BACHIR IBRAHIMI

RUE RABIAA ADAOUIA

BLVD DE LA GIRONDE

Avenue Hassan II 🖼

ZERKTOUNI

RUE DE REIMS

RD-PT DE L'EUROPE

BLVD DE LA

PL. LEMAIGRE DUBREUIL

RÉSISTANCE

RUE HADJ

ROUTE

DE

RUE MOHAMED AL FIDOUZI

RUE SEBTA

BLVD DU 2 MARS

RUE DE MADRID

RUE HATIM EL ASSAM

BLVD DE LONDRES

AMAR

IDRISSI

RIFFI

MÉDIOUNA

SALIM ECHERKAOUI

RUE DES HÔPITAUX

LES HÔPITAUX

RUE SEBTA

RUE DE ROUSSILLON

Parc Isesco

BOULEVARD

OMAR

EL

RUE AHMED EL FIGUIGUI

Royal Palace

RUE SIDI OKBA

RUE IE ABOU BAKER HAMED IBN ZAHAR

HABOUS

RUE DE

RUE DE VICTOR

L'ARGONNE

RUE RIF

RUE DE ROME

HUGO

BOULEVARD IMPERIAL

RUE IMAM KASTALANI

RUE ABDEL MOUMEN

RUE TARIQ IBN ZIAD

BLVD DU 2 MARS

RUE LA LANDE

RUE SALONIQUE

RUE AMSTERDAM

RUE CONSTANTINOPLE

⑥

Quartier Habous (New Medina) ⑩

① 🏛️ 🕌

HASSAN II MOSQUE

◉ B1 **🏠 Blvd Sidi Mohammed Ben Abdallah** **🕐 Daily** **📞 (0522) 48 28 89/86**

Jutting over the Atlantic ocean on a man-made platform, the awesome scale and dramatic location of the magnificent Hassan II Mosque are sure to impress anyone who visits, but get a little closer and you'll soon find that, as is typical of the Moorish style, the magic is in the detail.

With a minaret that soars 200 m (656 ft) into the sky, the Hassan II Mosque is said to be the tallest religious building in the world. It beautifully blends traditional Moorish architecture with 20th-century innovation, from the lasers that shine east towards Mecca to the sliding roof and the glass floor through which the Atlantic Ocean is visible below. It is possible to visit the mosque as part of a guided tour, of which there are several a day delivered in a number of languages. The highlight is the vast prayer hall, with its columns the size of giant redwood trees. Every surface is covered with exquisite decoration, from patterned marble floors and intricate tiling to carved wooden ceilings.

Rising dramatically above the Atlantic Ocean, the minaret is 25 m (82 ft) wide and 200 m (656 ft) high.

↑ Decorative marble interior, featuring carved stucco and *zellij* tilework *(inset)*

Covering the columns of the prayer hall and doorways, marble is ubiquitous.

The minbar, or pulpit, located at the western end of the prayer hall, is particularly ornate. It is decorated with verses from the Qur'an.

↑ The imposing minaret, as viewed from the surrounding porticos, towers over the square

Above two mezzanines and hidden from view, the Women's Gallery extends over 5,300 sq m (57,000 sq ft) and can hold up to 5,000 worshippers.

The cedar-panelled interior of the dome over the prayer hall glistens with carved and painted decoration.

The Royal Door is decorated with traditional motifs engraved on brass and titanium.

Columns

Seen from the exterior, these are double doors in the shape of pointed arches framed by columns. Many are clad in incised bronze.

Mashrabiyy screenwork at the windows protects those within from prying eyes.

The stairway to the Women's Gallery features decorative woodcarving, multiple arches and marble, granite and onyx columns.

Hammam

Able to hold 25,000 faithful, the prayer hall measures 200 m (656 ft) by 100 m (328 ft). The central part of the roof can be opened to the sky.

↑ Cutaway illustration detailing the interior of the Hassan II Mosque

35,000

The number of craftsmen that worked tirelessly to complete this ambitious building project.

EXPERIENCE MORE

② Avenue des Forces Armées Royales

◉ D3 ⬛ South of the old medina, running between Place Oued el-Makhazine and Place Zellaga

Lined with high-rise buildings, major hotels such as the Sheraton, airline offices and travel agents, and towering, futuristic glass structures, this avenue marks the boundary of the commercial district. Further development is planned for its continuation towards the Hassan II Mosque.

③ Place des Nations Unies

◉ D3 ⬛ South of the old medina

At the beginning of the 20th century, this was still no more than a market square, a place that, by evening, would become the haunt of story-tellers and snake charmers. Today, it is the heart of the new town, a hub where major thoroughfares converge.

When the square was laid out in 1920, it was known as Place de France, but was later renamed. Beneath the arcades of 1930s' apartment blocks are rows of brasserie terraces and souvenir shops. In the north-east corner of the square, the original clocktower was built in 1910, demolished in 1940 and then rebuilt in 1992 to an identical design. At the time that it was erected, the clock symbolized colonial rule, indicating to the population that it should now keep in time with an industrial society.

At the Hyatt Regency Hotel, pictures of Humphrey Bogart and Ingrid Bergman, stars of the famous film *Casablanca* (1942), hang on the walls. In the southeast corner of the square is the Excelsior Hotel, embellished with Moorish friezes and balconies, which was the first of Morocco's Art Deco hotels and is one of the square's finest buildings. In 1934, the 11-storey Moretti Milone apartment block, at the corner of Boulevard Houphouët Boigny, became the first high-rise building in central Casablanca. The boulevard, lined with shops and restaurants, runs from the square to the port. At the end, on the right, the *marabout* of Sidi Belyout, patron saint and protector of Casablanca, stands in stark contrast to the neighbouring buildings.

> 💬 **INSIDER TIP**
> ## Eating Straight from the Sea
>
> At lunchtime a cluster of cafés at the Marché Central serve grilled fish fresh from the port, a stone's throw away. Alternatively, buy your fish in the market and take it to one of the stalls to have it cooked.

④ Boulevard Mohammed V

◉ E3 ⬛ Running from Place des Nations Unies to Boulevard Hassan Seghir

Running through the city like a spine, this boulevard links Place des Nations Unies with the railway station in the east of the city. When it was built in 1915, it was intended to be the major artery through the commercial heart of Casablanca. On both sides, covered arcades house shops and restaurants.

A raised strip sections off traffic and widens into a square level with the **Central Market**. The high-rise buildings here are notable for their façades, which feature loggias, columns, *zellij* tilework and geometric carvings. Particular to the buildings of this period is the mixture of styles: Art Deco, seen in the white façades of simple design (*p114*), and the typically Moroccan decorative style. Among the finest of these buildings are three residential blocks: the Glaoui, on the corner of Rue el-Amraoui Brahim; the Bessonneau, opposite the

←

The Zevaco Dome and clocktower of the old medina in Place des Nations Unies

Visitors relaxing in the tropical gardens of Place Mohammed V →

busy market; and the Asayag building, on the corner of Boulevard Hassan Seghir.

Another particular feature of Boulevard Mohammed V is its covered arcades, which are similar to the shopping arcades built during the same period (the 1920s) along the Champs-Élysées in Paris. Among the most interesting of these arcades is the Passage du Glaoui, which links Boulevard Mohammed V to Rue Allal ben-Abdallah. Lit by prismatic lamps, the arcade is punctuated by glass rotundas. Passage Sumica, opposite Passage du Glaoui, is closer to the Art Deco style. This runs through to Rue du Prince Moulay Abdallah, which also contains some notable 1930s' apartment blocks. This pedestrianized street, lined with boutiques and eateries, is very popular with shoppers.

In Rue Mohammed el-Quori, off Boulevard Mohammed V, stands the Rialto, a renovated cinema renowned for its fine ornamentation, stained-glass windows and Art Deco lighting.

Central Market

🏠 Boulevard Mohammed V
🕐 7am–2pm daily

5

Place Mohammed V

🗺 D3 🧭 North of the Parc de la Ligue Arabe

The administrative heart of the city, Place Mohammed V exemplifies the architecture of the Protectorate, combining French monumentality with Moorish sobriety.

The Préfecture, overlooked by a Tuscan-style campanile (bell tower), stands on the southeastern side of the square. Its buildings are set around three courtyards, each with a tropical garden. The central stairway is framed by two huge paintings by Jacques Majorelle (p243) depicting the festivities of a *moussem* and a performance of the *ahwach*, a Berber dance.

Behind the Préfecture stands the Palais de Justice (law courts). The strong verticality of the Moorish doorway, with its awning of green tiles, contrasts with the horizontal lines of the arcaded gallery, which are emphasized by a carved frieze running the length of the building.

Two buildings set slightly back abut the façade of the law courts on either side. On the right is the Consulat de France, whose immaculate gardens contain an equestrian statue of Marshal Lyautey, which stood in the centre of the square until Moroccan independence. On the left, in the northeastern corner, is the Cercle Militaire. To the north is the post office, fronted by an open arcade decorated with *zellij* tilework and semicircular arches; this leads through to an Art Deco central hall within.

Opposite, along Rue de Paris, an area of greenery gives a more picturesque feel to the square and provides a popular spot for a stroll. At certain times of day, the monumental fountain at the centre plays music and has light displays.

> **Place Mohammed V exemplifies the architecture of the Protectorate, combining French monumentality with Moorish sobriety.**

CASABLANCA'S MAURESQUE ARCHITECTURE

In 1907, innovative architects set to work to create buildings in a range of contemporary styles, and Casablanca began to look like a huge building site. By the early 1920s, numerous teams of architects were working in the city. Whatever the style, avant-garde tendencies were often counterbalanced by a traditional Moroccan style.

As the architects drew on the repertoire of Art Nouveau, Art Deco and Neo-Classicism, which were fashionable at the time, they also took inspiration from the Moorish style that Europeans found so fascinating. Towards the end of the 1920s and into the early 1930s, a new taste for simplicity became apparent. Emphasizing shape and outline at the expense of decoration, this gave prominence to the interplay of convex and concave shapes, and to balconies and bow windows. Another significant driving force was the expectations of the colonial population and European speculators, resulting in lifts, bathrooms, kitchens and parking areas becoming commonplace.

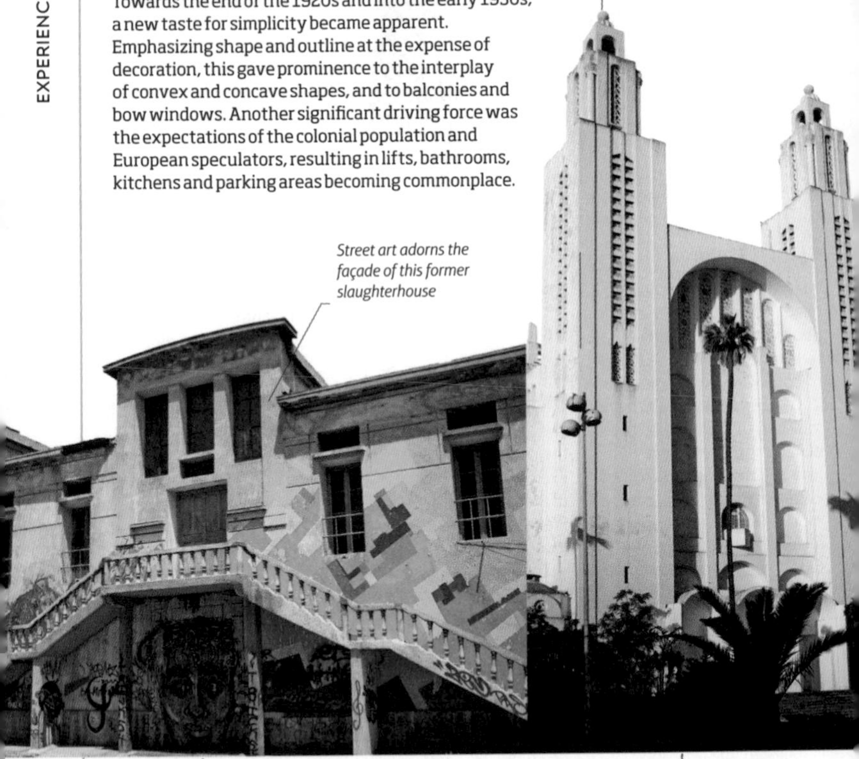

Domed bell chambers straddle the Sacré-Coeur's arched entrance

Street art adorns the façade of this former slaughterhouse

Architectural Highlights

Fabrique Culturelle des Anciens Abattoirs

△ One of the largest employers in the working-class neighbourhood of Hay Mohammadi was the slaughterhouse. It closed in 2000 and since then this surprisingly grand building on Avenue Jaafar Barmaki, with a wonderfully ornate Art Deco gateway-like entrance has been renovated. It now operates as a *fabrique culturelle*, or culture factory, offering work and exhibition spaces for local artists.

Église du Sacré-Coeur

△ Casablanca's most well known landmark after the Hassan II Mosque, its city centre cathedral is a striking fusion of Neo-Gothic and Art Deco, with local Moroccan elements. It was designed by Marseille architect Paul Tournon and took a quarter of a century to build. After independence in 1956, it was no longer used as a church and is now an arts centre (p116).

← The lavish interior of the Art-Deco Lynx Cinema, Casablanca

Did You Know?

A campaign to protect the city's architecture and name it a UNESCO World Heritage Site is underway.

Semicircular arches and traditional Moorish stucco on the exterior of the Grande Poste

Grande Poste

▲ This is no ordinary post office. The Grande Poste on Place Mohammed V was built in the early 1900s during the French protectorate. This highly decorative building, which features mosaics, a loggia of semicircular arches and intricate *zellij* tilework, could easily be mistaken for an important cultural monument. While the outside is impressive, the original Art-Deco interiors are also worth a look. The building still functions as the main post office in Casablanca.

Cinema Rialto

▲ Looking like it belongs on Miami's South Beach, the Rialto Cinema on Rue Mohammed El Quorri is perhaps Casablanca's most strikingly Art-Deco edifice. It was built in 1930 and as well as screening movies it has hosted musical stars including Edith Piaf and Josephine Baker, who showed up to entertain American troops in 1943. It has been renovated numerous times over the years and is still showing films.

↑ The nave of the Église du Sacré-Cœur, formerly a Catholic church and now a cultural centre

There is a small permanent exhibition of Moroccan art from the second half of the 20th century, supplemented by regularly changing temporary exhibitions of both Moroccan and international artists. The institution is operated by the nonprofit Fondation ONA, one of the country's primary cultural foundations, whose major shareholders are the Moroccan royal family. It is easy to find: look for the dual towers of the Casablanca Twin Centre, and the villa is just to the east, across the road.

6

Parc de la Ligue Arabe

◉ D4 ◉ South of Place Mohammed V (between Boulevard Rachidi and Boulevard Mohammed Zerktouni)

This huge garden incorporates café terraces and is a good spot to get some air. Avenues lined with impressively tall palm trees, ficus, arcades and pergolas frame some stunning formal flowerbeds. The streets surrounding the park, including Boulevard Moulay-Youssef, Rue d'Alger and Rue du Parc contain Art Nouveau and Art Deco houses.

Northwest of the park stands the **Église du Sacré-Cœur**. A white concrete twin-towered building with an Art Deco flavour to its façade, it is now deconsecrated and used for cultural events.

To the southeast stands the Église Notre-Dame-de-Lourdes. Its stained-glass windows depict scenes from the life of the Virgin Mary against motifs taken from

Moroccan carpets. They are the work of G. Loire, a master-craftsman from Chartres. To the southwest is the Villa des Arts, displaying contemporary Moroccan paintings.

Église du Sacré-Cœur

◉ Rond-point de l'Europe ◉ Only for concerts and other cultural events

7

Villa des Arts

◉ C4 ◉ 30 Boulevard Brahim Roudani, near Parc de la Ligue Arabe ◉ 9am-7pm Tue-Sun ◉ fondation ona.com

Another of Casablanca's elegant Art Deco buildings that has been put to good use, this 1934 villa is now a serene centre for the arts. It is approached through a sculpture garden with lush green lawns, giant palm trees and a central fountain feature. Inside, it has two floors of coolly minimal galleries showcasing modern art.

8

Abderrahman Slaoui Foundation Museum

D3 **12 Rue du Parc, close to the Cathédrale Sacré-Coeur** **10am-6pm Tue-Sat** **musee-as.ma**

Abderrahman Slaoui (1919–2001) was a businessman, traveller and patron of the arts. The museum that bears his name occupies a charming 1940s' Art Deco house, located at the heart of downtown. Over multiple floors, it displays his collection of Orientalist posters, jewellery and assorted decorative items. This unique and personal amassing of frequently dazzling and often curious items includes many beautiful vintage advertising and travel posters, a number of which were designed by French artist Jacques Majorelle, whose former home and garden can be visited in Marrakech (p242). Other displays present illuminated Korans and manuscripts, ceramics from Fès, lustrous coloured glassware, exquisite Berber jewellery and even fish made of segmented copper.

↑ Jewellery and Koran box at the Abderrahman Slaoui Museum

Temporary exhibitions complement the musuem's dazzling permanent collection. There is also a stylish top-floor tearoom.

9

Old Medina

D2 **Between Boulevard des Almohades and Place des Nations Unies**

At the beginning of the 20th century, Casablanca consisted only of the old medina, which itself had no more than a few thousand inhabitants. The walls around the old town were originally pierced by four gates, though only two of them survive today. Bab Marrakech and Bab el-Jedid, on the western side, face onto Boulevard Tahar el-Alaoui. A daily market, with jewellers, barbers, public letter-writers and so on, stretches out along the length of the walls.

Opposite the fishing harbour is the sqala, a fortified bastion built in the 18th century and one of the few remaining tokens of the reign of Sidi Mohammed ben Abdallah, who built much of the old medina. Behind the bastion, a *marabout* (shrine) with a double crown of merlons contains the Tomb of Sidi Allal el-Kairouani, who became Casablanca's first patron saint in 1350. Bab el-Marsa (Gate of the Sea), which opens onto Boulevard des Almohades, also dates from the 18th century. It was at this spot that the French disembarked in July 1907 to restore order to a rioting city, catalysing the process of French colonial rule in the region.

↑ A trader selling teapots and other accessories at the daily market in the old medina

10

Quartier Habous (New Medina)

☑ F5 ⚐ Southeast of the city centre, near Boulevard Victor Hugo

In the 1930s, in order to address the problem of an expanding urban population and to prevent Casablanca's underprivileged citizens from being forced to settle in insalubrious quarters, French town planners laid out a new medina (Nouvelle Medina). Land to the south of the existing city centre earmarked for this development was given over to the Habous, the administration of religious foundations, hence the new town's name.

This new town – which did not, however, forestall the later development of shanty towns – was built in the traditional Arab style at the same time as obeying modern town planning and public health regulations. It contains public areas, such as a market, shops, mosques, a *kissaria* and baths, as well as private dwellings (arranged around a courtyard separated from the street by a solid wall).

The new medina is another facet of colonial town planning during the Protectorate, and its flower-filled, arcaded streets offer the opportunity for an amble through an especially scenic quarter of the city. While the most modest houses are located around the market, the finest are set around the mosque.

Northeast of the medina are the copper and brass Souk and Chez Bennis, Casablanca's most famous patisserie, which sells pastries known as *cornes de gazelle* (gazelle's horns), fritters and *pastilla*. There are also shops specializing in curios and collectors' items, and they can be good places to find Art Deco objects. A wide range of Moroccan rugs and carpets is also on sale at the weekly auction in the carpet souk.

Northwest of the Quartier Habous is the **Mahakma du Pacha**, a formal tribunal and today one of the city's eight

MYTHS AND MOVIES

The much-loved film *Casablanca* (1942), which was entirely shot on a studio lot in Hollywood, has little to do with its namesake. Not even the American writers of the play on which it was based, *Everybody Comes to Rick's*, visited Morocco. The city now has a bar named after the eponymous club: Rick's Café *(right)*, on Boulevard Sour Jedid. As in the film, it is American owned, it does have a resident pianist, and yes, he does play the iconic "As Time Goes By."

1755

The year Casablanca was hit by the Lisbon earthquake, followed by a powerful tsunami.

préfectures (administrative headquarters). The building, which centres around a tall tower and two courtyards, is a fine example of the adaptation of traditional Arab architecture to modern needs. The traditional Arabic decoration of its 64 rooms is the work of Moroccan craftsmen: it consists of carved stucco and *zellij* tilework on the walls, carved cedarwood panels on the ceiling and wrought iron on the doors.

The elegant **Royal Palace**, on the fringes of the Quartier Habous and set in extensive gardens, was built in the 1920s by the Pertuzio brothers, whose aim was to create a luxuriously appointed yet modern dwelling.

Mahakma du Pacha
🏛 Boulevard Victor Hugo

←
A visitor capturing the richly decorated walls and arches of the Mahkama du Pacha

Royal Palace
🏛 Between Boulevard Victor Hugo and Rue Ahmed el-Figuigui 🚫 To the public

---

⓫
Port

🗺 D2 🏛 East of the old medina

Casablanca is Morocco's main port. Built during the Protectorate, it is one of the largest artificial ports in the world. A groyne protects it from the pounding of the ocean that destroyed several earlier constructions. The port is equipped with ultra-modern commercial, fishing and leisure facilities.

Access to the port complex is via the fishing harbour. On the seafront in the port itself, as well as along the avenue leading down to it, some excellent seafood restaurants are to be found.

A multimillion-dirham development of towering hotels, restaurants, shops, offices and apartments, together with a marina, is changing the shoreline between the port and the Hassan II Mosque.

STAY

Riad Jnane Sherazade
This tranquil villa, set in lovely gardens, offers modern comforts and a traditional hammam

🗺 E5 🏛 8 Rue de Belgrade, Habous
📞 (0522) 82 44 44

ⓓ ⓓ ⓓ

Hyatt Regency
The city's landmark hotel with the most central location and superb five-star facilities, including three restaurants.

🗺 D3 🏛 Place des Nations Unies
🌐 hyatt.com

ⓓ ⓓ ⓓ

Le Doge Hotel & Spa
Stylish boutique hotel in a 1930s townhouse. Guests have free access to the hammam, sauna and hot tub.

🗺 D3 🏛 9 Rue du Doctor Veyre
🌐 hotelledoge.com

ⓓ ⓓ ⓓ

↑ The Royal Palace in Casablanca, surrounded by beautiful Mediterranean-style gardens

DRINK

Petit Pouchet
Faded French-style bar-café once frequented by Edith Piaf and Antoine de Saint-Exupéry.

🔢 E3 🏠 Cnr Boulevard Mohamed V & Rue Mohamed el-Qory

Dh Dh Dh

Sky 28
This opulent rooftop bar with fabulous views over the city serves great cocktails and hosts live music and DJs.

🔢 B4 🏠 Kenzi Tower Hotel, Boulevard Mohamed Zerktouni
📞 (0522) 97 80 00

Dh Dh Dh

12

Corniche d'Aïn Diab

🔢 X9 🏠 West of the Mosque of Hassan II

The Corniche d'Aïn Diab has been an upmarket part of Casablanca since the 1920s. Running from El-Hank Lighthouse in the east, to the Marabout of Sidi Abderrahman in the west, this coastal avenue is lined with a succession of tidal swimming pools, hotels, restaurants, fashionable nightclubs and an institute of thalassotherapy (a type of treatment involving seawater, mud, algae and seaweed).

The earliest establishments to be built here – with the needs of a wealthy clientèle in mind – opened in the 1930s. A string of public beach clubs, each one rivalling its neighbour, lines the Corniche, offering a variety of pools and restaurants. The most modern and fashionable of them all is the Tahiti Beach Club.

At the foot of the hill of Anfa, near the Palais Ibn Séoud, the foundation of the same name houses a mosque and one of the most comprehensive libraries on the continent. At the western end of the Corniche, 3 km (2 miles) further on, the Marabout of Sidi Abderrahman, perched on a rock, is accessible only at low tide. It attracts many Muslim pilgrims in search of a cure for nervous disorders.

13

Anfa

🔢 C5 🏠 Northwest of the city

Occupying a hill that overlooks Casablanca from the northwest, Anfa is a residential quarter with wide avenues lined with floral decorations, where luxurious homes with terraces, swimming pools and lush gardens bring to mind Beverly Hills in California.

← The Marabout of Sidi Abderrahman, at the of the Corniche d'Aïn Diab

A visit to the kasbah and the fish market can be followed by a stroll along the seafront. From the port, the clifftop walk offers fine views of the sea and Mohammedia.

Since the 1930s, villas have been built here, and they constitute a catalogue of successive architectural styles and evolving fashions.

It was at the Hôtel d'Anfa, now demolished, that the historic meeting between US president Franklin D. Roosevelt and British prime minister Winston Churchill took place in January 1943, during World War II, at which the date of the Allied landings in Normandy was decided. Although they got wind of the meeting, the Germans were misled by the literal translation of the word "Casablanca". Under the impression that the location was to be the White House in Washington, they failed to prevent it from going ahead.

During the meeting, President Roosevelt also formally pledged his support to Sultan Mohammed V in his aim to obtain independence from France, thus opening new avenues for Morocco in the postwar period.

14

Casablanca Twin Center

📍 B4 📍 At the intersection of Boulevard Zerktouni and Boulevard el-Massira

Dominated by its two soaring skyscrapers, the East Tower and West Tower, this extensive complex is both proof and a symbol of the city's economic importance. Located at an intersection leading to the main residential districts, these twin structures are the tallest buildings in Morocco and comprise numerous offices and shopping malls as well as a hotel. By its outward appearance no less than in its infrastructure, and by its proximity to some of the city's greatest landmarks, the complex is a statement on the role that Casablanca plays on both the national and international stages.

15

Mohammedia

📍 F1 📍 28 km (17 miles) northeast of Casablanca
🚗 🚌

At the beginning of the 20th century, Mohammedia (formerly Fedala) was no more than a kasbah. This changed in the 1930s, when its port began to receive oil tankers. Today, petroleum accounts for 16 per cent of all Moroccan port traffic. Although the flaming chimneys of the refineries blight the landscape, this large town, now part of greater Casablanca, is still residential. It has a golf course and a yacht club. Its fine beaches and friendly atmosphere have helped to turn Mohammedia into an upmarket coastal resort for wealthy Moroccans.

16

Musée du Judaïsme Marocain

📍 E2 📍 81 Rue Chasseur Jules Gros, Quartier de l'Oasis ⏰ 10am–5pm Mon–Fri (summer: to 6pm), 11am–3pm Sun 🌐 jewishmuseum casa.com

The modernized Museum of Moroccan Judaism, the only one of its kind in the Arab world, contains displays of scarves, kaftans, prayer shawls and other religious objects, and a reconstructed Moroccan synagogue.

From Roman times up to independence in 1956, Morocco had a sizeable Jewish community. Today numbering some 5,000, Morocco's Jews occupy prominent positions in the spheres of politics, economics and culture.

↑ The Casablanca Twin Center towers facing a busy intersection

Blue fishing boats moored in the port of Essaouira

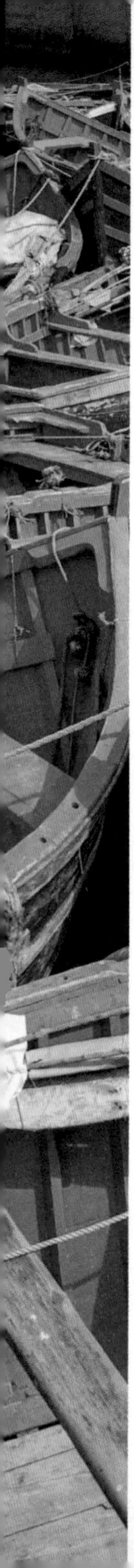

SOUTHERN ATLANTIC COAST

Morocco's Southern Atlantic coastal area contains many smaller towns and resorts, which are especially attractive to those who wish to escape the frenetic activity of the imperial cities.

This region, more than almost any other part of Morocco, has always had contact with the outside world. The Phoenicians, then the Romans, established trading posts here. The Portuguese and the Spanish built military strongholds and centres of trade along the coast, whose topography also made it a haven for pirates. Fortified towns such as El-Jadida, Safi and, most especially, Essaouira bear witness to the Spanish and Portuguese contribution to Morocco's history. Under the French Protectorate *(p68)*, the region became the country's economic and administrative centre. Today, this stretch of coastline is very industrial and visibly oriented towards the modern world.

The coastal road to Essaouira passes stunningly beautiful deserted beaches that are ideal for surfing. It winds on to Agadir, Morocco's most popular coastal destination.

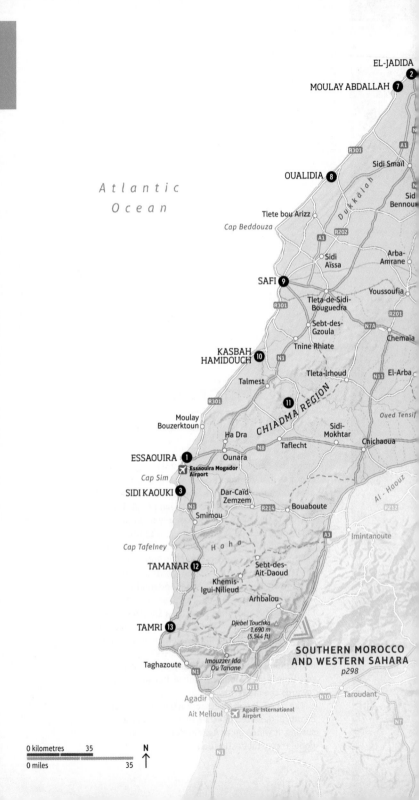

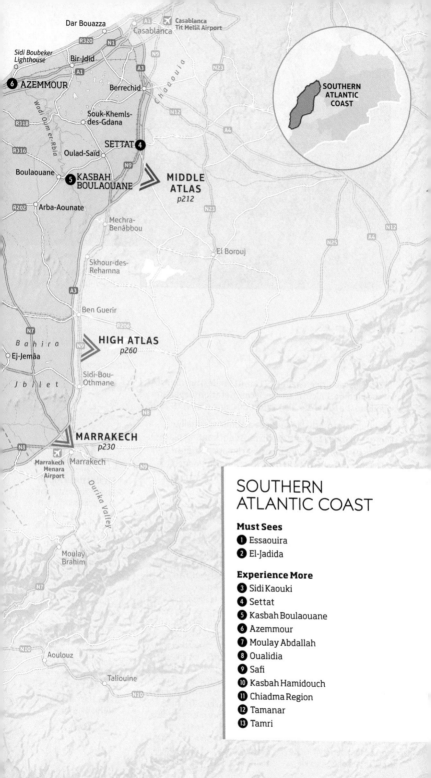

SOUTHERN ATLANTIC COAST

Must Sees
❶ Essaouira
❷ El-Jadida

Experience More
❸ Sidi Kaouki
❹ Settat
❺ Kasbah Boulaouane
❻ Azemmour
❼ Moulay Abdallah
❽ Oualidia
❾ Safi
❿ Kasbah Hamidouch
⓫ Chiadma Region
⓬ Tamanar
⓭ Tamri

A cluster of fishing boats floating beneath one of Essaouira's sea bastions

❶

ESSAOUIRA

🅰B4 **✈Essaouira-Mogador** **🚌1 km (0.5 miles) northeast of the medina; link to Marrakech coach station (departure opposite the Hôtel des Îles)** **🛈Rue du Caire, (0524) 78 35 32**

Essaouira, formerly Mogador, is a quintessentially Moroccan town and one of the most enchanting places in the country. It enjoys a pleasant climate and, although it is a mecca for artists and surfers, it has managed to escape the overspill of mass tourism from Marrakech.

In the 7th century BC, the Phoenicians founded a base where Essaouira now stands, and in the 1st century BC, Juba II, founder of the Roman city of Volubilis (p198), made it a centre of the manufacture of purple dye. The Portuguese established a trading and military bridgehead here in the 15th century and named it Mogador. The town itself, however, was not built until around 1760, when Sultan Mohammed III set up a naval base here. The town, the harbour and the fortifications were designed and built in the style of European fortresses by renowned French architect Théodore Cornut, who had worked for Louis XV. On the small group of islands known as the Îles Purpuraires, visible from the coast, there is a bird sanctuary for gulls and threatened species. Phoenician, Attic and Ionian amphorae found on the Île de Mogador, and now displayed in the Musée de l'Histoire et des Civilisations in Rabat (p86), prove that were traders here from the 7th century BC. In the 1st century BC, Juba II set up a centre for the production of purple dye, from which the islands take their name. Highly prized by the Romans, the dye was obtained from the murex, a type of mollusc. The ruins of a 19th-century prison are also visible. Some 12 km (7.5 miles) south of Essaouira, the beach at Sidi Kaouki (p132) is popular with surfers. A mausoleum, here contains the tomb of a *marabout* (holy man) who, according to legend, had the power to cure infertile women. An annual pilgrimage, with many devotees, takes place here in mid-August.

① Ramparts

The outer walls on the seafront, which have bevelled crenellations, were designed to protect the town from naval attacks and thus betray influences from European fortifications. By contrast, the inner walls, which have square crenellations like those found around Marrakech, are more Islamic in style. These are built in stone and roughcast with a facing of earth. The walls surrounding the medina are pierced by Bab Doukkala on the northeastern side, Bab Marrakech on the eastern side and Bab Sebaa on the southern side.

② Sqalas

Essaouira boasts two *sqalas* (sea bastions): Sqala du Port in the south and Sqala de la Ville in the northwest. The latter is lined with Spanish cannons and was built by Théodore Cornut on the site of Castello Real, a castle constructed by the Portuguese in about 1505. The esplanade, where scenes from Orson Welles' film *Othello* were shot in 1949, commands dramatic views of the ocean and the Îles Purpuraires across the bay. A passage leads from the bastion to the former munitions stores, which now house marquetry workshops.

③ Port

The Porte de la Marine, leading to the docks, is crowned by a classical triangular pediment and is dominated by two imposing towers flanked by four turrets. From the 18th century, 40 per cent of Atlantic sea traffic passed through Essaouira. It became known as the Port of Timbuctu, being the destination of caravans from sub-Saharan Africa bringing goods for export to Europe. Once one of Morocco's largest sardine ports, it now provides a living for only 500 or so families. But it still has its traditional shipyard, where seagoing vessels are made by hand out of wood. Visitors can also watch the fish auction and sample grilled sardines fresh from the day's catch.

> **The esplanade, where scenes from Orson Welles' film *Othello* were shot in 1949, commands dramatic views of the ocean and the Îles Purpuraires across the bay.**

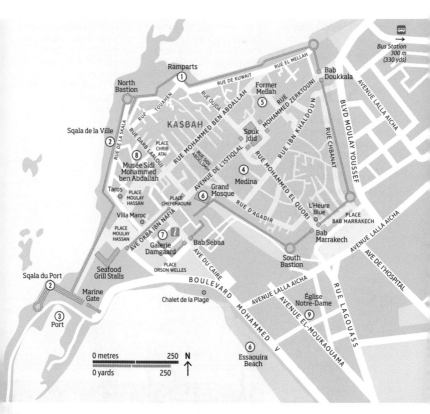

④
Medina

The layout of Essaouira is unusual. As with elsewhere in Morocco, the medina is a labyrinth of narrow passages; the town itself, by contrast, has straight, wide streets laid out at right angles and cut by gateways. The Grand Mosque is situated in the heart of the medina. Further north, Souk Jdid is divided into four by the intersection of two thoroughfares: there is a daily souk for fish, spices and grains, and a souk for secondhand items and collectables, known as *joutia*.

⑤
Former Mellah

⌂ From Bab Doukkala, via Rue Mohammed Zerktouni

Having risen to prominence and prosperity in the 18th and 19th centuries, the Jewish community in Essaouira came to hold an important economic position in the town, and Jewish jewellers were renowned. The town's former *mellah* is no longer inhabited by Jews, but the former houses of Jewish businessmen can still be seen on Rue Darb Laalouj; they are now converted into shops. In contrast to Muslim houses, they are fronted by balconies opening onto the street and some have lintels inscribed in Hebrew. Rue Mohammed Zerktouni, the main street in the quarter, has a lively market. Leaving by Bab Doukkala, you will pass the austere Jewish cemetery, which is worth a visit. (Keys are available on request from the caretaker.)

⑥
Essaouira Beach

Essaouira's beach, south of the town centre, is known as one of the finest in Morocco. All through the summer, the trade winds keep this part of the coast surprisingly cool. At times, however, the blustery winds are so strong that they drive people to seek shelter in the medina. At the estuary of Wadi Qsob, on the far side of the beach, vestiges of the thick system of defences built on a rocky promontory by Sultan Sidi Mohammed are visible. Although they have crumbled, the walls can still be made out.

Did You Know?

Essaouira has an "Orson Welles Square" honouring the time the director spent here filming *Othello*.

By tracing the wadi upstream, after a tumbledown bridge, you reach the village of Diabet. It is also accessible via the road to Agadir, turning off to the right after 7 km (4 miles). Of interest here are the ruins of Dar Soltane Mahdounia, a palace built by Sidi Mohammed ben Abdallah in the late 18th century, now almost entirely engulfed in sand. A common belief (happily perpetutated by locals) is that It inspired Jimi Hendrix (who visited Diabet in 1969) to write the song "Castles in the Sand", but more keen-eyed historians will note that Hendrix released the song two years before he even arrived in Morocco.

Surfers will particularly enjoy the many beaches each side of Essaouira. Thanks to the enterprise of dynamic local associations, Morocco is

STAY

Villa Maroc
Essaouira's original boutique hotel is a warren of rooms, courtyards and terraces with views over the port.

⌂ 10 Rue Abdellah Ben Yassine, Medina
Ⓦ villa-maroc.com

Ⓓ Ⓓ Ⓓ

L'Heure Bleue
The top hotel in town is a former mansion, done out in colonial style, with all the facilities you could ever desire.

⌂ 2 Rue Ibn Batouta, Medina Ⓦ heure-bleue.com

Ⓓ Ⓓ Ⓓ

becoming increasingly popular with surfers and windsurfers. (The Océan Vagabond café is a good place to hire surfing equipment.) The windiest time of year, and therefore the best time for surfing and wind-surfing, is April to September. However, while the air is always pleasantly warm, the water is rather cool. South of Essaouira, at Cap Sim (beyond Diabet) and at Sidi Kaouki, and to the north, at Moulay Bouzerktoun, the waves are powerful, and safe only for the experienced. Also to the south, at Tafelney (beyond Smimou), there is a magnificent bay where the water is warmer. In spite of the constant gusty wind, it is easier to get into the water on the beach at Essaouira, as the waves are much gentler.

THE GNAOUA WORLD MUSIC FESTIVAL

Every June, Essaouira's population is swollen by about 200,000 people as music fans and revellers roll into town for four days and nights of concerts. It began back in 1998 as a celebration of the music of the gnaoua (or gnawa), the descendants of African slaves, who are renowned for their spiritual music. Over the years the scope has grown and now all kinds of musicians from all over the world take part, and the whole town turns into one big party. Find out more at *www.festival-gnaoua.net*.

⑦
Galerie Damgaard

⌂ Avenue Oqba Ibn Nafia
☎ (0524) 78 44 46   🕘 9am–1pm & 3-7pm daily

A generation of self-taught painters and sculptors has transformed Essaouira into an important centre of artistic activity. Essaouira's medina is now packed with boutiques and galleries. Many talented artists – some of them former fishermen and farmers – were brought to the public's attention by the Dane Frederic Damgaard. Once an antique dealer in Nice, from 1988 he devoted his energies to the art produced in Essaouira, running his own gallery in the medina until he retired in 2006. On display is the work of artists from the humblest walks of life. Among the best known are Zouzaf, Ali Maïmoune, Rachid Amarlouch, Fatima Ettalbi and Mohammed Tabal, a Gnaouan known as "the trance painter". Others to be discovered include the expressionist known simply as Ali, whose style is midway between naïve and Brutalist, and his son Ben Ali. All of these artists draw inspiration from Essaouira's cultural variety, and reflect the traditions of different schools. In Morocco and throughout the world, many exhibitions and other projects have been devoted to the painters of Essaouira.

⑧
Musée Sidi Mohammed ben Abdallah

⌂ Rue Darb Laalouj
🕘 9am-6pm daily

This small but well-curated ethnographic museum is laid out in a 19th-century house, which was the pasha's resi-dence and the town hall during the Protectorate, and is almost worth the trip alone. With a strong focus on Berber culture, it contains many fine displays of ancient crafts, weapons and jewellery. There are artifacts from reli-gious brotherhoods, Moorish musical instruments and some stunning examples of Berber and Jewish costumes in silk, velvet and flannel. Carpets illustrating the tradi-tional weaving of local tribes are also on show.

←

Sunset over Essaouira's beach, one of the finest in Morocco

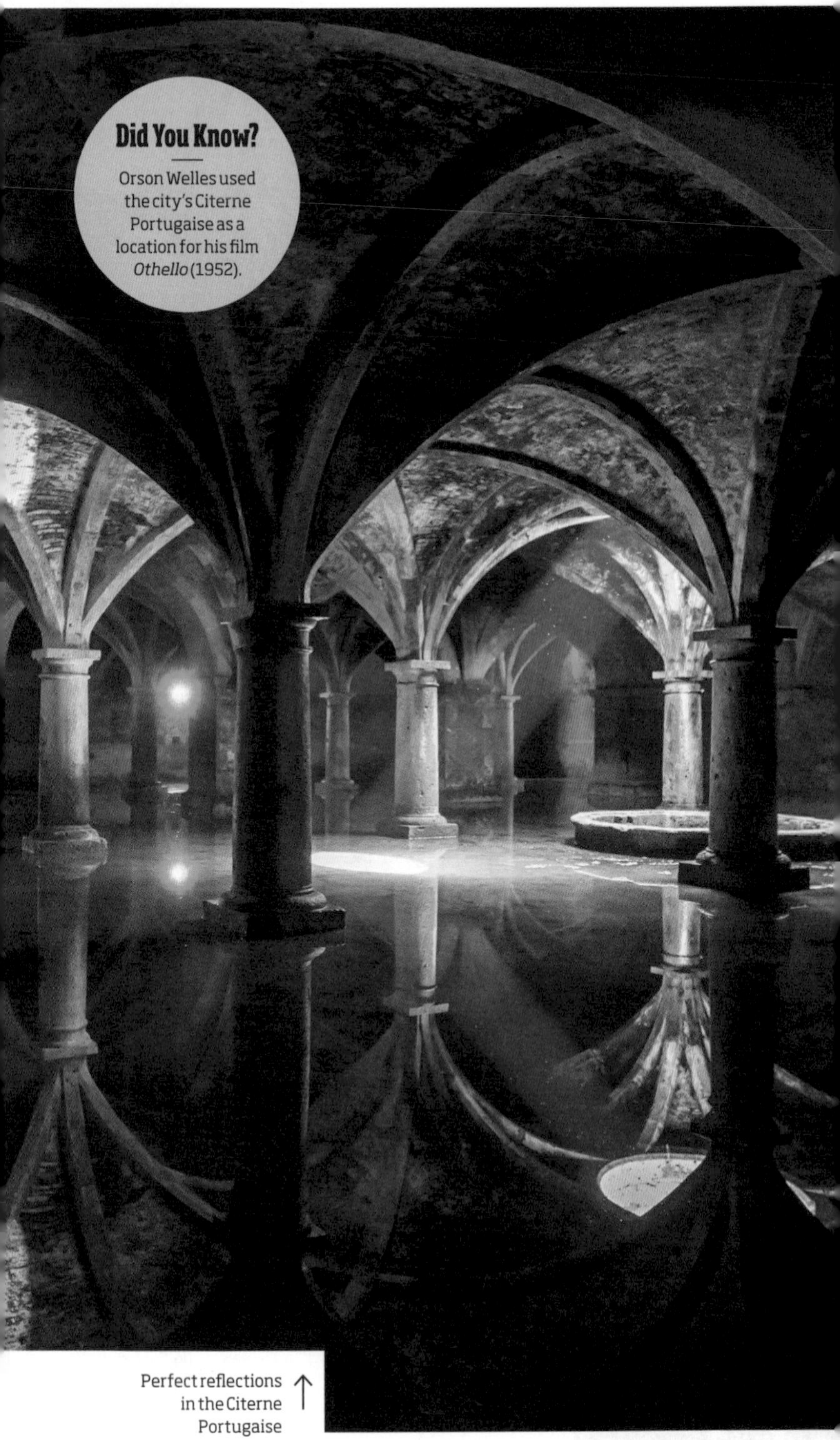

Did You Know?

Orson Welles used the city's Citerne Portugaise as a location for his film *Othello* (1952).

Perfect reflections in the Citerne Portugaise ↑

②

EL-JADIDA

🗺B2 🏬🚍 ℹ️20 bis, Ave Maukawama & Place Mohammed V; (0523) 34 47 88

Lying between Casablanca and Essaouira, the small coastal city of El-Jadida is an appealing mix of a historic medina with fortified sea-walls, fine beaches and plenty of excellent seafood. With far fewer tourists than its neighbouring cities and some wonderful historic sights, El-Jadida is a great place to kick back for a couple of days.

The Story of El-Jadida

The Portuguese settled here in 1502 and built a fort named Mazagan. In time, the town became a major centre of trade, and ships from Europe and the East anchored here to take on provisions. In 1769, the sultan Sidi Mohammed expelled the Portuguese, who destroyed it with explosives as they fled. It was resettled by local Arab tribes and a large Jewish community from Azemmour at the beginning of the 19th century.

Old Town Highlights

Entry into the UNESCO World Heritage listed old town is through a gateway that leads to Place Mohammed ben-Abdallah. The seawalls are fortified with four bastions that were rebuilt after the Portuguese destroyed the town in 1769, and a walk along the ramparts offers lovely panoramic views.

At the centre of the old town is the Citerne Portugaise (Portuguese cistern). Designed in the Manueline Gothic style, the cistern was constantly fed by fresh water so as to guarantee the town's water supply in the event of a prolonged siege. It was rediscovered by chance in 1916 when a shopkeeper was knocking down a wall to enlarge his premises. The mirror-like reflections of the architecture in the still water are a truly captivating sight.

↑ Fortifications of the old Portuguese city of Mazagan

INSIDE THE CITERNE PORTUGAISE

The Portuguese built the foundations of this underground cistern in 1514. First an arsenal, then an armoury, it was converted into a cistern after the citadel was enlarged in 1541. The cistern is open daily (admission fee required).

A well, 3.5 m (11.5 ft) across, was sunk through the central span, allowing daylight to enter.

Five lines of columns support the vaults.

The cistern takes the form of a square 34 m by 33 m (111 ft by 108 ft).

The 25 pillars are reflected in the stagnant water.

↑ The mausoleum of Marabout Sidi Kaouki situated on the beach

EXPERIENCE MORE

③
Sidi Kaouki

🏔B4 🚗12 km (7.5 miles) south of Essaouira

Sidi Kaouki is a small, sleepy seafront village with a fine, if windswept, beach. Appearing to rise up out of the water is the tomb of the *marabout* (holy man), who, according to legend, cured infertile women. An annual pilgrimage takes place here in mid-August. This is also a popular surf centre, with a number of rental kiosks in the village. Locals offer horse and camel rides along the beach. In the winter months, the local river, just a short walk from the village, becomes home to wild flamingos.

④
Settat

🏔C3 🚌🚉 ℹAvenue Hassan II, El-Haram building; (0523) 40 58 05

Set on a crossroads between north and south, Settat is the capital of Chaouia and the economic hub of the province, a coastal plain known as Morocco's grainstore. While the north of the region is famous for its fertile agricultural land, the southern part is given over to livestock (*chaoui* means "breeder of sheep").

When Moulay Ismaïl built the Kasbah Ismaïla at the end of the 17th century, the security and stability of the region – which was traversed by major caravan routes – were strengthened. The sultan would stay in the kasbah on his travels between Fès and Marrakech. Vestiges of the building can still be seen in the modern town.

Today, Settat offers little of interest to tourists. However, under the aegis of Driss Basri, a native of the region and Minister of the Interior for almost 20 years, it stood as a model of urban development in the 1990s. The merits of this distinction can be seen from Place Hassan II, in the town centre, in the arrangement of open spaces and pedestrianized shopping areas, and in buildings combining Art Deco and Moorish styles.

Of greater interest is the tiny village of Boulaouane, which can be reached by road from Settat. The journey to Boulaouane is a foretaste of the semi-arid southern landscapes. Barbary fig trees line the roads, and donkeys carry barrels of local wine.

⑤
Kasbah Boulaouane

🏔C3

Located in a meander of Wadi Oum er-Rbia, this stunning kasbah stands on a promontory in the heart of a wide

> **The journey to Boulaouane is a foretaste of the semi-arid southern landscapes. Barbary fig trees line the roads, and donkeys carry barrels of local wine.**

forested area. It was apparently built by the Almohads, who made it an imperial stopping place on the road running along the coast and inland to Fès. At the beginning of the 16th century, it was the scene of a battle that halted the Portuguese advancement towards the interior. Moulay Ismaïl revitalized the village by choosing to build a kasbah here in 1710 – an attempt to pacify and control the region.

The stone-built fortress is encircled by a crenellated wall set with bastions and pierced by an angled gate with three pointed arches. Above the gate is an inscription of Ismaïl's name and the date of the kasbah's foundation.

This gate, which accommodated sentries, is the only point of entry into the fortress. It leads through to the sultan's palace, built around a central courtyard with rather elaborate mosaic decoration. Beside the palace, a square tower, now disfigured by cracks, afforded a vantage point over the surrounding territory. Disused vaulted armouries were used for storing food supplies. The mosque is now in a very bad state of preservation. Next to it is the tomb of Sidi Mancar, whom the region's inhabitants still revere, since he is believed to have had the power to cure paralysis and sterility.

BOULAOUANE WINE

Connoisseurs consider Gris de Boulaouane, a rosé with an orange tint, one of the best Moroccan wines. Although the Romans successfully grew vines here, the establishment of Islam hindered the upkeep of the vineyards. Under the French Protectorate, the vineyards were revived, but their quality soon deteriorated. In the 1990s, old vines were dug up and new stock planted. Today, Moroccan vineyards are found in the district of Boulaouane, the Doukkala region, the foothills of the Atlas and along the Atlantic coast. The grapes are hand-harvested at the end of August, and the wine is exported mostly to Europe.

Ceaselessly battered by the elements, the kasbah has suffered a great deal of deterioration over the centuries. It was declared a historic monument in 1922. The mosque and city walls are undergoing restoration work.

The region is also famous for its tradition of falconry, a sport still practised today by falconers from several important local families.

---

⑥
Azemmour

🅰 B2 🚌 ℹ Avenue Mohammed V

An ancient Almohad town located on the left bank of the Wadi Oum er-Rbia estuary, Azemmour is also known by the name of Moulay Bouchaïb – the town's patron saint, who, in the 12th century, was also patron saint of the trade that flourished between the town and Málaga in Spain.

In 1513, the Portuguese took control of the town. The fort that they built became the kasbah that can be seen today. They abandoned the town when Agadir fell in 1541.

Despite its year-round gentle climate and coastal location, Azemmour has few hotels, and not many tourists come here. The narrow white streets of the medina are peppered with architectural features recalling the former Portuguese presence – the style of the doors being particularly prominent in this respect. The town also has a tradition of Portuguese-style embroidery, which features dragons and lions depicted face to face, an exclusively Moroccan motif. The mellah (Jewish quarter), once within walls, is now derelict. The synagogue, however, has a notable pediment with an inscription in Hebrew.

Eight kilometres (5 miles) north on the coastal road, the Sidi Boubeker lighthouse offers a view of the town's defences. Haouzia beach, starting 2 km (1.5 miles) southeast of Azemmour, stretches from the Oum er-Rbia estuary to El-Jadida. Along the way it passes a forest of eucalyptus, pine and mimosa with flowering cacti.

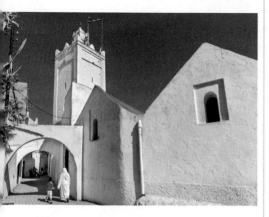

↑ Whitewashed walls of Azemmour mosque give the town a Mediterranean feel

Man strolling past portugese-style doorways, Azemmour

7

Moulay Abdallah

🅰B3 🏠11 km (7 miles) south of El-Jadida and 82 km (51 miles) north of Oualidia

The origins of this fishing village lie in a 12th-century Almohad settlement, then known as Tit. The old site's impressive ruins can still be seen today, together with a minaret dating from the same period as that of the Koutoubia Mosque in Marrakech (p234). The settlement was a *ribat*, or fortified monastery, built around the cult of the saint Moulay Abdallah, and its purpose was to guard the coast. It became a busy port, but it was destroyed in the early 16th century to prevent the Portuguese, who were at Azemmour, from taking it.

The burgeoning fishing industry revived the village, which then assumed the name of the saint in whose honour it was established. The *moussem* (a meeting of the Doukkala tribes) held here every year in August is famed for its fantasias and for its orchestral and folkloric spectacles that last throughout the night.

From the coast road leading south from Moulay Abdallah you can see the huge industrial installations of the mineral port of Jorf Lasfar, the largest of its kind in Africa.

8

Oualidia

🅰B3 🚍

This small coastal resort takes its name from the sultan El-Oualid, who built an impressive kasbah here in 1634. The rather unattractive town centre leads through to a stunningly beautiful beach on the edge of a lagoon. Swimming is safe here, but on either side the sea is rough and foaming. This is one of the best beaches on the Atlantic coast for surfing, particularly for beginners. Among the summer villas here is the residence built for Sultan Mohammed V.

The town is an important centre of the oyster industry. A visit to the oyster farms (*parcs à huitres*), particularly **Oyster Farm No 7**, is a pleasant way to pass some time and a good opportunity to sample some local treats. The Ostrea restaurant and hotel is also located here.

The coastal road running south along the clifftop leads to Cap Beddouza and Safi.

Oyster Farm No 7 and Ostrea

🏠On the El-Jadida Road 📞(0523) 36 64 51; Ostrea: (0664) 49 12 76

9

Safi

🅰B3 🏠🚍 𝒊Tourist office, Rue Imam-Malek & main market, Avenue de la Liberté; (0524) 62 24 96

An important Moroccan port since the 16th century, the

Waves hitting the cliffs of the Atlantic coast near Safi →

town of Safi is today an industrial centre and a major sardine-processing port. It owes its importance to the growth of the fishing industry and to the processing and exporting of phosphates, but it is probably best known for its exceptional pottery, found the world over. A rapidly expanding town, Safi has an alluring medina, and the traces of its Portuguese history are prevalent.

The area covered by the medina takes the form of a triangle, whose widest side faces onto the coast. Rue du Souk, which is lined with shops and workshops, leads to Bab Chaaba (Gate of the Valley). Near the Grand Mosque, south of the medina, is the Portuguese Chapel, originally the choir of Safi's cathedral, which was built in the 16th century and was the first of its kind outside Portugal.

Overlooking the sea is the small fortress of **Ksar el-Bahr**, also known as the Château de la Mer (Castle of the Sea),

Did You Know?

During WWII, American forces occupied the town of Safi in Operation Blackstone.

which served as a residence for the Saadi sultans in the 17th and 18th centuries before the French took control of the region. On the esplanade are rows of cannons cast in Spain, Portugal and Holland.

On the hill just behind the medina, the citadel, known as the Kechla, encloses a mosque and garden dating from the 18th and 19th centuries. Since 1990, the Kechla has housed the **Musée National de la Céramique**, which contains displays of traditional and modern ceramics, including blue-and-white wares made in Safi, pottery from Fès and Meknès, and pieces by the Algerian pottery master Boujmaa Lamali, who lived and worked in Safi for almost 50 years and introduced the revolutionary techniques now considered typical of Moroccan pottery.

In the Colline des Potiers (Potter's Hill), on the edge of the medina in the Bab Chaaba district, you will find craftsmen making the traditional ceramic wares that have made Safi famous. Finished pieces are displayed and offered for sale in the commercial showrooms, and visitors can follow the various stages of pottery production at the training school, from a simple mound of clay to a hand-painted masterpiece, or commission an original.

Ksar el-Bahr
🕘 9am-noon & 2-6pm daily

Musée National de la Céramique
🏛 Kechla 🕘 10am-6pm Wed-Mon

OUALIDIA OYSTERS

Lovers of seafood the world over hold Oualidia oysters in especially high esteem. The species of edible oyster that has earned Oualidia its reputation is related to those from the Marennes-Oléron region of France and were imported in the 1950s. Oyster Farm No 7, which was set up in 1992 in the lagoon on the El-Jadida road, is one of the most modern in Morocco. The oysters and other shellfish farmed here are raised according to stringent European health and hygiene regulations.

⑩

Kasbah Hamidouch

🅰 B3 🚗 29 km (18 miles) south of Safi on the coast road

This kasbah is part of a system of fortified outposts that Moulay Ismaïl established to control the region and accommodate travellers. It is encircled by an outer wall, within which stand a mosque and other buildings, now in ruins. An inner wall, set with square towers and reinforced by a dry moat, surrounds a courtyard lined with shops, various houses and a chapel.

11

Chiadma Region

⚠ X9

The territory of the Chiadma, in the provinces of Safi and Essaouira, is inhabited by Regraga Berbers. They are reportedly descended from the Seven Saints, a group of scholars, who, during a journey to Mecca in the 7th century, were directed by the Prophet Mohammed to convert the Maghreb region to Islam. In spring, the Regrada make a 40-day commemorative pilgrimage, ending at the small village of Ha Dra.

A souk, one of the most authentic markets in the area, takes place in Ha Dra on Sunday mornings. Grain, spices, animals and a wide range of goods, mostly food, are offered for sale.

ARGAN OIL

The argan, a tenacious, twisted North African tree, has a multitude of uses. Being a hard wood, it is ideal for charcoal; camels and goats find the leaves and fruit delectable; and the vitamin-rich oil extracted from the kernel can be used in cosmetics for its anti-ageing properties. In medicine it is used to combat arteriosclerosis, chicken pox and rheumatism. A few drops are enough to bring out the flavour of salads and *tajines*, and it is used as fuel for lamps.

12

Tamanar

⚠ B4

The small town of Tamanar, which extends along its one main street, is a regional administrative centre and the effective capital of the argan industry. The production of the oil originated here, and the region has been classified as a UNESCO Biosphere Reserve due to the forests of argan found throughout. It is at the heart of Haha territory, home to a settled yet dynamic Berber population that was self-governing in the 15th century.

On the way out of the village, near Café Argana, is a store selling locally produced argan oil. The highly organized women who run it show the fruits of their labour in a friendly atmosphere and sell their products in a cooperative.

Between Smimou (where there is a picturesque souk on Sundays) and Tamanar, a small sign saying "Tafadna" indicates the route to Tafelney. Two-thirds of the way along this road, the landscape takes on a majestic beauty. The road comes to a sudden stop at a magnificent bay, where fishermen can often be seen mending their nets on the beach.

To the left, a huddle of identical shanty houses are home to thousands of birds. To those with a taste for remote spots, the strange beauty of this place will have a strong appeal.

↑ Blue fishing boats lining the beach in the town of Taghazoute, near Tamri

13

Tamri

⚠ B4

This village is located on the estuary of a river that in the winter months is fed partly by the waterfall at Imouzzer des Ida Outanane. There is an extensive banana plantation. On the left, as you approach Tamri from the north, an inland road leads to a major birdwatching area, where Audouin's gulls, Barbary falcons, Lamier's falcons, sparrows and various other species can be seen.

About 19 km (12 miles) north of Agadir is Taghazoute, a fishing village that is popular with surfers. It was also colonized by the hippy movement, and, on the way out of the village, you can see curious signs saying "Banana Village" and "Paradise Valley" – names given by those who followed in the footsteps of Jimi Hendrix.

Did You Know?

In times of drought, puppets decorated with white flowers are placed in the Chiadma's fields to bring rain.

A DRIVING TOUR
IMOUZZER DES IDA OUTANANE

SOUTHERN ATLANTIC COAST

Imouzzer des Ida Outanane

Locator Map
For more detail see p124

Length 40 km (25 miles) **Stopping-off point** Hôtel des Cascades at Imouzzer has relaxing gardens and a restaurant

This tour follows a very scenic river valley with many natural swimming pools surrounded by palm trees. From Agadir, a winding road leads to Imouzzer village, set on a hilltop in the foothills of the High Atlas, with waterfalls said to be the highest in northern Africa. It is the heart of the territory of the Ida Outanane, a confederation of Berbers whose traditional speciality is gathering honey.

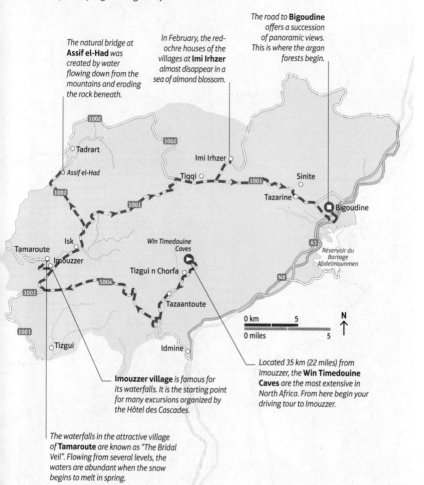

The road to **Bigoudine** offers a succession of panoramic views. This is where the argan forests begin.

The natural bridge at **Assif el-Had** was created by water flowing down from the mountains and eroding the rock beneath.

In February, the red-ochre houses of the villages at **Imi Irhzer** almost disappear in a sea of almond blossom.

Tadrart

Assif el-Had

Imi Irhzer

Tiqqi

Sinite

Tazarine

Bigoudine

Isk

Win Timedouine Caves

Réservoir du Barrage Abdelmounmen

Tamaroute

Imouzzer

Tizgui n Chorfa

Tazaantoute

0 km 5
0 miles 5

N

Tizgui

Idmine

Located 35 km (22 miles) from Imouzzer, the **Win Timedouine Caves** are the most extensive in North Africa. From here begin your driving tour to Imouzzer.

Imouzzer village is famous for its waterfalls. It is the starting point for many excursions organized by the Hôtel des Cascades.

The waterfalls in the attractive village of **Tamaroute** are known as "The Bridal Veil". Flowing from several levels, the waters are abundant when the snow begins to melt in spring.

Interior details of the Hôtel Continental, Tangier

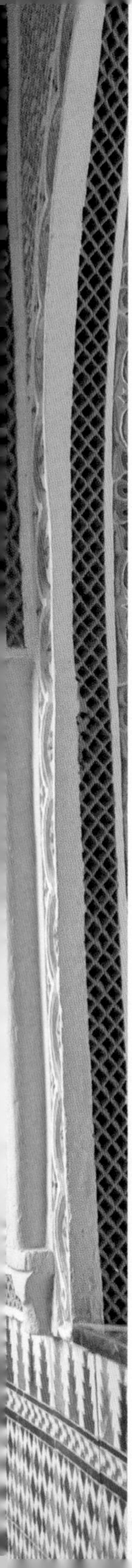

TANGIER

The history of Tangier is inextricably linked to its strategic location on the Strait of Gibraltar. The Phoenicians established a port here in the 8th century, and it was later settled by the Carthaginians. In 146 BC, Tangier, known as Tingis, became a Roman town and the capital of Mauretania, to which it gave the name Tingitana.

In 711, Arab and Berber forces gathered here to conquer Spain. By the 14th century, the town was trading with Marseille, Genoa, Venice and Barcelona.

In the 19th century, Morocco was the object of dispute between European nations. When Kaiser Wilhelm II denounced the *entente cordiale* between France and Britain in 1905, the stage was set for Tangier's transformation into an international city. This was sealed by the Treaty of Algeciras (1906), after which the diplomatic corps in Tangier took over Morocco's political, financial and fiscal affairs. When colonial rule was established in 1912, Spain took control of the northern part of the country. Tangier, however, remained under international administration until 1956, when it was returned to the now-independent Kingdom of Morocco. Its time as an international zone was very much the city's heyday; during this time its image as a romantic and sensuously exotic place was reflected in literature and on the big screen.

TANGIER

Experience

1. Kasbah
2. Kasbah Museum of Mediterranean Cultures
3. Ramparts
4. Rue Es-Siaghine
5. Petit Socco
6. Tomb of Ibn Batuta
7. Grand Mosque
8. Hôtel Continental
9. American Legation Museum
10. Grand Socco (Place du 9 Avril 1947)
11. Galerie d'Art Contemporain Mohamed Drissi
12. Fondouk Chejra
13. Anglican Church of St Andrew
14. Rue de la Liberté
15. Place de France and Place de Faro
16. Boulevard Pasteur
17. Ancien Palais du Mendoub
18. Quartier du Marshan
19. Café Hafa
20. Colline du Charf
21. Bay of Tangier

Eat

1. Anna & Paolo
2. Le Nabab
3. Populaire Saveur du Poisson

0 metres 200
0 yards 200

N

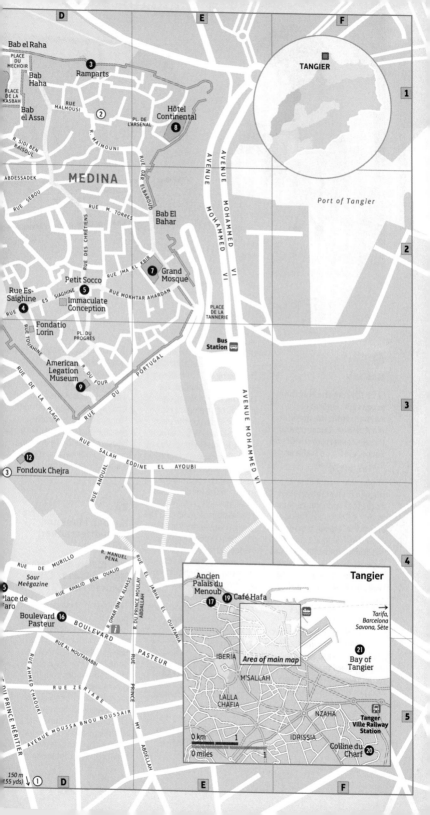

EXPERIENCE

1

Kasbah

C1 **From the Marshan, accessible via Bab el-Kasbah; from the medina, via Rue Ben Raissouli and Bab el-Assa; from the Grand Socco, via Rue d'Italie and Rue de la Kasbah**

The kasbah was built on the site of a Roman settlement. Its present appearance dates from the Portuguese period and that of Moulay Ismaïl (p202). With its quiet streets and friendly inhabitants, it has a special character, and its walls and gates command stunning views over the strait, the bay and the city.

Place de la Kasbah was once the *méchouar*, where the sultan or his pashas held public audiences. It is also the location of the Dar El-Makhzen, the former palace that is now a museum, and of the Kasbah Mosque, whose octagonal minaret is clad in coloured tiles. Its present form dates from the 19th century; the *mendoub* (the Sultan's representative in Tangier) led Friday prayers here. Also on the square is the Dar ech-Chera, the former tribunal, fronted by an arcade of three white marble columns. The large fig tree growing against the wall of an elegant house is supposed to be the place where Samuel Pepys wrote about Tangier in his diary in the 17th century.

Bab el-Assa (Gate of Bastinado) leads from the square to the medina. It was set at an angle so as to make it more difficult to attack. The gate gets its name from the *bastinado* (caning the soles of the feet) that was once the punishment of criminals. In the lobby, between the two porches, stands a fountain decorated with mosaics, stuccowork and woodcarving. Gnaouas, distantly related to those found in Marrakech and Essaouira, regularly perform music and dance here. In the evening, audiences can talk with them about their musical traditions and their repertoire. From the lobby, a narrow passage reveals a small *derb* (alleyway) lined with very fine houses, while beyond the gate is a view over the city.

€8 Billion

The cost of the proposed tunnel linking Spain and Morocco via the Strait of Gibraltar from Tarifa to Tangier.

2

Kasbah Museum of Mediterranean Cultures

C1 **Place de la Kasbah** **(0539) 93 20 97** **9am-6pm Wed-Mon**

The Kasbah Museum is laid out in the Dar el Makhzen, a former sultans' palace built in the 17th century by Ahmed ben Ali, whose father Ali ben Abdellah al Hamani Errifi liberated Tangier from the British settlers in 1664. The palace was remodelled and enlarged several times in the 17th and 19th centuries. Bit el-Mal, the treasury – a separate room with a glorious painted cedar ceiling – contains large

←

A local man walking through Bab el-Assa, which leads to a stunning view of the city

18th-century coffers with a complex system of locks.

A gallery leads to the palace itself. It is built around a central courtyard paved with *zellij* tilework and surrounded by a gallery supported by white marble columns with Corinthian capitals. The seven exhibition rooms opening onto the patio display artifacts evoking the material history of Tangier from prehistoric times to the 19th century. These include bone and stone tools, ceramics, terracotta figurines and Phoenician silver jewellery.

The Voyage of Venus, a Roman mosaic recovered from the ruins of the ancient city of Volubilis *(p198)*, is displayed in the museum's courtyard. Reproductions of several famous bronzes from the Musée de l'Histoire et des Civilisations (formerly named the Musée Archéologique) in Rabat *(p86)* are also on display. One room is devoted entirely to Morocco's major archaeological sites, while another is filled with fascinating replica maps of enormous proportions tracing ancient trade routes, dating as far back as 1154. On the upper floor, the prehistory and history of Tangier and its environs, from the Neolithic period to its occupation by foreign powers, are presented through displays of grave goods, pottery and coins. Adjacent to the palace is a delightful Andalusian Garden, perfect for a peaceful stroll.

---

❸
Ramparts

📍 **D1** ⌂ **Place de la Kasbah, accessible via Bab el-Bahar**

On the side of the square facing the sea, opposite Bab el-Assa, stands Bab el-Bahar (Gate of the Sea), built into the walls in 1920. From the terrace there is a breathtaking view of the port, the Mediterranean Sea and, on a particularly clear day, even the Spanish coast on the other side of the Strait of Gibraltar.

The walkway, starting on the left, follows the outside of the ramparts and leads to the impressive Borj en Naam fort, which, although closed to the public, is impressive when viewed from afar. Continuing along the seafront through residential districts, the route leads to Hafa.

TOP 5 **TANGIER TEAHOUSES**

Café Baba
📍 D1 ⌂ Rue Zaitouni
The locals' and celebs' choice for mint tea for over 75 years.

Café Central
📍 D2 ⌂ Petit Socco
Revisit Burroughs and Kerouac in the literary Tangier of old.

Cinémathèque de Tanger
📍 C3 ⌂ Place du 9 Avril (Grand Socco)
Arthouse café with fresh juices, pastries and Wi-Fi.

Gran Café de Paris
📍 C4 ⌂ Place de France
Once a meeting place for literati, now known for *The Bourne Ultimatum*.

Café Hafa
Iconic café featuring a sprawling terrace with views across the Mediterranean straight *(p152)*.

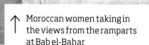

↑ Moroccan women taking in the views from the ramparts at Bab el-Bahar

④

Rue Es-Siaghine

📍 D2 🔗 Running from the Petit Socco to the Grand Socco

This street was once the *decumanus maximus*, the main axis and busiest thoroughfare of the Roman town. It led from the harbour out through the southern gate, marked today by Bab Fahs. Lined with cafés and bazaars, the street is as lively now as it would have been in antiquity.

The small administrative building at No 47, with a courtyard planted with orange trees, was from 1860 to 1923 the residence of the *naib*, the Moroccan high official who served as an intermediary between the sultan and foreign ambassadors. The Spanish Church of the Immaculate Conception (La Purísima), at No 51, was built by the Spanish government, work beginning in 1880. It was used by the whole city's Christian community, as well as by foreign diplomats. It is now used for social activities.

Further up the street, on the left, is Rue Touahine, which is lined with jewellers' shops and which leads to the **Fondation Lorin**, an arts centre housed in a disused synagogue. On display here are newspapers, photographs, posters and plans relating to the political, sporting, musical and social history of Tangier since the 1930s. Temporary exhibitions of paintings also take place here.

Fondation Lorin

🏠 44 Rue Touahine 📞 (0539) 93 03 06 🕐 10:30am–1:30pm & 3:30–7:30pm Sun–Fri

---

⑤

Petit Socco

📍 D2 🔗 Accessible via Rue Es-Siaghine or Rue Jma el-Kbir

Known today as Souk Dakhli, Petit Socco probably corresponds to the area on which the forum of Roman Tingis once stood. It was a country souk, where people would come to buy food, and with the arrival of the Europeans at the end of the 19th century it became the pulsing heart of the medina. This was where business was done; diplomats, businessmen and bankers, whose offices were located around the square or in the close vicinity, could be seen in the cafés, hotels, casinos

💬 INSIDER TIP
Exploring the Medina

There are a number of walks through Tangier's medina, marked by colour-coded signs. The yellow route will take you from the south of the medina at Petit Socco all the way to the American Legation.

and cabarets of Petit Socco. The Fuentes, a café-restaurant and hotel, now gives but a faint impression of these halcyon days. From the 1950s, the hub of city life shifted to Ville Nouvelle, leaving the square to a few writers, and to idlers, smokers of kif and shady traffickers. Nowadays Petit Socco is a lovely place to wander, admire colourful architecture and take in the city's bohemian vibe over a cup of Morocco's signature sweet mint tea.

---

⑥

Tomb of Ibn Batuta

📍 C2

The Marco Polo of the Islamic world, Ibn Batuta was born in Tangier in 1304. As an adult, the Berber Muslim made an arduous *hajj* (pilgrimage) to Mecca and just kept on going, dedicating his life to exploring the world. In the end, he spent over 30 years travelling across North and West Africa, Central and Southeast Asia, reaching as far as China. Towards the end of his life he recorded his experiences in a book usually referred to as *The Travels*, an invaluable historical resource, even today. A modest tomb in the medina, a 20-minute walk from Petit Socco, is supposed to be his final resting place. It is a simple, single-room structure, and the greatest satisfaction comes from simply having found it.

↑ Visitors and locals wandering through the busy, winding streets of Petit Socco

7
Grand Mosque

📍 E2 🏠 Rue Jma el-Kbir
🚫 To non-Muslims

The Grand Mosque, built on the site of a Portuguese cathedral, probably also overlies a former Roman temple dedicated to Hercules. Dating from the reign of Moulay Ismaïl, it was enlarged in 1815 by Moulay Sliman. Sultan Mohammed V led Friday prayers here during a visit to Tangier in the 1940s, when he also made a historic speech in the Mendoubia grounds. Opposite, the state primary school (established during the French Protectorate) is a former Merinid medersa that was remodelled in the 18th century.

Nearby, the Borj el-Hadjoui commands a view of the port and a pair of Armstrong cannons, each weighing around 20 tonnes. They were bought from the British in Gibraltar, but were never used.

8
Hôtel Continental

📍 E1 🏠 36 Rue Dar el-Baroud
📞 (0539) 93 10 24 🕐 Daily

The **Hôtel Continental**, located opposite the port, is one of Tangier's oldest hotels. The building's architectural style, its open terraces and its Andalusian-style lounges give this establishment great appeal. Its patrons have included writers, film producers and painters – among them Edgar Degas.

9
American Legation Museum

📍 D3 🏠 8 Rue d'Amérique
📞 (0539) 93 53 17 🕐 10am–5pm Mon–Fri, 10am–3pm Sat

The American Legation Museum consists of a suite of rooms that originally formed part of the residence that

↑ Guests enjoying a quiet meal in the balcony restaurant at Hôtel Continental

Moulay Sliman presented to the United States in 1821, and which served as the US Consulate for the next 140 years. Another suite, on several floors looking out onto a garden, was presented by a Jewish family: the site was pivotal in rescuing thousands of Jewish refugees from Europe during World War II. The doors, windows and ceilings have been skilfully decorated by craftsmen from Fès.

The rooms contain engravings of Gibraltar and Tangier, old maps, and paintings by Yves Brayer, Claudio Bravo and others, were given to the legation by Marguerite McBey, wife of James. One wing is devoted to Paul Bowles, author of *The Sheltering Sky*, who lived in Tangier for over 50 years. Through photographs, early editions and recordings, the rooms give an overview of his life. A reference library is also available for scholars on North Africa, and there is an ongoing literacy programme for the women of Tangier.

Nowadays Petit Socco is a lovely place to wander, admire colourful architecture and take in the city's bohemian vibe over a cup of Morocco's signature sweet mint tea.

10

Grand Socco (Place du 9 Avril 1947)

C3

Officially known as Place du 9 Avril 1947 in memory of the historic speech that King Mohammed V made in that year in support of Moroccan independence, Grand Socco (meaning "big souk" – *socco* being a Spanish corruption of the Arabic word, souk) is the link between the medina and the Ville Nouvelle. With an elegant fountain at its central point, and lined with towering palm trees, Grand Socco is a busy market square that acts as a convivial meeting place for the city's inhabitants. Numerous lively

> **INSIDER TIP**
> **Book Ahead**
>
> On arrival in Tangier, you will be inundated by those offering to "guide" you to your hotel. This is rarely genuine, or free. Be confident, and say "no thanks". Hotels and riads will almost always organise a transfer.

cafés, restaurants and teahouses surround the cobbled square. It also acts as a transportation hub, and is always full of *petit taxi* drivers competing for business.

The square comes to life in the evenings, when, every night, street vendors spread out their wares on the ground – extensive displays of a huge variety of second-hand goods and all manner of trinkets.

A colourful market, where peasant women in striped *foutas* (scarves) and wide-brimmed straw hats come to sell fresh fruit and fowl, takes place above the square, near the Anglican Church of St Andrew, at the end of Rue d'Angleterre. The minaret of the Mosque of Sidi Bou Abib, decorated with polychrome tiles, dominates the skyline in the south-west. Just off the main

The buzzing atmosphere in Fondouk Chejra, colloquially known as the Poor People's Souk or the Weavers' Souk, is that of an Oriental bazaar.

square is the iconic **Cinema Rif**, originally built in 1938 and restored in 2005. An Art Deco gem, the cinema now operates as the Cinémathèque de Tanger. It is a cultural hotspot for the city's film-buffs, screening a mix of mainstream and arthouse films, and hosting numerous creative workshops and film-themed events throughout the year such as the Tangier National Film Festival and the African Film Festival of Tarifa-Tangier. The cinema café is a popular hangout for the city's youth and local creatives.

Northwest of the square, near Bab Fahs, the grand double gateway that gives entrance to the medina, are the delightful Mendoubia Gardens. They contain the former residence of the *mendoub*, who was the sultan's representative in Tangier when the city was under international administration from 1923–56. The building now houses a local chamber of commerce, while the gardens are a large public park, a welcome relief from the chaotic buzz of city life. The park is surrounded by attractive colonial buildings. At the top of the tallest hill, there is a monument commemorating the speech made by Mohammed V in 1947, in which he formally requests independence for Morocco.

Cinema Rif
🏠 3 Rue de La Liberté
🌐 cinemathequede tanger.com

←

The multicoloured minaret of the Mosque of Sidi Bou Abib overlooking the square

ARTISTS AND WRITERS IN TANGIER

Many artists and writers from Europe and the United States have come to Tangier in search of stimulation. Most notably, painters Eugène Delacroix and Henri Matisse, and authors William Burroughs and Mohammed Choukri were drawn by the atmosphere, freedom and sense of adventure that this international port city projects. The Expressionist and companion of Matisse, Charles Camoin, reputedly rediscovered his joy of painting in Morocco, *Minaret à Tanger* (1913) being one of several works completed here.

⑪ ⚲

Galerie d'Art Contemporain Mohamed Drissi

⑨ B4 ⬛ Rue d'Angleterre
☎ (0539) 93 60 73 ⏰ 9am–4pm Tue–Sun

Formerly the Museum of Contemporary Art, the gallery reopened in 2006 and was renamed in homage to the influential Moroccan artist. It hosts regular exhibitions by Moroccan and international artists. The museum, whose five galleries occupy a grand villa, was originally constructed to house the British Consulate at the end of the 19th century. A small pagoda in the garden in front of the building sits over a fountain dedicated to Sir Reginald Lister, former British Delegate to Morocco. It is now one of the most prestigious state galleries in Morocco, with a mission to preserve and disseminate contemporary Moroccan art.

⑫

Fondouk Chejra

⑨ D3 ⬛ Rue de la Liberté, accessible via the steps below the level of the Hôtel el-Minzah

The buzzing atmosphere in Fondouk Chejra, colloquially known as the Poor People's Souk or the Weavers' Souk, is that of an Oriental bazaar. Above the shops on the ground floor, the rooms that were once used by travellers and passing tradesmen have been converted into weavers' workshops, where the white-and-red fabric that is typical of the Rif is produced by hand (and foot) on giant wooden looms. The original layout of the former *fondouk*, or caravanserai (a roadside inn providing accommodation for travellers and their caravans) is difficult to make out, the central courtyard having been much altered.

⑬

Anglican Church of St Andrew

⑨ C3 ⬛ Rue d'Angleterre
⏰ 9:30am–12:30pm & 2:30–6pm daily; keys obtainable from the caretaker

Built on land that Moulay Hassan donated to fulfil the needs of a large British population in Tangier, the Anglican Church of St Andrew was completed in 1894. The interior is a curious mix of styles, but the Moorish one dominates.

The lobed arch at the entrance to the choir, and the ceiling above the altar, which is decorated with a quotation from the Gospels in Arabic, are of particular interest. The bell tower, strikingly similar in shape to that of a minaret, overlooks the cemetery. Among those buried here are Walter Harris, a journalist and correspondent for *The Times*, and Sir Harry Mclean, a military adviser to the sultans.

A plaque at the west end of the church commemorates Emily Kean, who came to Tangier from Britain in the 19th century, married the *shorfa* (sherif) of Ouezzane, a revered holy town, and devoted her life to the welfare of the people of northern Morocco.

↑ The English flag waving above the Anglican Church of St Andrew

Treasures glinting in one of the many antique shops that line Rue de la Liberté ↑

14

Rue de la Liberté

📍 C3

This street runs from Place du 9 Avril 1947 (or Grand Socco) to Place de France and Ville Nouvelle. While it was formerly known as Rue de Fès, then as Rue du Statut, its current moniker dates from the beginning of Moroccan independence in 1956 (p64).

At the southern end of the street, the French Consulate is set in the centre of a pleasant and attractive park, and the classical arcade of the façade is offset by decoration in the traditional Moorish style.

In the **Galerie Delacroix**, housed in the French Cultural Institute next door, temporary exhibitions are organized by the Institut Français. The Hôtel el-Minzah is one of the most

Did You Know?

Tangier was gifted to King Charles II of England on his marriage to Princess Catherine of Braganza, Portugal.

illustrious hotels in Morocco, with an Andalusian-style courtyard and gardens, and comfortable lounges and bars. Winston Churchill, Paul and Jane Bowles, Jean Genet and Hollywood stars from Rita Hayworth to Errol Flynn all stayed in this magical place at one time or another.

Just off the main street, opposite the El Minzah Hotel, is the Bazaar Tindouf, where you can while away the hours marvelling at floor-to-ceiling trinkets and antiquities – a haggler's paradise.

Galerie Delacroix
🏠 86 Rue de la Liberté
📞 (0539) 93 21 34 🕐 11am–1pm, 4–8pm Tue–Sun

15

Place de France and Place de Faro

📍 C4-D4

Place de France is a major meeting place for the inhabitants of Tangier. The Café de Paris was the first establishment to open outside the medina. Among its regular customers were Paul Bowles, Tennessee Williams and Jean Genet, as well as foreign

diplomats. The café has remained a bustling hub of city life. Very near Place de France, on Avenue Pasteur, is Place de Faro (named after the Portuguese town twinned with Tangier in 1984), complete with cannons pointing across the sea towards Spain. It is one of the few places to have escaped the attentions of developers and offers a view of the medina and ferry traffic in the harbour and the strait.

16

Boulevard Pasteur

📍 D4

Boulevard Pasteur is Ville Nouvelle's main artery and its economic centre. Later in the day, the avenue is given over to the Spanish custom of *paseo*, a leisurely evening stroll. The Moroccan tourist office at No 29 occupies the first building to be constructed on the avenue, while the villa at No 27 houses the **Great Synagogue**. The famous

→

The lavish colonial villa of Ancien Palais du Mendoub, once home to Malcolm Forbes

Librairie des Colonnes, the bookshop at No 54, has lost some of its former prestige and importance. Once a regular haunt of Tangier's intellectuals and writers such as Paul Bowles, Jean Genet, Samuel Beckett and William Burroughs, the chic and stylish bookshop is still a much-loved city landmark, where lectures, signings and other special events are held regularly.

The Gran Teatro Cervantes (accessible from Avenue Pasteur, which is reached along Rue du Prince Moulay Abdallah and via steps continuing from it) is one of North Africa's major theatres, and it was here that the greatest singers and dancers of the age performed. The building, with an Art Deco façade, is in a bad state of repair. Restoration has been delayed by disputes between the city and the Spanish state, which had agreed to finance its upkeep.

Great Synagogue
🏠 27 Blvd Pasteur

Librairie des Colonnes
🏠 54 Blvd Pasteur
🕙 10am–8pm Mon–Sat
🌐 librairie-des-colonnes.org

17

Ancien Palais du Mendoub

📍 E4 🏠 Avenue Mohammed Tazi (in the northwest of Ville Nouvelle) 🚫 To the public

The Mendoub was the sultan's representative during the international administration of Tangier. While his main residence was the Mendoubia, near Grand Socco, this palace, built in 1929, was used mostly for receptions and special functions. It was acquired in 1970 by the American multi-millionaire Malcolm Forbes, founder of *Fortune* magazine. It then became a luxury residence where Forbes threw lavish parties frequented by such international luminaries as Elizabeth Taylor, Calvin Klein and Henry Kissinger. The house also contained a display of Forbes' 120,000-piece collection of toy soldiers. The palace stood in for a villainous arms dealer's lair in *The Living Daylights* (1987), starring Timothy Dalton as James Bond. It is now owned by the state and used as a residence for visiting VIPs from abroad.

EAT

Anna & Paolo
Intimate and friendly family-run trattoria serving authentic Italian dishes, including fresh fish.

📍 D3 🏠 77 Ave Prince Héritier, Ville Nouvelle
📞 (0539) 94 46 17

ⓓⓗ ⓓⓗ ⓓⓗ

Le Nabab
This cosy eatery serves great local cuisine. Hard to find, but worth the effort.

📍 D1 🏠 4 Rue Al Kadiria, Medina
📞 (0661) 44 22 20

ⓓⓗ ⓓⓗ ⓓⓗ

Populaire Saveur du Poisson
Small restaurant with no menu; everyone is served four courses of whatever seafood the chef has in that day.

📍 D5 🏠 2 Escalier Waller, Ville Nouvelle
📞 (0539) 33 63 26

ⓓⓗ ⓓⓗ ⓓⓗ

decor seem to have changed since then. Assorted tables and rush matting are laid out on terraces rising in tiers from the edge of the cliff, offering a breathtaking view of the strait. Writers and musicians, from Paul Bowles and William Burroughs to The Beatles and The Rolling Stones, have all visited this iconic café.

18 Quartier du Marshan

◻B2 **⌂Rue Mohammed Tazi, Rue Assad Ibn Farrat, Avenue Hassan II (in the western part of the kasbah)**

Being removed from the bustle of the medina and of Ville Nouvelle, the Quartier du Marshan was an attractive residential area where high-flying officals and the *shorfa* (sherif) of Ouezzane built their palaces and grand villas in the late 19th century. The Italian Consulate (Rue Assad Ibn Farrat), its walls covered in *zellij* tilework, reputedly housed Italian general and nationalist, Garibaldi, in 1849–50. On the edge of the strait,

↑ Trees framing the view out on to the strait from the Café Hafa terrace

the Marshan ends at the limits of Hafa, a less affluent residential district with a great deal of local character, up on the sea cliff.

19 Café Hafa

◻E4 **⌂Rue Mohammed Tazi (in a narrow street opposite the football stadium, leading towards the sea)**

Café Hafa opened in 1921, and neither the furniture nor the

20 Colline du Charf

◻F5 **⌂In the southeast of the city**

A hill rising to a height of about 100 m (328 ft), the Colline du Charf (Charf Hill) commands the most impressive and most complete view of Tangier. The panorama stretches from Cap Malabata in the east to La Montagne, which rises over the old town to the west. From here the beach appears as a strip lining the bay, and the white, densely packed medina seems to cling to the hillside as it slopes down towards the port, while the high-rise blocks of Ville Nouvelle stand tall along

its wide avenues. Poorer residential districts stretch out southwards: in among them, at the foot of the hill, you can see Plaza Toro, whose bullrings are now used for public functions.

Further north is the Syrian Mosque, with an unusual style of minaret that is rarely seen in the Maghreb. The mosque-like building on the hill was a busy café during Tangier's international period. A favourite form of relaxation for the inhabitants of Tangier is to stroll to the top of the hill and gaze out over the strait.

Bay of Tangier

F5

The Bay of Tangier, a splendid crescent-shaped bay likened to the Baie des Anges in Nice or to Copacabana beach in Rio de Janeiro, stretches from the port to the residential districts and resorts just outside the city, to the first spurs of land that mark the bay's most eastern extremity.

Avenue d'Espagne, which runs along the bay, is lined with hotels, from small guesthouses to large modern establishments. Dotted with the blues, reds and whites of the boats and the ochre, green and orange of the fishing nets, the town's small fishing harbour is a colourful sight to behold, and the freshly caught fish that is offered there daily makes a delicious meal. It was on Avenue d'Espagne that Bernardo Bertolucci shot scenes for his 1990 film *The Sheltering Sky*. Many literary works, by William Burroughs and others, took shape in the small guesthouses here. The French philosopher Michel Foucault would stay at the

Hôtel Cecil, while Samuel Beckett preferred the Solazur.

The proximity of the city and the rivers that flow into it unfortunately make the beach here the most polluted in Morocco. For swimming and sunbathing, it is better to make for Cap Spartel and the Grottes d'Hercule, where there are many attractive little bays separated by rocky outcrops. Cap Malabata, where there are coves sheltered by stands of pine, is an easy day trip from the city, or, further east, the beaches at Sidi Khankroucht and Ksar es-Seghir offer some of the best surf in Morocco.

↓ The sprawling city of Tangier viewed from the ancient kasbah

MEDITERRANEAN COAST AND THE RIF

The great mountainous crescent of the Rif forms a natural barrier across northern Morocco, separating much of the Mediterranean coast from the interior. Inaccessible and intricately partitioned, the Rif has always resisted conquest, though not always successfully.

The Spanish, to whom the region fell when Morocco was divided up under the French Protectorate *(p68)*, came face to face with this intransigence during the uprisings of 1921–6, and they were soundly defeated at Anoual in 1921. The history of the Rif and its coastline is closely linked to that of Spain. For Morocco, the Mediterranean became a bridgehead for the conquest of Spain. From the 15th century, Portuguese occupation, followed by that of the Spanish, cut Morocco off from the Mediterranean and accelerated its decline. Spain still maintains a foothold in Ceuta and Melilla, and on a few rocky islets, and Morocco is working closely with Spain and Europe to tackle problems of illegal trafficking and emigration here. The increase of tourism in Tangier and Ceuta has resulted in dramatic changes to the area, including a modern port and airport.

MEDITERRANEAN COAST AND THE RIF

Must Sees

1. Tetouan
2. Chefchaouen
3. The Rif

Experience More

4. Ketama
5. El-Jebha
6. Cap Spartel
7. Cap Malabata
8. Ksar es-Seghir
9. Grottes d'Hercule
10. Ceuta
11. Torres de Alcalá
12. Al-Hoceima
13. Ouezzane
14. Nador
15. Cap des Trois Fourches
16. Melilla
17. Moulouya Estuary
18. Saïdia
19. Zegzel Gorge
20. Oujda

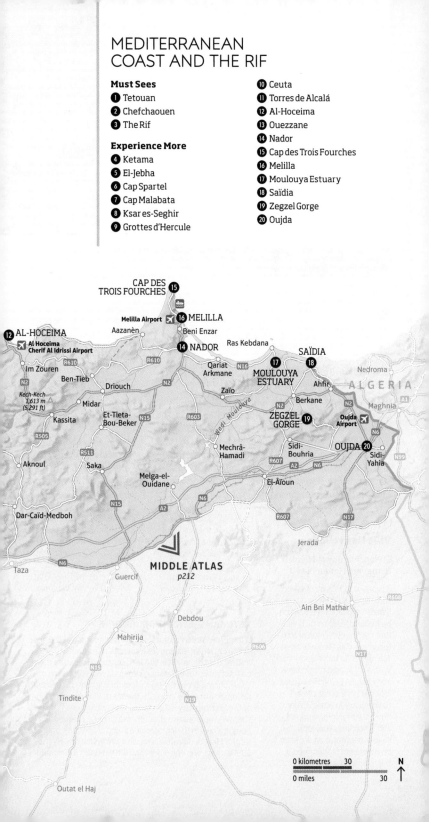

↑ Tetouan's Ville Nouvelle and Jbel Dersa providing the backdrop to the medina

❶

TETOUAN

🅰D1 ✈5 km (3 miles) 🚋Tnine-Sidi-Lyamani
🚌 30 Boulevard Mohammed V; (0539) 96 19 15

In the words of Arab poets, Tetouan is "the daughter of Granada". Built partly on the slopes of Jbel Dersa, the town was inhabited by Jewish refugees from Granada in the 15th century, then by Andalusian Moors in the 17th century. Up to the 18th century, it was a centre of thriving trade with Europe, becoming a city-state comparable to Florence or Venice. Later, the Spanish made it their capital during the Protectorate.

① Ville Nouvelle

🏛 Place Moulay el-Mehdi & Boulevard Mohammed V

It is on Place Moulay el-Mehdi, sometimes still referred to as Place Primo (after the Spanish politician José Primo de Rivera), that the Spanish colonial architecture of Ville Nouvelle (New Town) is at its most eloquent. With a main post office, bank and church (1926), the square looks like any other central town square in Spain. Elegant homes with doors, windows and balconies with Moorish-style ornamentation are seen on Boulevard Mohammed V, the town's principal artery.

Place Hassan II links Ville Nouvelle and the medina. Modern tiling has replaced the old mosaic decoration of the royal palace on the side of the square nearest the medina. Both the boulevard and the square come to life in the evenings with the *paseo* (promenade), a Spanish custom that is more deeply ingrained in Tetouan than anywhere else in Morocco.

---

② 🏛🖼 Musée Archéologique

🏛 Avenue Ben H'sain, near Place Hassan II 📞(0539) 96 73 03 🕐9am–4pm Wed–Mon

The collections of Tetouan's Archaeological Museum contain objects discovered at Volubilis, Lixus and Thamuda, a Roman site on the outskirts of Tetouan (on the road to Chefchaouen). Several mosaics are on display, including a depiction of the Three Graces of classical mythology, as well

TETOUAN'S JEWISH POPULATION

A large Jewish community, expelled from Spain at the end of the Christian Reconquest, settled in Tetouan, thrived and reached its height in the 16th century. Exploiting their contacts in Europe, Tetouan's Jews played a central role in the economic life of the town, and through them it became an important trade link with the West. At the beginning of the 19th century, subjected to violence and heavy taxes, the Jews repaired to a quarter of their own, the *judería*. Marginalized in their professional and social lives, many left for Melilla, Gibraltar, Iran, and Latin America. By the 1990s, there were no more than 200 Jews left in Tetouan.

as pottery, coins, and bronzes. The most interesting exhibits – ancient inscriptions, mosaic floors and Muslim funerary stelae with the Star of David – are laid out in the garden.

---

③ 🏛 Medina

🅰 Entry through Place Hassan II, then via Rue Ahmed Torres to the southeast

Tetouan's medina, a UNESCO World Heritage Site, is the most clearly Andalusian in all Morocco. Emigrants from Spain in the 15th and 17th centuries implanted their architectural traditions here, including a taste for wrought-iron decoration and doors with elaborate metal fittings.

The aroma of spices, freshly sawn wood and *kesra* (bread) fills the narrow streets, squares and souks, which bustle with carpenters, tanners and sellers of secondhand goods. Rue El-Mokadem (between Place Souk el-Fouqui and Place Gharsa el-Kebira) is densely packed with shops, but is also noteworthy for its impressive white buildings and its paving. Sellers of fabrics and pottery fill the small shady square where the El-Houts Souk takes place. It leads to the former *mellah*, where the balconied houses have large windows, wrought-iron gates and arcaded façades.

---

④ 🖼 🕌 Musée d'Ethnographie

🅰 Zankat Sqala, near Bab Oqla 📞 **(0539) 97 05 05** 🕐 **9am–4pm Wed–Mon**

Occupying a bastion built in 1828, the museum is laid out as an Andalusian palace with a garden, a fountain clad in *zellij* tilework, and red-tiled awnings. The furniture, crafts, costumes and musical instruments typify the town's traditions. Tetouani rooms with marriage scenes have also been recreated.

The Craft School, opposite Bab Oqla, occupies a Moorish-style residence. Specializing in local traditions, the school teaches leatherwork, mosaic-making, carpet-weaving and plasterwork. The work is exhibited in a domed hall.

EAT

Blanco Riad Hotel
Modern Moroccan cuisine served in a charming riad patio and garden in Tetouan's medina. The restaurant is popular among locals and visitors, so be sure to book ahead.

🅰 **Rue Zawiya Kadiria** 🆆 **blancoriad.com**

Ⓓⓗ Ⓓⓗ Ⓓⓗ

Restaurant Cap Marina
Offering a fine ocean view from the interior and the outdoor terrace, the Cap Marina serves an array of Moroccan, Mediterranean and international cuisine.

🅰 **Marina Smir, Route de Sebta** 🆆 **marina smirhotel.com**

Ⓓⓗ Ⓓⓗ Ⓓⓗ

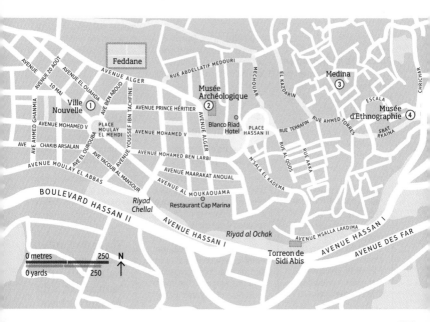

↑ Children sitting in a peaceful blue square in Chefchaouen's medina

2

CHEFCHAOUEN

🅰D1 🚌From Tangier

Chefchaouen nestles in the hollow of two mountains – ech-Chaoua (The Horns) – from which it takes its name. It was founded in 1471 by Idrissid *shorfa* (descendants of the Prophet Mohammed) as a stronghold against the Portuguese. Steep narrow streets with bright blue buildings, small squares, ornate fountains, decorative doorways and red-tiled roofs make this a delightful town.

① 💻 🛍

Place Uta el-Hammam

All the streets of the medina converge in this pleasant square, making it one of the focal points in the city. It is lined with trees and paved with stones and pebbles, and in the centre stands a fountain decorated with arches and crowned by a pavilion of green tiles. With a plethora of shops and cafés, this is an ideal place for a relaxed stroll.

---

②

Grand Mosque

🏛Place Uta el-Hammam
🚫To non-Muslims

Chefchaouen's Grand Mosque was founded around the 16th century and has been remodelled several times since. The later minaret, which dates from the 17th century, has a distinctive octagonal shape and is decorated with three tiers of plain and lobed arches on a painted ochre background. The uppermost tier is decorated with *zellij* tilework.

③

Fondouk

🏛Corner of Place Uta el-Hammam & Rue Al-Andalus

The *fondouk* still serves its original purpose, taking in travellers and passing traders. It is a building of strikingly simple design, with a gallery of semicircular arches lining the pebble-paved courtyard. The only contrast to this simplicity is provided by the main entrance, surmounted by an awning and framed by a broken horseshoe arch and interlacing arches.

---

④ 🏛

Kasbah and Museum

🏛West corner of Place Uta el-Hammam ⏰10am–5pm Wed–Mon (till 1pm Fri)

The kasbah, with its crenellated walls of red beaten earth and ten bastions, is the heart of the town. The fortress was

> **The kasbah, with its crenellated walls of red beaten earth and ten bastions, is the heart of the town.**

📷 PICTURE PERFECT
Spanish Mosque

Follow the trail out of the medina's east gate, across the river and up the hill to the Spanish Mosque. Your reward for the 30-minute walk is the terrific views of Chefchaouen below.

begun in the 15th century by Moulay Ali ben Rachid and completed by Moulay Ismaïl in the 17th century, showing an Andalusian influence. A delightful garden is laid out within, with good views of the walls and the rampart walk. The Musée Ethnographique occupies the residence in the garden. This is a traditional Moroccan house with a court-yard and gallery on the first floor. The museum contains displays of pottery, armour, embroidery, costumes, musical instruments and palanquins, as well as a collection of painted wooden chests.

↑ Sacks of colourful paint powder, in Chefchaouen

⑤ 🏛

Medina

A small street running between the kasbah and the Grand Mosque leads to the Souïka district, the oldest in town with the finest houses. The name *souïka*, meaning "little market", comes from the district's *kissaria*, where there are many small shops along its narrow streets.

The medina contains more than 100 weavers' workshops. Indeed, Chefchaouen is famous for the woollen *jellabas* woven here, as well as for the red-and-white-striped fabrics worn by the women of the Jebala, a tribe of the western Rif. One such workshop is located in Rue Ben Dibane and is conspic-uous for its exterior stairway.

⑥ 🖥

Ras el-Ma and the Mills

The steep streets of Al-Andalus leading towards the mountain pass through Bab Onsar, the town's northeast gateway.

Beyond is the spring of Ras el-Ma, now enclosed by a build-ing. This underground spring

WHY SO BLUE?

Although founded in 1471, Chefchaouen did not take on its distinc-tive colour until 1492, when the town took in an influx of Jews fleeing the Spanish Inquisition. They brought with them a tradition of painting buildings blue because, it is said, the colour mirrors the sky and reminds them of God.

was the reason the town's first inhabitants settled here. It also accounts for the town's lush gardens and powers the mills. Steps leading towards the metalled road run along-side the wash-houses, then the mills, whose origins go back to the arrival of the town's Andalusian refugees.

The route then leads to the bridge across Wadi Laou, a semicircular arch with bevelled buttresses. With its cascades, wash-houses and cafés, this is one of the most pleasant quarters of Chefchaouen.

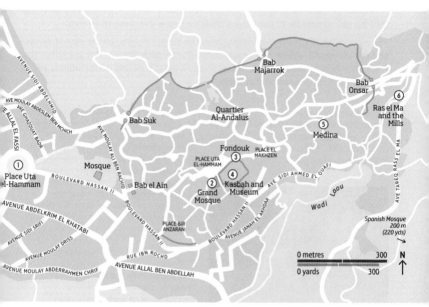

3

THE RIF

🅐 D1-E1 ℹ️ Casa Hassan, 22 Rue Targui, Chefchaouen; www.casahassan.com

The mountains of the Rif rise sharply from the Mediterranean to the east of Tangier and roll in rugged fashion all the way to the border with Algeria. Not as high as the Atlas, they nonetheless offer stunning scenery, great trekking opportunities and picturesque hilltop towns and villages.

This region is well known for its atmospheric and beautiful medinas, notably Chefchaouen *(p160)*. Covering an area of some 30,000 sq km (11,580 sq miles), it offers much else besides. Among its natural wonders are high mountains,

capes, gorges and curious rock formations. Ramblers and those with four-wheel-drives can visit the protected fir forests of the Talassemtane National Park, where popular destinations include the small villages of El-Kelaâ and Akchour, starting points for some excellent walks. Further east, Route N2 commands breathtaking views of the mountains and isolated villages as it climbs toward Mount Tidirhine, the highest point in the Rif at 2,448 m (8,034 ft).

←

The isolated mountains of the Talassemtane National Park are a tranquil home for Barbary macaques

EXPERIENCE MORE

4
Ketama

⚑ D2 ⚐ 107 km (66 miles) east of Chefchaouen on the N2, the Route des Crêtes (Ridge Road)

Located in the heart of a forest, Ketama was once a popular summer and winter resort known for its hunting and fishing, but the presence and perseverance of the illegal kif and hashish salesmen that have coopted the town, and the law enforcement they attract, will give most visitors cause to move on.

Leaving the town, the road leading eastwards reveals the slopes of Jbel Tidirhin (or Jbel Tidiquin), the highest peak in the Rif mountain range. In the valleys, the houses have pitched roofs, with a covering of planks and corrugated metal, the modern substitute for thatch. In some villages, such as Taghzoute, the ancient craft of leather embroidery has been passed on through the generations and is still very much alive.

Did You Know?

Morocco reputedly produces half of the world's hashish; most of it is grown in the Rif.

5
El-Jebha

⚑ D1 ⚐ 137 km (85 miles) east of Tetouan along the coastal road N16; 73 km (45 miles) from Ketama on the N2 then the P4115

The small fishing town of El-Jebha nestles at the end of Fishermen's Point. Its one-storey, cube-like houses, covered in white roughcast, give it something of a Mediterranean air. To the right of the harbour, where *lamparo* boats (which use lamps to attract fish) are moored, is Crayfish Cove, an ideal fishing spot. On the left, a soft sandy beach stretches away towards the west.

← In spring, the Rif is awash with colour as wildflowers burst into bloom

KIF

Kif (cannabis) crops underpin the Riffian economy. Although growing and smoking it are tolerated on a localized basis, its commercial exploitation is illegal, resulting in a major smuggling trade, which the Moroccan authorities are fighting with assistance from the European Union.

↑ A small boat moored in the cove near the small town of El-Jebha, a perfect spot for fishing

↑ The famous Cap Spartel lighthouse sits some 300 m (1,000 feet) above sea level

6
Cap Spartel

D1 🚗 **14 km (9 miles) west of Tangier**

From Tangier, the road leading to Cap Spartel runs through La Montagne, the city's western suburb, which is bathed in the perfume of eucalyptus and mimosa. Long walls surround the residences of Moroccan, Kuwaiti and Saudi kings and princes and the luxury villas dating from the golden age of Tangier's international period. Beyond stretch forests of holm oak, cork oak, umbrella pine, mastic tree, broom and heather, which all flourish here, watered by the highest rainfall in Morocco.

At the cape is the promontory known in antiquity as Cape Ampelusium, or Cape of the Vines, and a lighthouse

dating from 1865. From beneath the lighthouse, there is a breathtaking view of the stretch of ocean where the Mediterranean and Atlantic meet, and on an especially clear day you can see the strait and coast of Spain all the way from Cape Trafalgar to the Rock of Gibraltar.

7
Cap Malabata

D1 🚗 **12 km (7.5 miles) east of Tangier**

The route out of Tangier skirts an area of large tourist hotels and continues eastwards round the curve of the bay. Soon after a tiny estuary, at the edge of the road, are the remains of a 16th-century fortress, from which Moroccan soldiers could watch and attack the Portuguese, Spanish and English occupiers as they approached of Tangier. Nearby, white crenellated walls surround the lush and extensive grounds of the Villa Harris. It was once the residence of Walter Harris, a journalist and diplomatic correspondent for *The Times*. Harris chronicled life in Tangier for many years at the turn of the 20th century. After his death, the resplendent villa was given to the people of Tangier and it was briefly

a casino before being shut down. Its future is now uncertain.

The road ascending the hills passes through pine forests and by many small coves with cafés blessed with an old-world charm. Just before the cape, a strange medieval-style building appears, the work of a whimsical Italian, who left it unfinished in the 1930s.

The view from Cap Malabata is stunning, especially in the morning, looking westwards over the city and suburbs of Tangier and across to the Straits of Gibraltar, and eastwards to Jbel Moussa.

💬 **INSIDER TIP**
Getting Around

If you don't have a car, Cap Spartel and Cap Malabata are best reached by *grand taxi* from the nearest town. A round trip from Grand Socco in Tangier will set you back around Dh 200. Be sure to agree your fare before setting off.

→ The conspicuous Jabala women at the Saturday Souk in Ksar es-Seghir

Ksar es-Seghir

D1 **33 km (20 miles) east of Tangier**

A town with a small fishing harbour and a fine beach, Ksar es-Seghir faces the Spanish town of Tarifa across the Straits of Gibraltar. The souk that takes place here every Saturday is filled with women of the Rif, conspicuous in their red-and-white-striped *foutas*.

Forts have stood on this well-sheltered spot on an estuary since the 17th century, and it was from here that Moroccan troops set sail for Spain, and the Almohads made it an important centre for shipbuilding. In a small forest are the remains of a town built by the Merinids in the 14th century. The Portuguese held the town from 1458 to 1549, and strengthened it with new fortifications that reached as far as the sea.

Grottes d'Hercule

D1 **5 km (3 miles) southwest of Cap Spartel**

At the place known as Achakar, the sea has carved impressive caves out of the cliff. The people who, from prehistoric times came to these caves, knapped stones here and quarried millstones for use in oil presses. The opening to the caves, facing out onto the sea, is a cleft shaped like a mirror image of Africa.

According to the legend, Hercules slept here before performing one of his 12 labours – stealing the golden apples from the Garden of the Hesperides – and it was long thought to be bottomless. The location of the legendary garden belonging to these nymphs of darkness and guarded by a dragon with 100 heads is said to be further south, near Lixus.

The best time to visit the caves is in the late afternoon,

↑ Ancient quarry marks lining the walls of the Caves of Hercules

after which the light of the setting sun can be enjoyed from the cafés nearby. Further south, beneath the level of the caves, are the Ruins of Cotta (1st century BC to 3rd century AD). With vats for salting fish, making *garum* and producing purple dye, this was one of the largest industrial centres of the Punic and Mauretanian periods.

> **A few dozen trawlers are usually moored in Al-Hoceima's small harbour; in the evenings, the *lamparos* are lit up, ready for a night's fishing.**

⑩ Ceuta

🗺 D1 🚗 63 km (39 miles) east of Tangier ℹ Calle Edrissis, Edif Baluarte de los Mallorquines; www.destinoceuta.com

Standing on a narrow isthmus between Monte Hacho and the mainland, Ceuta occupies a favourable location opposite Gibraltar. The Rock of Gibraltar and Monte Hacho are the two legendary Pillars of Hercules.

From the 12th century onwards, the town was visited by traders from Genoa, Pisa, Mareille and Catalonia among others. In 1415, Ceuta became a Portuguese enclave, then passed to Spain in 1578. Today it is an important garrison town. Its livelihood depends mainly on the tax-free trade that its status as a free port allows. Ceuta (like Melilla) is a self-governing town within the Spanish state. Morocco views the Spanish presence as anachronistic and claims sovereignty.

The 12-km (7.5-mile) circuit of Monte Hacho (part of it is accessible by road) affords views over the town, the mountains and coast of the Rif and Gibraltar, especially from the lighthouse at Punto Almina. The Castillo del Desnarigado, a fortress that is now a military museum, encloses the Ermita de San Antonio. This chapel draws a large pilgrimage on 13 June each year.

The Plaza de Africa is, in architectural terms, the centre of the town, where the main public buildings are concentrated. The cathedral, whose present appearance dates from the 18th century, stands on the site of a Grand Mosque. A range of religious paintings and liturgical objects are on display in its museum.

Nuestra Señora de Africa (Church of Our Lady of Africa) was built in the early 18th century, also on the site of a mosque, in an arresting Baroque style. On the high altar stands a statue of the Virgin, patroness of Ceuta, who is believed to have saved the town from the plague in the 16th century. The treasury contains some fine paintings, banners and 17th-century illuminated books.

The Ayuntamiento (town hall) will be of interest to visitors for its paintings by Mariano Bertuchi, known as "the great painter of the Protectorate."

The **Museo Municipal El Revellín** (Archaeological Museum) is laid out above underground passages dug in the 16th and 17th centuries to supply the town with water. The displays include Neolithic, Carthaginian and Roman pottery, including amphorae, as well as coins and armour.

Through maps, photographs and visual displays, the **Museo de la Legión** documents the activities of the Spanish Foreign Legion and its efforts in 1921–6 to subdue the Rif uprising and the rebel leader Abdel Krim. The legion, formed in 1920, suffered serious losses during this war.

Museo Municipal El Revellín

⊕ 🏛 On the corner of Paseo de Revellín and Calle Ingenieros 📞 (0956) 51 73 98 🕐 11am–2pm, 5–9pm Tue–Sat (11am–2pm public hols)

Museo de la Legión

⊕ 🏛 Paseo de Colón 🕐 9am–5pm Mon–Sat

↑ The Baroque frontispiece of Nuestra Señora de Africa, facing on to its chequered forecourt

← Fishing boats moored in the pretty harbour of Al-Hoceima

The souk at Im Zouren, 17 km (10 miles) east on the road to Nador, is unusual: for the first few hours in the day, only women may go there. Both Im Zouren and Beni Bou Ayach, large market towns on the road out of Al-Hoceima, have a slightly unreal appearance, created by largely empty residential blocks painted in ochres, blues, greens and pinks. The towns come to life for only a few weeks of the year, when emigrant workers who base themselves in Germany and the Netherlands return home.

⑪ Torres de Alcalá

🅐D1 🚗144 km (89 miles) from Chefchaouen and 72 km (45 miles) from Ketama on the N2 then the P5205

Located on the estuary of Wadi Bou Frah, the fishing village of Torres de Alcalá lies at the foot of a peak crowned by a five towers – the ruins of a Spanish fortress dating to the 16th century. About 5 km (3 miles) further east is Peñon de Velez de la Gomera, a tiny island fortress attached to the mainland by a narrow spit of sand, one of several of its kind found on the coast of North Africa. Held by the Spanish from 1508 to 1522, it later became a hideout for pirates and privateers during Turkish occupation. A convict station under the Protectorate, it remains under Spanish sovereignty today.

Some 4 km (2.5 miles) west of Peñon de Velez de la Gomera is Kalah Iris, a cove that is now part of Al-Hoceima National Park and is an oasis of calm outside the summer season, though new developments are underway.

⑫ Al-Hoceima

🅐E1 ✈17 km (10 miles) SW 🚌 ℹ Zankat Al Bahia; (0539) 98 11 85

This ancient port, seat of the emirate of Nokour during the Middle Ages, was long the object of dispute between European traders. The modern town was founded in 1926 by José Sanjurjo, a lieutenant general of the Spanish Army, in the spot where his garrison landed, and was known initially as Villa Sanjurjo.

The town's location is one of the most beautiful along Morocco's Mediterranean coast. Whitewashed houses line the bay – an almost perfect semicircle between two hilly promontories. The coastline to the east, opposite Peñon de Alhucemas, a small island held by Spain, commands the most impressive view of the bay.

A few dozen trawlers are usually moored in Al-Hoceima's small harbour; in the evenings, the *lamparos* are lit up, ready for a night's fishing. Plage Quemado, stretching out in front of the town, is better than other nearby beaches.

TOP 5 NORTH COAST BEACHES

Cap Spartel
🅐D1 🚗West of Tangier
Many small coves with sandy beaches, from which Robinson Beach stands out as ideal.

Mrissa
🅐D1 🚗East of Tangier
Fine, soft sand beneath Cap Malabata, sheltered by stands of pine.

M'diq
🅐D1 🚗South of Ceuta
Down to earth, with a shell-scattered beach and blue-and-white-trimmed seafront.

Martil
🅐D1 🚗East of Tetuoan
A backdrop of lush green mountains and a pleasant boardwalk lined with cafés.

Saidia
🅐D1 🚗Northwest of Oujda
One of the loveliest Mediterranean beaches in Morocco, unusually overlooked by a kasbah.

↑ Stunning views and aquamarine waters at Cap des Trois Fourches

⑬ Ouezzane

🅐D2 🚗60 km (37 miles) south of Chefchaouen 🚌

Known for its textiles (*jellabas* and carpets) and olive oil, this large market town spreads out over the slopes of Jbel Bou Hillal, in an extensive landscape of olive groves and plantations of fig trees fed by abundant springs.

In the 15th century, the mainly Andalusian town also counted many Jews among its inhabitants. In 1727, a descendant of Sultan Idriss II established the religious brotherhood of the Taïbia, whose influence spread throughout Morocco, Algeria and Tunisia. In the 19th century, the *shorfa*

💬 **INSIDER TIP**
Charanna Beach

Just beyond the Cap des Trois Fourches, Charana beach is a favourite among the locals. To get there requires a car, and beachgoers must follow a steep, winding dirt trail by foot to reach the pristine sands, secluded coves and shallow lagoon that extends below the hillside.

(sherif) played a prominent religious and political role in Morocco. The sherif of Ouezzane's policy of openness also assisted trade relations with France. The *Zaouia* (Green Mosque) and, with its *zellij*-covered minaret, the Mosque of Moulay Abdallah Cherif, founder of the Taïbia brotherhood, attract many pilgrims.

Jews also come to Asjen, 8 km (5 miles) west of the town, to venerate the tomb of Rabbi Abraham ben Diouanne, who died in about 1780. The pilgrimage that takes place 33 days after Easter is an oppurtunity for Morocco's Jewish community to acknowledge its allegiance to the king.

---

⑭ Nador

🅐E1 🚗154 km (96 miles) east of Al-Hoceima, 13 km (8 miles) south of Melilla 🚌🚢

With wide avenues, shops, a multitude of cafés, restaurants and hotels, banks and residential blocks, Nador, somewhat unexpectedly, has all the trappings of a major town.

Nador's dramatic economic growth has been fuelled both by its traditional industries, such as metallurgy, and by modern ones, namely textiles, chemicals and electrics. The waves of emigration that have affected the whole of the eastern Rif have also contributed significantly to Nador's development. While immigrants here are key investors and consumers, funds sent home by foreign workers have swelled the town's economy.

Nador's proximity to the Spanish enclave of Melilla also accounts for the town's prosperity, through illegal trafficking. Through well-oiled channels, goods cross the border at many points, including Beni Enzar, the border post nearest Melilla. Small consignments cross over here several times a day, packed in trucks

or loaded on to the backs of women and children. The goods are then disposed of in broad daylight in two huge markets in Nador.

Beni Enzar, on the edge of Nador, is the foremost fishing port on the Mediterranean coast, and it also has modern naval dockyards.

---

⑮ Cap des Trois Fourches

🅐E1 🚗30 km (18 miles) from Melilla by road then track

The road from Beni Enzar to the Cap des Trois Fourches offers some stunning views of Melilla and the Mediterranean. The part of the cape beyond the Charrana lighthouse is one of the most beautiful promontories in Morocco.

The cape is lined with bays and beaches nestling against the rocky coast. However, the coast road is a challenging drive, so care should be taken.

→ Melilla's city walls, lighthouse and harbour on a rocky peninsula

> **Puerta de la Marina, the main entrance to the fortress, leads to a tracery of alleys, vaulted passages, steps and small squares, some with a chapel or church.**

⑯

Melilla

🗺 E1 **🚗 167 km (104 miles) east of Al-Hoceima and 153 km (95 miles) northwest of Oujda** **🚌** **ℹ Information office near Plaza de Toros; (952) 67 54 44**

Although 40 per cent of the population of the Spanish town of Melilla is Moroccan, the way of life here is still very Andalusian.

It was once a Carthaginian, then a Roman, trading post. Melilla was a busy port during the Middle Ages and has been in Spanish hands since 1497. Under the Protectorate, Melilla underwent rapid development thanks to its status as a free zone. However, Moroccan independence and the closure of the border with Algeria cut it off from the hinterland. While consumer demand has contributed to a thriving illegal trade, which creates the appearance of prosperity, the town is now experiencing economic difficulty.

Set on a rocky peninsula and enclosed within 16th- and 17th-century walls is the fortress of Melilla la Vieja. Puerta de la Marina, the main entrance to the fortress, leads through to a tracery of alleys, vaulted passages, steps and small squares, some with a chapel or church.

The church of La Purísima Concepción, in the northwest of the old town, contains some fine Baroque altarpieces; on the high altar stands an 18th-century statue of Our Lady of Victory, patron saint of Melilla. Behind the church and along the ramparts is the **Museos de Historia, Arqueología y Ethnografía**. Here, Melilla's

Phoenician, Carthaginian and Roman periods are represented by ceramics, coins and bracelets discovered nearby. Various stone implements from the western Sahara are also exhibited here.

The circular Plaza de España links the old town with the new. Avenida del Rey Juan Carlos is the new town's busiest street.

Museos de Historia, Arqueología y Ethnografía
⊛ 🏛 Plaza Pedro de Estopinan 🕐 Summer: 10am-2pm & 5-9pm Tue-Sat; winter: 10am-2pm & 4-8pm Tue-Sat, 10am-2pm Sun 🌐 museomelilla.es

⓱
Moulouya Estuary

🅰F1 🅰From Nador to Ras Kebdana, then on to Saïdia, road N16

The whole area between the Bou Areg lagoon and the estuary of Wadi Moulouya is a rich and fascinating nature reserve. A great variety of birds – including dunlin, plover, oystercatcher, little egret, redshank, black-tailed godwit and flamingos, terns, and different species of gulls – come to spend the winter in this marshy area. The dunes are home to woodcock, plovers, herons and storks.

> GREAT VIEW
> ### Beni-Snassen Mountain Road
>
> This mountain road winds up the hillsides and threads its way above dramatic precipices. Some days there is a view of the Angad plain, where the town of Oujda was built. At the highest point, Jbel Fourhal is partly covered with forests of holm oak and scarred by areas of limestone scree.

The vegetation in this area is equally diverse: spurge and sea holly grow on the dunes, while glasswort, reeds and rushes cover the marshes, which are the habitat of dragonflies, grasshoppers and sand spiders.

⓲
Saïdia

🅰F1 🅰50 km (31 miles) northwest of Oujda 🚌

At the northern extremity of the fertile Triffa plain, an agricultural and wine-growing region, is the little town of Saïdia, located on the Wadi Kiss estuary. The last 20 km (12 miles) before the river reaches the sea constitutes the border between Morocco and Algeria, making it strategically useful to Sultan Hassan I, who built a kasbah here at the end of the 19th century.

Saïdia is a coastal resort with one of Morocco's longest and most beautiful beaches, edged with mimosa and eucalyptus, earning the town the name "Blue Pearl". Being one of the country's most popular attractions, it has several modern hotels overlooking the beach these are

quickly booked up in summer. In July and August the beach becomes crowded with Moroccan tourists, who flock here for the annual Festival des Plages, a folk arts festival with an eclectic programme of artists, live music and events.

⓳
Zegzel Gorge

🅰F1 🅰Berkane, 60km (37 miles) from Oujda

Some of the country's most dramatic scenery can be experienced on the route from Berkane to Taforalt. The mountain follows the course of the fast-flowing Wadi Zegzel river as it carves its way through deep gorges and cuts along valleys and red, sloping hillsides. Many caves have been hollowed out of the cliff by the action of water, such as the Grotte de Tghasrout and the Grotte du Chameau (Camel Cave). The latter was carved out of

←

The illuminated entrance to the Medina Saidia Shopping arcade

↑ Sun setting on the ramparts and palms on Oujda's promenade

the mountain-side by an underground hot stream and contains several great halls of impressive stalactites and stalagmites. Continuing along this road there are breathtaking views of the Beni-snassen mountains, dotted with villages and *marabouts*. Grown on terraces carved into the hillside, almond trees are widely cultivated in this region. Their blossom adds a splash of colour to the otherwise harsh, high limestone environment. Road P6017 then road N2 lead back to Oujda, or Berkane via Ahfir, a small town established by the French in 1910. Though it is possible to find a decent meal in Ahfir, it is best to take a picnic, as shops and restaurants are relatively few and far between.

㉑

Oujda

**Ⓐ F2 ✈ 15 km (9 miles)
🚉 🚌 ℹ Place du 16 Août
1953; (0536) 68 56 31, and
railway station**

The history of Oujda has been shaped by its geographical location on a crossroads. In the Ville Nouvelle, the main

shops, banks and several large brasseries with spacious terraces, are concentrated around Place du 16 Août 1953, with its municipal clocktower, and on Avenue Mohammed V.

The medina, still partly enclosed by ramparts, is much smaller than that of Fès and Marrakech, is easy to explore, being small enough to wander about in. Rue el-Mazouzi, a major axis, crosses the medina from west to east, ending at Bab Sidi Abdel Ouahab. Various souks are located on this main street, or wind their way off it.

The *kissaria*, which is lined with arcades, has shops selling various types of textiles, kaftans and velvets as well as looms and skeins of wool. The small squares where the El-Ma Souk (Water Market) and the Attarine Souk take place contain trees and fountains, and are the living centre of the medina.

The **Musée Ethnographique**, outside the ramparts, contains local costumes and items relating to life in the region.

STAY

Blanco Riad

A former Spanish consulate then home of the ruler of Tetouan, now the city's first boutique hotel.

**Ⓐ D1 🏠 25 Rue Zawiya
Kadiria, Tétouan
🌐 blancoriad.com**

Lina Ryad & Spa

Attractive Andalusian-style quarters in the heart of Chefchaouen's ancient medina, with a gorgeous hammam and swimming pool. Rooms are spacious and bright, with fantastic views of the surrounding peaks.

**Ⓐ D1 🏠 Avenue Hassan I,
Quartier Andalous,
Medina, Chefchaouen
🌐 linaryad.com**

Casa Hassan

Beautiful pastel-coloured, traditional riad in the medina, with an excellent sister restaurant sitting just across the street.

**Ⓐ D1 🏠 22 Rue Targhi,
Medina, Chefchaouen
🌐 casahassam.com**

Just 6 km (4 miles) east of Oujda is Sidi Yahia, an oasis with abundant springs. Nearby is the tomb of Sidi Yahia ben Younes, patron saint of Oujda. Venerated by Muslims, Jews and Christians alike, he is often equated with John the Baptist.

Musée Ethnographique
**⊕ 🏠 Parc Lalla Meriem
📞 (0536) 68 56 31
🕐 Daily**

FÈS

Located between the fertile lands of the Saïs and the forests of the Middle Atlas, Fès is the oldest of Morocco's imperial cities. It is the embodiment of the country's history and its spiritual and religious capital, and as such was declared a UNESCO World Heritage Site in 1981.

Idriss I founded Madinat Fas, on the right bank of the River Fès, in 789. In 808, his son, Idriss II, built another establishment, El-Alya (High Town), on the left bank. In 818, both received hundreds of Muslim refugees expelled from Córdoba and Kairouan, in Tunisia. Within a few years, thanks to these two communities, the two towns became central to the Arabization and Islamization of Morocco.

In the mid-11th century, the Almoravids united the two towns, only for the Almohads to take what was then a city in 1145, after a long siege. Fès then became the country's foremost cultural and economic metropolis, thanks in large part to the founding of its university. In 1250, the Merinids raised Fès to the status of imperial capital. To the west of the old city they established a new royal one, Fès el-Jedid (New Fès). Conquered by the Alaouites in 1666, Fès was spurned by Moulay Ismaïl, who chose Meknès as his capital. The city's decline continued until the early 20th century.

When the Protectorate was established in 1912, the Ville Nouvelle (New Town) was built. This was populated by the prosperous citizens of the old medina, while the rootless and poor crowded into the old city of Fès el-Bali.

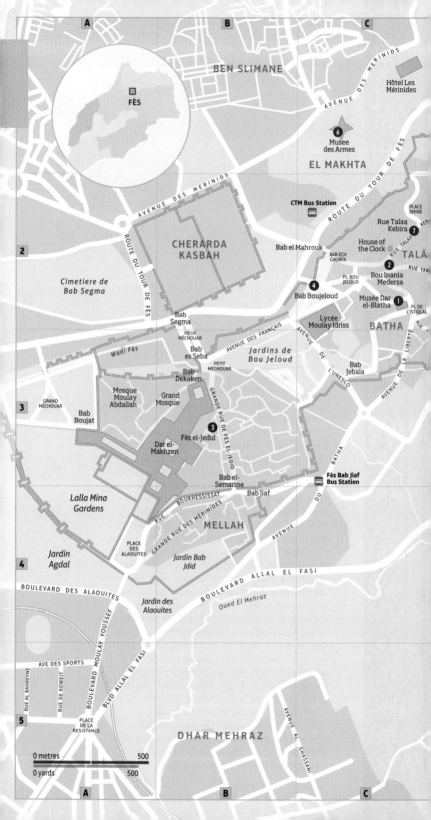

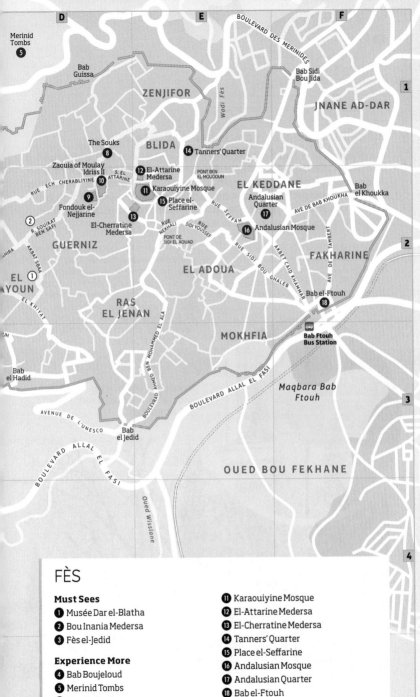

FÈS

Must Sees

① Musée Dar el-Blatha

② Bou Inania Medersa

③ Fès el-Jedid

Experience More

④ Bab Boujeloud

⑤ Merinid Tombs

⑥ Musée des Armes

⑦ Rue Talaa Kebira

⑧ The Souks

⑨ Fondouk el-Nejjarine

⑩ Zaouia of Moulay Idriss II

⑪ Karaouiyine Mosque

⑫ El-Attarine Medersa

⑬ El-Cherratine Medersa

⑭ Tanners' Quarter

⑮ Place el-Seffarine

⑯ Andalusian Mosque

⑰ Andalusian Quarter

⑱ Bab el-Ftouh

Eat

① Fez Café

② NUR

① ⟨⟩ ⟨⟩

MUSÉE DAR EL-BLATHA

⊙ C2 ⌂ Place du Batha ☎ (0535) 63 41 16 ⊙ 9am–4pm Wed–Mon

The palace of Dar el-Batha was begun by Moulay el-Hassan in 1873, and completed by Moulay Abdel Aziz in 1897. Moulay el-Hassan, who wanted to make the palace a residence worthy of being used for official receptions, added an imposing courtyard covered with coloured tiles and featuring a large fountain. He also laid out a large and very fine Andalusian garden. Despite many later alterations, the traditional Moorish features of this building have survived.

In 1914 the French scholar Alfred Bel – a specialist on Near and Far East and Arab cultures – made the first bequest to the future ethnographic museum. The following year, the beautiful palace – a work of art in its own right – became the official museum of local crafts (Musée des Arts et des Traditions). The collecton is shown in two large sections, one displaying archaeological exhibits and the other on ethnography, featuring the arts and crafts of Fès and neighbouring areas. Particularly notable is the display tracing the development of architecture in Fès, from the Idrissid period to that of the Alaouites.

← A beautiful wooden Berber door, carved and painted with intricate designs

GALLERY GUIDE

The collections are divided into two large sections. The ethnographic section occupies eight rooms with exhibits on the art of the book, ceramics, paintings, textiles, jewellery, wooden doors, genealogy and objects from everyday life. The archaeological section is found in the remaining four rooms and contains displays of *zellij* tiels and ceramics, wood used in architecture, archaeology relating to Islam and funerary stelae. There is also a workshop where visitors can watch woodcarvers at work.

↑ Stunning symmetrical tiles and archways in the palace's inner courtyard

↑ The peaceful Andalusian gardens, added to the design by Moulay el-Hassan

Collection Highlights

Rural Crafts

▽ Objects of everyday life from various regions of Morocco are exhibited in Room 6, including pottery made by the women of the Rif, carpets from the Middle Atlas and fine Berber jewellery *(below)*, such as brooches, pectorals, necklaces, rings and bracelets. All these show the skills and inventiveness of Moroccan craftsmen and craftswomen.

Woodwork

▷ The furniture in Room 4 shows both the range of woods used (cedar, thuya, almond, walnut, ebony, citron and mahogany) as well as the artisans' incredible skills. Here visitors will find designs using many different techniques: carved and painted or leather-covered furniture, and furniture with iron fittings, marquetry decoration and mother-of-pearl and ivory inlay. One highlight is a fine 14th-century Moorish chest, made to hold the most valuable pieces of a bride's trousseau as they were carried to her new home.

Ceramics

▽ The original location of the potters' souk, next to the Karaouiyine Mosque, is proof of the respect with which the makers of the famous Fès blue and white ware were held. As well as this pottery, Room 2 contains dishes and *jebbana* (traditional earthenware vessels) with polychrome decoration over a white tin glaze, or with *sboula* (herringbone) or *chebka* (scale) motifs.

2

BOU INANIA MEDERSA

📍 C2 🏛 Rue Talaa Kebira 🕐 9am–6pm daily (except during prayer times)

This is the largest and most sumptuously decorated *medersa* ever built by the Merinids. Constructed between 1350 and 1355 by the sultan Abou Inan, the one-storey building is a mosque, cathedral, students' residence and school combined, with the varied functions reflected in its architectural complexity.

That the Bou Inania Medersa has a *minbar* (pulpit) and minaret is an indication of the ambition of its builder, Sultan Abou Inan. He intended his grand monument to be not just a theological college, but a rival in religious authority to the city's great Karaouiyine Mosque. While simple in plan, with a square courtyard flanked by two small, square *iwans* (halls) and a larger prayer hall, every surface of the building is covered in complex decoration. Visitors enter directly into the courtyard, which is the building's most outstanding feature. Its floor is marble, while the walls are decorated in a harmonious combination of *zellij* tiling and carved plaster and wood. The prayer hall is divided from the courtyard by a long, narrow pool.

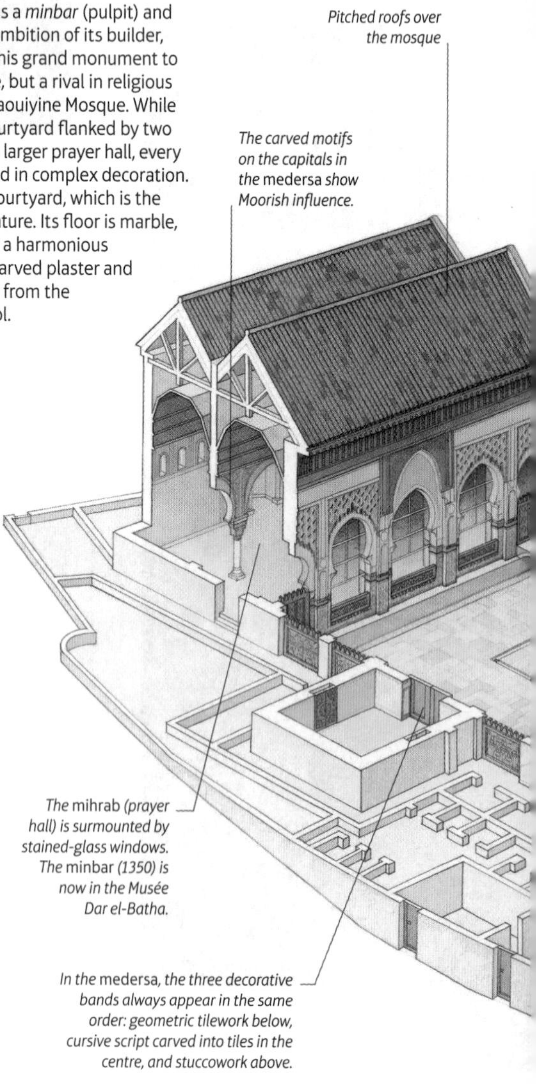

THE MEDERSA

The *medersas* of Fès, home to some of the greatest scholars in the country, were the most highly esteemed in Morocco. Primarily residential colleges, they were both an extension of the great university-mosque and an important cultural and religious institution dedicated to the study of religion, law, science and also the arts.

Pitched roofs over the mosque

The carved motifs on the capitals in the medersa show Moorish influence.

The mihrab (prayer hall) is surmounted by stained-glass windows. The minbar (1350) is now in the Musée Dar el-Batha.

In the medersa, the three decorative bands always appear in the same order: geometric tilework below, cursive script carved into tiles in the centre, and stuccowork above.

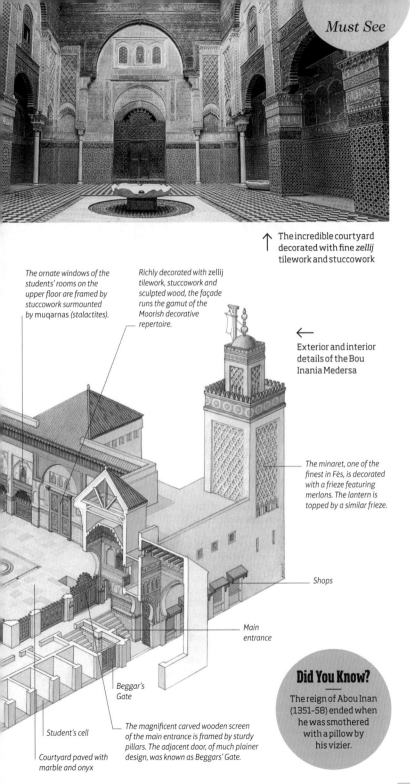

↑ The incredible courtyard decorated with fine *zellij* tilework and stuccowork

The ornate windows of the students' rooms on the upper floor are framed by stuccowork surmounted by muqarnas (stalactites).

Richly decorated with zellij tilework, stuccowork and sculpted wood, the façade runs the gamut of the Moorish decorative repertoire.

← Exterior and interior details of the Bou Inania Medersa

The minaret, one of the finest in Fès, is decorated with a frieze featuring merlons. The lantern is topped by a similar frieze.

Shops

Main entrance

Beggar's Gate

Student's cell

Courtyard paved with marble and onyx

The magnificent carved wooden screen of the main entrance is framed by sturdy pillars. The adjacent door, of much plainer design, was known as Beggars' Gate.

Did You Know?

The reign of Abou Inan (1351-58) ended when he was smothered with a pillow by his vizier.

The splendid main gateway to the Dar el-Makhzen palatial complex ↑

3 🍴 🖥 🛍

FÈS EL-JEDID

📍 B3

Meaning New Fès or White Fès, Fès El-Jedid was built in 1276 by Merinid princes as a stronghold against the threat of the rebellious Fassis. It was the administrative centre of Morocco up to 1912. Today, Fès el-Jedid consists of several distinct units: the royal palace and the Moulay Abdallah Quarter in the west; in the south, the *mellah*, or Jewish quarter – a maze of dark, narrow streets; and the Muslim quarters in the east.

① Dar el-Makhzen

🚫 To the public

Surrounded by high walls, this vast palatial complex in the centre of Fès el-Jedid was the main residence of the sultan, together with his guard and his retinue of servants. Part of the palace is still used by the king of Morocco when he comes to stay in Fès.

The main entrance to the complex, on the huge Place des Alaouites has a richly ornamented Moorish gateway and exquisitely engraved bronze doors, which are permanently closed. The walls enclose a disparate ensemble of buildings: palaces arranged around courtyards; official buildings, notably the Dar el-Bahia, where Arab summit meetings are held; the Dar Ayad el-Kebira, built in the 18th century by Sidi Mohammed ben Abdallah; administrative and military buildings; the Lalla Mina Gardens; a mosque; and a *medersa*, built in 1320.

② Moulay Abdallah Quarter

🚪 Accessible via Bab Boujat or Bab Dekaken

Completely closed off on its western side by the palace walls and the ramparts of Fès el-Jedid, this quarter has two gateways linked by a central thoroughfare with a lattice-work of narrow streets leading off it. Bab Dekaken, the east gate, leads to the former *méchouar* (parade ground) and Bab Boujat, the west gate, pierces the city's walls. Nearby, in the main street, stands the Grand Mosque, a Merinid building dating from the 13th century that houses the necropolis of the sultan Abou Inan. Also on this street, in the direction of Bab Boujat, stands the Mosque of Moulay Abdallah, which was built in the mid-18th century.

> **The Bab el-Semarine (Gate of the Farriers) is a monumental vaulted gateway, beneath which a souk for all sorts of food takes place.**

③
Grande Rue de Fès el-Jedid and the Muslim Quarters

🚹 Accessible via Bab el-Semarine to the south and Bab Dekaken to the north

The Muslim quarters – Lalla Btatha, Lalla Ghriba, Zebbala, Sidi Bounafaa, Boutouil and Blaghma – are the principal components of the urban agglomeration that Fassis know as Fès el-Jedid. The quarters are enclosed by the walls of Dar el-Makhzen to the west, and by a double line of walls to the east. Two gateways lead into the Muslim quarters; Bab Dekaken, on the northern side, is a simple opening in the fortifications. On the southern side is the Bab el-Semarine (Gate of the Farriers), a monumental vaulted gateway, beneath which a souk for all sorts of food takes place; the stalls are laid out in the old Merinid grain stores.

The two gates are connected by Grande Rue de Fès el-Jedid, the main north–south artery

←

Wall and side entrance to Dar-el-Makhzen royal palace complex

through the city. The street, covered by a cane canopy at its northern extremity, is lined with shops. This congested thoroughfare is the economic centre of the royal city. At intervals it is flanked by quiet residential quarters with a maze-like layout typical of Muslim towns.

On the western side of the street, a small quarter huddles around the Lalla el-Azhar Mosque (Mosque of the Lady Flower), which was built by the Merinid sultan Abou Inan in 1357. On the eastern side are the humble quarters inhabited by families of old warrior tribes. There are two important mosques here: Jama el-Hamra (Red Mosque) with a 14th-century minaret, and Jama el-Beïda (White Mosque).

←
Interior of the Danan
Synagogue located in the
Mellah (Jewish quarter)

⑤

Danan Synagogue

🏛 Rue Der el-Feran Teati
🕘 9am–5pm daily
🕘 Jewish Cemetery: Sat

The 17th-century synagogue,
the property of a family of
rabbis from Andalusia, looks
as if it has been squeezed in
between the houses in the
mellah. The building has
some mosaic tile decoration,
influenced by Islamic design.

Entered via a simple
doorway indistinguishable
from the neighbouring
houses, the synagogue's
interior is divided into four
aisles. A trap door in the aisle
on the far right opens onto a
steep stairway that leads
down to a *mikve* – a bath for
ritual purification where the
faithful were cleansed of their
sins. Above this fourth aisle is
the *azara*, the women's gallery,
which offers an overall view
of the synagogue. It is worth
going out onto the terrace for
a sweeping view of the Mellah,
and of the white tombs of the
Jewish cemetery below.

There is no entrance fee to
the synagogue, but a small
donation is requested.

④ 🍴 🛍

Mellah

🏛 Accessible via Place des
Alaouites or Bab el-Mellah

Bab el-Semarine, then Bab el-
Mellah leads into the Mellah,
the Jewish quarter of Fès. The
name *mellah* probably comes
from the Arabic word for "salt
marsh", the terrain on which
the quarter grew.

Thought to be the first
Jewish enclave to be
established in Morocco, this
quarter was originally located
in the northern part of Fès el-
Bali, in the El-Yahoudi Quarter
next to the Karaouiyine district.
In the early 13th century the
Merinid rulers moved it near
the palace, to the site of a
former kasbah that was once
occupied by the sultan's
Syrian archers. The rulers of
Fès had undertaken to protect
the Jewish community in
return for an annual levy
collected by the state
treasury. The Jewish quarter's
new location afforded the
inhabitants greater security.

With its souks, workshops,
schools, synagogues and a
cemetery, the quarter
flourished, providing the
Jewish community with

strong social cohesion and
unrivalled opportunities for
social advancement. Like the
Muslims elsewhere, most of
the Jews in the district were
grouped according to their
craft speciality. Thus, the
Berber Andalusi author and
diplomat Leo Africanus
mentioned metalworking
in his book *Descrittione
dell'Africa (Description of Africa)*
in the mid-16th century,
recording that only the Jews
worked with gold and silver.
Today, the Jews of Fès have
left to settle in Casablanca or
have emigrated abroad, to
Israel in particular.

Exploring the *mellah*
reveals a striking contrast
with the Muslim quarters. In
architectural terms it is another
world – buildings are higher,
narrower and more closely
spaced. The present
boundaries of the Jewish
quarter were established
only at the end of the 18th
century, during the time of
the Alaouite sultan Moulay
Yazid, and the space available
was small. As a result, the
inhabitants were forced to
build two-storey houses
around tiny courtyards, and
space to move around in was
very restricted.

⑥ 🛍

Rue Bou Ksissat

🏛 Accessible via Bab el-
Semarine or Place des
Alaouites

A central rectilinear axis, lined
with various workshops and a
kissaria, divides the Mellah
into two. All the commercial
activity in the quarter takes

→
The Vieux Méchouar,
with the ramparts of
Bab Al Makina behind it

place in this street (formerly known as Rue des Mérinides), which was once the economic and spiritual centre of the Mellah. The street is lined with jewellery shops.

Rue Bou Ksissat separates the Mellah from the Dar el-Makhzen. With its luxury residences, this was once the aristocratic area. The design of the houses here is the most unified and harmonious in the Mellah. The rows of houses open onto the street, each house having a workshop on the ground floor. The upper storeys are fronted by the generously proportioned, finely carved wooden balconies that are characteristic of the Jewish architecture of Fès.

⑦
The Méchouars

Méchouars are wide, walled parade grounds used on ceremonial military occasions. Processions and ceremonies, such as acts of allegiance and the acknowledgment of the royal right to rule, are also performed here. There are three such esplanades in Fès. The Grand Méchouar, in the northwest, also known as the Méchouar de Bab Boujat, is an extensive parade ground. The Méchouar de Bab Dekaken (Gate of the Benches), or Vieux

Did You Know?

The Fès Festival of World Sacred Music is held annually in summer in Bab Al Makina.

Méchouar, in the northeast, is a rectangular esplanade with the high ramparts of Bab Al Makina on one side. It links Bab Segma, the Merinid gate, and Bab el-Seba. It is here that the population gathered at sunset to watch dancers, musicians and storytellers. The Petit Méchouar, the smallest of the three, links the Méchouar de Bab Dekaken and Dar el-Makhzen. It can be reached through Bab el-Seba (Gate of the Lion), which once defended the entrance to the palace.

On Avenue des Français, just south of Bab el-Seba, a narrow street on the right, reachable through an opening in the wall, leads, after about 150 m (165 yards), to a large *noria* (waterwheel) built in 1287 by the Andalusians.

Bal Al Makina was an arsenal, established by Moulay el-Hassan in 1855 with the help of Italian officers. It was built on the west side of the Méchouar de Bab Dekaken. Having fallen into disuse, the Makina was eventually restored. It is now used as a concert hall and conference venue.

⑧
Kasbah Cherarda

🅰 North of the town, accessible via Bab Segma

Once known as the Kasbah el-Khmis (Thursday Fort), after the El-Khmis Souk which took place along the northern and eastern walls, this kasbah was built by Moulay Rachid in the 17th century. Its present name is derived from a former kasbah built nearby by a Cherarda caid (chief) to defend his tribe's grain stores. With Bab Segma and Bab Dekaken, the kasbah formed a system of fortifications that controlled the road to Meknès and Tangier, and protected Fès el-Jedid and the intersection with Fès el-Bali.

Enclosed within crenellated walls set with sturdy square towers, the kasbah has two monumental gateways, one on the western and the other on the eastern side. The kasbah now contains a hospital and an annexe of the Karaouiyine university. Beneath the walls on the southern and western sides, in an area where Almoravid and Almohad grain stores once stood, are the tombs of the Bab el-Mahrouk cemetery. Among them is the small Mausoleum of Sidi Boubker el-Arabi.

EXPERIENCE MORE

4
Bab Boujeloud

⚐ C2 ⌂ Place du Pacha el-Baghdadi

Enclosed within high walls, the large Place Pacha el-Baghdadi links the medina and Fès el-Jedid. On one side of the square stands Bab Boujeloud. Built in 1913 in the Moorish style, this fine monumental gate consisting of three symmetrical horseshoe arches is the main entrance into Fès el-Bali.

With the development of heavy artillery, the fortified gates of Fès came to be seen merely as decorative, contributing to the city's prestige and helping to justify the levy of city taxes. A rich scheme of geometric patterns, calligraphy, interlaced floral motifs and glazed tilework of many colours graces the façade. From this entranceway the silhouette of the minaret of the Bou Inania Medersa *(p178)* can be seen to the left.

5
Merinid Tombs

⚐ D1 ⌂ North of the medina

Standing on a hill among olive trees, cacti and blue agaves, the 16th-century ruins that overlook Fès el-Bali are those of a Merinid palace and necropolis. Ancient chroniclers made note of their magnificent marble and coloured epitaphs. Today, the tombs are dilapidated, and the area is popular with petty thieves, but it offers an impressive view of the city and is well worth the climb. Parts of the curtain wall date from the Almohad period (12th century), notably Borj Kaoukeb.

The tombs overlook a tiered cemetery, which stretches as far as Bab Guissa, an Almohad gateway from the 13th century.

8,000

The number of pieces of weaponry exhibited in the Musée des Armes.

6
Musée des Armes

⚐ C1 ⌂ Borj Nord ☎ (0535) 64 75 66 ⏰ 9am–1pm Tue–Sun

Borj Nord was built in 1582 on the orders of the sultan. From its vantage point over the city, the fortress both defended and controlled Fès el-Bali. In 1963 the collection of weapons from the Musée Dar el-Batha *(p176)* was transferred here to create the Museum of Arms. Much of the collection comes from the Makina, the arsenal built by Moulay Hassan I at the end of the 19th century, although it was enriched by donations from various Alaouite sultans.

Collections are exhibited in 16 rooms, running chronologically from prehistory up to the middle of the 20th century. Moroccan weapons are well represented and demonstrate the technical knowledge of the country's craftsmen.

←

Visitors entering the busy medina thorugh the grand archways of Bab Boujeloud

Intricate wooden carvings lining the courtyard of the Fondouk el-Nejjarine →

7

Rue Talaa Kebira

C2 **Reached via Bab Boujeloud**

This thoroughfare, whose name means "Great Climb", is lined with small shops along almost its entire length. It is continued by the Ras Tiyalin and Aïn Allou souks and by spice markets. The street passes the *kissaria* and ends at the Karaouiyine Mosque (*p188*). Running parallel to it at its southern end is Rue Talaa Seghira ("Short Climb"), which joins up with Rue Talaa Kebira at Aïn Allou. These streets are the two principal cultural and economic thoroughfares of Fès el-Bali.

Opposite the Bou Inania Medersa stands Dar el-Magana (House of the Clock), built by the ruler Abou Inan in 1357. It contains a water clock built by Fassi craftsmen during the Merinid period.

Not far from here, level with a covered passage in the Blida Quarter, is Zaouia el-Tijaniya, containing the tomb of Ahmed el-Tijani, master of *Tariqa el-Tijaoniya* (The Way), a doctrine that spread widely throughout the Maghreb and sub-Saharan Africa. Further on are three musical instrument workshops. Makers of stringed instruments have almost completely disappeared from Fès; the only one remaining is in Rue Talaa Seghira, opposite Dar Mnebhi; it still makes traditional *ouds* (lutes). Beyond is the skin-dressers' *fondouk*, which contains leather workshops.

Across the Bou Rous bridge stands the Ech Cherabliyine Mosque (Mosque of the Slipper-Makers), distinguished by its elegant minaret.

8

The Souks

D1

The souks of Fès el-Bali spread out beyond the Ech Cherabliyine Mosque. The location of each reflects a hierarchy dictated by the value placed on the various goods on offer. Every type of craft has its own street, or part of a street, which has resulted in a logical but relatively complex layout. While the El-Attarine Souk sells spices, there is also a Slipper Souk and a Henna Souk, laid out in an attractive shaded square. A plaque records that the Sidi Frej *maristan*, a specialist teaching hospital once stood on the square. Built in 1286, it was the largest of its kind in the Merinid empire. In the 16th century, Leo Africanus, known today for his accounts of his travels, worked there as a clerk for two years.

9

Fondouk el-Nejjarine

D2 **Place el-Nejjarine** **(0535) 74 05 80** **9am–6pm daily**

Not far from the Henna Souk, the impressive Fondouk el-Nejjarine is one of the most renowned buildings in Fès. Built by the *amine* (provost) Adeyel in the 18th century, this former caravanserai (roadside inn) provided food, rest and shelter to traders in luxury goods arriving from the interior. Classed as a historic monument in 1916, it is now a UNESCO World Heritage Site. Its restoration was part of the preservation programme carried out on the whole medina. Its three floors house the privately run Musée du Bois (Museum of Wooden Arts). Among the displays are carved doors from the magnificent Bou Inania Medersa.

> **INSIDER TIP**
> **Luxury Goods**
>
> The *kissaria*, near the Zaouia of Moulay Idriss, is a gridwork of streets where shops sell luxury goods. Some of the fine silks and brocades, kaftans and jewellery on offer here supply the international market.

Traditional tannery in the old medina of Fès el-Bali

⑩
Zaouia of Moulay Idriss II

◊ D2 ◊ To non-Muslims; respectful glimpses possible through open doors

The Zaouia of Moulay Idriss II, containing the tomb of the second Idrissid ruler (thought to be the founder of Fès) is the most venerated shrine in Morocco. Built in the centre of the city at the beginning of the 18th century, during the reign of Moulay Ismaïl, the building was restored in the mid-19th century. The pyramidal dome that covers the saint's tomb and its polychrome minaret give it a majestic silhouette. The courtyard of the mosque contains a fountain that consists of a white marble basin on a shaft, richly decorated with *zellij* tilework. The *horm*, the perimeter wall around the *zaouia*, is also holy. The narrow streets leading to the shrine are barred at mid-height by a wooden beam to prevent the passage of beasts of burden. The *horm* also made the shrine an inviolable place, so that in the past outlaws would find sanctuary here.

At the end of each summer, during a *moussem* lasting two to three days, the *zaouia* attracts not only the inhabitants of Fès but also people from the countryside and mountain-dwellers, who all come to receive a blessing and *baraka* (beneficient force). The crowd is made up of pilgrims and beggars, as well as nougat, candle and incense sellers, whose goods are used as tomb offerings.

ARABIC CALLIGRAPHY

Islam traditionally forbids all figurative representation, and since the 8th century this prohibition has encouraged the use of decorative calligraphy as an art form. Islamic calligraphy is closely connected to the revelation of the Koran: the word of God is to be transcribed in a script far finer than secular writing. The importance of this art form in Islamic civilization is visible in the carved, painted or tiled friezes that decorate the walls and domes of mosques and medersas, as well as the thousands of scientific literary and religious calligriphic manuscripts preserved in public and private libraries.

---

⑪
Karaouiyine Mosque

◊ E2 ◊ Rue Bou Touil ◊ To non-Muslims

Established in 859, and significantly enlarged over the centuries , the Karaouiyine Mosque is one of the oldest

A woman sitting in the tomb of Moulay Idriss II, the most venerated shrine in Morocco

and most illustrious of its kind in the western Muslim world. A centre of teaching, it is also considered by UNESCO to be the oldest continually operating university in the world; it remains the seat of the Muslim university of Fès. Named after the quarter in which it was built, which was a home to refugees from Kairouan in Tunisia, it was founded by Fatima bint Mohammed el-Fihri, a religious woman who donated her worldly riches for its construction. Its prayer hall can hold up to 20,000 people, although it is impossible to gain an accurate impression of the mosque's size, so snugly is it embedded within neighbouring buildings. Non-Muslims have to content themselves with a glimpse through whichever of the mosque's 14 street doors happen to be open at the time, but be respectful.

12 🛇 El-Attarine Medersa

📍 E2 🏛 Opposite the Karaouiyine Mosque 📞 (0535) 62 34 60 🕐 8:30am–noon, 2:30–6.30pm daily

The El-Attarine Medersa (Medersa of the Spice Sellers) stands in the neighbourhood of the Karaouiyine Mosque and the El-Attarine Souk. Along with the Bou Inania Medersa, it is considered to be one of the wonders of Moorish architecture. Built between 1323 and 1325, it has all the elements specific to a medieval Muslim school.

→
Colourful tilework on the façade of Karaouiyine Mosque

> **Established in 859, the Karaouiyine Mosque is one of the oldest and most illustrious of its kind in the western Muslim world.**

The Medersa's decorative entrance leads to a courtyard paved with intricate *zellij* tilework in a two-colour pattern of brown and white, and enclosing an ablutions fountain. A cladding of polychrome tiles covers the base of the courtyard's four interior walls and its columns. A door with exquisite fittings leads from the courtyard through to the prayer hall, which contains a mihrab. The prayer hall has a highly embellished ceiling, walls with luxuriant stuccowork and *zellij* work, and lintels with intricate epigraphic decoration.

The students' rooms, looking on to the courtyard from the upper floor, have windows fronted by turned wooden railings. The terrace offers a view of the courtyard of the Karaouiyine Mosque.

13 🛇 El-Cherratine Medersa

📍 X9 🏛 Rue El-Cherratine

Located southeast of the Karaouiyine Mosque, in Rue el-Cherratine (Street of the Ropemakers), this medersa was built by Moulay Rachid, the first Alaouite sultan, in 1670. Although it is similar to the Merinid medersas in structure, it is less elaborately decorated. Adding to the building's austerity are the high, narrow residential *douiras*, which stand in three corners of the courtyard. The tiny cells inside were for the students.

Entry into the medersa is through beautiful double doors cased in bronze. The doors open on to a passageway with a fine carved and painted wooden ceiling, which in turn leads to the Moorish courtyard.

⑭ Tanners' Quarter

⑨E1 ⌂North of Place el-Seffarine

The Chouara, or Tanners' Quarter, is almost medieval. Tanning has traditions that go back thousands of years. The process turns animal hides (mostly goat or sheep, but occasionally cow and even camel) into soft, rot-proof leather, which is passed on to the leatherworkers. The methods by which this is achieved are the same as they have always been. They involve repeatedly softening the skins in vats of various noxious ingredients, including pigeon droppings. It is easy to find the tanneries – just follow your nose.

If you can bear the unpleasantly strong smells, from the Derb Chouara (Tanners' Alley) a staircase leads up to the Terrase de Tannerie. From here you can view the honeycomb-like arrangement of pools and busy workers from a safe distance. The different hues in the various vats are the due to the dyes used to colour the leather. About 50 families work here and the trade is passed on from father to son.

On the terrace is a large collective shop selling the finished products of the tanneries in the form of bags, coats and slippers in butter-soft leather.

___

⑮ Place el-Seffarine

⑨E2

Fès is the centre of brass and silverware production in Morocco. The workshops of brass-workers and copper-smiths lining Place el-Seffarine have been here for centuries. The pretty fountain with *fleur-de-lis* decoration, probably built by French convicts in the 16th century, is worth a look.

North of the square is the 14th-century **Karaouiyine Library**, which was set up on the orders of the sultan Abou Inan. It was used by the greatest Moorish men of learning, including the philosopher and doctor Ibn Rushd, known as Averroës, the philosopher Ibn Tufayl, the historian Ibn Khaldoun and the 6th-century traveller Leo Africanus. The manuscripts that once formed part of the library's collection have been transferred to the Moroccan Royal Library in Rabat. Further on, to the right, is the 16th-century Tetouani Fondouk, which accommodated traders and students from Tetouan.

Place el-Seffarine leads to Rue des Teinturiers (Dyers' Street), which runs parallel to the *wadi* and is where skeins are hung out to dry.

Karaouiyine Library

⌂Place el-Seffarine ☎(0535) 62 34 60 ⏱10am–4pm Mon–Thu, 9am–1pm Fri

___

⑯ Andalusian Mosque

⑨E2 ⌂Accessible via Rue el-Nekhaline or Bab el-Ftouh and Rue Sidi Bou Ghaleb ⊗To non-Muslims

According to legend, this mosque was established in the 13th century by Mariam el-Fihri, sister of the founder of the Karaouiyine Mosque, and by the Andalusians from the Karaouiyine Quarter. The

1280

The year El-Seffarine Medersa was built. It is the oldest *medersa* in Morocco that is still in use.

→

A coppersmith working on cookware at a workshop in Place el-Seffarine

Merinids added a fountain in 1306 and established a library here in 1416. Non-Muslims can only admire the building from the exterior; notable are the great north entrance, with a carved cedar awning, and the domed Zenet minaret.

17

Andalusian Quarter

⑨ E/F2

The Andalusian Quarter did not undergo the same development as the Karaouiyine Quarter, located on the opposite bank of Wadi Fès and better provided with water. Nevertheless, this quieter, more residential part of the city has monuments that are worth a visit.

The **El-Sahrij Medersa**, built in 1321, takes its name from the large water basin in one of the courtyards. This is considered to be the third-finest medersa in Fès after the Bou Inania and the El-Attarine medersas. The Mausoleum of Sidi Bou Ghaleb, in the street of the same name, is that of a holy man from Andalusia who lived and taught in Fès in the 12th century.

El-Sahrij Medersa

🏛 ⌂ Rue Sidi Bou Ghaled 📞 (0535) 62 34 60 🕐 9am–5pm Wed–Mon

18

Bab el-Ftouh

⑨ F2 ⌂ Southeast of the medina

Literally meaning "Gate of the Aperture", the huge Bab el-Ftouh is also known as the Gate of Victory. This leads through to the largely residential Andalusian Quarter. Originally built in the 10th century by a Zenet emir, it was altered in the 18th century, during the reign of Alaouite ruler Sidi Mohammed ben Abdallah. Outside the ramparts, on a hill opposite the city, is the Bab el-Ftouh cemetery, where some of the most illustrious inhabitants of Fès are buried.

←

The enormous Bab el-Ftouh gateway leading to the Andalusian Quarter

---

EAT

Fez Café
Set in the courtyard of Le Jardin des Biehn riad, this secret garden eatery serves inventive French-Moroccan fusion dishes.

⑨ D2 ⌂ 13 Akbat Sbaa, Douh 📞 (0535) 63 50 31 🕐 Noon–3pm, 7:30–10pm daily

🏷 🏷 🏷

NUR
Creative Moroccan cuisine prepared by a chef whose CV includes stints at elBulli in Spain and two-Michelin-starred Noma in Denmark.

⑨ D2 ⌂ Zkak Rouah 🕐 6:30–10pm Tue–Sun 🌐 nur.ma

🏷 🏷 🏷

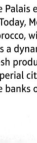

MEKNÈS AND VOLUBILIS

Located between the fertile plain of the Rarb and the Middle Atlas, Meknès and Volubilis lie at the heart of an agricultural area that has been Morocco's grain store since ancient times. The historical importance of the two cities can be clearly seen in the ruins of Volubilis, capital of Mauretania Tingitana and the most important archaeological site in Morocco, as well as in the grandeur of the Moorish buildings in Meknès.

From the time of its foundation in the 10th century to the arrival of the Alaouites in the 17th century, Meknès was just a small town overshadowed by Fès, its neighbour and rival. It was not until Moulay Ismaïl's reign, which began in 1672, that Meknès first rose to the rank of imperial city, and the sultan ordered the building of gates, ramparts, mosques and palaces worthy of such an honour. This ambitious building programme continued throughout his reign and involved robbing the ruins of Volubilis and the Palais el-Badi in Marrakech.

Today, Meknès is one of the largest cities in Morocco, with a population approaching a million. It is a dynamic economic centre, renowned for its fresh produce, olives, wine and mint tea. The grand imperial city stands alongside the new town, on the banks of Wadi Boufekrane.

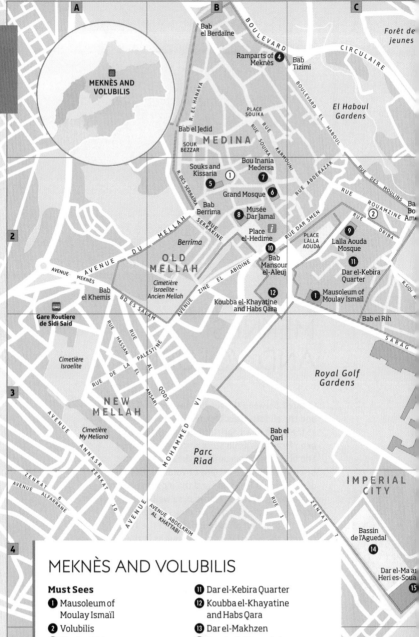

MEKNÈS AND VOLUBILIS

Must Sees

1 Mausoleum of Moulay Ismaïl

2 Volubilis

3 Moulay Idriss

Experience More

4 Ramparts of Meknès

5 Souks and Kissaria

6 Grand Mosque

7 Bou Inania Medersa

8 Musée Dar Jamaï

9 Lalla Aouda Mosque

10 Bab Mansour el-Aleuj and Place el-Hedime

11 Dar el-Kebira Quarter

12 Koubba el-Khayatine and Habs Qara

13 Dar el-Makhzen

14 Bassin de l'Aguedal

15 Dar el-Ma and Heri es-Souani

16 Haras de Meknès

17 Sidi Kacem

18 Khemisset

19 Zerhoun Massif

Eat

① Kenza

② Le Collier de la Colombe

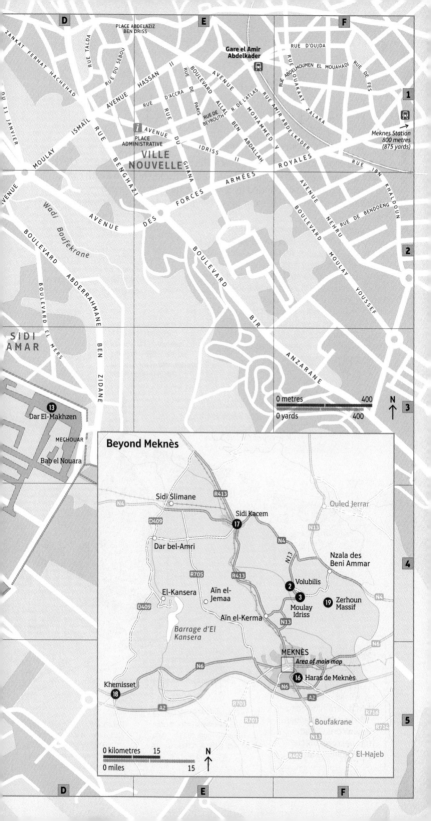

PLACE ABDELAZIZ
BEN DRISS

**Gare el Amir
Abdelkader**

RUE D'OUJDA

Meknes Station
800 metres
(875 yards)

ZANKAT FERHAT HACHEHAD

DU 11 JANVIER

RUE TALDA

RUE DU SEBOU

AVENUE HASSAN II

ISMAIL MOULAY

RUE BENGHAZI

RUE D'ACCRA

RUE DE PARIS

BOULEVARD ALLAL BEN ABDALLAH

AVENUE

RUE DE LATLAS

RUE XMIR ABDELKADER

RUE DE BEYROUTH

RUE MOHAMMED V

RUE DU GHANA

AVENUE DU IDRISS II

RUE ABDELMOUMEN EL MOUAHADI

RUE OUAKAAT ZALAKA

RUE DE FÈS

i AVENUE

PLACE
ADMINISTRATIVE

**VILLE
NOUVELLE**

FORCES ARMÉES

ROYALES

AVENUE NEHRU

RUE IBN KHALDOUN

AVENUE

DES

AVENUE

BOULEVARD MOULAY YOUSSEF

RUE DE BENDOENG

BOULEVARD ABDERRAHMANE

Wadi Boufekrane

BOULEVARD

BIR

ANZARANE

SIDI
AMAR

BOULEVARD EL MERS

BEN ZIDANE

0 metres   400

0 yards   400

N ↑

13 Dar El-Makhzen

MECHOUAR

Bab el Nouara

Beyond Meknès

Sidi Slimane

R413

Sidi Kacem

17

Ouled Jerrar

N4

D409

N13

Dar bel-Amri

N4

Nzala des
Beni Ammar

R705

R413

2 Volubilis

3

19 Zerhoun
Massif

N4

El-Kansera

Aïn el-
Jemaa

Moulay
Idriss

D409

Aïn el-Kerma

N13

Barrage d'El
Kansera

N6

MEKNÈS
Area of main map

N6

Khemisset

16 Haras de Meknès

N6

A2

18

A2

R701

R716

R701

Boufakrane

R714

0 kilometres   15

N13

0 miles   15

R402

El-Hajeb

N ↑

❶
MAUSOLEUM OF MOULAY ISMAÏL

📍 C2 📍 Rue Sarag, Meknès ⏰ 9am–noon & 3–6pm daily

The most bloodthirsty ruler in Moroccan history, Moulay Ismaïl (1672–1727) spent the latter part of his life making sure that when his own death came he would be buried surrounded by splendour. He built this lavish mausoleum, which is a fine example of Islamic architecture and design.

Once through the highly ornate entrance, you will pass through a series of yellow courtyards, a sequence intended to create a sense of calm. These lead to a suite of burial chambers decorated with a blaze of polychromatic tiling in a style similar to the Saadian Tombs in Marrakech (p256). The wife of Moulay Ismaïl and his son Moulay Ahmed al-Dahbi, as well as the sultan Moulay Abderrahman (1822–59), are all buried here. The tomb chamber is often visited by locals seeking good baraka (blessings).

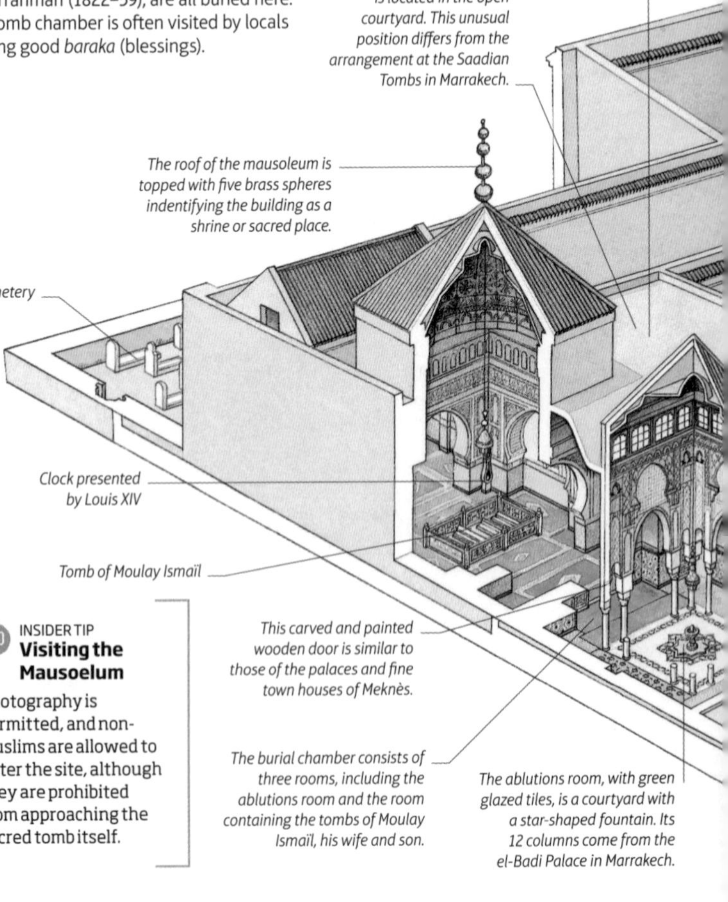

The floor of the prayer hall is covered with mats on which worshippers kneel to pray or to reflect before going into the burial chamber.

The mausoleum's mihrab is located in the open courtyard. This unusual position differs from the arrangement at the Saadian Tombs in Marrakech.

The roof of the mausoleum is topped with five brass spheres indentifying the building as a shrine or sacred place.

Cemetery

Clock presented by Louis XIV

Tomb of Moulay Ismaïl

💬 INSIDER TIP
Visiting the Mausoelum

Photography is permitted, and non-Muslims are allowed to enter the site, although they are prohibited from approaching the sacred tomb itself.

This carved and painted wooden door is similar to those of the palaces and fine town houses of Meknès.

The burial chamber consists of three rooms, including the ablutions room and the room containing the tombs of Moulay Ismaïl, his wife and son.

The ablutions room, with green glazed tiles, is a courtyard with a star-shaped fountain. Its 12 columns come from the el-Badi Palace in Marrakech.

↑ The mausoleum façade, decorated with beautiful mosaic tiles

This imposing carved stone entrance doorway, surmounted by an awning and a pyramidal roof, indicates the importance of the royal building.

En route to the burial chamber you pass through several empty, peaceful courtyards, which are decorated in a sober style.

Did You Know?

Moulay Ismaïl is alleged to have fathered a total of 867 children.

← Plan showing the layout of the Mausoleum of Moulay Ismaïl

Open courtyard

The lower part of the walls of the rooms leading into the burial chamber is covered with traditional zellij tilework – mosaics of glazed polychrome tiles.

→ Fountain in the opulent interior of the mausoleum

② ⟨⚔⟩ ⟨🏛⟩ ⟨🖼⟩

VOLUBILIS

📍 F4 🚗 31 km (19 miles) northwest of Meknès; 5 km (3 miles) from Moulay Idriss
🕐 8am–one hour before sunset daily 🚌 Bus from Meknès to Moulay Idriss, then by *grand taxi* to the site

Founded in the 3rd century BC, Volubilis was the capital of the ancient kingdom of Mauretania. When Mauretania was annexed by the Romans in AD 45, Volubilis became one of the most important cities in the province of Mauretania Tingitana. It has some of the finest Roman ruins in Morocco.

Exploring Volubilis

During its heyday under the Romans Volubilis was an affluent city. This is seen in the remains of the beautiful 2nd-century forum, basilica and capitol and the sophisticated town houses paved with mosaics. The site also features baths, oil presses, bakeries, aqueducts, drains and shops that evoke the inhabitants' daily lives. After Rome withdrew from Mauretania in the 3rd century, the city declined. It was inhabited by Christians, Jews and Greeks and then became an Islamic settlement under Idriss I in 788. By the 11th century Volubilis was abandoned after the seat of power transferred to Fès.

Gordian Palace

House of Dionysus and the Four Seasons

Decumanus maximus

The House of the Labours of Hercules is named after a mosaic found here depicting the Greek hero's 12 labours.

Aristocratic quarter

The House of Columns is arranged around a huge peristyle courtyard with a circular pool. Columns with twisted fluting and composite capitals front the grand reception room.

Bestriding the decumanus maximus, the triumphal arch overlooks plantations of cereals and olive trees. The fertile plain to the west of Volubilis has provided the area with grain and oil since antiquity.

House of the Dog

House of the Athlete

Macellum (market)

58

The number of oil presses discovered at Volubilis, showing the value of olive oil to the city's economy.

Plan showing the layout of the ancient city of Volubilis ↑

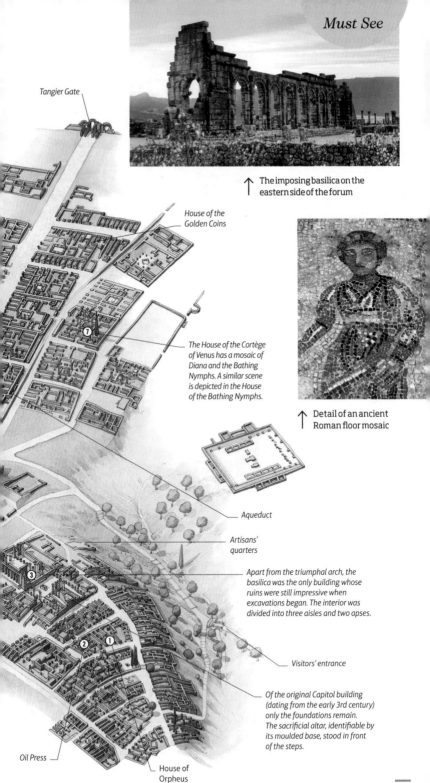

Tangier Gate

↑ The imposing basilica on the eastern side of the forum

House of the Golden Coins

The House of the Cortège of Venus has a mosaic of Diana and the Bathing Nymphs. A similar scene is depicted in the House of the Bathing Nymphs.

↑ Detail of an ancient Roman floor mosaic

Aqueduct

Artisans' quarters

Apart from the triumphal arch, the basilica was the only building whose ruins were still impressive when excavations began. The interior was divided into three aisles and two apses.

Visitors' entrance

Of the original Capitol building (dating from the early 3rd century) only the foundations remain. The sacrificial altar, identifiable by its moulded base, stood in front of the steps.

Oil Press

House of Orpheus

① The House of Orpheus

Located in the southern quarter of the city, the House of Orpheus is remarkable not only for its size but for the rooms that it contains. Opposite the entrance is a large peristyle courtyard, with a slightly sunken square pool that is decorated with sea creatures. The *tablinum*, looking onto the courtyard, is the main reception room; the centre is paved with the Orpheus Mosaic, the largest of the circular mosaics that have been discovered in Volubilis. Orpheus is depicted charming a lion, an elephant and other animals with his lyre. The house also has an oil press with purification tanks, as well as private areas. These have further rooms paved with mosaics in geometric patterns and bath suites with hypocausts (underfloor heating).

The centre of the *tablinum* in the House of Orpheus is paved with the Orpheus Mosaic, the largest of the circular mosaics that have been discovered in Volubilis.

② Oil Press

The reconstruction of an oil press near the House of Orpheus shows how this device worked in Roman times. The olives were crushed in a cylindrical vat by the action of a millstone fixed to a vertical axis. The resulting pulp was emptied into rush or esparto baskets laid beneath planks of wood on which pressure was exerted by means of a beam that acted as a lever. The oil ran out along channels and into purification tanks set up outside. Water poured into the tanks forced the better-quality oil to float to the surface. It was then poured off into large earthenware jars for local use or for export.

③ The Forum, Basilica and Capitol

Like the other major public buildings in the heart of the city, the unusually small forum dates from the early 3rd century. It was the focal point of public life and administration, as well as a meeting place where business was done. It is continued on its western side by the *macellum*, a market that was originally covered.

On the left of the entrance, from the direction of the oil press, stands the stele of Marcus Valerius Servus, which lists the territory that the citizens of Volubilis possessed in the hinterland.

On the eastern side of the forum, a short flight of steps and three semicircular arches leads into the basilica. This was the meeting place of the curia (senate), as well as the commercial exchange and tribunal, and somewhere to take a stroll. On the capitol, south of the basilica, public rites in honour of Jupiter, Juno and Minerva were performed.

> **RECONSTRUCTION OF VOLUBILIS**
>
> Many of the ancient ruins were badly damaged during a major earthquake in 1755. Excavations and restoration began in the late 19th century and continue to this day, although extensive areas still remain to be explored. So far, only the centre of the city has been excavated.

→

Close-up of an ancient Roman carved capital in Volubilis

↑ Well-preserved Roman mosaics, a key feature of the ruins in Volubilis

④
House of the Athlete

The athlete that gives this house its name is the *desultor*, or chariot jumper, who took part in the Olympic Games. He would leap from his horse or his chariot in the middle of a race and remount or get back in immediately.

The mosaic here depicts the *desultor* as a parody. The naked athlete is shown bestriding a donkey backwards, and holding a *cantharus*, a drinking vessel given as a prize. The scarf, another emblem of victory, flutters in the background.

⑤
House of the Dog and House of the Ephebe

The House of the Dog, behind the triumphal arch on the western side, is laid out to a typical Roman plan. A double doorway opens onto a lobby leading through to the atrium. This room contains a pool and leads in turn to a large dining room, or *triclinium*. In 1916, a bronze statue of a dog was discovered in one of the rooms off the *triclinium*. Opposite the House of the Dog stands the House of the Ephebe, where a beautiful statue of an ivy-wreathed ephebe (youth in military training) was found in 1932. This, together with the statue of the dog are now in the Musée de l'Historie and des Civilisations in Rabat *(p86)*.

⑥
Aristocratic Quarter

Fine houses, such as the elegant House of the Columns, House of the Knight and House of the Labours of Hercules, constituted the aristocratic quarter. The House of Dionysus and the Four Seasons and the House of the Bathing Nymphs have high-quality mosaics. The Gordian Palace, named after Emperor Gordian III (238–44) and probably the residence of the Roman governor, is notable for the 12 columns that front it and the horseshoe-shaped pool with almost perfectly semicircular outlines.

⑦
Cortège of Venus

Busts of Cato the Younger and Juba II were found south of the city's main road, the *decumanus maximus*. The mosaic depicting the Cortège of Venus, which paved the *triclinium*, is displayed in the Kasbah Museum of Mediterranean Cultures in Tangier *(p144)*. Some of the mosaics have motifs very similiar to those seen in Berber carpets today.

⑧
Triumphal Arch and Decumanus Maximus

According to the inscription that it bears, the triumphal arch was erected in AD 217 by the governor Marcus Aurelius Sebastenus in honour of Caracalla and his mother Julia Domna. Above the inscription, at the top of the monument, ran a frieze and a band, and the whole was crowned by a chariot drawn by six horses.

The arch, which stands over 8 m (26 ft) high, was reconstructed in 1933. It faces west onto the plain and east onto the *decumanus maximus*. This main axis through the city leads from the triumphal arch in the southwest to the gateway known as Tangier Gate in the northeast.

Parallel with the *decumanus maximus*, and a few metres away on its southern side, ran an aqueduct, substantial parts of which survive. This brought water from a spring 1 km (0.6 mile) from Volubilis to the city's baths and fountains.

↑ Triumphal arch, situated at the end of the *decumanus maximus*, the city's main street

3

MOULAY IDRISS

📍 F4 🏠 3 km (30 miles) north of Mecknès 🚌 From Mecknès

The holy city of Moulay Idriss clings to two rocky outcrops at the foot of the Zerhoun Massif. Built around the sacred tomb of Moulay Idriss I, this pretty, white-washed town is of huge national importance. A peaceful and picturesque place for the majority of the year, it bursts into life each August when thousands of pilgrims arrive for the annual *moussem*.

> 💬 INSIDER TIP
> **Volubilis by Foot**
>
> It is possible to walk from Moulay Idriss to the nearby Roman site of Volubilis *(p198)* via a scenic mountain footpath. The 4-km (2.5-mile) route skirts the hillside, and affords spectacular views of the town and the surrounding landscape.

Fleeing the persecution of the Abbassid caliphs of Baghdad, Morocco's first Islamic leader and most revered saint, Moulay Idriss, found sanctuary in Oualili (Volubilis). A direct descendant of the Prophet Mohammed, he founded the first Arab-Muslim dynasty in Morocco. He died in 791 and was buried in the town that now bears his name. In the 16th century the town began to prosper, and it was still in the process of developing in the 17th century, during the reign of Moulay Ismaïl, when he endowed it with defensive walls, a monumental gate, Koranic schools, fountains and a new dome for the mausoleum.

Due to its holy status, Moulay Idriss remained closed to non-Muslims until 1912, and they were not allowed to stay overnight until 2005. As such, it has managed to remain somewhat of a tranquil backwater in comparison to other tourist favourites, and retain its peaceful and spiritual charm.

←

The town of Moulay Idriss,
perched on the foothills
of the Zerhoun Massif

The Mausoleum of Moulay Idriss

Conspicuous with its green-tiled roof, the Tomb of Idriss I,
around which the town clusters, is closed to non-Muslims.
However, a the terrace near the Mosque of Sidi Abdallah el-
Hajjam, which perches above the town, offers splendid views
of the town and the mausoelum. Its unusual cylindrical minaret
is covered with green tiles and verses from the Koran.

↑ Beautifully tiled entrance to
the Mausoleum of Moulay Idriss

> **MOUSSEM OF
> MOULAY IDRISS**
>
> Moulay Idriss is the
> setting for Morocco's
> most celebrated
> *moussem*, or religious
> festival, in which
> thousands of Muslims
> make a pilgrimage to
> this holy town during
> the month before
> Ramadan. Colourful
> banners, Moroccan
> flags and pictures of
> the King are erected
> throughout the town.
> Traditional music is
> played as a procession
> winds its way through
> the medina. The
> energy is infectious,
> and all are welcome to
> join the party.

EXPERIENCE MORE

4

Ramparts of Meknès

🅰B1 🅽Encircling the medina, Meknès

Protected by three stretches of wall several kilometres long, the medina has the appearance of a sturdy fortress set with elegant gates. Bab el-Berdaïne (Gate of the Pack Saddle Makers), on the northern side, was built by Moulay Ismaïl. It is flanked by protruding square towers crowned by merlons, and stylized flowers in *zellij* tile-work decorate its exterior façade. West of the gate, the walled cemetery contains one of the most highly venerated

Did You Know?

Alouite sultan Moulay Ismail intended Meknès to become Morocco's answer to Versailles.

mausoleums in Morocco – that of Sidi Mohammed ben Aïssa, founder of the brotherhood of the Aïssaoua.

On the southern side of the cemetery stands Bab el-Siba (Gate of Anarchy) and Bab el-Jedid (New Gate, although in fact it is one of the oldest in Meknès). Further south is Bab Berrima, which leads into the medina's principal souks. To the west stands Bab el-Khemis (Thursday Gate), which once led into the mellah, now non-existent. The remarkable decoration of the façade is on a par with that of Bab el-Berdaïne.

The layout of the medina, a medieval labyrinth, is identical to that of the other imperial cities. There are a few main thoroughfares. Rue Karmouni, which runs north to south, links Bab el-Berdaïne with the spiritual and economic heart of the medina. Rue des Souks runs from Bab Berrima, in the west, to this centre, which is marked by the Grand Mosque and the Bou Inania Medersa, one of the few religious sites in Morocco to which non-Muslims can gain access.

5

Souks and Kissaria

🅰B2 🅽Rue des Souks, Meknès 🕐Daily

A network of small streets lined with shops, the souks are a fascinating encapsulation of the 17th- and 18th-century Moroccan urban environment. Rue des Souks, near Bab Berrima, is filled with hardware merchants *(akarir)*, corn chandlers *(bezzazine)* and fabric sellers *(serrayriya)*, while metalsmiths *(haddadin)* are to be found in the old Rue des Armuriers. Bab Berrima leads through to Souk En-Nejjarine, the Carpenters' Souk, which is next to that of the brass- and coppersmiths, and to the Cobblers' Souk *(sebbat)*.

The En-Nejjarine Mosque, built by the Almohads in the 12th century, was given a new minaret in 1756. Set back from the En-Nejjarine Souk, in the Ed-Dlala Kissaria, is a Berber souk. Every day from 3pm to 4pm, the mountain-dwellers of the Middle Atlas come to auction carpets and blankets.

↑ Driving through the twin towers of the Bab el-Khemis gateway in Meknès

↑ A visitor admiring the intricately decorated Bou Inania Medersa, at the heart of the medina

⑥ Grand Mosque

🅰B2 🕌Rue des Souk es Sebbat, Meknès ⏰Daily 🚫To non-Muslims

The Grand Mosque, which stands near the souks and the Bou Inania Medersa, was established during the reign of the Almoravids in the 12th century and remodelled in the 14th century. The main façade is pierced by an imposing doorway with a carved awning. The beautiful green-glazed terracotta tiles of the roof and of the 18th-century minaret are particularly striking, the bright sunlight giving them a translucent appearance.

⑦ 🔧 Bou Inania Medersa

🅰B2 🕌Rue des Souks es Sebbat, Meknès ⏰8am-noon, 3-6pm daily

This Koranic school opposite the Grand Mosque was established by the Merinid sultans in the 14th century. The building is divided into two parts with a long corridor between them. On the eastern side is the medersa proper, while on the western side is an annexe for ablutions (now no longer in use). The main entrance is crowned by a flat-sided dome and faced with horseshoe arches that feature impressively delicate stuccowork decoration.

A corridor leads to a beautiful courtyard, in the centre of which is a pool. While three sides of the courtyard are lined with a gallery, the fourth opens on to the prayer hall. The green-tiled awnings, the sophisticated carved wood, stuccowork and *zellij* tilework, as well as the mosaic-like tiled floor, make the courtyard an entrancing sight.

The prayer hall itself remains unaltered. Students' cells fill the rest of the ground floor and the upper floor. The terrace offers a fine view of the medina and the Grand Mosque next to the medersa.

⑧ Musée Dar Jamaï

🅰B2 🕌Place el-Hedime 📞(0535) 55 88 73 ⏰10am-5:30pm Wed-Mon

This museum of Moroccan arts is set in a delightful palatial residence that is worth the modest admission price alone. Built at the end of the 19th century, the palace is decorated with intricate plasterwork and *zellij* tilework. It has a courtyard with two pools and a shady Andalusian garden planted with orange trees and tall cypresses.

The collection includes carved and painted wood, ceramics, carpets and embroidery from around the country, kaftans, belts and jewellery. Highlights include a finely carved 17th-century minbar (pulpit) that originally stood in the Grand Mosque. Also worth close inspection is the room devoted to metalwork. While ceramics reached their apogee in Fès, the craftsmen of Meknès were distinguished masters of damascening. The technique consists of covering a metallic surface with a filigree of gold, silver or copper, and is still very much alive today.

On the upper floor is a sumptuous reconstruction of a traditional Moroccan salon complete with carved wooden dome ceiling and luxurious rugs and cushions.

↑ The Moroccan flag waving in front of Lalla Aouda Mosque

9

Lalla Aouda Mosque

🅰C2 🅰Place Lalla Aouda, Meknès ⬤Daily ⬤To non-Muslims

The first major place of worship to be built by Moulay Ismaïl, in 1680, this mosque is one of the few of the sultan's projects to have survived intact. The building has three doorways. Two on the northwestern side open out on to the former *méchouar* (parade ground), and a smaller one, on the side of the mosque where the mihrab is located, leads to a corridor running behind the mosque, probably the sultan's private entrance.

10

Bab Mansour el-Aleuj and Place el-Hedime

🅰B2 🅰South of the medina, Meknès

Bab Mansour el-Aleuj (Gate of the Victorius Renegade) is so named for the Christian who designed and built it. Standing

→

Visitors admiring the iconic Bab Mansour el-Aleuj from the Place el-Hedime

like a triumphal arch before the imperial city, it pierces the walls of the kasbah and leads to Place Lalla Aouda and the Dar el-Kebira Quarter.

Of monumental proportions and distinguished for its decoration, Bab Mansour el-Aleuj is the finest gate in Meknès, or even in Morocco. It was begun by the sultan Moulay Ismaïl in about 1672 and completed during the reign of his son, Moulay Abdallah, in 1732. An intricate pattern of interlacing motifs is carved in relief on a background of predominantly green mosaics and tiles. The cornerpieces are filled with sgraffito floral decoration incised into dark-glazed terracotta. The gate is framed by protruding loggia-style towers. Temporary exhibitions are sometimes held here.

Place el-Hedime (Square of Ruins) links the medina and the kasbah. It was laid out on the ruins of the Merinid kasbah that Moulay Ismaïl razed to make space for the palaces, water tanks, gardens, stables, arsenals and forts with which he planned to surround himself. The square is now lined with modern residential buildings that are

not in keeping with its historic character. Nearby, to the left of the square, is a covered food market.

11

Dar el-Kebira Quarter

🅰C2 🅰Behind Place Lalla Aouda (between Bab Moulay and the Lalla Aouda Mosque), Meknès

This quarter forms part of the so-called Imperial City, or Kasbah of Moulay Ismaïl. Covering an area four times as large as that of the medina, the whole quarter is a testament to the grand ambitions of this enterprising sultan. Protected by a double line of walls and monumental angled gates, the Imperial City has the appearance of an impregnable *ksar* (fortified village). It contains wide avenues and large squares, palaces with attractive pools and extensive gardens, as well as administrative buildings enclosed within their own ramparts.

The Imperial City comprises three complexes: Dar el-Kebira, Dar el-Medrasa and Ksar el-Mhanncha. Dar el-Kebira, the

Quarter of the Large House, is located southeast of the medina. It was the first palatial complex of the Imperial City that Moulay Ismaïl ordered to be built, in about 1672. It stands near Place Lalla Aouda, probably on the site of the former Almohad kasbah. The complex was cut off from the urban bustle by a double wall and by Place el-Hedime.

Each palace in Dar el-Kebira contained a harem, hammams, kitchens, armouries, ovens and mosques, interlinked by a somewhat haphazard network of open or partially covered alleys. Today, the ancient heart of the Imperial City, which is partly in ruins, has become a poor district that has been filled with shanty dwellings.

The Mausoleum of Moulay Ismaïl, the Lalla Aouda Mosque and a monumental gate near Bab Bou Ameïr are the last surviving vestiges of the ostentatious complex that the sultan had envisaged.

The second complex, which is now in complete ruins, was the Dar el-Medrasa. The palace comprised suites of residential rooms, some of which were used exclusively by the sultan and his harem.

↑ Paintings in Habs Qara, a medieval prison hidden beneath the streets of Meknès

12 🚶

Koubba el-Khayatine and Habs Qara

🅰B2 🏠Place Habs Qara, Meknès ⏰9am–noon, 3–6pm daily 🚫Public hols

This imperial pavilion was originally used to receive diplomats who came to negotiate the ransom of Christian prisoners. The building is crowned by a conical dome decorated with geometric and floral motifs.

Behind the pavilion are the former underground storage areas that were converted into the Christian Prison, or Habs Qara. The prisoners, probably Europeans captured by the corsairs of Rabat, were made to work on the sultan's building projects. Chroniclers have recorded that thousands of convicts were once incarcerated in these underground galleries, which were later partly destroyed by an earthquake.

13

Dar el-Makhzen

🅰D3 🏠Place Bab el-Mechouar, Meknès 🚫To the public

This royal complex was formerly known as the Palace of the Labyrinth, named after a white marble pool fashioned as a labyrinth. In contrast to Dar el-Kebira and Koubba el-Khayatine, the complex has a neat and compact layout.

It is divided into eight parts and surrounded by walls set with bastions. In the centre stands a monumental gate, the fulsomely decorated Bab el-Makhzen (Gate of the Warehouse), built by Moulay el-Hassan in 1888. A second gate, Bab el-Jedid (New Gate), was made on the north-western side. Features of the complex include a *méchouar* and Kasbah Hadrach, the former barracks of the sultan's army of slaves.

14

Bassin de l'Aguedal

🅰C4 🏠Aguedal Quarter, Meknès

This *sahrij* (water reservoir) was built by Moulay Ismaïl to supply water to the palace and the Imperial City, its mosques, hammams, gardens and orchards. The women of the harem, so it is said, would sail on it in their pleasure boats. Only a few stretches of its walls survive. The spot has suffered some unfortunate alterations in an effort to create a place where the people of Meknès could come to walk.

Pottery and tajines for sale in Place el-Hedim, Meknès

↑ A berber man standing in one of the 29 aisles of Heri es-Souani

⓯
Dar el-Ma and Heri es-Souani

📍 C4 🏠 L'Agdal Quarter, Meknès ⏰ 9am–noon, 3–6pm daily

Dar el-Ma, the Water House, held the town's water reserves and was another of Moulay Ismaïl's grandiose projects. The huge barrel-vaulted building contains 15 rooms, each with a *noria* (water wheel) once worked by horses to draw underground water by means of scoops. The terraces offer a fine view of the city.

Dar el-Ma gives access to Heri es-Souani, the so-called Grainstore Stables, which are considered to be among the sultan's finest creations. As well as a network of underground passages, this monumental building, with 29 aisles,

---

💬 INSIDER TIP
People Pics

It's rude to take photos of anybody in any country without asking permission. Canny Moroccans may ask to be paid, so it's a good idea to establish a price (Dh 10 is about right) before snapping.

---

has thick walls to keep the temperature inside the grainstore at a constant low level. The ceilings collapsed during the earthquake of 1755.

⓰
Haras de Meknès

📍 F5 🏠 Zitoune Quarter, southwest of Meknès, from Dar el-Ma, 1 km (0.6 miles) towards Dar el-Beïda, turning right 400 m (440 yds) beyond Dar el-Beïda and continuing for 2 km (1 mile) to the south ⏰ 9am–noon, 2–6pm Mon–Fri

Although it cannot rival the modern studs in Rabat and Marrakech, Haras de Meknès is well known in Morocco. The stud was established in 1912 with the aim of improving bloodlines and promoting various Moroccan breeds of horses for use in racing, riding and fantasias.

The stud can accommodate 231 horses, ranging from pure-bred Arabs and Barbs to English thoroughbreds and Anglo-Arabs. A visit here may include seeing horses being put through their paces.

⓱
Sidi Kacem

📍 E4 🏠 46 km (29 miles) northwest of Meknès 🚍🚆 From Meknès

Sidi Kacem grew out of a military outpost that was set up in 1915 near a *zaouia* and the souk of the local Cherarda tribe. It is now an important agricultural and industrial centre on the plain of the eastern Rharb.

The three complexes that dominate the town bear witness to the history and economic activity of Sidi Kacem. One is the railway station, at the intersection of lines running between Rabat and Fès and Tangier and Fès. The second is the oil refinery

(initially for local, then for imported, fuel). Third are the grain silos, which are at the heart of a well-watered and productive region.

Sidi Kacem is a major centre of agricultural food production and of brickmaking. These industries have made the town an important banking and commercial hub.

⓲
Khemisset

📍 D5 🚍 From Meknès

This town was founded in 1924, on the site of a military outpost on the road from Rabat to Fès. Now a provincial capital, Khemisset is also the de facto "capital" of the confederation of the Berber-speaking Zemmour tribes of the Middle Atlas.

This is a good place to stop, since there are many cafés and restaurants. The town also has a crafts cooperative where you can buy regional specialities, such as carpets and mats woven in palm fibre or wool and a variety of hand-carved wooden objects. Every Tuesday, Khemisset is the

venue for one of the most important country souks in Morocco, playing host to almost 1,900 stalls.

---

⑲

Zerhoun Massif

▣ F4 ⌂ About 50 km (31 miles) northeast of Meknès

Zerhoun Massif forms part of an extensive range of hills bordering the southern side of the Rif and running from the region of Meknès to the environs of Taza in the east. It is said to be one Morocco's most beautiful mountains.

This pre-Riffian terrain, consisting mostly of clay and marl, is very susceptible to erosion caused by the move-ment of water through the landscape. As a result, a few outcrops of harder limestone and sandstone have emerged, one of which is Jbel Zerhoun, its highest point, whose gorges, peaks and cliffs are all the result of erosion.

Water is abundant here, a fact known to the Romans, who tapped the springs to supply Volubilis. Large villages have since grown up on these hillsides, along the line of the springs and at the foot of the massif. While fig, orange and olive trees grow on the higher slopes, corn and barley thrive in the valleys and on the lower hillsides. Some consider the olives produced here to be the best in Morocco. Enclosures (*zriba*) of loose stones or thorny branches, for small herds of cattle, sheep and goats, can be seen near the villages.

For Moroccans, Zerhoun is a holy mountain, the home of many religious men – the Tomb of Idriss I (*p202*) is found in the town that takes his name – and the setting of numerous stories and legends.

COUNTRY SOUKS

Around 850 rural country souks are held every week in Morocco, drawing people from miles around. Their main purpose is to allow townspeople to buy agricultural produce, craft items, and groceries. However, not only do they provide services, entertainment and food, the souks are also an important social occasion, a meeting place where rural dwellers can interact and share their news. The civic authorities also use these souks to set up temporary registry offices, post offices and health centres. Permanent shops that may appear on the site of a weekly souk sometimes lead to the establishment of a new town or village.

↑ The remaining columns of the basilica in the ancient town of Volubilis on the Zerhoun Massif

Thundering waterfalls, Cascades d'Ouzoud

MIDDLE ATLAS

A wild region of rare beauty, the Middle Atlas is surprisingly little visited. The great cedar forests that cover the mountainsides between deep valleys stretch as far as the eye can see. Bordered by the fertile plain of the Saïs and the cities of Fès and Meknès, and traversed by one of the main routes through to southern Morocco, the mountainous heights of the Middle Atlas are the territory of Berber tribes, whose population is thinly scattered over the area.

Flanked on its eastern side by Tazzeka National Park, the terrain is scarred with natural caves and gorges, while forests of cedar, holm oak and cork oak form a patchwork with the bare volcanic plateaux and small lakes brimming with fish.

The Oum er-Rbia rises in the heart of the mountains. The longest river in Morocco, it travels 600 km (375 miles) before reaching the Atlantic. To the west, the Middle Atlas abuts the foothills of the High Atlas. Here, the Cascades d'Ouzoud crash down 100 m (328 ft) to the bottom of a natural chasm wreathed in luxuriant vegetation.

Nicknamed the Switzerland of Morocco, the Middle Atlas is also home to some exquisitely scenic small towns at mid-altitude. Ifrane, which has stone-built chalets with red-tiled roofs, Azrou, a resort on the slopes of a cedar plantation, and Imouzzer du Kandar are among the most attractive; they also serve as bases for hikes and tours in the mountains.

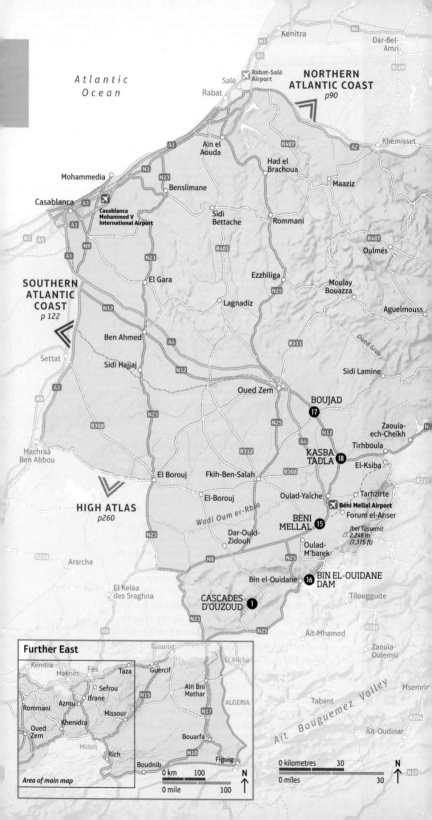

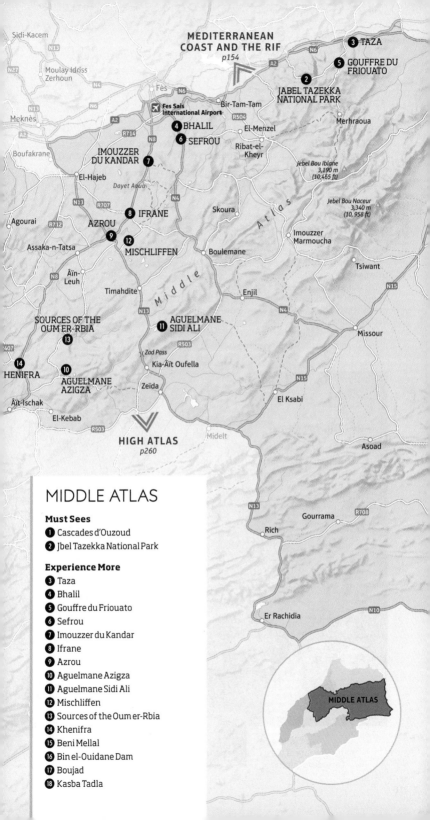

MIDDLE ATLAS

Must Sees

① Cascades d'Ouzoud

② Jbel Tazekka National Park

Experience More

③ Taza

④ Bhalil

⑤ Gouffre du Friouato

⑥ Sefrou

⑦ Imouzzer du Kandar

⑧ Ifrane

⑨ Azrou

⑩ Aguelmane Azigza

⑪ Aguelmane Sidi Ali

⑫ Mischliffen

⑬ Sources of the Oum er-Rbia

⑭ Khenifra

⑮ Beni Mellal

⑯ Bin el-Ouidane Dam

⑰ Boujad

⑱ Kasba Tadla

MIDDLE ATLAS

❶

CASCADES D'OUZOUD

🄰C3 🄷60 km (40 miles) southwest of Bin el-Ouidane on road R384, or 156 km (97 miles) from Marrakech via Demnate 🚐For Beni Mellal-Azilal then *grand taxi*

One of the most spectacular (and popular) sights in Morocco, the lush setting of these magnificent falls stands in stark contrast to their sunbaked surroundings.

Thundering down the valley's reddish cliffs and crashing off a series of rocky ledges to eventually fall into the canyon of Wadi el-Abid 100 m (328 ft) below, the Cascades d'Ouzoud are the largest waterfalls in Morocco, and arguably the most beautiful in North Africa. Visit in spring, when the river is at its highest, to experience this natural wonder at its most dramatic.

The waterfall can be reached along a rocky footpath from which visitors can marvel at the majestic falls and the permanent rainbow mist that hovers above the plunge pools. Bathing is permitted in the natural pools, while energetic visitors can hike further along the river bed, or embark on a more adventurous treck to the nearby Wadi el-Abid gorge.

> 🔍 HIDDEN GEM
> **Imi-n-Ifri**
>
> Just a short distance southwest of the falls is Imi-n-Ifri, a natural stone bridge that has been partly carved out by the river. A track leads down to the bottom of the chasm.

Did You Know?

The falls' Berber name translates as "the grinding of the grain" – a reference to the many mills that once operated here

The stunning natural beauty of the Cascades d'Ouzoud ↑

① Rocky outcrops are linked by ramshackle footbridges, while basic cafés and small fruit stands line the riverbank.

② Boats take visitors right to the base of the waterfalls.

③ Mist from the waterfalls creates an ideal environment for lush vegetation to grow, such as moss and fruit trees.

BARBARY MACAQUES

The Barbary macaque is the only primate (other than humans) that lives north of the Sahara, inhabiting parts of Morocco, Algeria and Gibraltar. As few as 6,000 remain in the wild, with between 4,000 and 5,000 living in Morocco, mostly in the Middle Atlas. They are easy to spot as they travel in large troupes. Be warned, they can be aggressive and will snatch food from your hands, whether it was meant for them or not.

❷

JBEL TAZEKKA NATIONAL PARK

Ⓐ E2 ⓦ tazekka.com

Just southwest of Taza, this expansive national park offers both beauty and grandeur, with scenery that includes thundering waterfalls, seasonal lakes, eerie caves and high mountain passes, as well as some exotic wildlife.

Established in 1950 to protect the cedar forests of Jbel Tazekka, this national park offers a spectacular tour southwest of Taza. In the middle of a valley of almond, cherry and fig trees are the Cascades de Ras el-Oued waterfalls. The winding road crosses the fertile plateau of the Chiker, a dry lake bed with calciferous rock structures. During the rainier months (November to April) it becomes a small lake (*dayet*) fed by underground water.

A short drive away are the Gouffre du Friouato caves (*p221*), one of the main attractions of the area. Possibly the most impressive caves in northern Africa – so vast they have still not been fully explored – they are also the only ones open to visitors.

The park is home to an abundance of animal and bird life, including the rare Barbary or Atlas deer, extinct in the wild until reintroduced into the park in 1994. There are also Barbary wild boar, crested porcupines, golden jackals and small, spotted, cat-like animals called genets.

> 🖼 GREAT VIEW
> ## Mountainous Heights
>
> Beyond the Bab Taka mountain pass, a narrow track leads over 9 km (5.5 miles) to the summit of Jbel Tazekka. From the peak there is a fine view north over the Rif's mountains, west over the plain of Fès and south to the higher foothills of the Middle Atlas and the snowy peaks of Jbel Boulblanc.

↑ Visitors descending into the Gouffre de Friouato caves

Did You Know?

The stunning
Ras el-Oued waterfalls
only flow between
November and April.

↑ The rushing waterfalls and green
riverbanks *(inset)* in spring,
Tazekka National Park

EXPERIENCE MORE

3

Taza

⚠E2 🚉From Oujda, Fès and Meknès 🚌From Nador, Al-Hoceima, Fès and Oujda
ℹ56 Avenue Mohammed V

Located on the route between Fès and Oujda, in the lower foothills of the Rif and the Middle Atlas, the town of Taza is a stopping place that seldom figures on the tourist route. It is, however, one of the oldest towns in Morocco.

Taza was founded in the 8th century by the Meknassa, a Berber tribe, and was regularly seized by sultans who wished to establish their authority

500

The approximate number of caves dotting the landscape around the village of Bhalil.

before going on to take Fès. The old town, built on a rocky hill, overlooks the new town below, which the French began to build in 1920. The walls surrounding the medina date mostly from the 12th century. Moulay Ismaïl, of the Alaouite dynasty, embellished the town and heightened its role as a military stronghold on the eastern frontier.

The Andalusian Mosque stands at the entrance to the medina, from where the main street runs through to the Grand Mosque. Founded by the Almohad sultan Abd el-Moumen in 1135, it is one of the oldest mosques in Morocco. It is closed to non-Muslims, who will have to settle with imagining the interior of the magnificent pierced dome and the fine bronze candelabrum.

There is a lively souk in the medina, as well as an unusually wide minaret. Bab er-Rih, in the north of the town, offers a splendid view of the orchards and olive trees below, the hills of the Rif and the slopes of Jbel Tazzeka.

4

Bhalil

⚠D2 🚌6 km (4 miles) northwest of Sefrou

Set on the side of a hill, the village of Bhalil is notable for its hundreds of unique cave houses, the majority of which are used for the storage of cattlefeed. Some of the caves, however, have been converted into comfortable homes for the local population. They stay relatively cool in summer and keep out the worst of the cold in winter. The caves are often used as salons, with bedrooms and bathrooms built adjacently or above in the conventional fashion, and fronted by a regular façade, so it is not obvious at first glance which of the houses are built around caves and which are not. However, visitors are usually approached on arrival by a local guide, who will offer a tour of the village for a small fee. There is a small, four-room guesthouse in the village where you can stay overnight.

↑ A small village Mosque nestled among the rolling hills of the Middle Atlas

5

Gouffre du Friouato

🅰E2 🅰22 km (13.5 miles) southwest of Taza

This natural chasm, which was first explored in 1934, is open to visitors, although sturdy walking boots are necessary. A flight of 500 slippery steps leads down to the cave. It contains galleries and halls filled with stalactites, stalagmites and other formations. The adjacent Chiker Caves are open only to speleologists.

6

Sefrou

🅰D2 🚌From Fès and Midelt

This ancient town has always stood in the shadow of Fès, the imperial capital. It takes its name from the Ahel Sefrou, a Berber tribe that converted to Judaism 2,000 years ago and was then Islamicized by Idriss I in the 8th century. In the 12th century, trade with the Sahara brought Sefrou prosperity. A century later, it became home to a large colony of Jews who had fled from the Tafilalt and southern Algeria. In 1950, a third of Sefrou's population was Jewish, but the majority of Jews emigrated to Israel in 1967, and the town is now mostly Muslim.

The town is bisected by Wadi Aggaï, which irrigates the surrounding fertile plain. Four bridges link the two parts of the town. South of the *wadi* is the mellah, the former Jewish quarter, a district of narrow winding streets. North of the *wadi* is the old medina, with its souks centred around the Grand Mosque and the *zaouia* of Sidi Lahcen Lyoussi, who became patron saint of Sefrou in the 18th century. On the north side of the town, just outside the ramparts, is a crafts centre where leather goods, pottery and wrought-iron items are made.

The road following the river west of Sefrou leads to the Kef el-Moumen Caves, a series of natural caves in the cliff face containing tombs that are venerated by both Muslims and Jews. One of them is said to be that of the prophet Daniel. The Wadi Aggaï Falls here bring a welcome freshness to the surrounding hills.

The green-roofed Koubba of Sidi bou Ali Serghine, to the west of town, offers a scenic view over Sefrou and the hills of Kandar. Nearby is the miraculous spring of Lalla Rekia, which is reputed to cure mental illness.

A minor road east of Sefrou leads to the small town of El-Menzel. The kasbah here overlooks the Sebou Gorge, which has impressively sheer cliffs.

↑ Relaxing in the walled *mellah* of Sefrou, a town steeped in Jewish history

7

Imouzzer du Kandar

🅰D2

The small hillside town of Imouzzer du Kandar overlooks the Saïss plain, which abuts the plateaux of the Middle Atlas. The dilapidated kasbah of the Aït Serchouchène, where the souk takes place, contains cave dwellings, of which the region has many. The caves were dug into the hillside and protected Berbers from enemy attacks. Some are still inhabited. The openings – no more than a small door and a few ventilation holes – are small to keep out the cold, and the spartan interiors have neither water nor electricity.

> 💬 INSIDER TIP
> ## Cherry Festival
>
> This celebration takes place at the end of the June cherry harvest. A colourful procession culminates in the coronation of the Cherry Queen, selected during a pageant that draws competitors from the across the country.

↑ The Middle Atlas mountains surrounding the regional market town of Azrou

❽ Ifrane

D2 **63 km (39 miles) south of Fès on road N8**
From Fès and Azrou
Avenue Mohammed V; (0535) 56 68 21

Established in 1929 during the Protectorate, Ifrane is a small town with more of a European than a Moroccan character. It is cool even in summer and may be snow-bound from December to March. On the descent into the valley, a green-roofed palace, the King's summer residence, comes into view. Al-Akhawaya University, inaugurated by Hassan II in 1995, has contributed considerably to the town's development.

Ifrane serves as the departure point for many tours, including a trip to the waterfalls known as the Cascades des Vierges, within the Ifrane National Park, 3 km (2 miles) west (follow the signs to Source Vittel), and north to the *zaouia* of Ifrane, which is surrounded by caves and *koubbas*.

Road R707 out of Ifrane, going up to the Tizi-n-Tretten Pass, leads to the Forêt de Cèdres. After running along the Mischliffen and Jbel Hebri, it reaches a legendary 900-year-old cedar, the Cèdre Gouraud.

❾ Azrou

D2 **48 km (30 miles) south of Ifrane on road N8**
From Meknès, Fès, Marrakech and Er-Rachidia
Ifrane; (0535) 566821

A large outcrop of volcanic rock at the entrance to the town gave Azrou (meaning "rock" in Berber) its name. Located at the crossroads of routes linking Meknès and Erfoud, and Fès and Marrakech, the town nestles in the centre of a geological basin, with Jbel Hebri to the southeast. It is circled by a dense belt of cedar and holm oak, where the Beni M'Gild, the most prominent Berber tribe in the region, came to spend their summers. These nomadic pastoralists decided to stay and founded the town.

Azrou is still a regional market town, with a large weekly souk. At the crafts centre items made of cedar, thuya, walnut and juniper are on sale, as are wrought-iron objects and the renowned carpets

made by the Beni M'Gild. During the Protectorate the town became a health resort, and highly reputed treatment centres are still found here. It is also the departure point for tours of the cedar forests and plateaux. The nearby lakes offer trout, pike and roach fishing (permits compulsory).

North of Azrou, the road to El-Hajeb runs along the edge of the Balcon d'Ito plateaux, offering good views of the "lunar" landscape. The Berber hill village of Aïn Leuh, 32 km

→ A visitor standing on a bridge at the waterfalls in Ifrane National Park

(20 miles) south of Azrou, hosts the Middle Atlas Arts Festival in July. There is a souk on Mondays and Thursdays.

10

Aguelmane Azigza

🅐D3 🄿12 km (7.5 miles) south of the sources of the Oum er-Rbia

The rivers whose sources lie in the heart of the Middle Atlas have formed lakes in the craters of extinct volcanoes. One such is Aguelmane Azigza. It is enclosed by cliffs and forests of cedar and holm oak and contains plenty of fish.

11

Aguelmane Sidi Ali

🅐X9 🄿Junction with N13

A right turn off road N13 from Azrou to Midelt leads you to Aguelmane Sidi Ali, a deep, fish-filled lake 3 km (2 miles) long and at high altitude. With Jbel Hayane rising above, it is surrounded by rugged hills and desolate pasture where the Beni M'Gild's flocks are brought for summer grazing. Continuing towards Midelt,

THE LIONS OF THE ATLAS

Before World War I, the roaring of lions in the Moroccan Atlas could be heard at dusk and during the night. Sadly, the last of the Atlas lions was killed in 1922. During the Roman period, lions were plentiful in North Africa. They flourished in Tunisia until the 17th century, although by 1891 not one remained. In Algeria, the last lion was killed in 1893. The lions of the Atlas were large, with a thick mane that was very dark or almost black. Because the genetic make-up of the Atlas lion is known, it should be possible to bring this extinct sub-species back to life. With this end in view, a breeding programme is under way, using lions bred in zoos and conservation areas, most particularly the zoo in Rabat.

the road climbs up to the Zad Pass, the highest in the Middle Atlas at 2,178 m (7,148 ft).

12

Mischliffen

🅐D2

A shallow bowl surrounded by cedar forests, Mischliffen is the crater of an extinct volcano. The villages here are out-numbered by the tents of the shepherds who bring their flocks for summer grazing. A winter sports resort (also called Mischliffen) has been set up among the trees. However, the facilites, which consist of just two ski lifts, are quite basic.

13

Sources of the Oum er-Rbia

🅐X9 🄿160 km (99 miles) from Fès and from Beni Mellal; note there are no hotels or petrol stations on road N8 between Azrou and Khenifra

A winding road runs above the valley of the Oum er-Rbia, then leads down to the *wadi* at the bottom of the valley. The river's sources – more than 40 springs that can be explored via footpath – form cascades that crash down the limestone cliffs, joining to form the Oum er-Rbia, the longest river in Morocco.

THE MOUNTAINS OF MOROCCO

With the Rif rising dramatically on the northern coast, the Middle Atlas and the High Atlas dominating the interior, and the lesser-known Anti-Atlas to the south, Morocco is a land dominated by mountains. In sharp contrast to the arid deserts and sunbaked valleys so often associated with Morocco's terrain, lush forests and verdant slopes command the country's higher ground. The climate here is permanently moist, and the vegetation particularly luxuriant, making it an ideal home for an abundance of wildlife, including a number of endemic plant and animal species.

HIKING IN THE HIGH ATLAS

Forming a barrier between the Mediterranean and Atlantic coastlines and the Sahara Desert, the soaring peaks of the High Atlas are by far the most breathtaking of Morocco's mountain ranges. Extending 2,500 km (1,600 miles) across the most northwesterly tip of the African continent, and rising to heights of 4,167 m (13,671 ft), the High Atlas are primarily inhabited by nomadic Berber populations. What's more, this spectacular mountain range, cut off from the chaotic clammer of city life, is surprisingly accessible from Marrakech. Many tour operators offer day trips or multi-day hikes with a guide, during which you will be able to see a wealth of wildlife. Popular routes include Jbel Toubkal Massif, North Africa's tallest peak *(p274)*. The summit can be reached in two days and climbing it does not require a high level of experience as a mountaineer. The only disadvantage is that this is where most hikers come in the high season, so you will not be alone. In the central High Atlas, the Ait Bouguemez Valley *(p264)* offers some fine trails. Starting from Demnate, the route is not particularly demanding and passes through a striking variety of landscapes, from lush valleys to precipitous peaks.

↑ The Tessaout valley, considered one of the most beautiful in the central High Atlas

↑ Forests of Atlas cedar are impressive for their sheer size, and the trees for their beauty and their height, which can exceed 50 m (164 ft)

Aleppo pine can grow to a height of 25 m (82 ft).

The carob produces sugar-rich pods that are a nutritious food for both humans and animals.

Argan

Kermes oak

MOUNTAIN FLORA AND FAUNA

Aleppo pine, carob, holme oak, and forests of Atlas cedar thrive on well watered slopes. The Barbary sheep, Africa's only wild sheep, inhabits the High and Middle Atlas. It can be seen in Jbel Toubkal National Park, which was created especially to ensure its survival. The Barbary stag was reintroduced in 1990. Three-quarters of the country's population of macaques live in the cedar forests of the Middle Atlas. Birdlife is plentiful, and includes the golden eagle, Moussier's redstart and the rare crimson-winged finch, which only nests at altitudes above 2,800 m (9,190 ft). Conservation efforts are underway in both Mediterranean and Saharan ecoregions to preserve Morocco's rich botanical diversity.

1 The Barbary sheep is threatened by poaching and competition from domestic stock.

2 Aleppo pine trees thrive on the steep mountain slopes.

3 Barbary macaques live in family groups in the High Atlas mountains.

→

Illustration depicting the varying terrain of Morocco's High Atlas mountain slopes

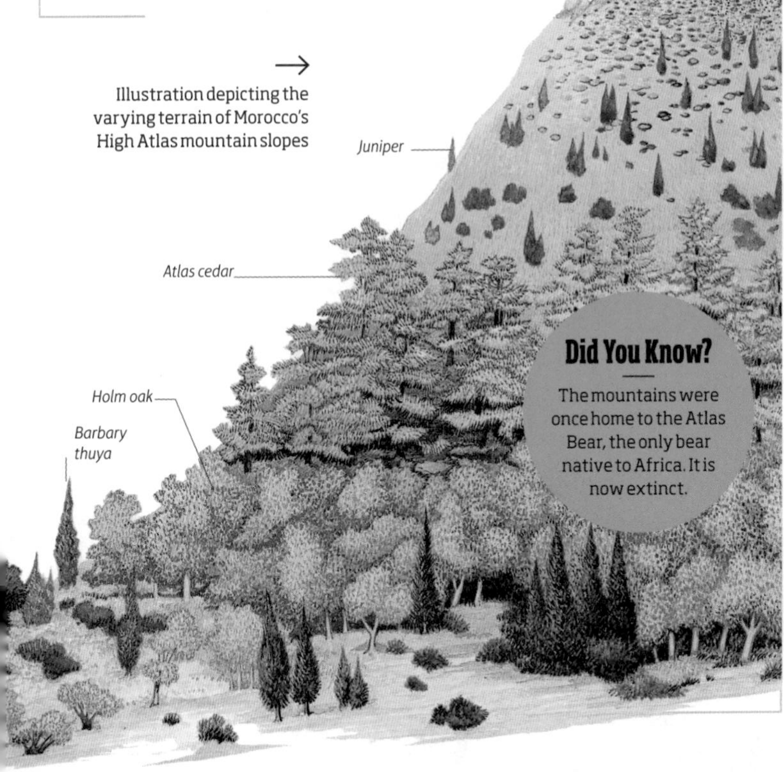

Juniper

Atlas cedar

Holm oak

Barbary thuya

Did You Know?

The mountains were once home to the Atlas Bear, the only bear native to Africa. It is now extinct.

14 Khenifra

D3 **160 km (99 miles) from Fès; 130 km (81 miles) from Beni Mellal** **From Fès and Marrakech**

In the folds of the arid hills and on the banks of the Oum er-Rbia stand houses painted in carmine red. Until the 17th century, Khenifra was the rallying point of the Zaïane tribe, which resisted French attempts to pacify the region. In the 18th century Moulay Ismaïl asserted his authority by building imposing kasbahs here. The livestock market is now one of the town's few interesting aspects.

The village of El-Kebab clings to a hillside 35 km (22 miles) southeast of Khenifra. Here craftsmen make pottery and carpets. Above the village is the hermitage where Albert Peyriguère, a doctor and companion to the French ascetic Charles de Foucauld, lived. A souk is held on Mondays.

15 Beni Mellal

D3 **30 km (18.5 miles) southwest of Kasba Tadla on road N8** **From Khenifra, Marrakech and Demnate** **Avenue Hassan II; (0523) 48 78 29 or (0529) 80 24 79**

The modern town of Beni Mellal lies at the foot of the Middle Atlas, on the edge of the great Tadla plain. Although it is devoid of any obvious appeal, it is still a convenient stopping place.

Inhabited by Berbers and Jews well before the arrival of Islam, the town was known successively as Day, Kasba Belkouche and Beni Mellal. In the 13th century, it stood on the border between Fès and Marrakech, which were the subjects of bitter dispute between the Merinid and Almohad dynasties.

The town is surrounded by orange groves (oranges from Beni Mellal are renowned),

GREAT VIEW
Ras el-Aïn

South of Beni Mellal, a road marked "Circuit touristique" leads to the Aïn Asserdoun springs. Make the short detour to Ras el-Aïn further up, where a stone-and-pisé tower offers a picturesque view of Beni Mellal and its orchards.

and olive groves stretch to the horizon. Beetroot and sugarcane have replaced bananas as cultivated crops. All are unusually well watered thanks to the Bin el-Ouidane dam.

The area around Beni Mellal has many waterfalls, springs, caves and wooded gorges populated by monkeys. About 10 km (6 miles) east, a road leads to Foum el-Anser, where a waterfall crashes into a gorge. The rockface here is marked by artificial caves, access to which is difficult. South of Beni Mellal, a hillside track leads up to Jbel Tassemit, which is the departure point for scenic mountain hikes. Hikers can also reach the Tarhzirte Gorge and the Wadi Derna valley, 20 km (12 miles) northeast of Beni Mellal.

16 Bin el-Ouidane Dam

C3 **43 km (27 miles) southwest of Beni Mellal on road N8, branching left on road R304**

From Beni Mellal the road climbs through wooded hills to reach the grandiose site of an artificial lake, the Bin el-Ouidane reservoir, the largest lake in Morocco. Fed by Wadi el-Abid and Wadi Ahansalt, it irrigates the intensively

← Waterfalls marking one of the sources of the Oum er-Rbia in the Khenifra hills

←

Cacti growing on the red hills surrounding the Ben el-Ouidane reservoir

cultivated Tadla plain, while the hydroelectric generator provides a quarter of Morocco's electricity. The turquoise waters of the lake, which are broken by spits of land and small islands, are surrounded by red hills, and the lakeshore is dotted with isolated houses.

Watersports and fishing are permitted, and Wadi el-Abid is suitable for kayaking and rafting in spring, when the water level is sufficiently high. A track leading from the lake ends at a rock formation known as La Cathédrale. This rock, with a covering of red soil and a setting among Aleppo pines, is well known to abseilers.

From here, Azilal and the Aït Bouguemez valley (p264) can be reached on road R304.

17

Boujad

D3 **24 km (15 miles) north of Kasba Tadla on road R312**

The holy town of Boujad, which is filled with *koubbas* (tombs) and shrines, is set in the Tadla plain, on the caravan route that once ran between Marrakech and Fès. It was established in the 16th century by Sidi Mohammed ech-Cherki, patron saint of Tadla, who built an important *zaouia* here. The saint and his descendants have always been highly venerated by the Beni Meskin and Seguibat, local Berber tribespeople. Resentful of this power, sultan Sidi Mohammed ben Abdallah razed the town in 1785. The *zaouia* was rebuilt in the 19th century and still houses the saint's descendants.

The tombs of the saintly dynasty can be seen around the market square in the north of the town. The largest, the Koubba of Sidi Othman, is open to visitors. There are many other mausoleums here, most notably that of the sheik Mohammed ech-Cherki, which is closed to non-Muslims.

On a promontory outside Boujad, in the direction of Oued Zem on the northern side of the town, stand five white *koubbas*, to which crowds of pilgrims come for annual gatherings.

18

Kasba Tadla

D3 **82 km (51 miles) southwest of Khenifra on road N8** **From Beni Mellal and Khenifra** **Beni Mellal**

The focal point of this former garrison town is, predictably, the kasbah, built by Moulay Ismaïl in the 17th century. So as to subdue rebellious tribes, he made his son governor of the province. The latter built a second kasbah. A double line of walls thus surrounds the town, enclosing two dilapidated mosques and the former governor's palace. Below the town, a 10-span bridge crosses Wadi Oum er-Rbia.

Plantations of olive trees cover the plain between Kasba Tadla and Khenifra, and many olive mills line the road at Tirhboula, 10 km (6 miles) from Khenifra. In the autumn, visitors can see the various stages in the oil-producing process and buy olive oil here.

El-Ksiba is an attractive village on the edge of the forest 22 km (13.5 miles) east of Kasba Tadla. It has a souk, which is very busy on Sundays. Beyond El-Ksiba, the road crosses the High Atlas via Imilchil, descending to Tinerhir in the south.

OLIVE OIL

In autumn, green, black and violet olives are harvested. A heavy grindstone turned by donkeys grinds them, and the resulting pulp is emptied into large porous containerss beneath the press. The oil seeps out and runs into vats, where, mixed with water, it floats to the surface, free of debris.

A DRIVING TOUR
INLAND LAKES

Length 60 km (37 miles) **Departure point** The town of Dayet Aoua, 6 km (10 miles) north of Ifrane on the N8, forking left to visit the lake of the same name

Three attractive lakes – Dayet Aoua, Dayet Ifrah and Dayet Hachlaf – lie 9 km (6.5 miles) south of Imouzzer du Kandar. A turning off road N8 leads to Dayet Aoua, which formed in a natural depression. The narrow road running along it leads to Dayet Ifrah, surrounded by a cirque of mountains, and on to Dayet Hachlaf. Beyond a forestry hut, a track on the right leads to the Vallée des Roches.

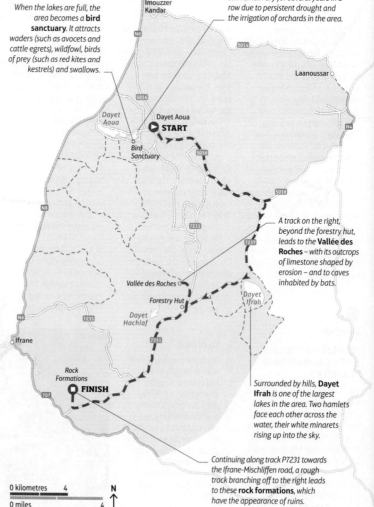

Dayet Aoua *lake sits in a natural depression surrounded by hills. It can remain dry for several years in a row due to persistent drought and the irrigation of orchards in the area.*

*When the lakes are full, the area becomes a **bird sanctuary**. It attracts waders (such as avocets and cattle egrets), wildfowl, birds of prey (such as red kites and kestrels) and swallows.*

Imouzzer Kandar

Laanoussar

Dayet Aoua

Dayet Aoua
START

Bird Sanctuary

*A track on the right, beyond the forestry hut, leads to the **Vallée des Roches** – with its outcrops of limestone shaped by erosion – and to caves inhabited by bats.*

Vallée des Roches

Forestry Hut

Dayet Hachlaf

Dayet Ifrah

Ifrane

Rock Formations
FINISH

*Surrounded by hills, **Dayet Ifrah** is one of the largest lakes in the area. Two hamlets face each other across the water, their white minarets rising up into the sky.*

*Continuing along track P7231 towards the Ifrane-Mischliffen road, a rough track branching off to the right leads to these **rock formations**, which have the appearance of ruins.*

0 kilometres 4
0 miles 4

N ↑

Canyon landscape in the
High Atlas; hikers by the
Dayet Aoua lake *(inset)*

MARRAKECH

Marrakech was founded in 1062 by Almoravids from the Sahara. These warrior monks soon carved out an empire that stretched from Algiers to Spain. In 1106, Ali ben Youssef hired craftsmen from Andalusia to build a palace and a mosque in the capital. He also raised ramparts around the city and installed *khettaras* (underground canals), creating an ingenious irrigation system that brought water to its great palm grove.

The Almohads took the city in 1147. Under their reign the Koutoubia, a masterpiece of Moorish architecture, and the kasbah were built. The Almohad dynasty collapsed, to the benefit of the Merinids of Fès, and for over 200 years Marrakech stagnated. It was not until the 16th century that the city was reinvigorated by the arrival of the Saadians, most notably by the wealthy Ahmed el-Mansour. The Saadian Tombs, the Ben Youssef Medersa and the remains of the Palais el-Badi mark this golden age. In 1668, Marrakech fell to the Alaouites, who made Fès, then Meknès, their capital.

However, with a population approaching a million, Marrakech remains the capital of the south of Morocco and, although it is now only Morocco's fourth city after Casablanca, Fès and Rabat, its fabulous palaces and luxuriant palm still hold a powerful fascination for visitors.

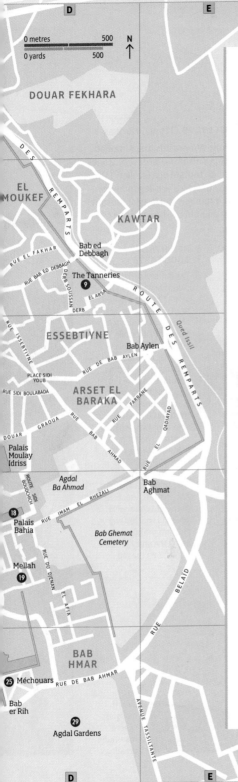

MARRAKECH

Must Sees

1. Koutoubia Mosque
2. Jemaa el-Fna
3. The Souks
4. Ben Youssef Medersa
5. Majorelle Garden

Experience More

6. Zaouia of Sidi bel Abbès
7. Zaouia of Sidi ben Slimane el-Jazouli
8. Chrob ou Chouf Fountain
9. The Tanneries
10. Jardin Secret
11. Musée de Marrakech
12. Dar Bellaj
13. Maison de la Photographie
14. Bab Doukkala Mosque
15. Mouassine Quarter
16. Koubba Ba'Adiyn
17. Dar Si Saïd Museum
18. Palais Bahia
19. Mellah
20. Palais el-Badi
21. Bab Agnaou
22. The Kasbah
23. Saadian Tombs
24. Dar el-Makhzen
25. Méchouars
26. Guéliz
27. Musée d'Art et de Culture de Marrakech (MACMA)
28. La Palmeraie
29. Agdal Gardens
30. Ménara

Eat

1. Night Market Food Stalls
2. Bakchich Café
3. Al Fassia
4. Nomad

Drink

5. Café de Épices

Stay

6. Dar Attajmil
7. Riad Berbere
8. La Mamounia

❶
KOUTOUBIA MOSQUE

📍B3 **🏠Place de la Koutoubia** **📞(0524) 43 61 31/79** **🚫To non-Muslims**

In about 1147, to mark his victory over the Almoravids, the Almohad sultan Abd el-Moumen set about building one of the largest mosques in the Western Muslim world. It was built on the site of a levelled 11th-century mosque, whose misalignment with Mecca – as legend goes – displeased the pious Almohads. Today it remains the largest mosque in Marrakech, an eye-catching meeting point in the heart of the city.

The "Booksellers' Mosque" takes its name from the manuscripts souk that once took place around it. Its exterior has been restored to reveal the original pink colour of the brick-work, which is made from splendid Guéliz stone. Inside, the prayer hall can accommodate some 20,000 faithful.

The Koutoubia's minaret, a masterpiece of Islamic architecture, was completed during the reign of Yacoub el-Mansour, grandson of Abd el-Moumen. Each side of the tower has a different decorative scheme, although all are adorned with flower motifs, arched windows and inscriptions. It later served as the model for the Giralda in Seville, and for the Hassan Tower in Rabat *(p84)*. The tower's interior contains a ramp used to carry building materials up to the summit.

←

The minaret's arched windows, surrounded by flower motifs

> ## HEIGHTS OF GOOD TASTE
>
> The Koutoubia minaret's continued dominion over the skyline is owed to an enlightened piece of legislation imposed by the city's former French colonial rulers. They decreed that no building in the Medina should rise above the height of a palm tree, and that no building in the New City should rise above the height of the minaret. The ruling still holds today; the tower stands 70 m (230 ft) high, in proportions that obey the canons of Almohad architecture (its height equals five times its width). Only Muslims are allowed to enjoy the unforgettable views from the top.

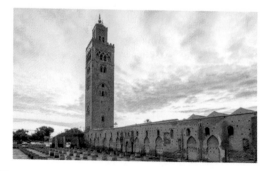

←

Sun setting over the mosque's spectacular rose-hued buildings

INSIDER TIP
Sneak Peek

Although access to the mosque is denied to non-Muslims, one of the doors on the east wall is often open, so visitors can peer through for a view of the prayer hall and its seemingly endless arcades of horseshoe arches.

↑ The minaret of Koutoubia Mosque, towering above the bustle of central Marrakech

235

2

JEMAA EL-FNA

C3 **East of Guéliz (off Avenue Mohammed V)**

For centuries, this unique and extraordinary square has been the nerve centre of Marrakech, its frenetic energy a symbol of the city, and its nightly events and storytellers a showcase of traditional Morocco.

Declared a UNESCO World Heritage Site in 2001, this lively square has a gruesome past: until the 19th century, criminals on whom the death sentence had been passed were beheaded here. Sometimes up to 45 people were executed on a single day, their heads pickled and suspended from the city gates.

No trace of this is left today, however. A market is held in the mornings, where medicinal plants, freshly squeezed orange juice and all kinds of nuts and confectionery are sold. From sunset, the life and bustle on the square reaches its peak. It becomes the arena of a gigantic, multifaceted open-air show. As the air fills with smoke from grilling meat and the aroma of spices, the square throngs with musicians, dancers and storytellers who draw in crowds of astonished onlookers.

EAT

Night Market Food Stalls

Every visitor to Marrakech should venture to the square at night to experience the unmissable chaos and clammer of the night market. Vendors jostle for your custom, but in reality all offer the same dishes of freshly grilled meats, fish, vegetables and local delicacies.

Jemaa el-Fna

Jemaa el-Fna, as viewed from one of the terraced restaurants surrounding the square ↑

1. Gnaoua musicians and dancers perform for onlookers at Jemaa el-Fna.

2. Locals and visitors descend on the square every evening to enjoy traditional Moroccan cuisine and experience the infectious energy of the night market.

3. These colourful leather slippers, known as *babouches*, are worn all over Morocco and can be picked up in any souk. Yellow is the traditional colour, but other colours and more elaborate designs are also available.

MARRAKECH'S ORAL TRADITION

Professional storytellers, or *halakat*, have been enchanting spectators on Jemaa el-Fna since the city was founded. They recite ancient Moroccan folk tales to rapt crowds that pay a few coins for the experience. Traditionally these oral expressions combine speech and gesture to teach, entertain and charm the audience. Nowadays only a few still work the square, and they have adapted their art for a contemporary audience. Café Clock *(p253)* in the Kasbah is keeping the tradition alive with authentic storytelling sessions every Monday and Thursday.

3 🍴 ☕ 🛍️

THE SOUKS

📍 C3 🏛️ Place Jemaa el-Fna (via Rue du Souk Smarine or Bab Doukkala) 🚌 Or *petit taxi* as far as the entrance to the souks, which must be explored on foot ⏰ 9am–7pm daily 🚪 Noon–4pm Fri

Marrakech's earliest inhabitants made their living from trade. Luxuries like gold and ivory came from the south, while leather, metalwork and ceramics went north. Trade continues to be the city's mainstay, with thousands of craftsmen making a living in the maze that fills the northern half of the medina. A wide range of goods is on offer, leatherwork being particularly prominent. Around this commercial hub are crafts such as blacksmithing, saddle-making and basketry. The tanneries and their rank odours are banished to the edge of the city. A trip to the souks is part history lesson, part endurance trial, testing just how long you can keep your money in your pocket.

① Souk Semarine

Entered via an elaborate arch just north of Jemaa El Fna, Souk Semarine is broad and covered with wooden trellising that patterns the street with shadows. Traditionally, this street specialized in textiles, but these days the cloth and clothing merchants are outnumbered by those selling trinkets and souvenirs.

② Rabha Kedima

Meaning "the old place", Rahba Kedima is where country folk sell fruit, vegetables and live chickens. There are also sellers of raffia bags and baskets. Around the edges are spice and "magic" stalls, where healers buy their supplies. A small passageway on the northern side leads through to the Criée Berbère.

> 📷 PICTURE PERFECT
> **Souk des Teintures**
>
> In Souk des Teintures, brightly hued skeins of freshly dyed wool are hung out above the alley to dry in the sun, an irresistible shot for photographers.

③ Criée Berbère

Up until French occupation, well into the 20th century, this partially roofed section of the souk was used for the buying and selling of African slaves. Fortunately, these days only carpets are auctioned here, every afternoon at 3:30pm. At other times throughout the day, carpets and rugs can be bought the usual way from the dozens of shops filling the surrounding alleys, collectively known as the Souk des Tapis, or Carpet Market.

④ Souk el-Attarin

Branching off Souk Semarine, the street that bears the name the "Spice Market" no longer trades in pungent powders,

←

Strips of sunlight breaking through the covered passage that divides Souk Semarine

perfumes and oils as it did in the old days but instead it is brimming with sellers of lamps, trays, teapots and mirrors as well as peddlers of inexpensive souvnirs. One narrow side street is wholly devoted to the sale of the colourful soft-leather slippers known as *babouches*.

---

⑤
Kissaria

Strung in between Souk el-Attarin and Souk el-Kebir (the northern extension of Souk Semarine) is this network of parallel, impossibly narrow alleys with covered souks known as *kissaria*. This is the deep heart of the souks of Marrakech, where among the traditional vendors of fabric and leather goods you will also find some surprisingly high-end designer boutiques (with price labels that match) offering quality homeware items such as lanterns, glassware, Berber rugs and antiques, as well as fashion and accessories.

↑ An assortment of lanterns glowing in Souk Haddadin

⑥
Souk Haddadin

At the northern end of Souk Attarin, the sound of hammering announces Souk Haddadin, the ironworkers' quarter. In dark, cavern-like workshops, craftsmen hammer hot metal, shaping it into lanterns, ashtrays, platters and the like.

---

⑦
Souk des Teintures

On the western edge of the souks, is Souk des Teinturiers, an area of dyers' workshops. Labourers rub dyes into hides from the tanneries *(p245)* and dunk wool into vats of variously coloured liquids. Oddly though, you'll find no fabric shops here, instead the area is populated with specialists in lanterns and ceramics.

NAVIGATING THE SOUKS

You will get lost in the souks. The alleys are narrow, winding and constantly branching, while landmarks are few. However, the area is relatively small and you're never more than a few minutes' walk back to Jemaa el-Fna. As such, a guide is not especially necessary. Any places you may be lead to are often only "the best" because they offer your guide the highest commission. Watch out for the constant stream of scooters and bicycles in the narrow lanes.

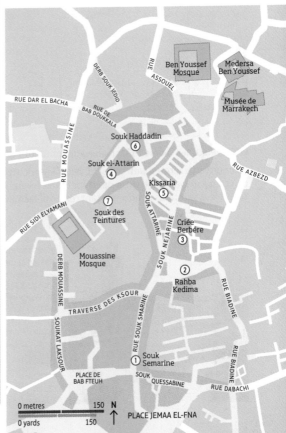

Did You Know?

Occupying 130 tiny rooms above the central courtyard, nearly 900 students studied here at any one time.

4

BEN YOUSSEF MEDERSA

📍 C2 🏠 Place Ben Yousseff 🕐 For renovation until 2019 🌐 medersa-ben-youssef.com

Elaborately decorated with colourful *zellij* tilework, stucco archways and intricately carved plasterwork, the sheer opulence of this former Islamic school is testament to its elevated status as an important centre of learning and religion.

This Koranic school is not only one of the finest but also one of the largest in the Maghreb. It was founded by the Merinid sultan Abou el-Hassan in the mid-14th century, and rebuilt by the Saadian sultan Moulay Abdallah in the 16th century. The *medersa* takes its name from the Almoravid mosque of Ali ibn Youssef to which it was once attached. For four centuries this mosque was the focal point of worship in the medina, and with the *medersa* it constituted an important centre of religion.

←

Green-tiled roof and minaret of Ben Youssef Mosque and Medersa

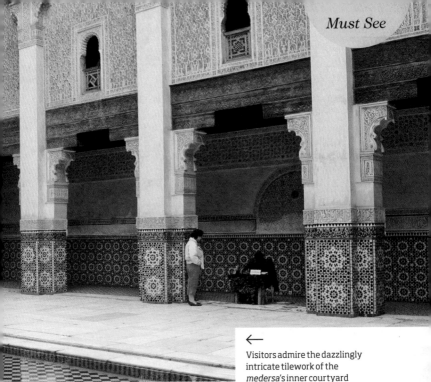

← Visitors admire the dazzlingly intricate tilework of the *medersa*'s inner courtyard

> **For four centuries this mosque was the focal point of worship in the medina, and with the *medersa* it constituted an important centre of religion.**

→ Study materials on display in one of the basic student cells that surround the courtyard

A masterpiece of Moorish design, this harmoniously proportioned *medersa* appears as it was originally intended, with no later alteration. The dome, decorated with exquisite stalactites, can be seen from the street. The main entrance, a bronze door topped by a carved cedar lintel, opens onto a mosaic-paved corridor, which in turn leads to an opulent courtyard complete with an ablutions pool. The walls are decorated with intricate *zellij* tilework and carved plaster. A magnificently ornate wooden doorway leads through to the large prayer hall, which is crowned by a pyramidal cedar dome and divided into three by marble columns The *mihrab* is decorated with verses from the Koran.

THE SAADIANS: MARRAKECH'S GOLDEN AGE OF ARCHITECTURE

The Saadians were a tribe from the Draa valley who dethroned the Merenids of Fès and made Marrakech their royal city. They established strong trading links with Europe and used the wealth they accrued to turn Marrakech into one of the most opulent cities in the Arab world. They rebuilt the city's Ali Ben Youssef Mosque and a *medersa* of the same name, and they created the lavish royal complex known as the Palais el-Badi *(p252)*.

5

MAJORELLE GARDEN

A5 ⌂ Avenue Yacoub el-Mansour (near the bus station) ⏰ Summer: 8am–5pm daily; winter: 8am–5:30pm daily 🖥 jardinmajorelle.com

The most famous of Marrakech's numerous gardens is a small paradise in the heart of the Ville Nouvelle. It is the legacy of expatriate French painter and self-proclaimed "gardenist" Jacques Majorelle, who created a beautiful botanical sanctuary to surround his studio.

In 1923, Jacques Majorelle fell in love with Morocco and in Marrakech he built himself a splendid Moorish villa, around which he laid out a luxuriant garden and Art Deco studio with pergolas and deep blue walls. After Majorelle's death, the property sadly fell into a state of disrepair.

Bought by the famous couturier Yves Saint-Laurent in 1980 and skilfully restored, the garden is divided by four walkways that cross each other to create parterres of brightly coloured tropical flowers. Besides yucca, bougainvillea, bamboo, laurel, geraniums, hibiscus and cypresses, it is home to over 400 varieties of palm tree and 1,800 species of cactus. Majorelle's studio has since been converted into a small museum, where more than 600 items illustrate aspects of traditional Berber culture. It also boasts a selection of Moroccan crafts such as antique carpets, Fassi ceramics, Berber doors, and engravings of Atlas villages and kasbahs by Jacques Majorelle himself.

Situated just next door to the gardens, the modern Musée Yves Saint Laurent displays some of the French couturier's best-known looks. There is also an arts centre and auditorium.

💬 INSIDER TIP
The Early Bird…

To avoid the crowds (and the stifling heat), plan to visit the garden early in the morning, when you will be able to enjoy the walkways and tranquil spaces as they were intended.

1 This fountain, surrounded by intricate mosaic tilework, is one of the many pleasant spots where visitors can sit and relax.

2 The iconic Art Deco Villa Majorelle, its walls painted in dazzling blues and bright yellow, is surrounded by towering cacti, palm trees and tropical flowers in full bloom.

3 Bordered by papyrus and home to various species of waterlily, a series of waterways runs through the garden, irrigating the land and nourishing the plants.

Did You Know?

The Majorelle name lives on in an electrifying shade of cobalt blue known as "Majorelle blue"

JACQUES MAJORELLE

The painter Jacques Majorelle was born in Nancy, in north-eastern France, in 1886. The son of Louis Majorelle, one of the leading figures of the École de Nancy, he was raised in the artistic milieu of Art Nouveau. After studying at the École des Beaux-Arts in Paris, Majorelle devoted himself to painting. He visited Morocco in 1919 and fell in love with its intense light and decided to settle in Marrakech. Finding endless fascination in the souks, kasbahs and villages of the High Atlas, he stayed in Morocco until his death in 1962.

←

The lush Majorelle Garden is home to a diverse array of plant life

EXPERIENCE MORE

6

Zaouia of Sidi bel Abbès

B1 Sidi bel Abbès quarter (north of the medina) To non-Muslims

From Bab el-Khemis, Rue Sidi Rhalem leads to the Zaouia of Sidi bel Abbès. The sanctuary is a focal point for the pilgrimage of the Seven Saints of Regraga, which was instituted by Moulay Ismaïl to obtain forgiveness for his depredations in Marrakech.

Sidi bel Abbès (1130–1205) is the city's most highly venerated patron saint. A disciple of the famous Cadi Ayad, he devoted his life to preaching and to caring for and defending the weak and the blind. Because of him, it was said throughout Morocco that Marrakech was the only city where a blind man could eat his fill.

In 1605, the Saadian sultan Abou Faris raised a mausoleum for the saint in the hope of curing his epilepsy. Moulay Ismaïl added a dome in the 18th century, and the mausoleum was altered again by Sidi Mohammed ben Abdallah a few years later.

The *zaouia* also includes a mosque, a hammam, a home for the blind, a small market, an abattoir and a cemetery. South of the *zaouia* is the El-Mjadlia (Passementerie) Souk, built in a covered alley during the reign of Sidi Mohammed ben Abderrahman, at the end of the 19th century. Going from here towards the centre of the medina, you will pass Bab Taghzout, an Almoravid gate that has been integrated into its surroundings.

7

Zaouia of Sidi ben Slimane el-Jazouli

B2 North of the medina (near Rue Dar el-Glaoui) To non-Muslims

After Bab Taghzout, if you follow Rue de Bab Taghzout, then take the first right, and then go right again, you will reach this *zaouia*, which also features in the Regraga pilgrimage. The mausoleum dates from the Saadian period and was remodelled in the late 18th century during the reign of Sidi Mohammed ben Abdallah.

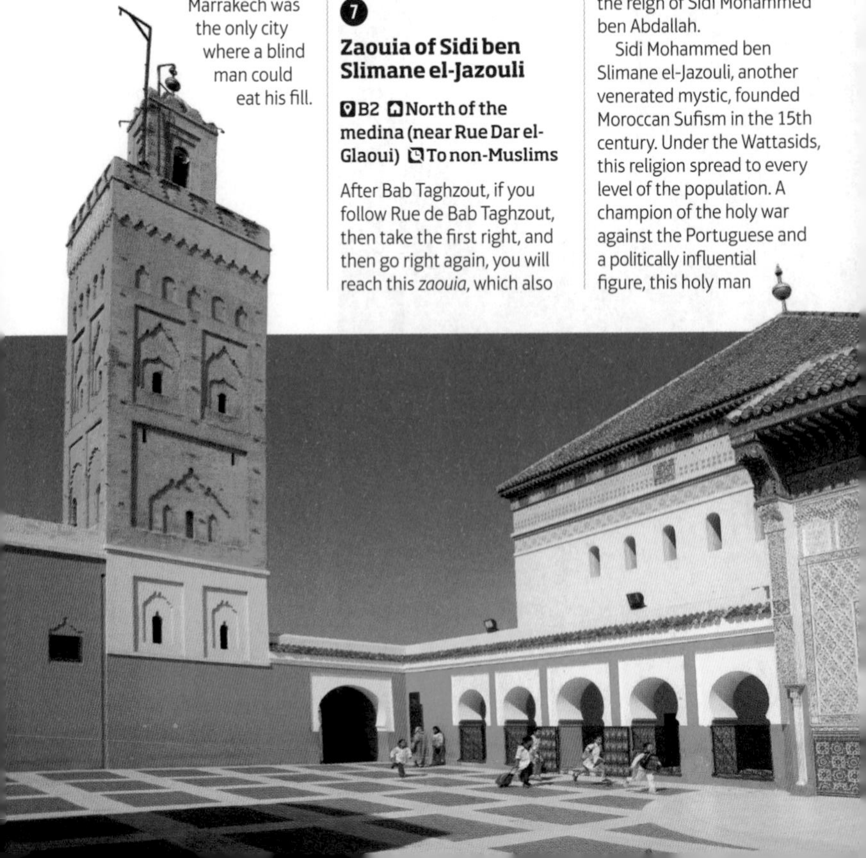

Sidi Mohammed ben Slimane el-Jazouli, another venerated mystic, founded Moroccan Sufism in the 15th century. Under the Wattasids, this religion spread to every level of the population. A champion of the holy war against the Portuguese and a politically influential figure, this holy man

DRINK

Café des Épices

This multi-floor caffeine pitstop is the perfect place to sit back and watch the world go by. A roof terrace overlooks the busy souk below.

C3 75 Derb Rahba Lakdima
cafedesepices.ma

gained thousands of devoted followers; his reputed powers even worried the sultan.

8
Chrob ou Chouf Fountain

◘ C2 ◪ Rue Amesfah, near the Mosque of Ben Youssef

As its name suggests (the Andalusian inscription on the lintel overhead translates as "Drink and Admire"), this Saadian fountain is one of the most beautiful in the medina. Declared a UNESCO World Heritage Site in 1985, it was built during the reign of Ahmed el-Mansour (1578–1603), and is shaded by a carved cedar awning with coloured *zellij* tilework and inscriptions in cursive and Kufic script exquisitely engraved into the wood.

In a town like Marrakech, located at the head of the pre-Saharan valleys, water was considered a very precious commodity. A complex underground network of channels, fed from sources in the Middle Atlas mountains, supplied the mosques and houses and kept the fountains flowing. Obeying the precepts of the Koran, according to which water must

be given to the thirsty, many of Marrakech's leading citizens financed the construction of fountains, which performed important social functions.

9
The Tanneries

◘ D2 ◪ Rue Bab Debagh, which is the eastern continuation of Rue du Souk des Fassis

The tanneries lie immediately south of Rue Bab Debagh. They are hidden from view of the street, but there is no mistaking the smell, which

↑ Young men working under the hot sun in the leather tanneries

intensifies on approach. You will easily find the alley that leads to the large yards filled with soaking and dyeing pits.

Though not as extensive as the tanneries of Fès, the tanneries of Marrakech are similarly ancient and have been on the same site since the city was founded, close to the Oued Issil river. As in Fès, you can observe the action at a distance from one of the terraces overlooking the yards. Owners of leather shops here sometimes kindly offer sprigs of mint to hold under your nose – you can accept without any obligation to make a purchase. Avoid the persistent self-appointed guides who haunt the area, as a guide is in no way necessary.

Rue Bab Debagh ends at Bab Debagh (Tanners' Gate), one of 19 gates that punctuate the salmon-pink *pisé* ramparts of the medina. It is the only gate to be named after a craft, demonstrating the historic importance of the leather trade to the city. A stairway gives access to the roof of the gatehouse. Unfortunately it is not possible to walk the tops of the city wall.

← The courtyard of the Zaouia of Sidi bel Abbès, and the intricately carved woodwork of the main entrance *(below)*

A chandelier dominating the inner courtyard of the Musée de Marrakech ↑

⑩
Jardin Secret

📍C3 🏠121 Rue Moussaine 🕐9:30am-7:30pm daily (Feb, Mar & Oct: to 6:30pm; Nov-Jan: to 6pm) 🌐lejardin secretmarrakech.com

Offering welcome respite from the chaotic clammer of the busy souks, this private garden was once part of an elegant palace complex that dates back almost 400 years. The original palace was destroyed at the end of the 17th century

---

GREAT VIEW
La Terrasse

For an extra 20-30Dh, visitors can climb to the top of the Jardin Secret's tower for a pleasant glimpse out accross the medina. The same view can be enjoyed for free from the sun terrace, where you can enjoy a refreshing mint tea, take photos and watch the world go by.

---

following the decline of the Saadian dynasty. It was then rebuilt in the mid-19th century by the *kaid* (local chief) Al-Hajj Abd-Allah U-Bihi, who insisted the layout should reflect that of the original Saadian era complex. Over the years, the palace changed hands many times, with ownership passing from chiefs to sultans to judges and even, at one point, to the head of the watchmakers' guild in Marrakech, before it once again fell into a state of severe disrepair. It wasn't until 2008 that a second restoration of the site was proposed.

Today, visitors can stroll through the palatial grounds, which boast fine examples of Islamic art and architecture alongside exotic and traditional Islamic gardens with numerous species of plantlife, browse the high-end gift shop and enjoy a light refreshment in the delightful Café Sahrij. A pretty pavillion is home to a permanent display on the fascinating history of the garden. It also hosts visiting photography and art exhibitions.

⑪
Musée de Marrakech

📍C2 🏠Place ben Youssef 📞(0524) 44 18 93 🕐9am-6:30pm daily

This museum is laid out in the Dar Menebhi, a palace built at the end of the 19th century by the grand vizier of Sultan Moulay Mehdi Hassan. The building is in the style of a traditional Moorish house.

The decorated door – which, as in many Moorish houses, is the only opening in the otherwise featureless external walls – leads through to an open courtyard with *zellij* tilework and three marble basins in the centre. The courtyard gives access to the rooms on the ground and upper floors.

The museum's collection is displayed in two wings. One contains contemporary art, Orientalist paintings and a series of original engravings of Moroccan subjects.

The second wing contains a rather haphazard display of objects: coins from the Idrissid period of the 9th century to

contemporary arts centre that hosts regular changing and usually quite fascinating themed exhibitions. It also has a varied programme of live concerts, storytelling sessions, song and dance, literary readings and theatre, as well as an attractive tearoom.

The name, Dar Bellarj, means "Stork's House", so called because it was formerly a hospital for the ubiquitous long-legged birds. Muslims in Morocco consider the stork sacred, and in old Berber legends they were thought to be humans that had been transformed into birds.

for example, have changed over the course of the last century. In addition to the historic photographs, the museum also presents temporary exhibitions dedicated to contemporary Moroccan photo art. On the upper floor, you can watch a colour documentary film from 1957, shot in Morocco, while another room has a small exhibition documenting the renovation of the riad itself. There is a ground-floor shop selling postcards and limited-edition prints and a delightful café on the rooftop terrace.

Did You Know?

The many holes in the city ramparts are there to support scaffolding during restoration work.

that of the Alaouites in the present day; illuminated copies of the Koran, including a 12th-century example from China and a 19th-century book of Sufi prayers; southern Moroccan jewellery; Tibetan dress; 17th- and 18th-century ceramics; and some fine decorated Berber doors.

12

Dar Bellarj

C2 7-9 Toualat Zaouiat Lahdar, Medina 9:30am-5:30pm Mon-Sat darbellarj.com

Just north of the main entrance to the Ben Youssef Medersa, this is a lively

13

Maison de la Photographie

C2 Rue du Souk des Fassi, Medina 9:30am-7pm daily maisondela photographie.ma

A renovated riad close to the Ben Youssef Medersa is the setting for this centre dedicated to the documentation of Morocco in photography. A museum of sorts, it holds an archive of more than 8,000 original images and documents (photographs, glass plates, postcards, newspapers and maps) dating from between 1870 and 1950, a selection of which is on permanent display. What becomes clear from perusing the images is how little parts of Marrakech,

↑ The upper and lower floors inside the Maison de la Photographie

⑭ Bab Doukkala Mosque

◉ B2 🏛 Rue de Bab Doukkala 🚫 To non-Muslims

This place of worship was built in the mid-16th century by the mother of the Saadian ruler Ahmed el-Mansour. Its slender minaret, crowned by four golden orbs, and its refined decoration are reminiscent of the Kasbah Mosque. Next to the building stands an ornate fountain featuring a bowl surmounted by three domes.

From here, Rue de Bab Doukkala, going towards the centre of the medina, leads to Dar el-Glaoui, the palace built by Thami El-Glaoui – the famous pasha of Marrakech and one of the richest and most powerful men in Morocco – in the early 20th century. One part of the building contains a library, while another is used to receive heads of state during official visits. The palace is reputed to have been the venue for some wild and extravagant parties.

The palace has several beautifully decorated courtyards lined with *zellij* tilework typical of the Moorish style, stuccowork, painted wood and *muqarnas* (stalactites). It also features a fine Andalusian garden planted with fruit trees.

⑮ Mouassine Quarter

◉ C3

North of Jemaa El Fna and west of the main souks, Mouassine is an ancient quarter of the medina that has become one of the most fashionable parts of Marrakech, boasting some of the most high-end riads and stylish boutiques. At its heart is the Mouassine Mosque. The Saadian sultan Moulay Abdallah established this place of worship, which was built between 1562 and 1573, on what is thought to be a former Jewish quarter, having relocated the Jewish population to the new mellah. The minaret, which is crowned by a gallery with merlons, is of strikingly simple design. The adjacent Mouassine Fountain, the largest and most ornate in the medina, consists of three large drinking troughs, two for animals and the third for people. The fountain is enclosed within a portico with decorative stuccowork and carved lintels. Just east of the fountain, an

> Mouassine is an ancient quarter of the medina that has become one of the most fashionable parts of Marrakech, boasting some of the most high-end riads and stylish boutiques.

arched gate leads through to the breathtaking Souk des Teinturiers, or Dyers' Souk *(p239)*. Here, skeins of wool in all manner of rainbow hues hang out to dry in the beating sun. In a city bursting with colour, this is surely the jewel in the Marrakech's colourful crown.

Between the mosque and the fountain is an old house, dating from the 17th and 18th centuries, that now serves as the Musée Mouassine. The museum's exhibits document the history of the neighbourhood, although the greatest attraction is the house itself, which is a fine example of 16th-century Saadian architecture, expertly restored to its former glory. A short film shows the key stages in the renovation process.

At the heart of the souks, the main street through the quarter is Rue Mouassine. A small west-leading alley off this street jogs and twists to

The tower of Koubba Ba-Adiyn and the interior stonework of the dome *(inset)*

deliver visitors to the large wooden door of Dar Cherifa, one of the most beautiful buildings in the medina. It is a stunning 15th-century riad that has been meticulously restored and returned to life as a gallery, workshop and performance space. You can order a mint tea here, which you can enjoy in the glorious galleried courtyard.

North of the mosque, at 192 Rue Mouassine, is a large *fondouk* (travellers' hostel) that was used in the film *Hideous Kinky* (1998) as the hotel at which Kate Winslett's character stays. At No 184, Souk Cherifa is the best shopping stop for designer clothes, accessories and homeware, with over 20 independent boutiques gathered together.

←

Tourists sheltering from the sun in a roof top café in the Mouassine Quarter

16

Koubba Ba'Adiyn

Q C2 **A** Place ben Youssef
C (0524) 43 61 31/43 62 39
O 9am–6pm daily

This brick-built dome is the only example of Almoravid architecture in Marrakech, making it most likely the oldest building in the city. Built by Ali ben Youssef in 1106, originally it formed part of a richly decorated mosque that was demolished by the Almohad dynasty upon over-throwing the Almoravids around 50 years later. Miracu-lously spared, the rectangular pavilion was rediscovered in 1948. It was found to contain an ablutions pool fed by three reservoirs. While the exterior is decorated with chevrons and pointed arches in relief, the interior is graced by scalloped and horseshoe arches and floral ornamentation. The *koubba* indicates how the city might have looked, as well as anticipating the creativity of Islamic architecture to come.

EAT

Bakchich Café
Lively, candy-coloured pit stop in the heart of the souk, serving tasty, well-priced local cuisine.

Q C3 **A** Rue des Banques, Kennaria, Medina **C** (0661) 48 86 92

Ⓓ Ⓓ Ⓓ

―――

Al Fassia
Simply the best Moroccan food in town at a restaurant run entirely by women.

Q A5 **A** 55 Boulevard Mohamed Zerktouni, Guéliz **W** alfassia.com

Ⓓ Ⓓ Ⓓ

―――

Nomad
A sleek, modern Moroccan eatery and rooftop cocktail bar featuring eclectic twists on local classics.

Q C3 **A** 1 Derb Arjaane, off Rahba Kedima, Medina **W** nomad marrakech.com

Ⓓ Ⓓ Ⓓ

Orange trees filling the
Moorish-style inner courtyard of the Palais Bahia ↑

17 🖉

Dar Si Saïd Museum

📍C3 🏠Riad Zitoune
Jedid 📞(0524) 38 95 64
🕐9–11:45am & 2:30–
5:45pm Wed-Mon

Commissioned by the brother
of Ba Ahmed, builder of the
nearby Palais Bahia, the 19th-
century Dar Si Saïd is a house
rather than a palace. It is
splendid nonetheless, with a
two-storey central building
arranged around courtyards
with graceful arcades. It also

↑ The cedar dome of the
Reception Room in
the Da Si Saïd Museum

has an Andalusian garden,
with a central pavilion and
fountain. While worth a visit in
its own right, particularly for
the painted wooden ceilings,
the house also serves as a
museum of decorative arts.

The exhibits include a fine
collection of carpets, chests,
weapons, ceramics, costumes
and jewellery illustrating the
skill of the craftsmen and
women of southern Morocco,
particularly of the High Atlas.
The sumptuous Reception
Room on the upper floor is a
jewel of Moorish design. The
cedar dome and the walls,
with *zellij* tilework and a stuccowork frieze, are a mesmerizing
sight. The room contains a
wooden candelabrum, a cedar
sofa and benches covered
with colourful fabric.

Some of the most interesting items are in the collection
of woodwork in the second
courtyard, including doors,
frontages and intricate
mashrabiyya (screenwork),
some of it painted in bright
colours. These architectural
elements, most of them carved
in cedar, originate from old
houses in Marrakech. Also
on display are archaeological
pieces and architectural fragments from Fès.

From the topmost floor
there is a view over the medina
and towards the High Atlas.

RIADS

A riad is a traditional
Moroccan townhouse
built around a central
courtyard. Over the
last 20 years, however,
in medinas throughout
Morocco, the term has
become synonymous
with boutique hotels.
These can be quite
humble, with just three
or four simple rooms
and few amenities.
They can also be rather
palatial affairs with 20
or more sumptuous
bedchambers, plus
pools, a hammam,
library and restaurant.
Whichever end of the
scale, they all offer a
personal and very
Moroccan experience.

---

18 🖉

Palais Bahia

📍D4 🏠Riad Zitoun Jedid
(medina) 📞(0524) 38 91 79
🕐9am–4:30pm daily

This palace, whose name
literally means "Palace of the
Favourite" or "Palace of the
Beautiful", was built by two
powerful grand viziers – Si
Moussa, vizier of Sultan Sidi
Mohammed ben Abderrahman,

and his son Ba Ahmed, vizier of Moulay Abdelaziz – at the end of the 19th century.

The complex consists of two parts, each built at different times. The older part, built by Si Moussa, contains apartments arranged around a marble-paved courtyard. It also has an open courtyard with cypresses, orange trees and jasmine, with two star-shaped pools.

The newer part, built by Ba Ahmed, is a huge palace without a unified plan. It consists of luxurious apartments looking on to courtyards planted with trees. To make it easier for the obese master of the house to move around, most of the apartments were located on the ground floor. The main courtyard is paved with marble and *zellij* tilework. It is surrounded by a gallery of finely fluted columns, while three fountains with bowls stand in the centre. This courtyard, once used by the viziers' concubines, faces the main reception room. It has a cedar ceiling painted with arabesques. The decoration of the palace apartments and of the council chamber is equally splendid.

Ba Ahmed hired the best craftsmen in the kingdom to build and decorate this palace. It is decked out with highly prized materials, such as marble from Meknès, cedar from the Middle Atlas and tiles from Tetouan. Not surprisingly, French Army general Marshal Lyautey chose to live here during the Protectorate.

Maison Tiskiwin, at 8 Rue de la Bahia, houses the **Bert Flint Museum**. This charming residence with a courtyard is an example of a traditional 19th-century Marrakech house. Here, Bert Flint, a Dutch anthropologist and art historian who fell in love with Morocco and settled here in the 1950s, amassed a huge collection of folk art and artifacts from around the Souss Valley and the Saharan region. He eventually donated the house and most of his collection to the university. Exhibits include pottery from the Rif, jewellery and daggers from the Anti-Atlas, and carpets from the Middle Atlas. The museum is not too far from the Dar Si Saïd, built by the brother of Ba Ahmed.

Bert Flint Museum
⊗ 🏠 8 Rue de la Bahia, Riad Zitoun Jedid 📞 (0524) 38 91 92 🕐 9am–12:30pm & 2:30–6pm daily

Doormen welcoming guests to the lobby at ↓ La Mamounia Hotel

STAY

Dar Attajmil
The cosiest of four-room riads, with a central courtyard shaded by a banana tree.

📍 B3 🏠 23 Rue Laksour 🌐 darattajmil.com

Riad Berbere
A fabulous renovated 17th-century property.

📍 C3 🏠 23 Derb Sidi Ahmed Benacer 🌐 leriadberbere.com

La Mamounia Hotel
The *grande dame* of Marrakech hotels – nothing compares to the hospitality and opulence of La Mamounia with its splendid Art Deco and Moorish decor.

📍 B4 🏠 Avenue Bab Jdid, Medina 🌐 mamounia.com

19
Mellah

◉ D4 ◎ East of Palais el-Badi and south of Palais Bahia

Once accommodating some 16,000 inhabitants, the former Jewish quarter of Marrakech was the largest *mellah* in Morocco until the country's independence. Previously located on what became the site of the Mouassine Mosque, the *mellah* was established in the mid-16th century by sultan Moulay Abdallah, and it was almost identical to the one in Fès *(p182)*. Until 1936, it was surrounded by a wall pierced by two gates, one opening east on to the cemetery, the other leading into the city. The jewellers' souk is held opposite the Palais Bahia *(p250)*.

20 ✍
Palais el-Badi

◉ C4 ◎ Hay Salam, Rue Berrima ◷ 9am–4:45pm daily

Five months after acceding to the throne, Ahmed el-Mansour decided to consolidate his rule and banish the memory of earlier dynasties. Having emerged victorious over the Portuguese at the Battle of the Three Kings in 1578, El-Mansour, "the Golden", ordered a luxurious palace to be built near his private apartments. It was to be used for receptions and audiences with foreign embassies. It was financed by the Portuguese, whom he had defeated in battle, and work continued until his death in 1603.

For a time, the palace was considered one of the wonders of the Muslim world. Italian marble, Irish granite, Indian onyx and coverings of gold leaf decorated the walls and the ceilings of the 360 rooms.

In 1683, Moulay Ismaïl demolished the Palais el-Badi and salvaged the materials to embellish his own imperial city of Meknès. Today, what remains of the palace are the empty shells of the pavillions and stables, the original cedarwood minbar of the Koutoubia Mosque *(p234)* and the tremendous central court, made up of several pools and sunken gardens planted with orange and citrus trees. You can climb up on to the ramparts for a better view.

99
The number of names there are for Allah. El-Badi, meaning "the incomparable" is just one of them.

21
Bab Agnaou

◉ B4 ◎ Rue de la Kasbah, opposite the Kasbah Mosque

Like its twin, Bab Oudaïa in Rabat *(p82)*, this monumental gate was built by Yacoub el-Mansour. Its name is Berber for "hornless black ram".

Protected by Bab el-Robb, the outer defensive gate, Bab Agnaou marked the main entrance to the Almohad palace, and its function was thus primarily decorative.

Although the gate no longer has its two towers, the façade still makes for an impressive sight. In the carved sandstone tinges of red meld with tones of greyish-blue.

The neatly sculpted façade consists of alternating layers of stone and brick surrounding

← The sizeable central court of the incomparable Palais el-Badi, with pools and sunken orange gardens

TOP 5 MEDINA SPAS AND HAMMAMS

Les Bains de Marrakech
🏠 2 Derb Sedra, Bab Agnaou ⏰ Daily
Affordable his 'n' hers with joint hammams.

Hammam Dar El Bacha
🏠 20 Rue Fatima Zohra
⏰ Men only: 7am–1pm; women only: 1–9pm
Old-school hammam with fine old buildings.

Hammam de la Rose
🏠 130 Dar El Bacha
🌐 hammamdelarose.com
Good mid-range option for affordable luxury.

Heritage Spa
🏠 40 Arset Aouzal, Bab Doukkala 🌐 heritagespa marrakech.com
Modern spa with a wide variety of treatments.

Spa MK
🏠 14 Derb Sebaai
🌐 maisonmk.com
One of the very top spa experiences in the city.

a horseshoe arch. The floral motifs in the cornerpieces and the frieze with Kufic script framing the arch are unusually delicate.

This is another example of the sober, monochrome style of decoration that is typical of Almohad architecture and that gives the gate a dignified and majestic appearance.

22
The Kasbah

📍 C4 🏠 Rue de la Kasbah, near Bab Agnaou; Kasbah Mosque: 🚫 To non-Muslims

The southernmost portion of the medina is notably quieter than elsewhere. It is home to three cemeteries and the stately precincts of the royal residence – off-limits to the public. The quarter is entered via Bab Agnaou, which leads directly to the Kasbah Mosque, also known as the Mosque of Moulay el-Yazid, after the Alaouite sultan.

Built by Yacoub el-Mansour (1184–99), the mosque is the only Almohad building other than Bab Agnaou to survive in Marrakech. Its distinctive minaret, a beautiful stone and brick construction in shades of ochre, was used as a model by later builders. Two-fifths of the tower are taken up by the lantern, which is crowned by three spheres. These are brass, but legend has it that they are gold, hence their popular name, the Golden Apples. In the lee of the southern wall are the Saadian Tombs. South of the mosque, along main Rue de la Kasbah is the Centre Artisanal, a huge store which sells handicrafts from Marrakech and the region. Prices are fixed, so you don't have to haggle. Further south is the excellent Café Clock, a funky little café with good food and entertainment.

→ The Kasbah Mosque with its distinctive minaret, viewed from Rue de la Kasbah

The Atlas Mountains seen from the rooftops of the Palais el-Badi

← Ahmed el-Mansour and his successors lying in eternal rest in the Saadian Tombs

The central Chamber of 12 Columns, a great masterpiece of Moorish architecture, is crowned by a remarkable dome of carved cedar with gold-leaf decoration. It is supported by 12 columns of Carrara marble. The walls are completely covered – the lower part by a graceful interlacing pattern of glazed tiles, and the upper part by a profusion of stuccowork. In the centre of the room lie Ahmed el-Mansour and many of his successors. The ivory-coloured marble tombstones are covered with arabesques and inscriptions arranged on two levels: above are verses from the Koran, below is a framed epitaph in verse. The third room, the Chamber of Three Niches, has an equally sumptuous decorative scheme. It contains the tombs of several young princes.

The second mausoleum has more modest proportions. It consists of a room with two loggias and a prayer hall. A carved cedar lintel links the columns of the loggias. In the prayer hall, the dome is a splendid sight. Filling a honey-combed niche in the burial chamber is the tomb of Lalla Messaouda, mother of Ahmed "the Golden".

23

Saadian Tombs

C4 Rue de la Kasbah
(0524) 43 61 31 9am–5pm daily

Although they were neglected for more than two centuries, the tombs of the Saadian dynasty constitute some of the finest examples of Islamic architecture in Morocco. Their style is in complete contrast to the simplicity of Almohad architecture, as the Saadian princes lavished on funerary architecture the same ostentation and magnificence that they gave to other buildings.

A necropolis existed here during the Almohad period (1145–1248), continuing in use during the reign of the Merinid sultan Abou el-Hassan (1331–51). The Saadian Tombs themselves date from the late 16th to the 18th centuries. Out of

respect for the dead, and even though he had been at pains to erase all traces of his predecessors, the Alaouite sultan Moulay Ismaïl raised a wall round the main entrance.

It was not until 1917 that the tombs were made accessible to the public. They consist of two mausoleums set in a garden planted with flowers symbolizing Allah's paradise.

The central mausoleum is that of Ahmed el-Mansour (1578–1603). It consists of three funerary rooms. The first room is a prayer hall divided into three aisles by white marble columns. The mihrab (which points to Mecca) is decorated with stalactites and framed by a pointed horseshoe arch supported by grey marble pilasters. The prayer hall is lit by the three windows of the lantern, which rests on a cedar base decorated with inscriptions.

24

Dar el-Makhzen

C5 Southeast of the Saadian Tombs
To the public

When Sidi Mohammed ben Abdallah arrived in Marrakech in the 18th century, he found

→ People going about their daily business in the upmarket area of Guéliz

the Almohad and Saadian palaces in ruins. He ordered this royal palace to be built in an extensive walled area in the kasbah, next to Palais el-Badi.

The building is notable because, unlike the other palaces in Marrakech, it took into account the perspective and dimensions of the terrain. Restored countless times, Dar el-Makhzen consists of several groups of buildings: the Green Palace (El-Qasr el-Akhdar), the Nile Garden (Gharsat el-Nil) and the main house (El-Dar el-Kubra), as well as outbuildings and several pavilions (menzah) in the park. The palace is still a royal residence today.

___

25
Méchouars

🇶 D5 🏛 Near Dar el-Makhzen

Dar el-Makhzen has three large parade grounds, known as *méchouars*, where royal ceremonies and other public gatherings are held. The inner *méchouar*, located south of the Dar el-Makhzen, is connected

> **The central Chamber of 12 Columns, a great masterpiece of Moorish architecture, is crowned by a remarkable dome of carved cedar with gold-leaf decoration.**

to the palace by Bab el-Akhdar and is linked to the Aguedal Gardens. The outer *méchouar*, east of the palace, is connected to the Berrima quarter by Bab el-Harri. The large *méchouar* south of the inner *méchouar* is outlined by a wall set with merlons.

___

26
Guéliz

🇶 A5 🏛 Northwest of the medina

Established during the Protectorate and taking its name from the hill that rises above it, Guéliz is the Ville Nouvelle (New Town) of Marrakech. This spacious commercial district has been put together in line with the principles of modern town planning. The wide avenues, large hotels, municipal

gardens, and cafés with shady terraces make Guéliz a lovely quarter to visit. Avenue Mohammed V, which runs between Guéliz and the medina, is lined with offices, banks, restaurants, bars, pavement cafés and shops.

Despite the number of modern buildings, a few vestiges of the European architecture introduced by the French remain. A notable example of this style, known as "Mauresque", is the Renaissance Café, on Place Abdel Moumen ben Ali. It is decorated in typical 1950s' style and has a dining area on the top floor with panoramic views. A large municipal fresh produce market takes place every day in Place du 16 Novembre. It is worth visiting the market to take in the lively atmosphere, as local shoppers purchase their fresh fruit, vegetables, herbs and spices.

27 🖌 Ⓜ 🖥 🛍

Musée d'Art et de Culture de Marrakech (MACMA)

📍A5 🏠Passage Ghandouri, 61 Rue Yougoslavie, Guéliz
🕐9am–7pm Mon–Sat
🌐museemacma.com

Opened in 2016, this is a smart art museum displaying the collection of its owner, the enthusiastic and hands-on Nabil El Mallouki. His passion is the work of the Orientalists. From the mid-19th to the mid-20th century, many European painters were attracted by the colour and, to their eyes, exoticism, of Morocco and its people and the beauty of its landscapes.

Hung in cool white and slate grey galleries are 80 or so works including pieces by Jacques Majorelle, Eugène Delacroix and Raoul Dufy. In addition to the main collection, the museum hosts regular temporary exhibitions featuring many Moroccan artists. It is a relatively small place, hidden in a shopping passage, but well worth seeking out for anyone with an interest in art. There is an attractive art bookshop and a literary café on site too.

The owner opened a sister museum to MACMA – the Orientalist Museum of Marrakech – on Kaat Benehid in the city's medina.

28

La Palmeraie

📍A4 🏠On the road to Casablanca, 22 km (14 miles) north of Marrakech

Legend has it that, after eating dates brought back from the Sahara, the soldiers of the 11th-century Almoravids spat out the stones around their encampment. The stones are supposed to have germinated and led to the creation of La Palmeraie (Palm Grove).

Covering an area the size of a small city, the grove consists of fields, gardens and orchards irrigated by ditches and wells supplied by underground channels known as *khettaras*. Tours can be taken by car or horse-drawn carriage.

Although it contains roughly 150,000 trees, the agricultural function of the grove is being pared away by developers, who are making inroads into it by building desirable residences here.

29

Agdal Gardens

📍D5 🏠Rue Bab Ahmar, via the outer méchouar near Bab Ighli 🕐Daily

This vast enclosed space contains an orchard planted with lemon, orange, apricot and olive trees. The historic gardens were laid out in the late 12th century by the Almoravids, who also installed two large irrigation pools connected by *khettaras*. Enlarged and embellished by the Almohads, and later the Saadians, the gardens were then completely neglected until the 19th century. At that point, the Alaouite sultans

←

Camels padding through the palm trees at La Palmeraie

The imperial gardens of Ménara, backdropped by the snowy peaks of the High Atlas

Moulay Abderrahman and Sidi Mohammed ben Abdallah restored the gardens and the pavilions, building gates into the surrounding wall and even diverting the course of Wadi Ourika to provide irrigation to the surrounding area.

While the public has free access to the gardens, the pavilions, on the northern side, are for the exclusive use of the king's guests. Dar el-Hana, the largest pool, is located south of the garden and dates from the Almohad period. The terrace of the small Saadian pavilion that stands next to it commands stunning views in two opposite directions: northwards across expansive olive groves, with the city in the background rising in tiers to the hill of Jbilet, and southwards to the serene and distant snowcapped peaks of the High Atlas.

Did You Know?

The Agdal Gardens' name derives from the Berber language and translates as "Walled Meadow".

30

Ménara

A5 🏠 **Avenue de la Ménara** 🕘 **9am–5pm daily**

A welcome haven of shade and coolness, this imperial garden enclosed within pisé walls is filled mostly with olive and fruit trees. In the 12th century, an enormous pool was dug in the centre of the garden to serve as a reservoir for the Almohad sultans. In the 19th century, Moulay Abderrahman refurbished the garden and built the pavilion with a green-tiled pyramidal roof. The ground floor is fronted by three arches opening onto the pool. The upper floor has a large balustered balcony on its north side.

This stunning building was used by the sultans for their romantic meetings. It is said that every morning they would toss the concubine that they had chosen the night before into the water.

Although the interior is rather plain, the building's overall conception and location are remarkable, and the view from any point within, with the peaks of the High Atlas serving as a backdrop, is quite unforgettable.

TOP 5 MARRAKECH BARS & CLUBS

Café Arabe
🏠 184 Rue Mouassine, Medina 🌐 cafearabe.com
Casual bar with a laid back vibe. Drink until late on the terraces.

Le Comptoir
🏠 Ave Echouhada, Hivernage 🌐 comptoirdarna.com
A raucous club, complete with belly dancers.

Grand Café de la Poste
🏠 Angle Blvd Mansour Eddahbi, Guéliz
Quirky little Café in a former colonial post office that transforms into a club at night.

Sky Bab
🏠 130 Angle Blvd Mansour Eddahbi, Guéliz 🌐 babhotelmarrakech.ma
Spacious rooftop bar at the luxurious Bab Hotel.

SkyBar
🏠 89 Angle Blvd Zerktouni, Gueliz
Perched atop the Hotel de la Renaissance, this sleek rooftop bar is one of the finest in town.

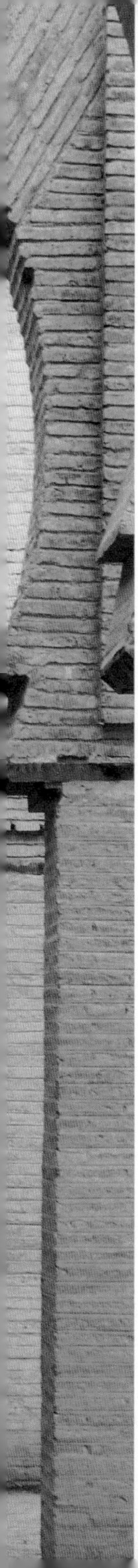

HIGH ATLAS

Extending from the plains of the Atlantic seaboard to Morocco's border with Algeria, the High Atlas forms an impregnable barrier some 800 km (500 miles) long and, in certain places, 100 km (60 miles) wide. Consisting of great massifs and steep valleys, desolate rocky plains and deep narrow canyons, the High Atlas has played a decisive role in Morocco's history.

From ancient times these mountains have been a place of refuge for populations fleeing from invaders. For centuries, nomads forced northwards by the desertification of the Sahara have come into conflict with the sedentary mountain-dwelling tribes, disputing possession of prized pasture. This tumultuous feudal past led to the development of a strikingly beautiful form of fortified architecture.

Today, although the Berbers no longer need to guard their safety, they still live in *tighremts*, old patriarchal houses with thick walls. Hamlets built of *pisé* (rammed earth) still cling to mountainsides, while every last plot of land is used to grow barley, corn, maize, turnips, lucerne (alfalfa) and potatoes – crops that can be cultivated at high altitudes. The Berbers channel river water to irrigate small squares of land and graze their flocks of sheep and goats.

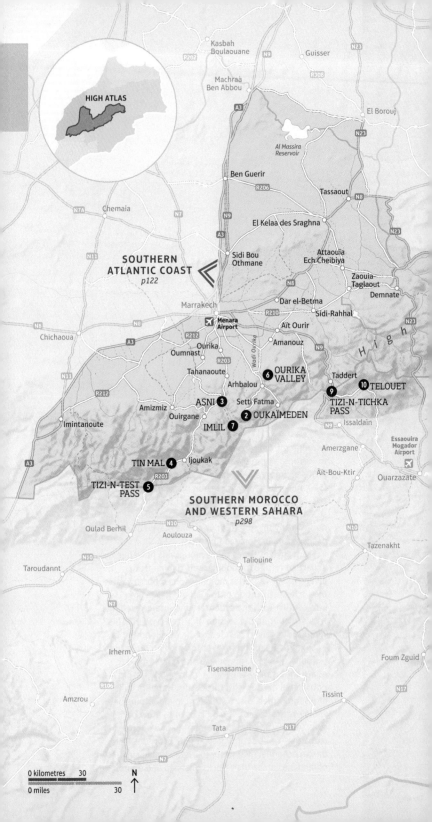

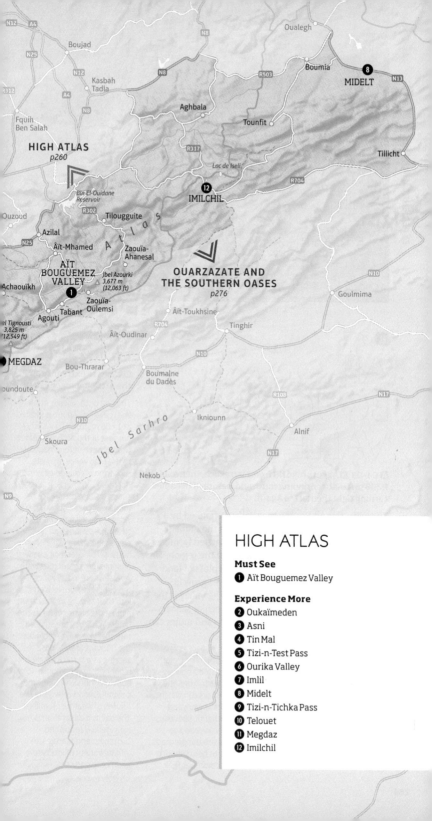

HIGH ATLAS

Must See
❶ Aït Bouguemez Valley

Experience More
❷ Oukaïmeden
❸ Asni
❹ Tin Mal
❺ Tizi-n-Test Pass
❻ Ourika Valley
❼ Imlil
❽ Midelt
❾ Tizi-n-Tichka Pass
❿ Telouet
⓫ Megdaz
⓬ Imilchil

❶ Ⓜ
AÏT BOUGUEMEZ VALLEY

🅰 C4-D3 🅰 Agouti; road N8 from Marrakech, then road R208 to Azilal, continuing south and, before Aït Mhamed, turning right then left to Agouti

The wide, flat Aït Bouguemez valley is flanked by a landscape of high, arid hilltops. This is the domain of the Aït Bouguemez tribe, who are settled farmers. The tribe is thought to be the oldest in the region. The valley is covered in meticulously tilled plots of land surrounded by ditches, and walnut trees grow in undulating fields of barley and corn. The valley is the starting point for hikes through spectacular scenery up to the massif of Jbel M'Goun. Guides and mules can be hired in Tabant and other villages.

Travelling through the Aït Bouguemez valley's villages can offer a fascinating insight into the daily lives of the local people and are home to many associations and cooperatives of artisans. The array of wares produced in the valley range from jewellery and traditional woven baskets to beautifully carved wooden handicrafts, such as boxwood bowls, as well as colourful rugs and carpets. Visitors can watch the artisans at work and pick up authentic souvenirs. The associations and co-operatives use the proceeds from sales to help support their local communities.

①
Agouti

🅰 Western extremity of the Aït Bouguemez valley

The first of the villages that line the valley, Agouti is located at 1,800 m (5,908 ft). As an outpost of the Aït Bouguemez tribe, it once defended access to the high valley against rival tribes. A ruined *igherm* (fortified communal granary), set on a sheer rocky promontory, towers above the village. The villagers once kept their possessions and their crops here. In the valley, many houses have electricity, as well as some form of running water. As elsewhere in the valley, the cube-like houses blend into their setting as they are almost the same colour as the landscape. They are stacked together like building blocks, the flat roof of the house serving as a terrace for the inhabitants of the house above. Visitors can see some beautiful wood ceilings in the houses of wealthier families. The painted decoration is executed by renowned craftsmen and features an infinite variety of intricate geometric patterns.

The Aït Bouguemez valley with hamlets surrounded by fields

② ⓜ

Aït Bou Oulli Valley

⌂ **West of Agouti**

From Agouti, a day trip can be made to the gorgeous Aït Bou Oulli valley on mule-back or by four-wheel-drive vehicle. A sheersided track leads down into the valley, whose name means "the people who raise ewes". The narrow wooded valley, thickly covered with walnut trees, winds the length of the *wadi*, which irrigates small fields for farming. Jbel Ghat, rising above the plain, is a peak with mythical associations to which the Berbers come on a pilgrimage in years of drought. Abachkou, an interesting, high-set village at the far end of the valley, is renowned for the beautiful white capes produced by the villagers and found nowhere else in Morocco.

Did You Know?

Houses in the valley bottom are built of *pisé* (raw earth), while those at a high altitude are of dry stone.

STAY

Touda Eco-Lodge
This rustic, homely Berber-owned lodge on a hilltop has eight rooms overlooking the Aït Bouguemez valley. It is the perfect trekking base, with plenty of home-cooked hearty Berber food at meal times.

⌂ Zawyat Oulmzi
ⓦ touda.co.uk

ⓓⓗ ⓓⓗ ⓓⓗ

Ecolodge Dar Itrane
Located in the peaceful viallge of Imelghas, this lodge has 17 rooms and is decorated in Berber style throughout. There are stunning views from its rooftop terrace.

⌂ Imelghas
ⓦ origins-lodge.com

ⓓⓗ ⓓⓗ ⓓⓗ

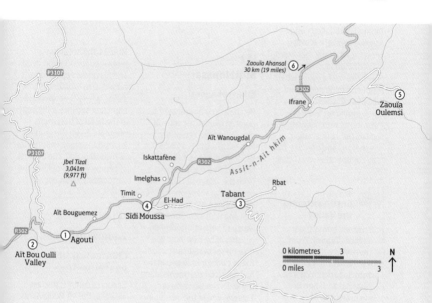

③

Tabant

📍 **East of Agouti**

Tabant is the valley's administrative centre. It is well known for its souk that takes place on Sundays, which is the only place in the valley where supplies can be purchased. Weekly deliveries arrive by truck, providing the local inhabitants with necessities, such as tea, coffee, sugar, matches, oil and utensils, that they cannot otherwise obtain.

> 💬 **INSIDER TIP**
> **Getting Around the Valley**
>
> The road is metalled as far as Tabant. From there you will need a four-wheel drive vehicle to reach Zaouïa Ahansal and then Bin el-Ouidane.

From the granary, it is possible to look over the rest of the valley, with the outlines of nearby villages dotting the surrounding hillsides.

④

Sidi Moussa

📍 **East of Agouti**

Perched on the summit of a pointed hill, in the centre of the Aït Bouguemez valley, Sidi Moussa granary is a UNESCO's World Heritage site. It is reached by a steep path from the village of Timit. This collective granary, one of three in the region, is a sturdy circular building with incorporated watch towers. In the interior, which is lit by loop-hole windows, a spiral staircase leads to the two upper floors. In the half-light, compartments along the walls can be made out. This was where the inhabitants kept their possessions. Sidi Moussa, the holy man renowned for his good deeds and his powers as a healer, is buried here. Women visit the shrine, where they spend the night and sacrifice a chicken in the hope of becoming pregnant. From the granary, it is possible to look over the rest of the valley, with the outlines of nearby villages dotting the surrounding hillsides.

⑤

Zaouïa Oulemsi

📍 **On the way from Agouti, on a narrow track**

Zaouïa Oulemsi is the last village in the Aït Bouguemez valley, which it overlooks

↑ Women arriving at the Sidi Moussa granary, a shrine to the *marabout*

33.4 kg
—
The weight of the largest carp caught in Lake Bin el-Ouidane (73.6 lb).

⑥

Zaouïa Ahansal

🏠 **On the track towards Bin el-Ouidane**

A track running along the continuation of the Aït Bouguemez valley goes up to the Tizi-n-Tirrhist Pass, at 2,629 m (8,628 ft). The mountains are very bare here. The track passes a petrified forest of juniper, with gnarled, dying trunks. Zaouïa Ahansal, consisting of some old *tighremts* and the tomb of its founder, Saïd Ahansal, dates from the 14th century, when the *marabout* movement loomed large in the history of this mountain region. *Zaouias* (sanctuaries set up around the tombs of *marabouts*, holy figures and the leaders of brotherhoods) were then protected holy places, where pilgrims and the needy found refuge. In exchange for the protection given by the *marabout*, the Berbers maintained the land around the *zaouïa*, were taught Arabic and received Koranic instruction. Heedless of the power of the sultans, the leaders of some *zaouias* controlled the lives of the mountain people, settling disputes over land ownership and imposing their will. Zaouïa Ahansal was a major influence on the local Berber populations, but the descendants of Saïd Ahansal came into conflict with the fiefs of the *caids* (chief of a defined territory) of the High Atlas. They held out against the French until 1934

The track continues for 40 km (25 miles) before reaching La Cathédrale, an impressive rock formation, followed by Lake Bin el-Ouidane. This lake is a popular place for fishing and is known for its huge carps. The water is also home to black bass, pike, zander, roach and tench.

from an altitude of 2,150 m (7,056 ft). It consists of low, red-hued drystone houses. Here, the snowfall comes early and tends to be heavy.

The village is the starting point for hikes to Lake Izourar, which lies in the heart of the mountains at an altitude of 2,500 m (8,205 ft). Many nomadic shepherds camp beside the lake, which is often dry in the summer months, when it turns into pasture, the use of which is carefully controlled to prevent over-grazing. The shepherds include the Aït Bouguemez, who come for the summer, living in the stonebuilt sheep-folds, and the Aït Atta, with their sheep, goats and camels, who come up to the High Atlas from Jbel Sarhro in summer. Seeking good pasture, they settle on the slopes of M'Goun, around Lake Izourar or on the Imilchil plateau, moving south again at the first frosts.

BERBERS OF THE HIGH ATLAS

The Berbers of the High Atlas are non-nomadic peasants. Many of them have a completely self-sufficient lifestyle. In some valleys mule tracks are the only channel of communication with the outside world. The inhabitants of these remote valleys live by the pattern of the seasons. In the autumn, they till the soil. In winter, they gather wood and weave woollen blankets. In spring, men dig and maintain irrigation channels. In summer, they harvest and thresh the grain.

EXPERIENCE MORE

❷ Oukaïmeden

🅰C4 🚗74 km (46 miles) from Marrakech on road P2017 🚌From Marrakech, then taxi ℹMarrakech; (0524) 43 61 31

A ski resort in winter and base for mountain hikes in summer, Oukaïmeden is a haven of fresh air, just over an hour from Marrakech. The resort is easily reached by a road that forks off to the right at the village of Arhbalou, with the

Ourika Valley on the left. Shaded by olive, oak and walnut trees, the road then winds upwards in a series of hairpin bends through a striking stony landscape. The chalets and winter sports facilities are in the village itself, encircled by several mountain peaks. From November to April, if the snow is sufficiently deep, a chair lift runs up to the summit. The resort offers long-distance and cross-country skiing too.

Engravings can be seen in the village and on the plateau. Dating from the Bronze Age, they depict mainly daggers, halbards, shields and humans.

About 2 km (1 mile) from the resort, the site of a transmission mast at an altitude of 2,740 m (8,993 ft) commands a magnificent view of the Atlas and the Marrakech plain. In the summer, Oukaïmeden is the starting point for hikes up to the Tizi-n-Ouaddi Pass, the village of Tacheddirt, and to Imlil and the Tizi-n-Test Pass.

❸ Asni

🅰C4 🚗42 km (26 miles) from Marrakech on road R203 🚌From Marrakech, then by taxi

With an interesting red-walled kasbah, Asni is the first large village on the road from Marrakech to the Tizi-n-Test Pass. Attractive orchards surround the village, and there are many mule tracks leading up to the plateaus in its vicinity.

A road leads from this small settlement to the village of Imlil, the starting point for hikes to Jbel Toubkal.

The very popular *moussem* at the town of Moulay Brahim, 5 km (3 miles) from Asni, takes place one to two weeks after the festival of Mouloud. Moroccans ascribe to the saint Moulay Brahim the power to cure infertile women. Pilgrims come to lay their gifts before his tomb and to hang small pieces of fabric from the shrubs here. When one of these fragments falls from the shrub, the woman who hung it may expect a child.

④
Tin Mal

B4 **About 25 km (15 miles) south of Asni on road R203** **Mosque: Daily, except Friday for non-Muslims; ask the caretaker in the village**

Isolated at the foot of the Atlas and situated uphill from the village, 10 km (6 miles) beyond Ijoukak on the Tizi-n-Test Pass road, the Mosque of Tin Mal, is the last remaining sign of the Almohad conquest in the 12th century.

Tin Mal, once a fortified holy town, was founded in 1125 by the Ibn Toumart, a religious leader of the Berber tribes of the High Atlas. From here, he fomented a holy war against the Almoravids.

The mosque was built in 1153 by Abd el-Moumen, Ibn Toumart's successor and the first Almohad ruler. In 1276, the town was sacked by the Merinids. Only the sumptuous mosque was left standing. It has since been restored and now, as a UNESCO World Heritage Site, it is one of the few religious buildings in Morocco open to non-Muslims. Its high walls and sturdy towers give it a fortress-like look. The arches, particularly the ones near the well-preserved *mihrab* (prayer niche), are one of the mosque's most striking features.

↑ Enormous arches inside the stark, fortress-like Mosque of Tin Mal

⑤
Tizi-n-Test Pass

B4

Beyond Asni, a small side road off to the right leads to Amizmiz, a pretty village with a ruined kasbah, set amidst olive trees. The souk here is renowned for Berber pottery

←

Skiers taking to the slopes of the popular Oukaïmeden resort on a winter's day

made in the village itself, and there is a lively market held every Tuesday.

A little further on R203 is Ouirgane, a resort whose coolness in summer makes it popular with the inhabitants of Marrakech. There are some rewarding walks in the area to nearby Berber hamlets and around a reservoir, and you can hire mountain bikes or arrange horse rides. The village has one or two good places to eat and accommodation for anyone wishing to spend a few days exploring. There is also a small Thursday market.

As the road climbs further up to the Tizi-n-Test Pass, snaking through red, almost purple terrain, the landscape becomes wilder. Starting from Ijoukak, keen hikers can reach the Agoundis Valley, walking in the direction of Taghbart and El-Maghzen, or make for the Jbel Toubkal massif. Beyond Ijoukak, the Tin Mal mosque is visible on the right.

Perched on arid outcrops below the pass are imposing deserted kasbahs that once belonged to the Goundafa, a powerful Berber tribe.

From November to April, the pass is sometimes blocked by snow. The descent offers a beautiful view of the Souss plain and of hills covered with argan trees.

STAY

Kasbah du Toubkal
This imposing fort on the slopes below North Africa's highest peak offers luxury and budget accommodation.

C4 **Imlil** **kasbahtoubkal.com**

Dh Dh Dh

Kasbah Tamadot
Luxury property in the Ouiragne Valley with landscaped gardens and fabulous views.

C4 **Asni** **virgin limitededition.com**

Dh Dh Dh

Ouirgane Ecolodge
The Berber-styled rooms at this peaceful retreat all have mountain views. Relax in the cosy lounge in front of the fireplace.

C4 **Maghira, Ouirgane** **ouirgane-ecolodge.com**

Dh Dh Dh

Ourika Valley

C4 68 km (42 miles) from Marrakech on road P2017 From Marrakech; Marrakech; (0524) 43 61 31

The trip to the Ourika valley, southeast of Marrakech, offers a pleasant tour of the lower foothills of the Atlas. Beyond the village of Tnine-de-l'Ourika, the valley becomes verdant, enriched by the fast-flowing river as it traverses the landscape. The largest souk in the valley takes place in the village on Mondays. All along the road that follows the course of the *wadi*, small houses, cafés, grocery shops and small hotels cling to the hillside. Gardens and plots of cultivated land shaded by many fruit trees are laid out along the valley bottom. Between the months of February and April, the fruit trees blossom and the valley is carpeted with wildflowers. The Ourika river is occasionally subject to sudden and devastating flooding, as seen in August 1995, when many houses were swept away. Beyond Arhbalou, the valley narrows and gently rises. The road comes to an end at the village of Setti Fatma, a good starting point for hikes. Seven waterfalls flow down the rocky scree above the village. The first of these is easy to reach by walking up the course of the *wadi*. The trek up to the others is over increasingly uneven ground, and some climbing is involved, so you will need strong walking boots. From that vantage point there is a magnificent view over Setti Fatma.

The village may also be used as the starting point for longer hikes to Jbel Toubkal and the Yagour Plateau, whose peak is well known for the hundreds of engravings that can be seen in the rock formations here. The tomb of Setti Fatma is the focus of a lively four-day *moussem* – one of the most important festivals in Morocco – that takes place in mid-August when Berbers from a wide area gather here on pilgrimage.

> Beyond the village of Tnine-de-l'Ourika, the valley becomes verdant, enriched by the fast-flowing river as it traverses the landscape.

→

Houses perched upon the dramatic snowy mountainside, Imlil

Hikers resting at a waterfall at Setti Fatma, one of seven flowing down to the village

7
Imlil

▲C4 🚗17 km (10.5 miles) from Asni on road P2015

An hour and 30 minutes by car from Marrakech, the small mountain village of Imlil sits at the head of the Aït Mizane Valley in the High Atlas. Its altitude makes it a popular base for hiking. Most people come here to tackle nearby Jbel Toubkal, the tallest mountain in Morocco, but there are many other hikes of differing lengths and degrees of difficulty. The shorter hikes are navigable on your own; for longer hikes a guide can easily be arranged in the village. The simplest trek is to a nearby waterfall, which is less than a mile from the village. Another mile beyond the waterfall is the village of Armoud, which has good views of the summit of Toubkal.

8 🖵

Midelt

▲D3 🚌From Meknès, Rabat, Erfoud, Er-Rachidia and Azrou

The small villages on each side of the road out of Midelt consist of traditional buildings that are very similar to those typical of southern Morocco. While it was no more than a modest *ksar* at the beginning of the 20th century, under the French Protectorate it became a garrison town.

Apart from a souk and some cafés, there is little of note in Midelt itself. However, the town is located at the foot of Jbel Ayachi, making it the starting point for tours. It enjoys a continental climate – very cold in winter and very hot in summer.

Beautiful Middle Atlas carpets, as well as fossils and mineral stones, are on sale in Souk Jedid. There is also a workshop in Kasbah Myriem, on the road to Tattiouine, where carpets, blankets and high-quality embroidery are produced. It used to be run by

Franciscan nuns, who taught the local Berber women these handicrafts, thus ensuring an income for many families.

The Cirque de Jaffar, a limestone gorge on the way out of Midelt, makes for the most interesting tour here. However, the tracks there and back, covering 79 km (49 miles), are tough going and passable only from May to October and only by four-wheel drive.

The track along the hillside is overshadowed by the imposing outline of Jbel Ayachi, which can be climbed without much difficulty. The Cirque de Jaffar is set in a wild landscape of cedar, oak and juniper growing in stony ground. The winding track passes through remote Berber hamlets. A turning off to the left, at the Mit Kane forestry hut, leads back to Midelt.

The track that continues west leads eventually to Imilchil. Disused lead and silver mines in the impressive Aouli Gorge, 25 km (15 miles) northeast of Midelt, have been sunk into the mountainside. They were abandoned in the 1980s, but the machinery remains.

Did You Know?

At an altitude of 2,260 m (7,417 ft), the Tizi-n-Tichka Pass is the highest road pass in Morocco.

9

Tizi-n-Tichka Pass

🅰B4 🚗From Marrakech or Ouarzazate on road N9 🚌Marrakech or Ouarzazate

Built by the French in the 1920s, this winding road runs through a landscape that is, by turn, arid, mineral-rich environments and fertile valleys. Pisé villages, in tones of red or grey, huddle at the foot of hillsides.

The first pass, Tizi-n-Aït Imger offers a panoramic view of the Atlas chain. Here, the road is lined with stalls selling pottery, mineral rocks and stones whose colours are a little too bright to be natural.

From here up to the Tizi-n-Tichka Pass crops gradually give way to a landscape of bare red soil. The mountains become rounder and the houses are built higher, with more decoration, anticipating those of the Moroccan south.

The grand fortified grainstore on the way out of Igherm-n-Ougdal is open to visitors.

Beyond Agouim, on the other side of the wadi, stands the restored kasbah at El-Mdint, its towers decorated with relief patterns. Palm trees come into view, and a wide stony desert plain with tones of pink and beige leads to Ouarzazate.

10

Telouet

🅰C4 🚗Accessible from road N9 🕐Daily

About 5 km (3 miles) along the road running down from the Tizi-n-Tichka Pass, towards Ouarzazate, a narrow minor road leads off to the left. It drops down into a steep valley, and 20 km (12 miles) further reaches the kasbah of Telouet.

This was one of the homes of Al-Thami el-Glaoui, pasha of Marrakech, whose fiefdom covered a large part of the High Atlas. El-Glaoui served Sultan Mohammed V, then switched to the French in 1912. His opposition to the sultan cost him dear; on his death his family was exiled and his possessions dispersed.

Thus it was that Telouet, a town with an illustrious past, has been the victim of neglect since 1956. The glazed tiles are disintegrating, the lookout towers crumbling, the walls cracking and the windows are shattered.

However, low-ceilinged, bare-walled corridors lead to two reception rooms that have miraculously survived the passage of time. They are vestiges of El-Glaoui's opulence. The Andalusian-style rooms have engraved stuccowork, painted cedar ceilings and doors, and colourful *zellij* tilework. Daylight entering through a glass-covered dome and a small window framed with decorative wrought iron lights the rooms from dawn to sunset.

From Telouet, a narrow, winding metalled road offers a picturesque route to the village of Aït Benhaddou (*p280*). In this fertile valley, planted with palm, fig and olive trees, and irrigated by Wadi Ounila, kasbahs signal the past importance of El-Glaoui's fiefdom. The charming village of Anemiter, standing at the head of the Ounila

On its eastern end, the chain of the High Atlas descends as if it had been crushed, forming a desert plateau surrounded by rolling mountains.

valley some 11 km (7 miles) from Telouet, is unusually well preserved for its age.

⑪ Megdaz

⚑ C4

The authentic and unspoilt Berber village of Megdaz lies at the remote heart of the central High Atlas, nestled on a mountainside. There is little to do here, but there is a small lodge at which you can break your journey and spend some time admiring the red earthen architecture particular to this corner of the wporld.

To reach Megdaz, leave Marrakech on road N8 to Fès, then after 12 km (7.5miles) fork right on to the R210 to Demnate. Follow signs to Imi-n-Ifri and, at the natural bridge (which is worth a look), take the right hand fork on the R307, towards Skoura.

⑫ Imilchil

⚑ D3 ⚑ Accessible via Kasba Tadla (on road N8) and El-Ksiba (on road R317)

On its eastern end, the chain of the High Atlas descends as if it had been crushed, forming a desert plateau surrounded

↑ The red earthen mosque in Megdaz, an archetypal Berber mountain village

by rolling mountains. Imilchil is at the heart of this sparsely populated region – the territory of the Aït Haddidou.

This group of semi-nomadic shepherds originally came from Boumalne du Dadès, located in the high Dadès valley, where some of them still live. They arrived in Morocco during the centuries immediately after the introduction of Islam, and there is evidence of their presence in the Boumalne du Dadès region during the 11th century. For several years they were in conflict with the powerful Aït Atta tribe in disputes over pasture, then settled in the Assif Melloul Valley in the 17th century.

The village of Imilchil is dominated by a sumptuously decorated kasbah. Its towers have a curious feature: the angles of the crenellation are set with finials resembling inverted cooking pots. This decorative device is also related to superstitious belief, as it gives protection against lightning and the "evil eye" and is a symbol of prosperity.

←

The Tizi-n-Tichka Pass Road snaking its way through the arid High Atlas landscape

The colourful tents of the great souk spread out across the wide plateau. Traders sell basketry, cooking utensils, blankets and handwoven carpets, metalware, clothing, basic foodstuffs, and other items. On the hillside, herds of cows and camels and flocks of sheep await buyers.

The twin lakes of Plateau des Lacs can be reached by following a long track that runs from El-Ksiba, crossing narrow gorges and undulating passes, or on a road via Rich, further east. The landscape is dotted with *tighremts* (kasbahs), and a splash of colour is provided by the emerald waters of lakes Tiselit and Iseli. In the summer, sheep are brought to the lush pasture here.

IMILCHIL MARRIAGE FAIR

The annual Marriage Fair, a *moussem* at which women choose a fiancé, takes place at the end of September at a spot known as Aït Haddou Ameur, some 20 km (12 miles) from Imilchil. The origin of the fair goes back to the story of two lovers, Hadda and Moha, who were members of rival tribes and kept apart by their parents. Their tears created two lakes, Iseli and Tiselit, on the Plateau des Lacs.

During the *moussem* young girls may talk freely with men from other tribes (albeit with a chaperone), and young couples can visit *adouls* (lawyers) to sign a betrothal agreement.

The event, which attracts huge crowds of tourists, has lost some authenticity. The parade of couples and the folk dances are a superficial aspect of what is in essence a great religious gathering.

HIKING ROUTES IN
JBEL TOUBKAL MASSIF

The unspoiled beauty and variety of hiking routes in the Toubkal massif make it a popular destination for day-trippers and seasoned mountaineers alike.

As well as the opportunity to climb to the top of Jbel Toubkal, at 4,167 m (13,676 ft) the highest peak in the Atlas, the Jbel Toubkal massif offers great scope for hikes lasting several days. Climbing Toubkal is not particularly difficult, but the fact that it is a high-altitude hike over rough terrain should be taken into account. From the Toubkal Refuge, the summit of Jbel Toubkal can be reached in about four hours. For the finest view over the High Atlas, aim to reach the summit in the late morning.

💬 INSIDER TIP
Exploring the Massif

Detailed maps of the area can be obtained at Imlil. Mules can also be hired for walks lasting several days.

↑ A traditional Berber village near Imlil, nestled in the Jbel Toubkal massif

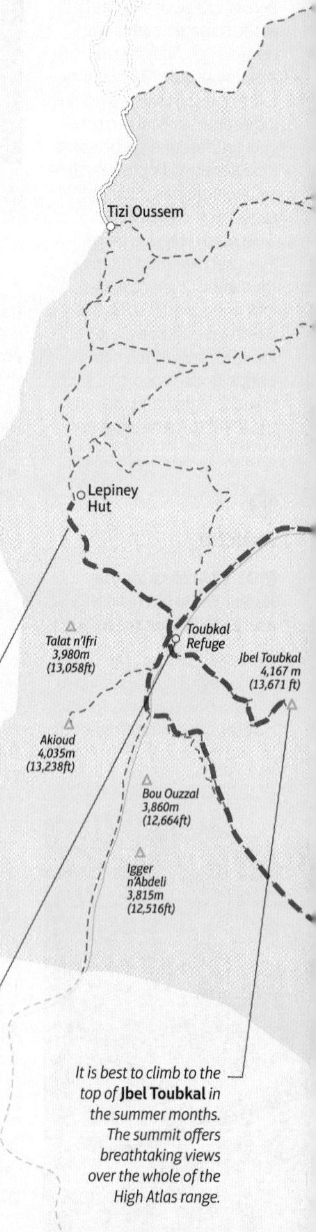

At 3,000 m (9,846 ft), **Lepiney Hut** is a handy base used by seasoned hikers and rock climbers.

Toubkal Refuge is the last stopping place before the four-hour trek to the summit of Jbel Toubkal. At 3,200 m (10,502 ft), it is open all year-round.

It is best to climb to the top of **Jbel Toubkal** in the summer months. The summit offers breathtaking views over the whole of the High Atlas range.

Tizi Oussem

Lepiney Hut

Talat n'Ifri
3,980m
(13,058ft)

Toubkal Refuge

Jbel Toubkal
4,167 m
(13,671 ft)

Akioud
4,035m
(13,238ft)

Bou Ouzzal
3,860m
(12,664ft)

Igger n'Abdeli
3,815m
(12,516ft)

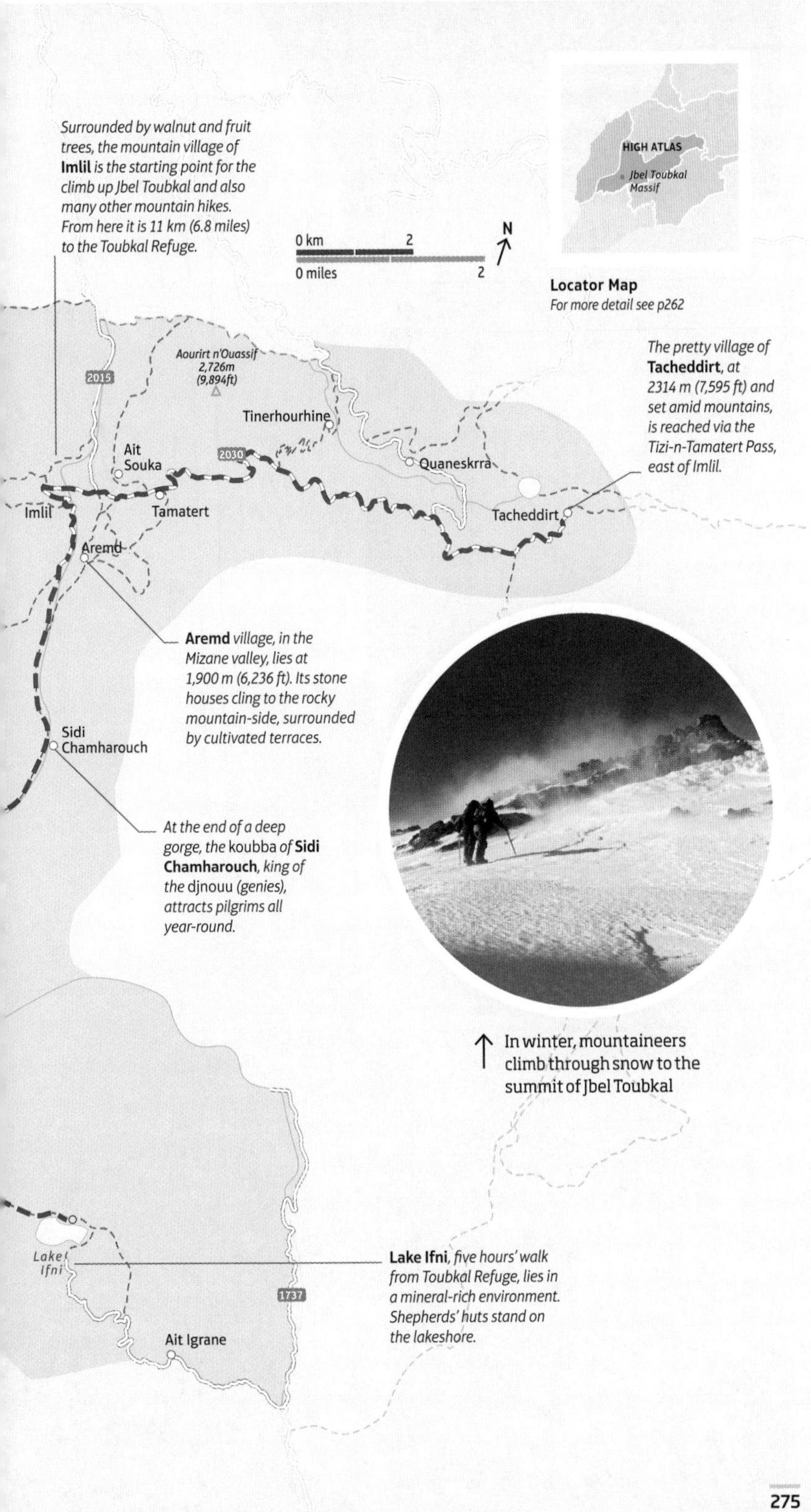

Surrounded by walnut and fruit trees, the mountain village of **Imlil** is the starting point for the climb up Jbel Toubkal and also many other mountain hikes. From here it is 11 km (6.8 miles) to the Toubkal Refuge.

0 km   2
0 miles   2

N

Locator Map
For more detail see p262

HIGH ATLAS

Jbel Toubkal Massif

Aourirt n'Ouassif
2,726m
(9,894ft)

2015

Tinerhourhine

Ait Souka

2030

Ouaneskrra

Imlil

Tamatert

Tacheddirt

Aremd

The pretty village of **Tacheddirt**, at 2314 m (7,595 ft) and set amid mountains, is reached via the Tizi-n-Tamatert Pass, east of Imlil.

Aremd village, in the Mizane valley, lies at 1,900 m (6,236 ft). Its stone houses cling to the rocky mountain-side, surrounded by cultivated terraces.

Sidi Chamharouch

At the end of a deep gorge, the koubba of **Sidi Chamharouch**, king of the djnouu (genies), attracts pilgrims all year-round.

↑ In winter, mountaineers climb through snow to the summit of Jbel Toubkal

Lake Ifni

1737

Ait Igrane

Lake Ifni, five hours' walk from Toubkal Refuge, lies in a mineral-rich environment. Shepherds' huts stand on the lakeshore.

Rose petals awaiting distillation, Dadès Valley

OUARZAZATE AND THE SOUTHERN OASES

This fascinating region at the southern edge of the High Atlas, where desert and mountains meet, is the birthplace of the great Moroccan dynasties. In the 11th century, Almoravid warriors, who came from the Sahara, set out from the south to extend their empire from Senegal to Spain. In the 16th century, the Saadians, who came from Arabia, left the Draa Valley to conquer Morocco. Lastly, the Alaouites, the dynasty that still holds power in Morocco today, settled in the Tafilalt region in the 13th century. Centuries of trade in gold, salt and slaves melded the local populations, so that Arabs, Berbers and Haratines lived side by side.

Life here centres on three great *wadis*, the Draa, the Dadès and the Ziz. These rivers have created stunning landscapes, carving gorges and canyons out of the sides of the High Atlas and Anti-Atlas. The date palm that brings welcome shade to small plots of corn and barley accounts for the region's wealth, and palm groves are punctuated by hundreds of kasbahs and *ksour*. These fortified villages and houses protected the sedentary populations against attack from nomadic tribes, and many of them are still inhabited today.

OUARZAZATE AND THE SOUTHERN OASES

Must See
1 Aït Benhaddou

Experience More
2 Ouarzazate
3 Taourirt Kasbah
4 Zagora
5 Draa Valley
6 Jbel Sarhro
7 Tamegroute
8 Mhamid
9 Skoura
10 El-Kelaa M'Gouna
11 Todra Gorge
12 Dadès Gorge
13 Tamtattouchte
14 Goulmima
15 Tinerhir
16 Boumalne du Dadès
17 Ziz Gorge
18 Source Bleue de Meski
19 Er-Rachidia
20 Erfoud
21 Merzouga
22 Tafilalt Palm Grove
23 Rissani

AÏT BENHADDOU

This fortified cluster of kasbahs is one of the most striking and best preserved in the country. It appears to tumble down the sloping left bank of the Wadi Mellah in a cascade of red mud-brick terraces, walls and towers. It is simply magnificent.

The once heavily fortified *ksar* of Aït Benhaddou is reached on foot from the village on the opposite bank of the river, and can easily be explored without a guide. Since the village was made a UNESCO World Heritage Site, some of its kasbahs have undergone restoration. Crenellated towers are decorated with geometric designs in negative relief, creating a play of light and shadow. Behind the kasbahs stand plain earth houses. Today, the *ksar* is inhabited by fewer than ten families.

Beyond Aït Benhaddou, a minor road leads to the ruined fortress of Tamdaght, once a kasbah inhabited by the Glaoui. Its towers are now inhabited by nesting storks. The road continues to Telouet, 32 km (20 miles) away.

↑ Intricate designs adorn the upper tiers of the town's ancient structures

PICTURE PERFECT
Aït Benhaddou at Golden Hour

Aït Benhaddou is at its most spectacular (and photogenic) during the hours of sunrise and sunset when the red mud-brick walls and towers practically glow in the warm, low light. Consider staying in the neighbouring village on the opposite bank of the Wadi Mellah to shoot this breathtaking *ksar* at golden hour.

① A man and his donkey descend the hillside from the front gate of Aït Benhaddou.

② A Berber woman weaves a carpet using traditional methods in a hilltop house.

③ Tools and trinkets are displayed within the fortified city walls.

CINEMATIC SCENERY

It seems that directors the world over are drawn to the drama of Aït Benhaddou, with the town featuring in numerous film and TV productions, including *Game of Thrones (p52)*. It's also a setting in films such as *Gladiator* (2000), Ridley Scott's *Kingdom of Heaven* (2005), Oliver Stone's *Alexander* (2004) and fantasy action blockbusters *Prince of Persia* (2009) and *The Mummy* (1999). Some of the guides here worked as extras on these sets, and have the photos to prove it.

←

Evening sunlight illuminates the *ksar* of Aït Benhaddou on the left bank of the Wadi Mellah

↑ Four Egyptian-style statues defending a film set at Atlas Film Studios in Ouarzazate

EXPERIENCE MORE

2
Ouarzazate

C4 From Marrakech, Tinerhir, Taroudant and Zagora Avenue Mohammed V; (0524) 88 24 85

A former garrison town of the French Foreign Legion, now a peaceful provincial town, Ouarzazate was founded in 1928. Located at the intersection of the Draa and Dadès valleys, with the Agadir region to the west, it is on the main route between the mountains and the desert. It is also a good base from which to visit Aït Benhaddou and the Skoura palm grove.

Avenue Mohammed V, the main street, crosses the town and leads to the Dadès Valley. The town has a great many hotels and restaurants, municipal gardens and the crumbling Taourirt Kasbah.

One of the area's main industries is film-making. Hundreds of films have been shot in this region, from David Lean's *Lawrence of Arabia*, through Scorsese's *Kundun*

and Oliver Stone's *Alexander*, to Ridley Scott's *Gladiator*. On the outskirts of town are **Atlas Film Studios** and **CLA Studios**, both of which offer tours to visitors. In the desert behind CLA is a large castle set that is featured in *Game of Thrones*.

About 10 km (6 miles) to the south is the Finnt Oasis, with fine pisé *ksour*. A little further on is the El-Mansour Eddahbi Dam, fed by the Dadès and Ouarzazate rivers, which join to form the Draa. The dam provides water for the golf course, the Draa's palm groves and electricity for the valley. About 7 km (4 miles) northwest of Ouarzazate is the majestic Tiffoultoute Kasbah, offering fine views from its terrace. In the 1960s it was converted

Did You Know?

The Southern Oases experience some of the most extreme heat in Morocco, with highs of 50°C (122°F).

into a hotel to provide rooms during the shooting of David Lean's *Lawrence of Arabia*. It is now a restaurant.

Atlas Film Studios

On road N9, 6 km (4 miles) northwest of Ouarzazate (0524) 88 22 23 8am-6:30pm daily (except during filming)

CLA Studios

On road N9, 5 km (3 miles) northwest of Ouarzazate (0544) 88 20 53 8am-6:30pm daily

3
Taourirt Kasbah

C4 Opposite the crafts centre on the road out of Ouarzazate leading to the Dadès Valley

Ouarzazate's only historic building, the Taourirt Kasbah, stands as a monument to Glaoui expansionism. At the beginning of the 20th century, the Glaouis were lords of the South and controlled access to the High Atlas. They were the first to assist with French expansion in the South. Begun in the 18th century and renovated in the 19th, the kasbah once housed the large Glaoui family and their servants.

The façade, consisting of high, smooth earthen walls, is pitted and decorated with geometric patterns in negative relief. Inside, a maze of staircases at every level of the building leads to rooms of various sizes lit by low windows. The larger rooms have plasterwork decoration featuring floral and geometric motifs, and colourful wooden ceilings. There are also some tiny rooms with low rush-matted ceilings, doorless arches, red-tiled floors and white walls.

→

Geometric patterns in negative relief adorning the façade of Taourirt Kasbah

> **Amazraou, set amid lemon, almond and olive trees on the southern side of the town, is a peaceful haven on the edge of the desert.**

Adjacent to the kasbah is a fortified former Berber village ksar, which probably predates the kasbah. It is inhabited by a busy population. In the narrow winding streets of this *ksar*, you will find an internet café, a former synagogue that now serves as a carpet shop, and a herbalist. The crafts centre opposite the Taourirt Kasbah offers an interesting range of carpets, stone carving, jewellery and pottery, all at relatively high prices.

④ Zagora

A D4 🚌 **From Ouarzazate**
🛈 **(0524) 88 24 85**

Established by the French authorities during the Protectorate, Zagora is the most convenient base for exploring this spectacular region. The famous sign saying "Timbuktu, 52 Days by Camel" evokes the great age of the trans-Saharan caravans, although the illusion is ever so slightly spoiled by the presence of a large concrete *préfecture* (town hall) just behind it.

The village of Amazraou, set amid lemon, almond and olive trees on the southern side of the town, is a peaceful haven on the edge of the desert. In the former *mellah*, the mosque stands next to the abandoned synagogue. Many of Amazraou's inhabitants continue the Jewish tradition of making silver jewellery.

By following a footpath from La Fibule hotel, the summit of Jbel Zagora (from which the town got it's name) can be reached in one hour. It is crowned by a military post and commands a breath-taking view of the valley. The remains of walls indicate the presence of the Almoravids in the 11th century.

Several hotels and tour companies offer excursions in four-wheel-drive vehicles or on camelback. Lasting from a day to two weeks, the tours take in the impressive Chigaga dunes south of Mhamid, and the town of Foum-Zguid, situated to the west of Zagora.

EAT

Douyria
The place for a comforting couscous and tajine - or something a little different, such as roasted goat or even camel, which is a a local delicacy in these parts.

A C4 🏠 **72 Avenue Mohammed V, Ouarzazate** 🌐 **restaurant-ouarzazate.net**

ⓓⓗ ⓓⓗ ⓓⓗ

La Kasbah des Sables
Enjoy a candlelit Berber banquet featuring an enticing mix of Moroccan cuisine and inventive French dishes.

A C4 🏠 **195 Hay Aït Kdif, Ouarzazate** 🌐 **lakasbahdessables. com**

ⓓⓗ ⓓⓗ ⓓⓗ

THE KASBAH

Kasbahs (*tighremt* in Berber) have long fulfilled the role of fortified castles. Housing the ruling family and their many servants within heavily guarded walls, the kasbah acted as a place of refuge for its inhabitants, both people and animals, in times of siege (a common occurence throughout Morocco's tumultuous and at times gruesome history), as well as affording protection from the cold and other threats to safety.

A TYPICAL KASBAH

A lordly residence or family dwelling, the kasbah is an imposing edifice, traditionally built to a square plan. While kasbahs in the mountain valleys are thick-set, those in the southern oases have a taller, more slender outline, and are often constructed from the distinctive red earth that colours the landscape. At each of the four corners are towers crowned with merlons rising above the height of the walls. Their dimensions being dictated by the size of the horizontally placed beams, the rooms are often longer than they are wide. The largest room is the reception hall, which often has a highly decorative painted ceiling and is reserved for men only. The stable and sheepfold are located on the ground floor, as is a fortified granary.

> **INSIDER TIP**
> **Crumbling Kasbahs**
>
> Taliouine and Telouet are home to some beautiful abandoned Glaoui Kasbahs. See them while you still can – these fragile buildings won't withstand the elements for long without proper maintenance.

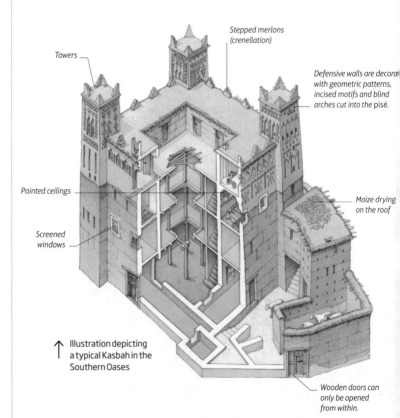

Towers

Stepped merlons (crenellation)

Defensive walls are decora~~te~~ with geometric patterns, incised motifs and blind arches cut into the pisé.

Painted ceilings

Maize drying on the roof

Screened windows

↑ Illustration depicting a typical Kasbah in the Southern Oases

Wooden doors can only be opened from within.

↑ The beautiful Amerhidil Kasbah at Skoura

↑ Timiderte Kasbah sitting on the left bank of Wadi Draa in the Draa Valley

⑤

Draa Valley

🅐D4 🅐200 km (124 miles) between Ouarzazate and Zagora on road N9

Rock engravings discovered near Tinzouline show that the Draa Valley was inhabited by warriors from prehistoric times. The valley, where buildings are in a good state of preservation, contains a wealth of *ksour* and kasbahs.

The road that runs between Ouarzazate and Agdz crosses the desert plateaus of Jbel Tifernine. Beyond Aït Saoun, hills of black rock give way to steep canyons, as the road climbs towards the Tizi-n-Tinififft Pass. To the north appear the foothills of the High Atlas, and to the east is Jbel Sarhro.

Agdz, an unassuming town on the edge of a palm grove, is convenient for a short stop. Between Agdz and Zagora, the road follows a string of oases.

About 6 km (4 miles) from Agdz, a track branching off to the left leads to the majestic *ksar* of Tamnougalt, which once controlled access to the trade routes of the Draa Valley. The interior reveals some striking frescoes, painted in pale colours for a film shoot.

Continuing along the left bank of the Draa, the track leads to the pisé village of Tamnougalt, with narrow, partly covered streets. You may want to bring a torch to view the superb painted ceilings of the kasbah. There is also a former *mellah* with a synagogue.

Back on the Draa Valley road, the elegant Timiderte Kasbah comes into view on the left bank of the *wadi*, backing on to Jbel Sarhro. Villages and *ksour* here are rarely signposted. In Tansikht, a narrow road turns off to the left towards Nekob, Jbel Sarhro and Rissani. The bridge over the *wadi* joins a track that passes through villages in the palm grove. To rejoin the road, you can ford the river in several places.

Still in the direction of Zagora, the road passes the Igdaoun Kasbah, with pyramid-shaped towers. At Tinzouline, a track to the right leads to a site with rock engravings, 7 km (4 miles) away.

The valley narrows as it approaches the Azlag gorge, to the right of which is a high, smooth cliff. Soon after, a signpost saying "Circuit Touristique de Binzouli" will lead you to the palm grove, which reaches Zagora on the other side of the river.

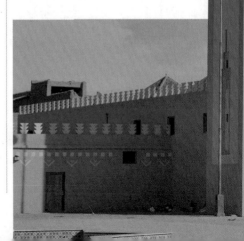

Ochre pisé *koubbas* line the valley, while cemeteries are filled with the vertical flat stones that are typical of Muslim graveyards. Between Tissergate and Zagora, the palm grove stretches to the distant foothills of Jbel Rhart.

6

Jbel Sarhro

D4 **98 km (61 miles) south of Ouarzazate; from Tansikht to Nekob on road R108, or from Boumalne du Dadès**

Jbel Sarhro is a wild and inhospitable region that is still off the tourist track. It is separated from the main Anti-Atlas chain by the Draa Valley to the west and from the High Atlas by Wadi Dadès to the north.

Jbel Sarhro is the territory of the Aït Atta, who, from the 17th and 19th centuries, were the most important tribe in southern Morocco. This seminomadic people never bowed to the power of the sultans, and they were the last to resist the French at the Battle of Bou Gafer in 1933. They usually live in *ksour* but use tents when they drive livestock to pasture.

Jbel Sarhro is a region of sheer rockfaces, undulating plateaux and blackish rocky escarpments. The rugged territory is crossed from north to south by tracks best tackled in a four-wheel-drive vehicle (routes are seldom signposted).

Guides can be hired at the Baha Kasbah in Nekob. The route from Nekob to the Tizi-n-Tazazert Pass is tricky, but the spot known as Bab-n-Ali has some striking rock formations. The track to Boumalne du Dadès crosses the Vallée des Oiseaux (Valley of Birds), home to over 150 species.

7

Tamegroute

D4

Surrounded by ramparts, the *ksar* at Tamegroute contains a Zaouia Nassiriya. This great Islamic learning centre was founded in the 17th century, and its influence extended throughout southern Morocco.

Beneath the arcades of the courtyard, near the entrance to the tomb of the founder Mohammed Bou Nasri, sick and disabled people gather, in the hope of being cured.

The holy man's works laid the foundations of the Koranic Library. A collection of priceless manuscripts displayed in one of the rooms includes an 11th-century gazelle-skin Koran, calligraphy with gold dust and saffron illuminations, and treatises on algebra, astronomy and Arabic literature.

The minaret of the *zaouia* in Tamegroute, and an interior mosaic *(inset)* ↓

In the potters' workshop outside, members of seven families produce traditional pots with a green glaze typical of Tamegroute ceramics.

About 5 km (3 miles) south of Tamegroute, and off to the left, are the Tinfou Dunes, an isolated ridge of sand rising up abruptly in the middle of the stony desert. Leaving Tagounite, a difficult track leads you to the foot of Jbel Tadrart and the beautiful Nesrate Dunes.

↑ A Bedouin man leading a caravan across the great expanse of the Sahara desert

8

Mhamid

△D4

This border post and small administrative centre is the last oasis before the great expanse of the Sahara. To the south stretches a stony desert, the Hammada du Draa. From Mhamid, Wadi Draa sinks below the sand to reappear on the Atlantic coast hundreds of miles to the west.

The ruins of a *ksar* indicate the former existence of a great caravan centre, from which Ahmed el-Mansour's armies set out in the 16th century to take Timbuktu.

Coming from Zagora, the Tizi-Beni-Selmane Pass offers a stunning view of Jbel Bani and the desert, whose covering of volcanic stone gives it its black appearance. A little further on, a track to the left leads to Foum-Rjam, one of the largest prehistoric necropolises in the Maghreb. Tumuli mark thousands of graves. About 45 km (28 miles) south of Mhamid, the Chigaga dunes, which can be reached only by four-wheel drive, stretch to the horizon.

9

Skoura

△C4 🚌From Ouarzazate and Tinerhir

The small sleepy town of Skoura is surrounded by an impressive palm grove, which was laid out in the 12th century by the Almohad sultan Yacoub el-Mansour. The most beautiful kasbahs in southern Morocco are to be found here. Some of these are still occupied, and some are attached to private houses. Many of Skoura's inhabitants, however, have moved into the breeze-block villages that line the road.

The Ben Moro Kasbah stands on the left of the road above Skoura. It was built in the 17th century and, now completely restored, has been converted into a guesthouse. The entrance to the palm grove is on the other side of Wadi Amerhidil. The grove can be explored on foot, by bicycle or on mule-back. The grove is irrigated by *khettaras* (underground channels) and wells dug at regular intervals. Ruined kasbahs stand among palm trees, fig trees, birch and tamarisk – whose tannin-rich flowers are used to process animal skins. The most imposing is the Amerhidil Kasbah, which was once owned by the Glaoui family and which dominates the *wadi*. The restored interior is now open to visitors. The kasbahs of Aït Sidi el-Mati, Aït Souss, El-Kebbaba and Dar Aïchil are also worth a visit.

Further east, Aït Abou, built in 1863 and the oldest kasbah in the palm grove, has six storeys and walls 25 m (82 ft) high. Its outbuildings have been turned into a small short-stay *gîte*. An orchard with pomegranate and fig trees provides the necessary shade for growing crops.

Twenty-five kilometres (15 miles) northeast of Skoura

→ The imposing Amerhidil Kasbah dominating the Skoura palm grove

> Ruined kasbahs stand among palm trees, fig trees, birch and tamarisk, whose tannin-rich flowers are used to process animal skins.

is the village of Toundout, where there are some highly decorated kasbahs. The Marabout of Sidi M'Barek served as a stronghold where the semi-nomadic people stored their crops under the protection of the saint.

A little way beyond Skoura, towards El-Kelaa M'Gouna, unexpected plantations of imported Australia grasses help to preserve moisture in the otherwise arid ground.

10
El-Kelaa M'Gouna

D3 **🛈** Guides' office, Ouarzazate; (0524) 88 24 85

This town, whose name means "fortress", is located in the heart of rose country. In the 10th century, pilgrims returning from Mecca brought *Rosa damascena* back with them to Morocco. These peppery-scented flowers have developed a resistance to the cold and dry conditions in which they are now grown. Each spring, rose-picking produces 3,000 to 4,000 tonnes of petals. The harvest is taken to two local factories. One of them, in El-Kelaa M'Gouna, is laid out in a kasbah, and it is open to visitors in April and May. While a proportion of the roses are used to make rose-water for local distribution, the rest are exported for use in the perfume industry.

The Rose Festival takes place after the harvest and is attended by all the inhabitants of the valleys of the Dadès. Young girls from El-Kelaa M'Gouna, accompanied by *bendirs* (tambourines), perform a sinuous dance, their long hair braided with coloured wool.

On the road out of town is a craft cooperative with about 30 workshops. Daggers are made here, the craftsmen continuing a Jewish tradition of making sheaths and dagger handles out of cedar or camel bone. The steel blades are made in the mountain village of Azlague, not far from El-Kelaa M'Gouna.

Between Skoura and El-Kelaa M'Gouna, kasbahs are set among greenery throughout the Dadès Valley. The modern concrete houses here contrast with the fine traditional buildings. Ruined kasbahs are now part of the local landscape. Many hikes and tours by four-wheel drive are organized from El-Kelaa M'Gouna, particularly to the Vallée des Roses and to the *ksar* at Bou Thrarar, a breathtaking mountain trek.

STAY

Kasbah Aït Ben Damiette
This lovingly restored, earth-built kasbah on the fringes of a remote palm oasis is the perfect desert retreat. A rich mix of traditional French and Moroccan cuisine is available at the hotel restaurant.

C4 **📍** Skoura **w** kasbahaitben damiette.com

ⓓⓗ ⓓⓗ ⓓⓗ

Kasbah Titrit
A stunning kasbah residence with terraces opening to spectacular mountain views and with an attached wellness area.

C4 **📍** Aït Benhaddou **w** kasbah-titrit.net

ⓓⓗ ⓓⓗ ⓓⓗ

Villa Zagora
A traditional villa on the edge of the desert with six elegant suites, plus a Berber tent on the roof for when you want to sleep under the stars.

D4 **📍** Zagora **w** mavillaausahara.com

ⓓⓗ ⓓⓗ ⓓⓗ

Xaluca Dadès Hotel
With panoramic views of the valley below, this exquisite hotel offers a rooftop pool, a spa, numerous sports facilities and a variety of bedroom suites. The hotel also organizes excursions around the High Atlas.

D4 **📍** El-Kelaa M'Gouna **w** xaluca.com

ⓓⓗ ⓓⓗ ⓓⓗ

⓫
Todra Gorge

🅰 D3

Sheer cliffs rise up dramatically each side of the narrow corridor that forms the Todra Gorge. These are the most impressive cliffs in southern Morocco, and they are well known to experienced mountaineers. Wadi Todra flows through this great geological fault and on into the Tinerhir palm grove.

Two hotels make it possible to stop overnight in the Todra

Gorge. The best time to view the gorge is in the morning, when the rays of the sun break through between the high cliffs on either side.

⓬
Dadès Gorge

🅰 D3 🚕 *Grands taxis* from Boumalne du Dadès

Bordered by greenery, Wadi Dadès stands out against the rocky landscape. Cultivated land on the banks of the *wadi* is surrounded by fig, almond and walnut trees and poplars.

About 2 km (1 mile) from Boumalne stands the Aït Mouted Kasbah, which once belonged to the Glaoui.

As the road rises, it passes some dramatic geological limestone folds that have been shaped by erosion. At the foot of these formations stand the ruins of the Aït Arbi Kasbah. Further on are the Tamnalt Kasbahs, whose towers

> 📷 PICTURE PERFECT
> **Dadès Gorge**
>
> There is a particular spot in the gorge where the road contorts through four tight switchbacks before snaking off along a rocky cliff high above the *wadi* floor. Stop at the top for a dramatic photo opportunity.

rise up against a backdrop of rocks that seem to be pressed together sideways like fingers.

Beyond Aït Oudinar, the road crosses Wadi Dadès, following the bottom of the gorge between sheer cliffs. It then runs along the edge of deep canyons, home to royal eagles and vultures. On the plateau, the valley widens again, and small villages overlook the riverbank.

The final stretch from Boumalne du Dadès before Msemrir passes through much wilder country. Beyond Msemrir, a track that is passable only by four-wheel drive leads east to the Todra Gorge and north to the High Atlas and Imilchil.

⓭
Tamtattouchte

🅰 D3 🚗 36 km (22 miles) north of Tinerhir

The picturesque village of Tamtattouchte is located at the other extremity of the Todra Gorge, its earth houses blending into the mountains. Here, small plots of land that stand out from their arid, rocky surroundings are irrigated by Wadi Todra. Tamtattouchte is the starting point of tracks to the Dadès Gorge to the west and Imilchil to the north, leading over

Wadi Todra flowing through the Todra Gorge as the sun hits the cliffs in the morning ↑

passes, through gorges, across plateaux and over mountains. Ask a local for information about the state of tracks negotiable by four-wheel drive, particularly after periods of rainfall. Be aware that no destinations are signposted.

14

Goulmima

D3 From Er-Rachidia and Tinejdad

In the heart of the Rheris oasis, about 20 *ksour* stand on the banks of Wadi Rheris surrounding the village of Goulmima.

The sturdiness of their fortifications make the *ksour* here unusual. Their towers are remarkably high and, when tribal feuds were rife, they protected the inhabitants against the incursions of the Aït Atta, who came to pillage their harvests.

The old fortified village of Goulmima, 2 km (1 mile) east on the road to Erfoud, is worth the detour. The Goulmima *ksar*, which exemplifies southern Moroccan defensive architecture, is surrounded by walls set with two massive towers. Cows and sheep are enclosed within small corrals outside. A gate set at an angle opens onto a second gate. On a small square within the walls stand

a mosque and the well that provides the *ksar* with water. The upper floors of some of the houses span the narrow streets, providing a strange contrast of light and shadow.

15

Tinerhir

D4 From Er-Rachidia and Ouarzazate, and *grands taxis* Hôtel Tomboctou, Ouarzazate; (0524) 88 24 85

This lively town, built on a rocky outcrop, lies midway between the Draa Valley and the Tafilalt. Its northern and southern sides are bordered by a lush palm grove at the foot of arid hills, which contain dozens of *ksour* and kasbahs.

With several silver mines in the vicinity, Tinerhir is a wealthy town known for its jewellery. To the west stands a kasbah once owned by the Glaoui, but

↑ The ruins of a kasbah rising up out of the rocks in the Dadès Gorge

now in a state of disrepair. To the southeast is Aït el-Haj Ali, the former mellah (Jewish quarter), whose houses make an interesting architectural ensemble. North of the town stretches a palm grove irrigated by Wadi Todra.

About 2 km (1 mile) from the bridge across the *wadi*, on the road to the Todra Gorge, a viewing platform commands a stunning view. Here, guides with camels offer their services, but you will need no help walking down into the Todra palm grove for a wonderful 12-km (7.5-mile) hike along the network of shady paths.

On the other side of the *wadi* are many semi-ruined *ksour*. The most interesting and most easily reached are Aït Boujane and Asfalou.

Further north, about 5 km (3 miles) before the start of the gorge, there is an alternative route to the palm grove via the Imarighen spring, the "Spring of the Sacred Fish". At El-Hart-n-Igouramene, south of Tinerhir, craftsmen produce bronze-coloured pottery. The road taking in El-Hart, Tadafalt and Agoudim offers views of many *ksour*, some of which are still inhabited.

Did You Know?

75 % of the Sahara's population live in oases, which occupy 2070 sq km (800 sq miles) of the desert.

THE SOUTHERN AND EASTERN OASES

South of the Atlas mountains, the Sahara begins. However, far from the barren dunescapes that one may expect, the valleys that lead yet further south, namely the Drâa, Dadès, Todra and Ziz, are peppered with lush date-palm oases; verdant havens where water is plentiful and life thrives in abundance. These pockets of civilization in this otherwise arid terrain follow the ancient trade routes that linked the imperial cities of Marrakech and Fès to Timbuktu, Niger and beyond.

IRRIGATION IN THE OASES

The existence of the oases depends on the presence of water, which is either supplied by rivers flowing down from the mountains or by an underground water table. Water rises naturally at the foot of dunes or is pumped by artesian wells along underground channels known as *khettaras*, an ancient and ingenious network with some covering considerable distances. Set in particularly hostile surroundings, oases are very fragile ecological environments that survive thanks only to ceaseless human intervention. Many dams are built to control the flow of water in the *wadis*, which, when they are in flood, can devastate plantations within a few hours. Irrigation is produced by *khettaras* and the water is either drawn from a well or forced to the surface by gravity. The exact amount of water needed for each crop is provided by *seguias*, man-made channels that criss-cross the oasis. Clay plugs are sometimes used to divert the water along particular routes. Crops such as tomatoes, carrots and lettuce, as well as fruit trees such as fig and apricot, thrive in the shade provided by the palm trees.

↑ The oasis town of Boumalne du Dadès in the lush Todra Valley

Clay plugs are used to direct the flow of water to other parts of the oasis.

Barley

Did You Know?

A single date palm tree can provide 30 to 100 kg (66 to 220 lb) of dates per year.

ANIMALS OF THE OASIS

The common bulbul, rufous bush robin, house bunting and doves are some of the more familiar birds seen in the oases. Toads frequent the banks of the watercourses, geckos and lizards cling to stone walls and the trunks of trees, and scorpions hide under stones. During the night, jackals occasionally approach places of human habitation. The fennec, horned viper and herbivorous lizard rarely venture beyond the dunes and rocks where they were born.

1 Young family of fennec foxes.

2 Venomous horned viper, native to the deserts of North Africa.

3 Herbivorous lizard, also known as the Moroccan rock lizard.

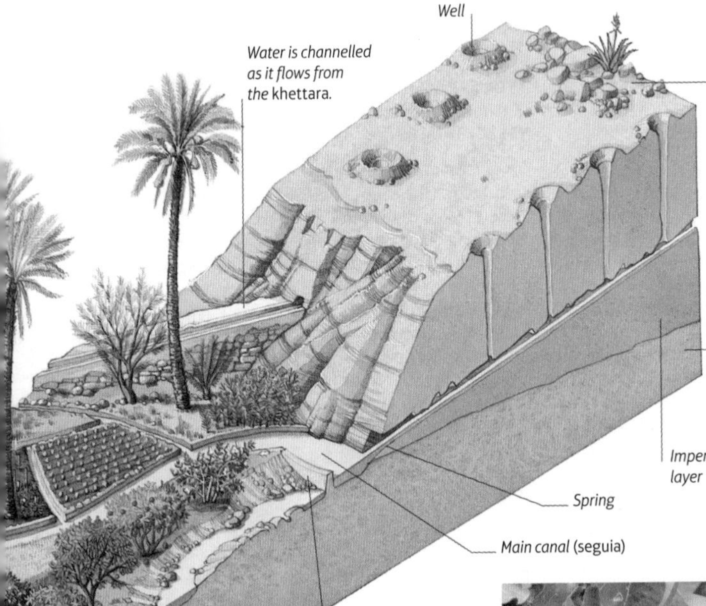

Well

Water is channelled as it flows from the khettara.

Arid zone

Clay

Impervious layer

Spring

Main canal (seguia)

Dam across the river, or wadi

Animal-skin container

→ Wild pears growing in an oasis in Southern Morocco

Wadi Ziz flows south from the High Atlas, carving its way through the mountains ↑

KSOUR IN THE OASES

The Ziz Valley is *ksar* country. The *ksar* (plural *ksour*) was developed as a stronghold against incursions from bandits and nomadic tribes that raided the oases when the harvests had been brought in. The design of these fortified villages is connected to this warlike past. The *ksar*, which usually overlooks an oasis, originally consisted of a central alley with houses on each side. Over time, it grew to become a village with a mosque, a *medersa* and granaries. Built of pisé and earth bricks, every *ksar* bears the stamp of its builders, who each used their own inticate patterns.

16
Boumalne du Dadès

D4 🛈 Tizzarouine Kasbah, Ouarzazate; (0524) 88 24 85

This pleasant stopping place is located at the edge of the desert plateau and at the beginning of the Dadès Gorge. From the edge of the plateau above the town, the view stretches over the Dadès Oasis. At Tizzarouine Kasbah, where there are also fine views, guides offer tours and camping trips in the High Atlas and Jbel Sarhro.

17
Ziz Gorge

E3 🚶 88 km (55 miles) south of Midelt on road N13

Wadi Ziz, which springs near Agoudal, in the heart of the High Atlas, runs east then obliquely south, level with the village of Rich. It then carves a gorge in the mountains, irrigates the Tafilalt then disappears into the Saharan sands. South of Midelt (*p271*), beyond the Tizi-n-Talrhemt Pass, forests give way to arid plains. The fortified villages of the Aït Idzerg tribe, as well as a few old forts of the French Foreign Legion, line the road.

The Tunnel de Foum-Zabel, or Tunnel du Légionnaire, was driven through the limestone rock here by the French Foreign Legion in 1927, thus opening a route to the south. The tunnel opens out onto the

↑ Wadi Ziz irrigating the the thirsty palm trees of the Tafilalt oasis

Ziz Gorge, whose impressive red cliffs jut into the Atlas. Two fine *ksour*, Ifri and Amzrouf, both surrounded by palm trees, stand here.

The Hassan-Addakhil dam, contained by a thick dyke of red earth, demarcates the lower foothills of the Atlas. Built in 1970, it irrigates the Tafilalt and Ziz valleys and provides power for Er-Rachidia.

Source Bleue de Meski

🅐E3 🅐23 km (14 miles) south of Er-Rachidia on road N13

The spring, located 1 km (0.6 miles) off the main road, is a reappearance of Wadi Ziz,

> The tunnel opens out onto the Ziz gorge, whose impressive red cliffs jut into the Atlas. Two fine *ksour*, Ifri and Amzrouf, both surrounded by palm trees, stand here.

which runs underground for part of its course. The blue spring waters flow from a cave at the foot of a cliff into a pool built by the French Foreign Legion. The spring provides water for local villagers and a natural swimming pool for the camp site in the palm grove.

The clifftop offers a view of the oasis and the ruined *ksar* of Meski. The road to Erfoud (*p296*) also offers fine views of the Ziz valley and the oases of Oulad Chaker and Aourfous.

🄳 Er-Rachidia

🅐D3 🚖 🚌From Erfoud, Midelt, Ouarzazate and Figuig 🄸Tourist office; (0535) 57 09 44

As a result of its strategic location between northern and southern Morocco, and between the Atlantic seaboard and Figuig and the Algerian border, Er-Rachidia became the main town in the province. Here the palm groves of the Ziz and Tafilalt begin, and this town stands at the start of the road to the south, making it a convenient stopping off point. Er-Rachidia, also an administrative and military centre, was built by the French in the early 20th century, when it was known as Ksar es-Souk. It gained its present name in 1979 in memory of Moulay Rachid, the first of the Alaouites to overthrow Saadian rule in 1666. Many *ksour* here were abandoned after 1960, when the Ziz broke its banks, causing serious floods and washing away land.

Although they are busy, the town's perfectly straight, gridlike streets hold scant appeal. A craft centre offers locally made pottery, carved wooden objects and rush baskets. Along the main throughfare are numerous shops, as well as restaurants and cafés.

GREAT VIEW
Meski and More

The clifftop at Source Bleue de Meski offers a view of the oasis and the ruined *ksar* below. The road to Erfoud also offers fine views of the Ziz Valley and of the oases of Oulad Chaker and Aoufous.

⑳
Erfoud

Ⓐ E4 🚌 **From Fès, Er-Rachidia, Midelt, Rissani and Tinejdad**

Before the development of the town began in 1930, the French had set up a military post here to watch over the Tafilalt Valley. The Berber tribes put up a long, drawn-out resistance, and the valley was one of the last parts of southern Morocco to surrender.

Erfoud's checkerboard layout is a vestige of its military past. This peaceful town, with an extensive palm grove, is the base for tours of the dunes of the Erg Chebbi desert. From the top of the eastern *borj*, a small bastion 3 km (2 miles) to the southeast, the view takes in a wide swathe of desert and palm groves.

In October, the Erfoud souk overflows with dates of every variety, and the three-day Date Festival takes place, with folk dances and processions of people in traditional costume.

Polished marble containing fossils is Erfoud's other main industry. The cutting workshop, the **Usine de Marmar**, is open to visitors. The road is also bordered with many small craters – the tops of shafts down to *khettaras*.

Usine de Marmar

Ⓐ E4 🅿️ **On road R702 to Tinejdad** ⏰ **8am-noon & 2-4pm Mon-Sat**

㉑
Merzouga

Ⓐ E4 🅿️ **53 km (33 miles) southeast of Erfoud**

The small Saharan oasis of Merzouga is famous for its location at the foot of the photogenic Erg Chebbi dunes. At sunrise or dusk, the half-light gives the sand a fascinating range of colours.

Although they are nearer to Rissani, both Merzouga and the Erg Chebbi dunes are easier to reach from Erfoud. A guide is not necessary, except when high winds whip up the sand. From Erfoud, going in the direction of Taouz, the road degenerates into a track after 16 km (10 miles). Beyond the Auberge Derkaoua, follow the line of telegraph poles, and the dunes come into view on the left. At Merzouga, camel drivers offer one-hour to two-day tours. Dayet Srji, a small lake west of the village, sometimes fills with water during the winter, after sudden rainfall. It attracts hundreds of pink flamingos, storks and other migratory birds.

㉒
Tafilalt Palm Grove

Ⓐ E4 🅿️ **South of Erfoud on road N13**

Stretching out along the bends of Wadi Rheris and Wadi Ziz from Erfoud, the Tafilalt oasis

SALT AND SLAVES

For centuries camel caravans transported precious items such as ivory, ostrich feathers and gold across the Sahara. These were traded for, among other things, salt mined in Morocco, which at one time was worth as much as gold. There was also extensive trade in human slaves. From the 10th to the 19th century as many as 7,000 slaves were transported northwards into Morocco.

nestles in a stretch of greenery, extending beyond Rissani. The oasis was once a welcome stopping-place for caravans, as they arrived exhausted after weeks in the desert.

Today, the inhabitants of the Tafilalt rely on it for their livelihood: the 800,000 date palms that grow here are renowned for their fruit. Unfortunately, since the early 20th century the trees have suffered from Bayoud palm sickness – caused by a microscopic fungus – and the effects of drought.

The October date harvest in the palm grove is a spectacular sight. Owners climb to the top of their trees, and, as the grove resonates with the sound of machetes, bunches of dates crash to the ground in large orange heaps (they turn brown as they ripen).

→
Camels striding across the coppery sand dunes of the Erg Chebbi desert

Symbols of happiness and prosperity, dates figure in many rituals and ceremonies.

The main prayer hall inside the Mausoleum of Moulay Ali Cherif

㉓
Rissani

E4 **From Meknès, Erfoud and Er-Rachidia**

This small town on the edge of the Sahara marks the end of the metalled road and the start of tracks into the desert. To the east is the Hammada du Guir, a stony desert notorious for its violent sandstorms.

Rissani, built close to the ruins of Sijilmassa, was once the capital of the Tafilalt. Sijilmassa is said to have been founded in 757–8 as an independent kingdom, becoming a major stopping place on the trans-Saharan caravan routes. Over the centuries, it became prosperous from trade in gold, slaves, salt, weapons, ivory and spices, reaching its peak in the 13th and 14th centuries. However, religious dissent and the instability of the rival tribes that regularly launched raids on the city led to its destruction. The first town had a *pisé* wall on stone foundations pierced by eight gates, and contained a palace, elegant houses, public baths and many gardens. A few vestiges of these emerge from the sand just west of Rissani.

The Rissani Souk is one of the most famous in the area. Donkeys, mules, sheep and goats are enclosed in corrals. Stalls are piled with shining pyramids of dates, as well as with vegetables and spices. Beneath roofs made of palm-matting and narrow *pisé* alleyways, jewellery, daggers, carpets, woven palm-fibre baskets, pottery and fine local leather items made from goat skins tanned with tamarisk bark are laid out for sale.

South of Rissani, a 20-km (12-mile) route marked by many *ksour* crosses the palm grove. After 2.5 km (1.5 miles) stands the Mausoleum of Moulay Ali Cherif, where the father of Moulay er-Rachid, founder of the Alaouite dynasty, is laid to rest. A courtyard leads to the burial chamber, to which non-Muslims are not admitted. Behind the mausoleum are the ruins of the 19th-century Abbar Ksar. This former residence once housed exiled Alaouite princes, the widows of sultans and part of the royal treasury.

About 2 km (1 mile) from the mausoleum stands the Oulad Abdelhalim Ksar, built in 1900 for the elder brother of Sultan Moulay Hassan. The monumental entrance opens onto a labyrinth of dilapidated rooms. The route takes in many other *ksour*, including those of Assererhine, Irara, Gaouz, and Tabassamt. The *ksar* built in Tinrheras, set on a promontory, also comes into view. The road leading to the Draa Valley via Tazzarine and Tansikht starts from Rissani.

Did You Know?

In 1927 Morocco sent 11 date palms to the US, from which every medjool date grown in America originates.

Tafraoute, in the beautiful valley of the Anti-Atlas

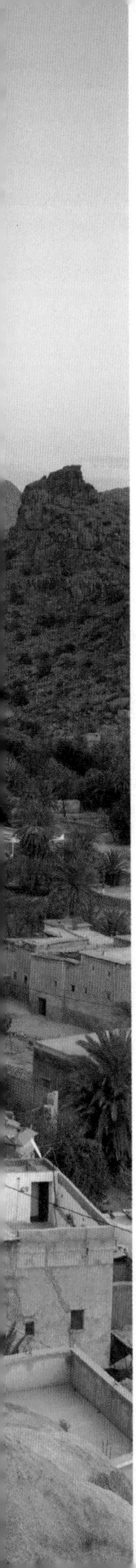

SOUTHERN MOROCCO AND WESTERN SAHARA

Six thousand years ago, hunters forced northwards by the desertification of the Sahara moved into southwestern Morocco, as shown by the thousands of rock engravings that have been discovered in the Anti-Atlas. The Arab conquest in the 7th century inaugurated the age of the independent kingdoms. An important point for trans-Saharan trade between Morocco and Timbuktu, the Atlantic coast was coveted from the 15th century by the Portuguese and the Spaniards, who eventually colonized it in the late 19th century, re-naming it Río de Oro (Golden River). When Spain withdrew from western Sahara in 1975, King Hassan II initiated the Green March, during which 350,000 civilians reasserted Morocco's claim to the region.

The great Souss plain, east of Agadir, lies at the heart of this isolated region. The commercially grown fruit and vegetables here are irrigated by the underground waters of Wadi Souss, and the surrounding argan trees provide food for herds of black goats. To the south, the Anti-Atlas is the final mountainous barrier before the Sahara. Its almost surreal geological folds, shaped by erosion, alternate with verdant oases. Stone-built villages, often with an *agadir* (fortified granary), cluster along *wadis* or at the foot of mountains. Further south, wide deserted beaches are cut off by lagoons that attract thousands of migratory birds.

SOUTHERN MOROCCO
AND WESTERN SAHARA

Must Sees

① Agadir
② Sidi Ifni

Experience More

③ Taroudannt
④ Igherm to Tata
⑤ Akka
⑥ Souss Massa National Park

⑦ Tiznit
⑧ Tafraoute
⑨ Tan Tan and Tan Tan Plage
⑩ Guelmim
⑪ Tarfaya
⑫ Laayoune

Atlantic Ocean

Mirleft

SIDI IFNI ②

N21

GUELMIM ⑩

Plage Blanche
El Abiar   Aït Bekkou

N1

El Ouatia
(Tan Tan Plage)   **TAN TAN** ⑨

Djebel Taskalouine

Dar-Chebika   *Wadi Draa*

N14

TARFAYA ⑪   *Reserve Naturelle Naila*   Sidi Akhfennir   M'sied

N1   Abetteh

As-Sakn

El Hagounia

Daoura

LAAYOUNE ⑫

Al Gada

Laâyoune Airport

N14   N17

N5

Esmara

**WESTERN
SAHARA**

Boucraa

N17

N5

MAURITANIA

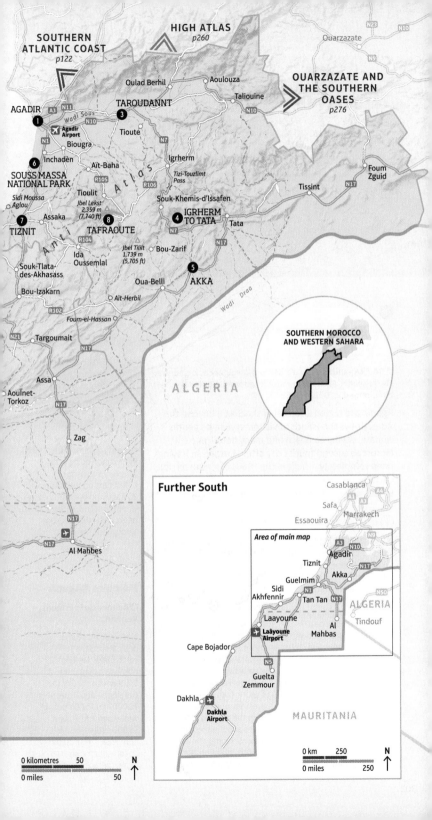

↑ The ruined hilltop kasbah overlooks sandy Agadir beach at sunset

①

AGADIR

🅰B4 🛫 Agadir El-Massira 🚌From Casablanca, Essaouira, Marrakech & Tiznit 🚹 Immeuble Ignouan, Boulevard Mohammed V; (0528) 84 63 77

Agadir, the regional capital of the South beyond the Atlas, draws thousands of visitors a year. Its gentle climate, sheltered beach and many hotels make it Morocco's second tourist city after Marrakech. Having been completely rebuilt in the 1960s after the terrible earthquake that destroyed the city, its wide-open spaces and modernity appeal to many holiday-makers.

① Nouveau Talborj

Agadir's modern centre, the Nouveau Talborj, was built south of the old city, which was completely destroyed in the earthquake of 1960. The main streets of the city centre run parallel to the beach. Pedestrian areas, lined with restaurants, shops and crafts outlets are concentrated around Boulevard Hassan II and Avenue du Prince Moulay Abdallah. There are some fine modern buildings, including the town hall and the stately law courts. The city's bright white buildings are interspersed by many splendid gardens.

② Musée Municipal du Patrimoine Amazighe

🏛 Avenue Hassan II, passage Ait Souss ☎ (0528) 82 16 32 ⏰ 9:30am–5:30pm Mon-Sat

This museum was opened on 29 February 2000, on the day of the commemoration of the reconstruction of Agadir, 40 years after the violent earthquake that destroyed the city. The museum exhibits everyday objects derived from the peoples of the Souss plains and the pre-Saharan regions. Among the exhibits is a rich collection of magnificent Berber jewellery,

superbly displayed alongside information on how the jewellery was made.

Just next door on Boulevard 20 Aout is an open air theatre, where Concerts, shows and music festivals take place throughout the year.

③ Mémoire d'Agadir

🏛 Avenue du Président Kennedy

This small museum is dedicated to the 1960 earthquake. Although it only had a magnitude of 5.8, (about a third of the city's population), between 12,000 and 15,000 people, were killed and around 35,000 people were left homeless. The museum documents the disaster in photographs.

④

Agadir Beach

South of the city, the sheltered beach, in a bay with 9 km (6 miles) of fine sand, is Agadir's main attraction, offering some of the safest swimming off Morocco's Atlantic coast. However, although the city enjoys 300 day of sunshine a year, it is often shrouded in mist in the morning. Sailboards, jet-skis and water scooters can be hired on the beach, and rides, on horses or camels, are also on offer. Many cafés and restaurants line the beach.

⑤

Vallée des Oiseaux

🏠 Avenue Hassan II 🕐 9am-noon & 3-6pm Tue-Sun

This open space in the heart of the city, laid out on a narrow strip of greenery, contains aviaries with a multitude of exotic birds. A small zoo features mouflons (wild mountain sheep) and macaques. There is also a play area for children.

⑥

Souk El-Had

🏠 Rue 2 Mars 🕐 6am-8:30pm Tue-Sun

A short walk southwest of the city centre, Agadir's "Sunday Souk" is a modern, walled market of around 6,000 stalls. The array of goods on offer is vast, from fresh fruit and vegetables to jewellery, home furnishings, and handicrafts. Good buys here include locally produced argan oil and saffron from the nearby region of Taliouine.

⑦

Old Kasbah

At an altitude of 236 m (775 ft), the hilltop ruins of the kasbah, within restored ramparts, offer a stunning view of Agadir and the bay. The kasbah was built in 1540 by Mohammed ech-Cheikh, to keep the Portuguese fortress under surveillance. It was restored in 1752 by Moulay Abdallah and accommodated a garrison of renegade Christians and Turkish mercenaries.

⑧

Polizzi Medina

🏠 Ben-Sergaou 10 km (6 miles) south of Agadir 📞 (0528) 28 02 53 🕐 9am-6pm daily

This medina was created by Coco Polizzi, an Italian architect, who used traditional Moroccan building methods. Houses, restaurants and local craft workshops are plentiful here.

↑ The Morrocan style Polizzi Medina lies just outside Agadir

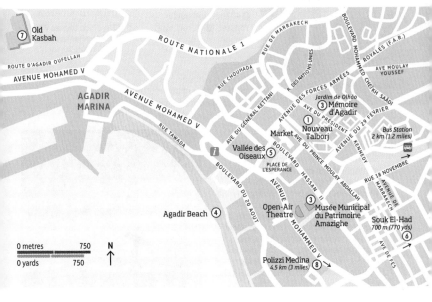

❷
SIDI IFNI

⬛A5 🚌From Tiznit 🛈ONMT Agadir; www.visitmorocco.com

From Tiznit, a scenic minor road leads to the Atlantic coast, which it follows until Sidi Ifni, a popular surf destination. Formerly a Spanish coastal enclave, the town has maintained an Iberian feel. It sits on the crest of a rocky plateau overlooking the ocean, and is buffeted by strong winds and often shrouded in sea mist.

Sidi Ifni's legacy of Spanish colonial rule is still tangible in many ways. At the town centre is Place Hassan II, previously named Plaza de España. On its north side are the former Spanish consulate and a sandcastle-like church, now the law courts. Facing them is the royal palace and town hall.

Beach Life

The beach is long, wide and somewhat wild compared to the sheltered city beach of nearby Agadir. It has a pleasant board-walk lined on the landward side by picturesque blue-and-white houses. At the northern end there is a small shrine, while to the south is the fishing port, where a lively fish market takes place. **Ifni Surf** offers surf lessons and board hire, as well as kayaking, paragliding and desert excursions. About 6 km (4 miles) north of Sidi Ifni is the beautiful Legzira Beach, best known for its impressive natural rock archways.

Ifni Surf

📍47 Avenue Moulay Youssef 🌐ifnisurf.com

←
Blue-and-white houses line the streets of this former Spanish enclave

EAT

Nomad
This laidback eatery serves grilled meats and fresh seafood, as well as a small selection of beer and wine. Plenty of choice for vegetarians.

📍5 Ave Moulay Youssef
📞(0662) 17 33 08
🕐Noon-3pm Tue-Thu, 6-11pm Sat & Sun

🅓🅓🅓

Municipal Market
As well as selling fresh fruit and vegetables, this market has a court-yard filled with stalls of freshly grilled seafood, straight from the boat.

📍Ave Mohammed V & Ave Hassan
🕐10am-10pm

🅓🅓🅓

WATERSPORTS AROUND SIDI IFNI

Sidi Ifni may be known for its laidback atmosphere and slow pace of life, but visitors looking for a hit of adrenaline should head for the beach. Strong Atlantic winds, broad sandy bays and a rocky coastline make Sidi Ifni, and nearby beaches at Legzira and Mirleft, excellent places for surfing and body boarding, among other watersports. The town is home to several surf camps, offering equipment rental and tuition for all levels.

1969
—
The year the Spanish returned the town of Sidi Ifni back to Morocco.

↑ Beautiful natural arches on Legzira Beach, 6 km (4 miles) from Sidi Ifni

EXPERIENCE MORE

3

Taroudannt

B4 **80 km (50 miles) east of Agadir** **From Casablanca, Agadir, Marrakech and Ouarzazate**

Enclosed within red-ochre ramparts and encircled by orchards, orange groves and olive trees, Taroudannt has all the appeal of an old Moroccan fortified town. It was occupied by the Almoravids in 1056 and in the 16th century became the capital of the Saadians, who used it as a base from which to attack the Portuguese in Agadir. Although the Saadians eventually chose Marrakech as their capital, they made Taroudannt wealthy through the riches of the Souss plain, which included sugarcane, cotton, rice and indigo.

Under the Alaouites, the town resisted royal control, forming an alliance with Ahmed Ibn Mahrez, the dissident nephew of Moulay Ismaïl. The latter regained control of the region by massacring the inhabitants.

Taroudannt is a generally peaceful town, except during the annual olive harvest, when it is enlivened by itinerant pickers. Its two main squares are Place Assarag and Place Talmoklate, where horse-drawn carriages can be hired for a tour of the ramparts. Set with bastions and pierced by five gates, they are in a remarkably good state of preservation, a part of them dating from the 18th century.

The souks, between the two squares, are the town's main attraction. The daily Berber market sells spices, vegetables, clothing, household goods, pottery and other items. In the Arab souk the emphasis is on handicrafts: terracotta, wrought iron, brass and copper, pottery, leather goods, carpets and Berber jewellery can be seen. Carvings in chalky white stone are a local speciality. Outside the ramparts is a small tannery, which is open to visitors. Its shop sells goat-skin and camel-hide sandals, lambskin rugs, soft leather bags, belts and slippers.

The peaks of the western High Atlas – particularly Jbel Aoulime – can be reached via road 7020, north of the town. The imposing Tioute kasbah

STAY

Dar el-Hossoun

An eco-friendly, traditionally styled guesthouse and restaurant, built by local artisans in gardens containing over 900 varieties of plants.

B4 **Taroudannt** **w** alhossoun.com

dominates the palm grove about 37 km (23 miles) southeast of town. This was the location for the 1954 film *Ali Baba and the Forty Thieves*. A restaurant adjacent to the kasbah rather spoils the site. On the banks of Wadi Souss, which attracts many migratory birds, stands the older Freija kasbah, now uninhabited.

Between Taroudannt and Ouarzazate, the road (N10) passes through a landscape of wild beauty. Plains covered with argan trees give way to the volcanic massif of Jbel Siroua, which bristles with peaks and where soft rocky folds alternate with plateaux.

Taliouine, a town between two mountain chains, has a stately kasbah once owned by the Glaoui. Though dilapidated, it is still inhabited. The town is at the centre of the world's biggest saffron-growing area. In Tazenakht, 85 km (53 miles) east of Taliouine, beneath Jbel Siroua, carpets with an orange weft are woven by the Ouaouzguite tribe.

↑ A woman photographing rock formations near Oua-Belli, where many prehistoric engravings can be found

❹
Igherm to Tata

🅰B4 🅰Road N10 east from Taroudannt, then road R109 to Tata 🚌Taroudannt, Tiznit, Agadir and Bouizarkane

A relatively new road (built in 1988), the N10 crosses the Anti-Atlas, passing through some remarkable landscapes. Between Taroudannt and Igherm, argan fields alternate with dry-stone villages overlooking terraced plantations.

Igherm, 94 km (58 miles) southeast of Taroudannt, is a large mountain village at an altitude of 1,800 m (5,908 ft). The village is the base of the Ida Oukensous tribe, who are

←

Local fruit and vegetables piled up at the daily Berber souk in Taroudannt

renowned for their dagger- and gun-making. The houses here are built of pink stone, their windows outlined in blue. Women dressed in black and wearing coloured headbands fetch water in tall copper jars (*situle*), which they carry on their heads.

Between Igherm and Tata the road crosses a rugged desert plain, with mountains of folded strata in hues of ochre, yellow and violet. The Tizi-n-Touzlimt Pass, at 1,692 m (5,553 ft), is followed by a succession of oases. In the Souk-Khemis-d'Issafen palm grove, women dressed in indigo can be seen walking around the well-watered gardens, except when the Thursday souk is on. Some 30 *ksour* stand in the great Tata palm grove, where Berber and Arabic are spoken.

Crossing Wadi Tata, which irrigates the grove, the road leads to Agadir-Lehne, where a stone *koubba* stands below a spring. Some 4 km (2.5 miles) further on are the Messalite caves, which are inhabited sporadically by shepherds.

❺
Akka

🅰B5 🅰62 km (39 miles) southwest of Tata on road N12

The Akka palm grove lies north of the village, while a dozen *ksour* are interspersed among the date palms and fig trees. On a hill is Tagadirt, a *mellah*, now in ruins, where the rabbi-adventurer Mardochée Abi Serour – who accompanied the French ascetic Charles de Foucauld on his peregrinations – was born in 1883.

The Aït-Rahhal springs in the palm grove supply the oasis. There is also a strange brick-built minaret dating from the Almohad period.

Many rock engravings can be seen near the village of Oua-Belli, southwest of Akka on road N12 to Bouizarkane, and at Foum-el-Hassan, 90 km (56 miles) further on the same road. You will need to hire a guide (details from Café-Hôtel Tamdoult in Akka). There are also many *igherm* (granaries), some dug into the cliff face.

↑ The edge of the Souss Massa National Park meeting the Atlantic Ocean

6

Souss Massa National Park

🅰B4 🚗65 km (40 miles) south of Agadir on road N1; 50 km (31 miles) north of Tiznit on road N1

The Souss Massa National Park extends along the banks of Wadi Massa, which, en route to the Atlantic, irrigates a large palm grove. This nature reserve, where river and sea water meet, the tides ebb and flow, and winter temperatures are mild, attracts hundreds of species of migratory birds.

The reed beds on the banks of the *wadi* are inhabited by greater flamingos from the Camargue, in southern France, and from Spain, as well as many other species. The primary purpose of the park was to preserve the bald ibis, a species threatened with extinction.

Did You Know?

The vertical poles on the walls of Tiznit's Grand Mosque are to help departed souls enter paradise.

Morocco is home to half the world's population of this curious pink-headed bird.

Only certain areas of the park are open to the public. Visitors should approach the *wadi* from Sidi Rbat. The best time to see the birds is early in the morning, from March to April and October to November.

7

Tiznit

🅰B5 🚗91 km (57 miles) south of Agadir on road N1 🚌From Agadir, Safi, Guelmim and Tafraoute 🚹ONMT Agadir

Located slightly inland from the coast, Tiznit is a small town where the proximity of both the Atlantic and the desert can be felt. In 1881, Sultan Moulay Hassan settled here in order to exert greater control over the Berber tribes of the Souss.

The town came to fame in 1912, when El-Hiba, a populist rebel leader, was proclaimed sultan of Tiznit in the mosque.

→

Jean Vérame's painted rocks rising out of the sparse, lunar landscape near Tafraoute

Opposed to the establishment of the Protectorate in Morocco, El-Hiba conquered the Souss by rallying the tribes of the Anti-Atlas and the Tuareg to his cause. He launched an attack on Marrakech, where he was repulsed by French troops.

It is possible to walk round the 5-km (3-mile) pink pisé ramparts that encircle the town. The *méchouar*, a parade ground that functioned as the pasha's reception courtyard, is lined with arcades beneath which are cafés and shops. Renowned craftsmen still work with silver here, as the Jews once did, producing chunky Berber jewellery and sabres with inlaid handles.

Sidi Moussa Aglou, 15 km (9 miles) northwest of Tiznit, is a fine beach used by surfers. Caves in the cliffs are used by local fishermen.

8

Tafraoute

🅰B5 🚗143 km (89 miles) southeast of Agadir Road N1 from Agadir then road R105; road R104 from Tiznit 🚌Tiznit and Agadir, or *grands taxis* 🚹ONMT Agadir

At an altitude of 1,200 m (3,938 ft), Tafraoute stands in the heart of a stunning valley of the Anti-Atlas. A cirque of

granite, whose colours change at the end of the day from ochre to pink, surrounds the town. The palm groves here are lush, and during the brief period of their flowering (two weeks in February) the almond trees are covered with clouds of pink and white blossom.

The square dry-stone houses consist of a central courtyard and a tower. They are rendered with pastel pink plaster, and their windows are outlined with white limewash.

Tafraoute is the territory of the Ameln, the best known of the six tribes of the Anti-Atlas. They are renowned for their acumen as traders. As spice merchants, they have spread throughout Morocco and also abroad. Limited local resources have forced them to leave their homeland. However, as soon as they can, the émigrés return to build comfortable houses.

Tafraoute is also a centre for the manufacture of round-toed slippers, in natural, red, yellow or embroidered leather.

Jean Vérame's painted rocks are found 3 km (2 miles) north of Tafraoute. These smooth, rounded rocks, painted by the Belgian artist in 1984, rise chaotically from a lunar landscape. Although their colours – red, purple and blue – have faded, the effect is still surreal.

About 4 km (2.5 miles) further north is the fertile Ameln Valley, carpeted with

SAFFRON

Saffron *(Crocus sativus)* is a bulbed herbaceous plant that belongs to the iris family and grows at altitudes of 1,200 to 2,000 m (4,000 to 6,600 ft). Harvesting takes place before sunrise and goes on for 15 to 20 days. It is a delicate process, involving the separation of the red stigmas that contain the colourant from the plant. After drying, some 100,000 flowers produce 1 kg (2.2 lb) of saffron, and just 1 gram is enough to colour 7 litres (12 pints) of liquid. Saffron is used in food, as a dye for carpets and pottery, and for dyeing hair and hands. It is also a medicinal plant that is thought to aid digestion and calm toothache.

orchards and with olive and almond trees. It is dotted with 26 Berber villages perching on the mountainside, above which runs a precipitous mountain chain culminating in Jbel Lekst. The highest village, Taghdichte, is the starting point for the ascent of Jbel Lekst.

North of Tafraoute, on the road to Agadir, is the *igherm* (communal granary) of Ida ou Gnidif, on the top of a hill. A little further on is the fortified village of Tioulit, looking down into the valley. About 3 km (2 miles) south of Tafraoute, a cluster of huge, strangely shaped rocks known as Napoleon's Hat overlooks the village of Agard Oudad. A one-day detour from Tafraoute leads to the Afella Ighir Oasis. Laid out along the *wadi*, it is filled with tiny gardens, palm trees and almond trees. The road becomes a rough track, and you will need a four-wheel drive to continue the journey.

9

Tan Tan and Tan Tan Plage

A5 **125 km (78 miles) southwest of Guelmim on road N1** **Agadir, Tarfaya and Laayoune**

The province of Tan Tan is sparsely populated by pastoral nomads and fishermen.

↑ Fresh oranges for sale at the Sunday souk in Guelmim

The road from Guelmim is good, but police checks are frequent since the region remains a military zone.

The desert town of Tan Tan has a certain raffish charm, with everything from shops and mosques to the *petits taxis* painted in blue or mustard. In the medina, Saharan-style bric-a-brac is for sale and there is a colourful Sunday souk. A *moussem* held in May or June, honouring local resistance hero Sheikh Ma el-Ainin, is the occasion of a huge camel market. At night, in tribal tents, women dance the *guedra* – a joyful blessing ritual particular to Southern Morocco. The word *guedra*, Arabic for "pot", refers to the makeshift drum used in the ritual.

On the coast, 25 km (15 miles) away, is Tan Tan Plage, where some low-key tourism development has begun.

Road R101 leads across the desert to Smara, about 245 km (152 miles) south of Tan Tan. Today no more than a garrison base, this legendary town put up fierce resistance to the expansion of French rule, with the town's imam calling for a holy war (*jihad*) against French colonialism in 1903.

> **HIDDEN GEM**
> ## Abaynou Hot Springs
>
> Located 14 km (9 miles) to the north of Guelmim are the Abaynou hot springs, which have pools for both men and women.

10

Guelmim

A5 **56 km (35 miles) south of Sidi Ifni** **(0528) 87 29 11** **From Agadir, Marrakech, Laayoune and Tan Tan, or grands taxis**

Also known as Goulimine, and sometimes the "Gateway to the Desert", this small settlement of red houses with blue shutters was an important centre on the caravan route from the 11th to the 19th centuries. Today, it is known chiefly for its camel souk.

The vast Plage Blanche (White Beach), some 60 km (37 miles) west of Guelmim, can be reached along tracks. The beautiful Aït Bekkou Oasis, 17 km (11 miles) to the southeast, is the largest in the area.

← Flamingos and storks flocking to the Dait Um Saad lake in the desert outside Laayoune

The desert town of Tan Tan has a certain raffish charm, with everything from shops and mosques to the *petits taxis* painted in blue or mustard.

11

Tarfaya

🚗 235 km (146 miles) south of Tan Tan 🚌 From Tan Tan or grands taxis

The spectacular route between Tan Tan and Tarfaya follows the coastline, where cliffs give way to dunes of white sand.

An expanding fishing port, Tarfaya was a stop on the Service Aéropostale, the French airmail service, in the 1920s and 1930s. There is a statue of airman Saint-Exupéry, who left vivid descriptions of flying over this desolate region in terrible sandstorms. It was also the rallying point for the Green March of 1975.

12

Laayoune

🚗 117 km (73 miles) south of Tarfaya 🛫 & 🚌 From Agadir, Dakhla and Tan Tan ℹ Avenue de l'Islam; (0528) 89 16 94

A large oasis on Wadi Sagia el-Hamra, Laayoune is today the economic capital of the Saharan provinces. Since Spain relinquished the territory in 1975 (*p69*), the town has reaped the benefits of ongoing investment and modernization.

On the outskirts of the city to the north, a large periodic lake known as Dait Um Saad provides a habitat for a great many migratory birds, such as flamingos and storks, in an otherwise barren environment. Dakhla, 540 km (335 km) to the south, stands on the tip of an attractive peninsula. The bay is one of the most beautiful places in the country and is an internationally renowned spot for kite surfing. Dakhla is the last town before the border with Mauritania, some 350 km (217 miles) away. Seek official advice before travelling to the border region.

DISPUTED REGION, WESTERN SAHARA

Western Sahara was colonised by Spain in 1884. When Spain withdrew in 1975, Morocco annexed the territory by staging the "Green March", a peaceful procession of 350,000 Moroccans into the region. The 570,000 native Sahrawis formed the Polisario Front, who launched a guerrilla struggle against the Moroccan occupation. The conflict lasted until a UN-brokered ceasefire in 1991, but it continues to flare up, most recently in 2011. At the present time, most of Western Sahara remains under the control of the Moroccan government and is known as the Southern Provinces. About 20 per cent of Western Sahara is controlled by the Sahrawi Arab Democratic Republic, but this has limited international recognition. The issue of a possible Sahrawi state is a key issue in ongoing peace talks.

NEED TO KNOW

Children on a local bus, Meknès

BEFORE
YOU GO

Forward planning is essential to any successful trip. Be prepared for all eventualities by considering the following points before you travel.

AT A GLANCE

CURRENCY
Dirham

(Dh)

AVERAGE DAILY SPEND

SAVE	SPEND	SPLURGE
600Dh	**1,1200Dh**	**1,800Dh**

BOTTLED WATER	COFFEE	BEER	DINNER FOR TWO
8Dh	**15Dh**	**40Dh**	**200Dh**

ESSENTIAL PHRASES

Hello	As-salaam aleikum
Goodbye	B'salaama
Please	Minfadlak/minfadlik
Thank you	Shukran
Do you speak English	Itkelim Ingleezi?
I don't understand	Mafayimtish

ELECTRICITY SUPPLY

Power sockets are type C and E, fitting two-pronged plugs. The standard voltage is 220 volts.

Passports and Visas

For tourist visits of up to three months, UK and most EU nationals, and citizens of the US, Canada, Australia and New Zealand do not need a visa to enter the country. Your passport must be valid for at least six months from your date of entry. Consult your nearest British embassy or check the **UK Government** website for up-to-date visa information specific to your home country.
UK Government
W gov.uk

Travel Safety Advice

Travel in Morocco is generally safe, although most official sources warn against travel in certain parts of the Western Sahara. Visitors can get up-to-date travel safety information from the **UK Foreign and Commonwealth Office**, the **US State Department**, and the **Department of Foreign Affairs and Trade** in Australia.
Australia
W smartraveller.gov.au
UK
W gov.uk/foreign-travel-advice
US
W travel.state.gov

Customs Information

An individual is permitted to bring the following into Morocco for personal use:
Tobacco products 200 cigarettes, 100 cigarillos, 50 cigars or 400 grams of tobacco.
Alcohol 1 litre of spirits and 1 litre of wine.
Perfume 150ml of perfume and 250ml of eau de toilette.

Insurance

It is wise to take out an insurance policy covering theft, loss of belongings, cancellation and delays. Morocco does not have any reciprocal health care agreements with other countries, so taking out comprehensive medical insurance is recommended.

Vaccinations

There are no required vaccinations for Morocco, although some health organisations recommend inoculations against hepatitis A and typhoid, which can both be contracted in Morocco through contaminated food or water.

Money

Debit cards and credit cards such as Visa and MasterCard are accepted in most shops and restaurants. American Express is less widely accepted. Be aware that credit cards often attract a surcharge of 5 per cent from Moroccan businesses. ATMs are widely available in towns and cities, although most will issue no more than 2,000Dh at a time. It is always worth carrying some cash, as many smaller businesses and markets, especially in more remote areas, still accept cash only. If you're travelling in out-of-the-way places, make sure you have enough cash to last until you get to a decent-sized town.

Tipping is an ingrained part of Moroccan society. Almost any service rendered will warrant a tip, known as baksheesh. Keep a stash of small denomination notes for this purpose.

Booking Accommodation

Morocco offers a huge variety of accommodation, from luxury five star hotels to budget hostels. All price ranges are catered for. Lodgings can fill up quickly in popular destinations such as Marrakech and Agadir, and prices are higher at peak times such as Easter, summer and Christmas. Make sure that your chosen accommodation has air conditioning if you are visiting between May and October, and heating in January and February. Campsites can be found in most towns and cities, and along the coast.

Travellers with Specific Needs

Outside of the five-star hotels and some of the more modern museums, not much in Morocco is wheelchair-accessible. In the medinas, roads are often rutted and crowded. Staircases often do not have bannisters. On the plus side, Moroccans are extremely accommodating and resourceful, and do their best to make things as easy as possible. The **Disabled Tourist Guide** website offers information and advice on travel in Morocco for those with specific needs.
Disabled Tourist Guide
w disabled-tourist-guide.com

Language

There are two official languages in Morocco – Arabic and Tamazight (Berber). The version of Arabic spoken is known as Darija, which is a dialect of standard Arabic. Most educated Moroccans also speak French. Signs in the country are in Arabic and French. Some also speak Spanish, especially in the north, in the areas that were once colonized by Spain. Many Moroccans, particularly those working in tourism, will also speak some English.

Closures

Fridays Some businesses close on the Muslim holy day, particularly in the souks and traditional parts of town.
Saturdays The official working week is Monday–Friday, and many business only open for a half day on Saturday.
Sundays All public businesses and banks are closed, as are many shops.
Public holidays Schools and public services are closed for the day; shops, museums and attractions either close early or for the day.

PUBLIC HOLIDAYS	
New Year's Day	1 Jan
Labour Day	1 May
Ramadan begins	6 May (2019) 24 Apr (2020)
Eid al-Fitr	5 Jun (2019) 24 May (2020)
Feast of the Throne	30 Jul
Eid al-Adha	12 Aug (2019) 31 Jul (2020)
Revolution Day	20 Aug
Youth Day	21 Aug
Islamic New Year	1 Sep (2019) 20 Aug (2020)
Green March Day	6 Nov
Independence Day	18 Nov

GETTING AROUND

Long-distance trains and buses connect the major towns and cities. To get away from the main highways consider hiring a car, or even a car and driver.

AT A GLANCE

TRAVEL COSTS

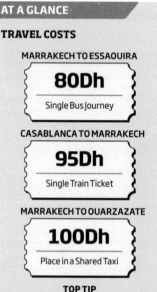

MARRAKECH TO ESSAOUIRA

80Dh

Single Bus Journey

CASABLANCA TO MARRAKECH

95Dh

Single Train Ticket

MARRAKECH TO OUARZAZATE

100Dh

Place in a Shared Taxi

TOP TIP
Avoid on-the-spot fines – be sure to stamp your ticket to validate your journey.

SPEED LIMIT

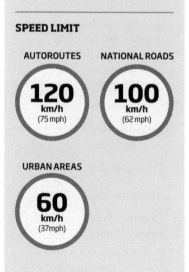

AUTOROUTES

120 km/h (75 mph)

NATIONAL ROADS

100 km/h (62 mph)

URBAN AREAS

60 km/h (37mph)

Arriving by Air

The busiest airports in Morocco with the most international flights are Mohammed V Airport in Casablanca, Marrakech Menara Airport and Agadir al Massia Airport, although Agadir mainly caters for package tourists. There are smaller airports at Rabat, Fès and Tangier, among other places, but they receive fewer direct international flights and flying into them from overseas is likely to involve a connection at Casablanca.

Domestic Air Travel

The national carrier **Royal Air Maroc** is the main domestic airline. It serves a multitude of airports including Agadir, Beni Mellal, Dakhla, Essaouira, Fès, Guelmim, Al-Hoceima, Laayoune, Nador, Ouarzazate, Oujda, Rabat, Er-Rachidia, Tangier, Tan Tan, Tetouan and Zagora. Internal flights are expensive compared to the train or bus and may not always be that much quicker as everything is routed through the hub of Casablanca. For comparison, a one-way flight from Marrakech to Fès will cost around £90 and take three hours, while a first-class ticket on the train costs around £26 and the journey takes eight hours.
Royal Air Maroc
W royalairmaroc.com

Train Travel

The train network in Morocco is not extensive but the service is excellent, benefitting from substantial investment. A single line running approximately north–south connects Tangier and Marrakech via Rabat and Casablanca, with an east–west link running via Meknès and Fès to Oujda on the border with Algeria. Fast, modern, air-conditioned *trains rapides climatisés* are operated by the Office Nationale des Chemins de Fer Maroccains (**ONCF**). Trains are frequent, comfortable, generally run on time and are cheap. In 2019, a new high-speed TGV is due to start running between Casablanca and Tangier that will more than halve the current four hours and 45-minute journey time. First- and second-

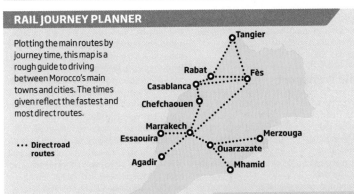

GETTING TO AND FROM THE AIRPORT

Airport	Distance to city	Taxi fare	Public Transport	Journey time	Price
Casablanca	16 miles (25 km)	200–300Dh	CTM Bus	45 mins	20Dh
Marrakech	4 miles (6 km)	70Dh	Bus No.19	15 mins	30Dh
Agadir	13 miles (21 km)	250Dh	Bus No.22	40 mins	30Dh

RAIL JOURNEY PLANNER

Plotting the main routes by journey time, this map is a rough guide to driving between Morocco's main towns and cities. The times given reflect the fastest and most direct routes.

··· Direct road routes

Agadir to Marrakech	3 hrs
Casablanca to Marrakech	3 hrs
Casablanca to Fès	3 hrs
Fès to Marrakech	8 hrs
Fès to Rabat	2.5 hrs
Marrakech to Essaouira	3 hrs
Marrakech to Ouarzazate	4 hrs
Ouarzazate to Merzouga	5 hrs
Ouarzazate to Mhamid	4.5 hrs
Tangier to Fès	4.5 hrs
Tangier to Chefchaouen	2.5 hrs

class options are offered, and there is also an overnight sleeper service between Tangier and Marrakech. Advance bookings can be made on the ONCF website, although It is usually possible to buy a seat on the day, particularly in second-class which has no seat reservations. Second class is perfectly adequate for short journey, but for longer distances it is worth paying more for first class.

ONCF
 oncf.ma

Long-Distance Bus Travel

Long-distance buses connect all major towns and cities. The main operators are **CTM** and **Supratours**. Buses are comfortable and cheap. On busy routes, such as Marrakech–Essaouira and Casablanca–Marrakech, book a few days ahead.

CTM
 ctm.ma

Supratours
 oncf.ma

Grand Taxi

An alternative to the long-distance bus is the *grand taxi*, or shared taxi. These are traditionally Mercedes saloons, although they are increasingly being replaced by people carriers, and operate like minibuses. They gather near bus stations or public squares with their destinations posted in the window or shouted out by the driver. Once the vehicle has filled up with passengers it leaves. The Mercedes cars take six passengers, the people carriers considerably more. The fixed-rate fares are generally a little higher than the bus but the advantage is that departures are typically far more frequent. The *grands taxis* often ply routes that are not well-served by the buses, including over the Tizi-n-Test and Tizi-n-Tichka passes, through the Ziz and Draa Valleys, and in the Rif Mountains. Be aware, however, that seatbelts are rare and drivers often don't adhere to speed limits.

Public Transport

The bigger towns and cities have public bus services. These are cheap (tickets can be as little as 5Dh) but routes are often limited and usually serve the suburbs rather than places that a visitor would want to go. Public buses can also be very overcrowded. Many Moroccans prefer to use taxis instead.

A tramway connects Rabat and Salé, crossing the Wadi Bou Regreg. The network has two lines with a total of 32 stations and is 19.5 km 12 miles) long. Tickets are available from the driver. There is also a tram system in Casablanca connecting the city centre to outlying residential areas.

Petit Taxi

Regular taxis (as opposed to the *grands taxis*) are known as *petits taxis*. They are usually small cars taking only three or four passengers. They are abundant in most Moroccan cities and can be flagged down on the street. *Petits taxis* are far cheaper than taking a taxi in Europe or the US. However, these taxis often do not have meters and it is necessary to negotiate a fixed price in advance with the driver. To avoid being exploited ask at your hotel what the correct fares are for local journeys. Some *petits taxis* in cities do have meters but drivers often do not want to turn them on. If this is the case, get out and find another taxi.

Petits taxis are not permitted to carry passengers beyond the limits of the city in which they operate. If you want to make a daytrip out of town you need to hire a *grand taxi*. To identify to which city a *petit taxi* belongs, each city's cabs are a particular colour. For example, in Marrakech they are all beige, while in Casablanca they are red and in Tangier they are blue.

Driving

With its magnificent scenery, much of Morocco is a pleasure to drive through and a car is by far the easiest way to explore beyond major cities. If you are not confident driving in a foreign country, then hiring a car and driver could be an option.

Driving to Morocco

It is possible to drive to Morocco via Spain taking a car ferry across the Strait of Gibraltar.

Driving in Morocco

The imperfect road network is constantly under improvement and the number of metalled roads means that a four-wheel-drive vehicle is no longer essential, even in the south. A greater hazard is Moroccan driving standards. Two-lane highways can frequently be filled by three or four vehicles jostling for position. Adherence to any sort of highway code often seems optional. Away from the main highways beware of obstacles such as donkeys, camels and livestock crossing. As a general rule, avoid driving at night, when carts and bicycles with no lights are a real hazard. Mountain passes can be hair-raising, with tight, hairpin bends and no safety barriers. Satellite navigation is available in Morocco for driving around major towns and cities.

In large towns and cities, an attendant wearing a small brass badge is assigned to every pavement. This *gardien de voitures* will help you to park, will watch your car in your absence and help you manoeuvre out of your parking place. Payment for this service varies according to how long the car is parked, and is at the driver's discretion.

Car Rental

Cities and airports are well provided with car-hire companies, including major international chains such as Avis, Europcar and Hertz. There are also plenty of local outfits, which, while cheaper, may not offer reliable vehicles or breakdown support. We recommend booking via a comparison site such as **Auto Europe** and checking online reviews of hire outfits. Aside from the credit card required for the deposit, to hire a car you must be over 21 and have a full driving licence.

Car rental rates are reasonable. Check the terms of your agreement carefully, especially clauses relating to insurance and cover in case of accident or theft. Also, be sure to check the state of the vehicle and ask for any damage to be noted before you drive off. Rental cars in Morocco are delivered empty of petrol and are returned empty. The major companies will allow you to pick up the vehicle in one city and drop it off in another.

An alternative to renting a car and driving yourself is to hire a car and driver. Most hotels have a list of recommended drivers. You could also negotiate a day rate with a *grand taxi* (*petits taxis* are not allowed beyond city limits). This can be a cost-effective way of getting around for groups.

Auto Europe
ⓦ autoeurope.co.uk

Rules of the Road

Drive on the right. The Moroccan highway code is based on the French system, giving priority to traffic from the right at roundabouts and junctions. Seat belts must be worn at all times by the driver and all passengers. In general, Moroccan drivers obey traffic lights, perhaps because most junctions are patrolled by a gendarme or policeman.

Cycling

Morocco is a terrific country for cycling due to its varied and interesting landscapes. Dedicated road tourers recommend the Rif Mountains, High Atlas and Southern Oases as particularly rewarding areas to explore on two wheels. They are also all relatively light on vehicular traffic. Roads are generally well surfaced, although in more remote countryside areas they can be potholed. It is best to have thicker-than-average tyres of at least 28mm or 35mm to cope with the terrain. It is wise to carry plenty of water and calorific snacks – there can be long stretches where you will find nothing to eat – as well as long-sleeve tops to protect from sunburn and a warm fleece for cold nights at higher altitudes.

There is a little in the way of support for cyclists, such as touring clubs or bicycle repair shops. You may prefer to travel with a specialist company such as **Morocco Bike Tours** or **Maroc Nature**, both of which can organise either day tours or longer rides, and provide bicycles and on-road support.

Morocco Bike Tours
ⓦ bike-morocco.com
Maroc Nature
ⓦ maroc-nature.com

Boats and Ferries

There are several options for sailing between Spain and northern Morocco across the Strait of Gibraltar. Africa Morocco Link (AML), Baleria and Transmediterránea all operate car ferry services from Algeciras to Tangier, with frequent daily sailings. The journey takes 1.5 hrs and prices start at around £100 for a car with two people. A company called Intershipping operates five ferries a day between Tarifa and Tangier, while GNV runs twice-weekly services between Barcelona and Tangier. The easiest way to reserve a space is via a specialist ferry booking site such as **aferry** or **Direct Ferries.**

aferry
ⓦ aferry.co.uk
Direct Ferries
ⓦ directferries.co.uk

Trekking

With its stunning mountains, Morocco is a superb destination for trekking. From Jebel Toubkal in the High Atlas to the Rif Mountains, there are plenty of beautiful landscapes to explore. Pack sturdy walking boots, sun cream, a sun hat and a waterproof and windproof jacket for trekking all year round. In June to August, wear long-sleeved shirts and bring a fleece or jumper for night time, when it can get chilly. During winter, be prepared for very cold weather and always take warm clothing, including a woolly hat and gloves.

It is recommended to hire a qualified guide – *guide de montagne.* As well as guiding you and keeping you safe, they will know local people and act as a translator. Official guides carry photo-identity cards and should be authorised by the l'Association Nationale des Guides et Accompagnateurs en Montagne du Maroc. They will have been trained in first aid. Fully qualified mountain guides can be found through the **Bureaux des Guides** in Imlil, Setti Fatma, Chefchaouen and the Aït Bougoumez Valley. Negotiate all fees before departure.

Bureaux des Guides
ⓦ bureaudesguidesimlil.com

On Foot

Town centres are easy to explore on foot and best appreciated at a relaxed pace, especially if you have time to enjoy the maze of narrow streets Take care when crossing roads.

CALÈCHE RIDES

Calèches
Several towns and cities, including Marrakech and Taroudannt, have horse-drawn carriages, known as calèches. Hiring one costs more than a *petit taxi,* but they can be a fun way of sightseeing. Official prices are posted at the carriage ranks.

PRACTICAL
INFORMATION

A little local know-how goes a long way in Morocco. Here you can find all the essential advice and information you will need during your stay.

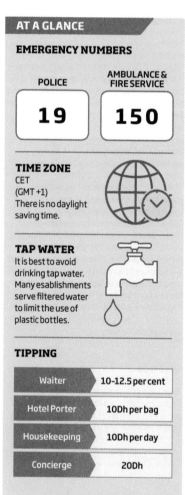

EMERGENCY NUMBERS

POLICE	AMBULANCE & FIRE SERVICE
19	**150**

TIME ZONE
CET
(GMT +1)
There is no daylight saving time.

TAP WATER
It is best to avoid drinking tap water. Many esablishments serve filtered water to limit the use of plastic bottles.

TIPPING

Waiter	10–12.5 per cent
Hotel Porter	10Dh per bag
Housekeeping	10Dh per day
Concierge	20Dh

Personal Security

Beware of pickpockets in crowded tourist areas such as the souks. In Marrakech visitors have had their bags snatched by thieves on scooters. Use your common sense and be alert to your surroundings. If you have anything stolen, report the crime as soon as possible at the nearest office of the tourist police (Brigade Touristique). Get a copy of the crime report to claim on your insurance. Contact your embassy or consulate if your passport is stolen or in the event of a serious crime or accident.

Health

For minor ailments go to a pharmacy or chemist, which are usually very well stocked and have knowledgeable staff. These are plentiful in towns and cities. If you have an accident or medical problem requiring non-urgent medical attention, ask at your hotel for a doctor, or go to the nearest hospital. Embassy websites sometimes list doctors and clinics. You will have to pay for medical treatment on the spot, including any supplies used.

Smoking, Alcohol and Drugs

Moroccan law prohibits smoking in most public buildings but this is rarely enforced.

Although Muslims are forbidden to drink alcohol, Morocco is a moderate Islamic country. It has bars – although not many – and most restaurants, especially those frequented by foreigners, serve beer, wine and spirits.

While hashish, known locally as *kif*, is illegal, plenty of Moroccans smoke it. Visitors may well be offered *kif* for sale, particularly in the Rif, but the penalty for buying or smoking hashish is ten years' imprisonment. It is best avoided.

ID

Visitors to Morocco are not required to carry ID at all times, but it is a good idea to keep a photocopy of the information pages of your passport on your person.

Visiting Places of Worship

Non-Muslims are not allowed inside mosques and religious shrines in Morocco. The one exception is the Hassan II Mosque *(p110)* in Casablanca and the old Tin Mal mosque *(p269)*, which non-Muslims can visit as part of a guided tour.

Religious Customs

Islam is the state religion, and the king of Morocco is the leader of the faithful. It is thus considered very bad form to criticize religion. It is also ill-mannered to disturb someone while they are at prayer. It is above all during Ramadan that certain rules must be obeyed. The fast of Ramadan is strictly observed in Morocco, and many dining establishments close during daylight hours as a result. Non-Muslims should avoid eating and drinking in public.

Dress Code

To avoid offence and being stared at, female visitors to Morocco should dress modestly, particularly when travelling outside the big cities. In practice, this means covering the shoulders and not wearing shorts. Dresses and skirts should be at least knee length. It is not necessary to cover your hair.

LGBT

Homosexuality is illegal in Morocco, and is technically punishable by up to three years of imprisonment. However, this is rarely enforced, and this law does not apply to non-Moroccan same-sex partners visiting the country. Morocco is, in fact, a popular holiday destination for members of the LGBT community. As with same-sex couples, LGBT travellers should use discretion. Public displays of affection by both gay and straight couples are generally frowned upon, and should be avoided since Morocco's largely Muslim population are extremely conservative in this regard.

Mobile Phones and Wi-Fi

Visitors can buy pay-as-you-go SIM cards from a variety of local providers. Many hotels and riads offer free Wi-Fi, as do many restaurants, cafés and train and bus stations.

Post

Main post offices, operated by Poste Maroc, are found in the centres of major towns and cities. Look for a yellow "PTT" sign or La Poste logo. You can also buy stamps at *tabacs*, the small tobacco and newspaper kiosks scattered about city centres. The postal system is fairly reliable, if not terribly fast.

Bargaining

You may bitterly disappoint a trader if you do not show a willingness to indulge in their ritual of bargaining, a custom that is very dear to them. Bargaining revolves around the considerable difference between the price quoted by the buyer and that offered by the seller, and the slow process by which the two arrive at a mutually fair figure. The whole process is treated like a game, so keep smiling, be polite and enjoy the spectacle. A third of the asking price is a good place to start. If you manage to get a good deal, you may feel that you have undercut the seller – don't worry, they wouldn't sell it if they weren't making a profit.

Taxes and Refunds

VAT of 20 per cent is levied on most goods and services. Visitors may be eligible for a refund on presentation of a receipt for purchases of over 2,000Dh. This service is available at Casablanca and Marrakech airports only.

WEBSITES AND APPS

www.visitmorocco.com
Morocco's official tourist board website provides excellent recommendations for accomodation, tours and trips.

www.moroccoworldnews.com
English-language news website

Careem
Casablanca's answer to UBER. Download the app before you travel in order to set up your account.

INDEX

GLOSSARY

adrar: mountain.

agadir: collective granary in the western Atlas.

agdal: large garden, orchard.

aguelmane: permanent natural lake.

ahidou: collective dance performed by the Berber tribes of the Middle Atlas and eastern High Atlas.

ahwach: collective dance performed by villagers of the western High Atlas and the Anti-Atlas.

aïd: festival.

aït: "son of", referring to a tribe or the region occupied by this tribe.

Ammeln: Berber tribe of the Anti-Atlas whose language is Chleuh (qv).

assif: river or watercourse.

bab: city gate.

baraka: divine blessing, which is passed down from parent to child. *Baraka* is also obtained by making a pilgrimage to a holy shrine.

bendir: drum consisting of a goatskin stretched over a frame.

bled: countryside, village.

borj: bastion or tower set at the corners of the defensive walls of fortified houses.

burnous: voluminous woollen hooded cloak worn by men.

cadi: religious judge, once having the power to impose *sharia* law.

caid: chief of a defined territory, subordinate to the governor of a province.

caliph: title held by a Muslim chief, designating Mohammed's successor.

chergui: hot, dry southeasterly wind.

Chikhate: female dancer from the Middle Atlas.

Chleuh: Berber tribe of the Atlas and Anti-Atlas. Also the language spoken by the tribes of these regions.

dahir: decree having the force of law in Morocco.

dar: house.

dayet: natural lake formed by underground water.

diffa: feast-day meal.

dirham: Moroccan unit of currency.

douar: hamlet.

emir: personal title meaning "he who commands".

erg: expanse of sand or ridge of dunes.

Fassi: inhabitant of Fès.

fiqh: Islamic legal code.

fondouk: in the past, hostelry for travelling merchants, their beasts of burden and their merchandise.

gebs: plaster that can be decoratively carved. Also known as stucco.

gurbi: house of semi-nomadic people, built with mud and branches.

Gnaoua: religious brotherhood of popular belief. Followers consider themselves to be the spiritual descendants of Bilal, an Ethiopian slave, whom the Prophet Mohammed set free before making him his muezzin (qv).

guedra: dance characteristic of the Goulimine region of Morocco, performed by kneeling women. Also the large drum that is played to accompany the dancers.

Hadith: collection of legends relating to the life, words and deeds of the Prophet Mohammed.

Hadj: pilgrimage to Mecca.

haik: long woman's wrap made from a single piece of fabric, worn draped around the body.

hamada: stony, arid plateau in the Sahara.

hammam: Traditional Moroccan bath.

hanbel: carpet or blanket woven by Berbers.

Hegira: starting point of the Muslim era, on 16 July 622.

henna: shrub grown for its leaves, which, among other things, are used in the manufacture of cosmetics.

igherm: communal fortified granary typical of the central High Atlas.

imam: Islamic leader of congregational prayer.

jbel: mountain.

jellaba: wide-sleeved, hooded garment worn by both men and women.

jemaa: village assembly of the heads of families in Berber tribes.

kaftan: long woman's garment secured at the front and decorated with passementerie and embroidery.

kasbah: fortified house with a single crenellated tower, or four crenellated towers, one at each corner of the walls.

khoubz: bread (usually a circular loaf).

khaima: tent made of woven goat-hair or camel-hair, used by the nomads of the Sahara and the semi-nomadic people of the Atlas.

khettara: underground channels for the provision of water, along whose course wells are sunk. Synonymous with foggara.

koubba: cube-like building crowned by a dome and housing the tomb of a venerated individual.

ksar (pl. *ksour*): fortified village surrounded by solid walls set with towers at the angles.

Lalla: title of respect given to women.

maalem: master-craftsman.

makhzen: central power, royal authority.

marabout: prestigious head of a religious brotherhood. By extension, the term also refers to the tomb of such a holy man.

mashrabiyya: wooden latticework panel used as a screen in front of balconies and in the windows of mosques and houses, to hide those within from view.

méchouar: parade ground at the entrance to a royal palace.

medersa: Koranic school with resident students.

medina: traditional Arab town enclosed by ramparts; from Medina, the city where the Prophet Mohammed found refuge from persecution.

mellah: Jewish quarter of a medina.

menzah: pavilion in a palace garden.

mihrab: niche in a mosque, indicating the direction of Mecca.

minaret: tower of a mosque from the top of which the muezzin (qv), or an electric recording, calls the faithful to prayer.

minbar: pulpit in a mosque, from which the imam (qv) leads Friday prayers.

moqqade: head of a village or of a religious brotherhood.

Mouloud: birthday of the Prophet Mohammed.

moussem: important annual festival involving a pilgrimage to the tomb of a saint, a commercial fair and popular entertainment.

muezzin: religious official who calls the faithful to prayer.

muqarna: decorative elements in the form of stalactites, made of stucco or wood and suspended from the ceiling.

nisrani: "Nazarene"– a Christian, or European.

pisé: mixture of sun-baked earth, grit and sometimes straw used as a building material in rural areas.

qibla: direction of Mecca, indicated in mosques by a wall in the centre of which is the mihrab (qv).

Ramadan: ninth month of the Muslim (lunar) year, during which Muslims are required to fast from sunrise to sunset.

reg: stony desert.

riad: traditional residence that is organized around a courtyard planted with trees and flowers.

ribat: fortified monastery from where Muslim warrior monks set out to spread the Islamic faith.

seguia: irrigation canal for distribution of water to crops.

serdal: brightly coloured scarf worn by Berber women, decorated with coins.

seroual: loose, calf-length trousers fastened at the waist and the knees, worn under the *jellaba* (qv).

shamir: long, wide-sleeved man's shirt worn under another garment.

sharia: religious law based on the teachings of the Koran.

sheikh: chief of a tribal subdivision or the leader of a religious brotherhood.

sherif (pl. shorfa): descendant of the Prophet Mohammed.

shorfa: *see sherif.*

souk: market, laid out according to the various goods and services that the stallholders offer.

sura: verse of the Koran.

tighremt: Berber word for a kasbah (qv). A fortified patriarchal house several storeys high with towers at the corners.

tizi: mountain pass.

wadi: river bed that is dry or semi-dry except in rainy season; river; river valley. Anglicized form of *oued.*

zakat: obligatory almsgiving. One of the five pillars of Islam.

zaouïa: seat of a religious brotherhood that gives religious instruction, the shrine where a *marabout* (qv) is buried.

zellij: geometric tilework, typically arranged in intricate, colourful patterns.

FRENCH PHRASE BOOK

IN EMERGENCY

Help!	Au secours!	oh se**koor**
Stop!	Arrêtez!	aret-**ay**
Call a	Appelez un	apuh-**lay** uñ
doctor!	médecin!	med**sañ**
Call an	Appelez une	apuh-**lay** oon
ambulance!	ambulance!	oñboo-**loñs**
Call the	Appelez la	apuh-**lay** lah
police!	police!	poh-**lees**
Call the fire	Appelez les	apuh-lay leh
department!	pompiers!	poñ-**peeyay**
Where is the	Où est l'hôpital	oo ay l'o**peetal** luh
nearest hospital?	le plus proche?	ploo **prosh**

COMMUNICATION ESSENTIALS

Yes	Oui	wee
No	Non	noñ
Please	S'il vous plaît	seel voo **play**
Thank you	Merci	mer-**see**
Excuse me	Excusez-moi	exkoo-**zay** mwah
Hello	Bonjour	boñ**zhoor**
Goodbye	Au revoir	oh ruh-**vwar**
Good night	Bonsoir	boñ-**swar**
Morning	Le matin	ma**tañ**
Afternoon	L'après-midi	l'apreh-**meedee**
Evening	Le soir	swar
Yesterday	Hier	eey**ehr**
Today	Aujourd'hui	oh-zhoor-**dwee**
Tomorrow	Demain	duh**mañ**
Here	Ici	ee-**see**
There	Là	lah
What?	Quel, quelle?	kel, kel
When?	Quand?	koñ
Why?	Pourquoi?	poor-**kwah**
Where?	Où?	oo

USEFUL PHRASES

How are you?	Comment allez-vous?	kom-moñ tal**ay voo**
Very well,	Très bien,	treh byañ,
thank you.	merci.	mer-**see**
Pleased to	Enchanté de faire	oñshoñ-**tay** duh fehr
meet you.	votre connaissance.	votr kon-ay-**sans**
See you soon.	A bientôt.	byañ-**toh**
Where is/are...?	Où est/sont...?	oo ay/soñ
How far	Combien de	kom-**byañ** duh
is it to...?	kilomètres d'ici à...?	keelo-**metr** d'ee-see-ah
Which	Quelle est la	kel ay lah **deer**-
way to...?	direction pour...?	ek-**syoñ** poor
Do you speak	Parlez-vous	par-lay voo
English?	anglais?	oñg-**lay**
I don't	Je ne	zhuh nuh kom-
understand.	comprends pas.	**proñ** pah
Could you	Pouvez-vous parler	poo-**vay** voo par-lay
speak slowly	moins vite s'il	mwañ veet seel
please?	vous plaît?	voo play
I'm sorry.	Excusez-moi.	exkoo-**zay** mwah

USEFUL WORDS

big	grand	groñ
small	petit	puh-**tee**
hot	chaud	show
cold	froid	frwah
good	bon	boñ
bad	mauvais	moh-**veh**
enough	assez	as**say**
open	ouvert	oo-**ver**
closed	fermé	fer-**meh**
left	gauche	gohsh
right	droite	drwaht
straight ahead	tout droit	too drwah
near	près	preh
far	loin	lwañ
early	de bonne heure	duh bon **urr**
late	en retard	oñ ruh-**tar**
entrance	l'entrée	l'on-**tray**
exit	la sortie	sor-**tee**
toilet	les toilettes, les WC	twah-let, vay-**see**
free, no charge	gratuit	grah-**twee**
Monday	lundi	luñ-**dee**
Tuesday	mardi	mar-**dee**
Wednesday	mercredi	mehrkruh-**dee**
Thursday	jeudi	zhuh-**dee**
Friday	vendredi	voñdruh-**dee**
Saturday	samedi	sam-**dee**
Sunday	dimanche	dee-**moñsh**

MAKING A TELEPHONE CALL

I'd like to place a	Je voudrais télé-	zhuh voo-dreh fehr
long-distance call.	phoner a l`etranger.	uñ oñter-oorboñ
I'll try again	Je rappelerai	zhuh rapel-
later.	plus tard.	**eray** ploo tar
Hold on.	Ne quittez pas,	nuh kee-**tay** pah
	s'il vous plaît.	seel voo play
Could you speak	Pouvez-vous parler	poo-**vay** voo par-
up a little please?	un peu plus fort?	**lay** uñ puh ploo for
local call	la communication	komoonikah-
	locale	**syoñ** low-**kal**

SHOPPING

How much	C'est combien	say kom-**byañ**
does this cost?	s'il vous plaît?	seel voo play
I would like ...	je voudrais...	zhuh voo-**dray**
Do you have?	Est-ce que vous avez?	es-kuh voo **za**vay
I'm just	Je regarde	zhuh ruh**gar**
looking.	seulement.	suhl**moñ**
Do you take	Est-ce que vous	es-**kuh** voo
credit cards?	acceptez les cartes	zaksept-**ay** leh kart
	de crédit?	duh kreh-**dee**
This one.	Celui-ci.	suhl-wee-**see**
That one.	Celui-là.	suhl-wee-**lah**
expensive	cher	shehr
cheap	pas cher,	pah shehr,
	bon marché	boñ mar-**shay**
size, clothes	la taille	tye

SIGHTSEEING

art gallery	la galerie d'art	galer-**ree** dart
bus station	la gare routière	gahr roo-tee-**yehr**
garden	le jardin	zhar-**dañ**
mosque	la mosquée	mos-**qay**
museum	le musée	moo-**zay**
tourist	les renseignements	roñsayn-**moñ** too-
information	touristiques, le	rees-**teek**, sandee-
office	syndicat d'initiative	ka d'eenee-syat**eev**
train station	la gare	gahr

STAYING IN A HOTEL

Do you have a	Est-ce que vous	es-kuh voo-**zavay**
vacant room?	avez une chambre?	oon shambr
double room,	la chambre à deux	shambr ah duh
with double bed	personnes, avec	pehr-**son** avek un
	un grand lit	groññ lee
twin room	la chambre à	shambr ah
	deux lits	duh lee
single room	la chambre à	shambr ah
	une personne	oon pehr-**son**
room with a	la chambre avec	shambr avek
bath, shower	salle de bains,	sal duh boñ,
	une douche	oon doosh
I have a	J'ai fait une	zhay fay oon
reservation.	réservation.	rayzehrva-**syoñ**

EATING OUT

Have you	Avez-vous une	avay-**voo** oon
got a table?	table de libre?	tahbl duh leebr
I want to	Je voudrais	zhuh voo-**dray**
reserve	réserver	rayzehr-**vay**
a table.	une table.	oon tahbl
The check	L'addition s'il	l'adee-**syoñ** seel
please.	vous plaît.	voo **play**
I am a	Je suis	zhuh swee
vegetarian.	végétarien.	vezhay-**tehryañ**
menu	le menu, la carte	men--oo, karto
breakfast	le petit	puh-**tee**
	déjeuner	deh-**zhuh**-nay
lunch	le déjeuner	deh-**zhuh**-nay
dinner	le dîner	dee-**nay**

NUMBERS

1	un, une	uñ, oon
2	deux	duh
3	trois	trwah
4	quatre	katr
5	cinq	sañk
6	six	sees
7	sept	set
8	huit	weet
9	neuf	nerf
10	dix	dees

MOROCCAN ARABIC PHRASE BOOK

Moroccan Arabic is unique to Morocco and is not understood by other Arabic speakers. Moroccans speak faster and abbreviate words. Pronunciation is gentler due to the influence of French.

IN EMERGENCY

Help!	**aawen**ooni
Stop!	**ow**kof!
Can you call a doctor?	momkin **kel**lem el ta**beeb**?
Call an ambulance!	**aay**eto **aa**la el isaaf
Can you call the police?	momkin kellem el po**lees**?
Call the fire department!	**aay**eto **aa**la el matafie
Where is the nearest hospital?	fin **kay**n akrab mos**tash**fa

COMMUNICATION ESSENTIALS

Yes	**na**-am
No	laa
Please	min **fad**lak
Thank you	se'hha / **shuk**ran
Excuse me	is**mah**lee
Hello / Peace be upon you	selaam
Goodbye	ma'eel sal**aa**ma
Good evening	ma**saal** kheer
Good morning	es**be'h elk**heer
Yesterday	**el** baareh
Today	el yoom
Tomorrow	gha**dan**
Here	hina
There	hinak
What?	shnoo?
When?	**im**ta?
Why?	a**lash**?
Where?	fayn?

USEFUL PHRASES

How are you?	wash**raak**?
I'm fine.	**laa**bas
Pleased to meet you.	metshar-fin
Where is/are...?	fayn...?
Which way to...?	ina te**rik...** ?
Do you speak English?	**tat**kalam engl**eeze-ya**?
I don't understand.	ana mafhim**taksh**
I'm sorry.	esme'h**lee**

USEFUL WORDS

big	**kbeer**
small	**sgeer**
hot	so**khoon**
cold	**baa**red
good	m**lee**'ha
bad	mashem**lee**'ha
open	maf**too**'h
closed	magh**look**
left	li**seer**
right	li**meen**
straight ahead	**nee**shan
near	qu**ray**ab
far	ba**eed**
entrance	do**khool**
exit	khrooj
toilet	towa**lett**
tonight	fel**leel**
day	ne**haar**
hour	**sa**'aa
week	sem**aa**na
Monday	el et**neen**
Tuesday	el t**laa**ta
Wednesday	el ar**be**'aa
Thursday	el kha**mees**
Friday	el **jo**mo'aa
Saturday	el **sa**bet
Sunday	el a'**had**

SHOPPING

How much is it?	kam else'**er**?
I would like...	ana 'hab**bayt** ...
Do you have?	an**dak**...?
This one	**haazi**
expensive	**ghaal**ya
cheap	rekhee**sa**

SIGHTSEEING

art gallery	gali**ree** daar
bus station	stas**yon** do boos
garden	el**jon**ayna
mosque	mas**jid**
museum	**moo**zi
tourist office	mek**tab** soy**aa**'h
train station	ma**hat**tat el tren
beach	**bhar**
guide	geed
map	kaart
park	baark
ticket	**te**kee

STAYING IN A HOTEL

Do you have a room?	en**ta** 'an**dak ghor**fa?
double room,	**ghor**fa le shakh**sayn**
with double bed	joj bioot
single room	**ghor**fa le shakhs **waa**'hid
with bathroom / shower	ma'al '**ham-maam** / **doosh**
I have a reservation.	ana me**reserve** hna

EATING OUT/FOOD

Have you got a table for...?	en**ta** 'an**dak towl**a le...?
I want to reserve a table.	brit re**serve** wahd tabla
The check please.	te'e**teeni** elfa**toora** min **fad**lak?
I am a vegetarian.	ana na**bati** wa la **aku**lu lehoum **wal**a hout
breakfast	if**tar**
lunch	reda
dinner	**aa**sha
steamed pot of vegetables with meat, etc.	ta**jeen**
hand-made couscous	**kus**kus
pastry filled with vegetables and meat, etc.	elbas**teela**
soup	'**hree**ra
meatballs with herbs	**kef**ta
fish	el'**hoot**
chicken	djaaj
meat	l'hem
vegetables	le**goom**/**kho**dra
water	**maa**'a

NUMBERS

1	**waa**'hid
2	zooj
3	t**laa**ta
4	arab**a**'aa
5	**kha**msa
6	**set**-ta
7	**seb**a'a
8	t**maan**ya
9	**tes**'aa
10	'**ash**ra
20	esh**reen**
50	kham**seen**
100	me**ya**

ACKNOWLEDGMENTS

The publisher would like to thank the following for their kind permission to reproduce their photographs:

Key: a-above; b-below/bottom; c-centre; f-far; l-left; r-right; t-top

123RF.com: Lukas Bischoff 77t; Sergei Bogomyakov 99bc.

4Corners: Kristel Richard 312-3.

akg-images: Philippe Maillard 67cr, 177cr.

Alamy Stock Photo: age fotostock 39tr, 81cra, 86b, 113t, 144t, 221t, 226bl, 229br, 244-5b; Jerónimo Alba 30tr, 176cl, 206-7, 208-9, 225cla, 283b; Leonid Andronov 133bl; arabianEye FZ LLC 104tl; ASK Images 119br, 165tr; Aurora Photos 164tl; Bill Bachmann 53t; Stefano Baldini 250bl; Stephen Barnes/Morocco 270tr; Jens Benninghofen 26t, 288tl; Sabena Jane Blackbird 50bl; Eduardo Blanco 218bl, 222-3b; blickwinkel 35cl, 218cra; Tibor Bognar 188bl; Brahim MNII 220b; Jordi Camí 166bl; Carefordolphins 38tl; Charles O. Cecil 180-1t, 297tr; Michelle Chaplow /Jardin Majorelle Marrakech © ADAGP, Paris and DACS, London 2018 242-3; Emanuele Ciccomartino 227br; Cosmo Condina 189br; Cultura Creative (RF) 205tl; Luis Dafos 47tr, 248b, 249t; Ian Dagnall 268b; Danita Delimont 62br, 132t, 222t; Wilf Doyle 117b; DPA Picture Alliance 54-5b; Igor Dymov 229; Roger Eritja 38-9b; Andrew Errington 278-9; Greg Balfour Evans 147t, 151b; Peter Forsberg 183b, / Africa 304cl; Jason Friend 217br; Funkyfood London - Paul Williams 53br, 105cr, 294-5t, 296-7b, /The Majorelle Garden botanical garden designed by French artist Jacques Majorelle © ADAGP, Paris and DACS, London 2018 243cra; Gaertner 136b, 288-9b; Robert Garrigus 281tr; Saverio Gatto 39cl; Grant Rooney Premium 238t; Paul Greaves 247br; Chris Griffiths 43cla, 63tl, 63cl, 269tr, 305; Derek Harris / A view of the old studio of Jacques Majorelle; now the Museum at Jardin Majorelle in Marrakech © ADAGP, Paris and DACS, London 2018 243cla; Chris Hellier 149br; hemis.fr / Christophe Boisvieux 164-5b, / Franck Charton 266-7t, / Jean Heintz 36b, / Ludovic Maisant 48-9c, 150t, / Lionel Montico 59t, 152tl, 162 -3, / Louis-Marie Preau 267br, / Bertrand Rieger 57br, 112bl, 115cl, 117tc, 120-1t, 170bl, / Gilles Rigoulet 138bl, /Jacques Sierpinski 121br, / Sylvain Sonnet 50-1t, 84t; Heritage Image Partnership Ltd 105cra; Ruth Hofshi 53cl; Peter Horree / Minaret à Tanger (1913) by Charles Camion © ADAGP, Paris and DACS, London 2018 149cla; Iconotec 56-7t, 168tl, 170-1t; imageBROKER 118bc, 264t, 286-7b, 287crb; Hassan II Mosque by Michel Pinseau © ADAGP, Paris and DACS, London 2018 17bl, 106-7; imageimage 148bl, 206tl; Images & Stories 210tl; Jam World Images 294br; JTB MEDIA CREATION; Inc. 133tr; Tetyana Kochneva 19t, 154-5; Karol Kozlowski 217tl; Alistair Laming 30cra; Gilles Larbi 89tl; MARKA 48-9t; Luz Martin 62cr; Mauritius Images Gmbh 246-7t; Ellen McKnight 65bc; Tuul and Bruno Morandi 41bl, 114cr, 115tl, 116tl, 310bl, 310-1t; Morocko 35t; Graham Mulrooney 87tr; National Geographic Image Collection 46tr, 118-9t, 137br, 293cla; North Wind Picture Archives 67br; Elena Odareeva 245bc, 282tl; PAINTING 51b; Ben Pipe 20t, 192-3; Fabian Plock / The famous colorful Painted Rocks near Tafraoute by Jean Verame © ADAGP, Paris and DACS, London 2018 308-9b; PM photos 101tr; Prisma Archivo 66bc; Luisa Puccini 33cl; QEDimages19bl, 172-3; Juergen Ritterbach 44clb, 250t; Robertharding 11cr, 32-3t, 40-1t, 49b, 63cr, 146bl, 152-3b, 240-1t, 253br, 257b, 294bl; Rowan Romeyn 42-3t; Grant Rooney 43br, 306b; Boaz Rottem 177cl; Peter Schickert 40bl, 185t; Mike P Shepherd 210-1b, 307tr; shoults 60-1t, 224cb, 273tc; Sean Sprague 54-5t; Dave Stamboulis 166-7t; Stockimo / Parisa 58tr; Paul Strawson 274cl; James Sturcke 11t; David Sutherland 65br, 241crb; Markus Thomenius 12t; Top Photo Corporation 95tr; Universal Images Group North America LLC / DeAgostini 62cl, 145bl; Lucas Vallecillos 32cra, 158t, 184bl, 190-1b, 207tr; Alvaro German Vilela 83tl; Vito Arcomano Photography 34tl; Andrew Walmsley 162bl; John Wang 96t; WENN UK 63bl; Wildlife Gmbh 62tr; Andrew Wilson 28cr; Jan Wlodarczyk 8-9b, 27t, 32tl, 41cr, 105b, 201br, 204-5b, 285, 290, 302t, 309cr, /Majorelle Gardens in Marrakesh, Morocco © ADAGP, Paris and DACS, London 2018 24crb; David Wootton 249cla; Marek Zuk 100b.

AWL Images: Mauricio Abreu 286t; Peter Adams 12clb; Neil Farrin 16c, 18clb, 72-3, 140-1; Cavalier Michel 23tl, 276-7; Doug Pearson 23cb, 298-9.

Bridgeman Images: AGIP 69bl, 77br; Buyenlarge Archive / UIG / Safi, Morocco 64t; De Agostini Picture Library / G. Dagli Orti / Labours of Hercules house, mosaic, Hercules kills King Diomedes on a horse, Roman Empire from 1st century ad 65cl, / Portuguese King Afonso V's taking of Asilah in Morocco, 15th century tapestry kept in the Collegiate Church of Pastrana, Spain 67tr; Louvre, Paris, France / Claudius, marble head, 41-54 AD 64br; Musee de La Presse, Paris / Abdication of Moulay-Hafid, Sultan of Morocco, cover illustration of 'Le Petit Journal', 25 August, 1912 68bc; Pictures from History / French colonial depiction in 'Le Petit Journal' of events in Morocco in 1912 resulting in the establishment of French colonial rule 68cr, / Berber general Tariq *ibn Ziyad, Muslim conqueror of southern Spain in 711* by Theodore Hosemann (1807-1875) 65tr, / *Qur'an sura 5, written in Maghribi script,*

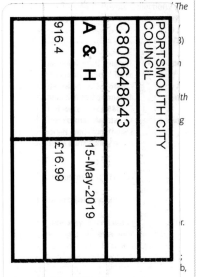

138tr; Laurens Hoddenbagh 97bl, 227tl; Javarman 130; Kasto80 44bl; Kicimici / Hassan II Mosque by Michel Pinseau © ADAGP, Paris and DACS, London 2018 110clb; Tetyana Kochneva 37b; Nataliya Kostenyukova 98-9t; Ernesto Jiménez Lucas 94br; milosk50 115cr; Elena Odareeva 56br, 203bl; Pdxnative 293tl; Philophotos 199tr; Saiko3p 178bl, 197t; Sandboarding 36tr; Smellme 225tl; Anibal Trejo 197br; Alvaro German Vilela 77cr, 78; Peter Wollinga 280-1b; Zlikovec 163bl; Zzvet 160t.

Getty Images: AFP / Fadel Denna 80-1b; Anadolu Agency 79br; Copyright Alengel 102-3; Walter G. Allgöwer 234cl; aprott 254-5; Atlantide Phototravel 237tr; Aurora Photos / Jason Langley 234bl; Alain Bachellier 37clb; Tim Gerard Barker 55crb; David Bathgate 62bl; Ben Pipe Photography 26cr; Walter Bibikow 86crb; Paul Biris 12-3b, 35br; John Seaton Callahan 13cr; Martin Child 24cr; ChrisHepburn 26-7t; Stefan Cristian Cioata 28cl, 31tl; Manuel Breva Colmeiro 2-3, 30-1c; Vincent Courceleaud 216-7b; Luis Dafos 79bl; danm 34br; Danita Delimont 153cl; Marcin Dobas 22, 260-1; encrier 27cl; EyeEm / Nicolas Ayer 4, /Siegfried Gehlhaar 235, / Teresa Henke 61cl; Michele Falzone 188t; Neil Farrin 82b; Federica Gentile 10-1b; Kodiak Greenwood 47br; Christopher Griffiths 8clb, 61br; guenterguni 256tl; Bartosz Hadyniak 281ca; hadynyah 45br; Roger de la Harpe 270-1b; Hugh Hastings 37tr; IP3 /

Aurelien Morissard 69cra; Jean-Philippe Ksiazek 63tr; Floris Leeuwenberg 17t, 90-1; Jean-Pierre Lescourret 258-9t; Lonely Planet / The Majorelle Gardens © ADAGP, Paris and DACS, London 2018 243tr; Lost Horizon Images 31tr; lubilub 28br; Lukasz-Nowak1 42b; David Ruiz Luna 258bl; Colin McConnell 46-7b; Fernando Vazquez Miras 134-5; Mlenny 186-7; Tuul & Bruno Morandi 114cl; Pavliha 6-7; Douglas Pearson 8cl, 26cl; Pixelchrome Inc 202-3t; Herman du Plessis 11br; RobertoGennaro 200br; Roc Canals Photography 128-9; roevin 58-9b; Bernd Schunack 57cl; Davide Seddio 290-1t; Abdelhak Senna 69br; Fadel Senna 60br; Starcevic 28t; stockstudioX 70-1; STR 69tr; uchar 24t; ugurhan 13t, 292cl, / Hassan II Mosque by Michel Pinseau © ADAGP, Paris and DACS, London 2018 24bl; Ullstein Bild 252-3t; Christine Wehrmeier 10clb, 33tr; Westend61 59cl; Rosmarie Wirz 224clb; A J Withey 225cl; xavierarnau 10ca, 48br.

iStockphoto.com: Ababsolutum 13br; Leonid Andronov 137tl; Marisa Arregui 87cr; Charles03 217cla, 217cra; Conan-Edogawa 280cra; Louis-Michel Desert 18tl, 122-3; fotoVoyager 275cr; gionnixxx 308tl; JohnnyGreig 239bl; JulieanneBirch 178-9t; manx_in_the_world 245tr; mrsixinthemix 272-3; nicolamargaret 126t; Pavliha 20bl, 212-3, 236-7b, 237cla; photooiasson 181bl; Fabian Plock 293br; RedPhotography 281cra; Republica 237cra; RobertoGennaro 199cr; SeanPavonePhoto / Hassan II Mosque by Michel Pinseau © ADAGP, Paris and DACS, London 2018 110cl; Sharrocks / Hassan II Mosque by Michel Pinseau © ADAGP, Paris and DACS, London 2018 111t; ViliamM 168-9b; John_Walker 191tr; Jef Wodniack 30tl.

La Mamounia: 251b.

Mohammed Vi Museum Of Modern And Contemporary Art: 81tl.

Press Association Images: Empics / Steve Etherington 62tl.

Rex by Shutterstock: Moviestore Collection 52tl, 52br; Sipa 63br.

RMN: *Audience donnée à Meknès par le sultan du Maroc Moulay Ismaïl à François Pidou, chevalier de Saint-Olon, ambassadeur extraordinaire de Louis XIV. 11juin 1693* by Martin Pierre Denis 68tl.

Robert Harding Picture Library: Jordan Banks 161cl; Gavin Hellier 21, 230-1; Travel Collection 129tr.

Royal Mansour: 47cl.

Photo Scala; Florence: Dar El-Batha Museum 117br, 177cra.

Front Flap:
Alamy Stock Photo: Jens Benninghofen cla; **Getty Images:** John Seaton Callahan bl; Pavliha tc; encrier cra; Davide Seddio cb; uchar br.

Cover images:
Front and spine: **iStockphoto.com:** undefined undefined.
Back: **Alamy Stock Photo:** Paul Strawson cla; **AWL Images:** Neil Farrin c; **Getty Images:** Paul Biris tr; **iStockphoto.com:** undefined bc.

For further information see:
www.dkimages.com

**The information in this
DK Eyewitness Travel Guide is checked regularly.**
Every effort has been made to ensure that this book is as up-to-date as possible at the time of going to press. Some details, however, such as telephone numbers, opening hours, prices, gallery hanging arrangements and travel information, are liable to change. The publishers cannot accept responsibility for any consequences arising from the use of this book, nor for any material on third party websites, and cannot guarantee that any website address in this book will be a suitable source of travel information. We value the views and suggestions of our readers very highly. Please write to: Publisher, DK Eyewitness Travel Guides, Dorling Kindersley, 80 Strand, London, WC2R 0RL, UK, or email: travelguides@dk.com

Penguin
Random
House

Main Contributors Andrew Humphreys, Rachida Alaoui, Jean Brignon, Nathalie Campodonico, Fabien Casenave, Gaëtan Du Chatenet, Alain Chenal, Carole French, Emmanuelle Honorin, Maati Kabbal, Mohamed Métalsi, Marie-Pascale Rauzier, Richard Williams

Senior Editor Alison McGill

Senior Designer Laura O'Brien

Project Editor Danielle Watt

Project Art Editors Bess Daly, Tom Forge, Ben Hinks

Designer Van Lee

Factchecker Mary Novakovich

Editors Matthew Grundy Haigh, Rachel Thompson

Proofreader Clare Peel

Indexer Hilary Bird

Senior Picture Researcher Ellen Root

Picture Research Ashwin Adimari, Tim Draper, Sumita Khatwani, Susie Watters, Harriet Whitaker

Illustrators Chapel Design & Marketing Ltd., Chinglemba Chingbham, Surat Kumar Mantoo, Arun Pottirayil, T. Gautam Trivedi, Mark Arjun Warner

Cartographic Editor James Macdonald

Cartography Dave Pugh, Fabrice Le Goff, Quadrature Créations

Jacket Designers Maxine Pedliham, Bess Daly, Simon Thompson

Jacket Picture Research Susie Watters

Senior DTP Designer Jason Little

DTP George Nimmo, Azeem Siddiqui, Tanveer Zaidi

Senior Producer Stephanie McConnell

Managing Editor Rachel Fox

Art Director Maxine Pedliham

Publishing Director Georgina Dee

First edition 2002

Published in Great Britain by Dorling Kindersley Limited, 80 Strand, London, WC2R 0RL

Published in the United States by DK Publishing, 1450 Broadway, 8th Floor, New York, NY 10018

Copyright © 2002, 2019 Dorling Kindersley Limited
A Penguin Random House Company
18 19 20 21 10 9 8 7 6 5 4 3 2 1

A CIP catalog record for this book is available from the British Library.

A catalog record for this book is available from the Library of Congress.

ISSN: 1542 1554
ISBN: 978 0 2413 6010 1

Printed and bound in China.

www.dk.com